D1244614

FV

WITHDRAWN

THE BATTLE OF BELMONT

THE BATTLE OF

BELMONT

GRANT STRIKES SOUTH

Nathaniel Cheairs Hughes, Jr.

THE UNIVERSITY OF NORTH CAROLINA PRESS

Chapel Hill ✳ London

The paper in this book
meets the guidelines for
permanence and durability
of the Committee on
Production Guidelines for
Book Longevity of the
Council on Library Resources.

95 94 93 92 91 5 4 3 2 1

Library of Congress Cataloging-in-Publication
Data
Hughes, Nathaniel Cheairs, Jr.
The Battle of Belmont : Grant strikes South /
by Nathaniel Cheairs Hughes, Jr.
p. cm.
Includes bibliographical references and index.
ISBN 0-8078-1968-9 (cloth : alk. paper)
1. Belmont (Mo.), Battle of, 1861. I. Title.
E472.28.H84 1991
973.7'31—dc20 90-26401
CIP

To

my wife and partner,

BUCKY,

veteran of many battles

CONTENTS

Preface   xiii

Acknowledgments   xv

Chapter 1. What I Want Is to Advance   1

Chapter 2. Grant and McClernand   8

Chapter 3. Cairo   14

Chapter 4. Polk and Pillow   26

Chapter 5. Columbus   36

Chapter 6. Down the River to Look for a Fight   45

Chapter 7. Walke   60

Chapter 8. Turn Out! Turn Out!   65

Chapter 9. My Heart Kept Getting Higher and Higher   78

Chapter 10. Nothing out There but Yankees   93

Chapter 11. Every Man Was Now His Own Captain   114

Chapter 12. Fighting the Same Ground over Again   134

Chapter 13. Surrounded! Surrounded!   147

Chapter 14. A Perfect Storm of Death   164

Chapter 15. Pumpkins in a Cornfield   178

Chapter 16. A Glorious Repulse   189

Chapter 17. It Will Not Do to Smile in Triumph   198

Appendix 1. Organization of Forces at the Battle of Belmont   209

Appendix 2. Beyond Belmont   215

Notes   221

Bibliography   277

Index   297

ILLUSTRATIONS

Brig. Gen. Ulysses S. Grant   6

Brig. Gen. John A. McClernand   11

Col. John A. Logan   17

Col. Napoleon B. Buford   20

Col. Jacob G. Lauman   24

Maj. Gen. Leonidas Polk   28

Brig. Gen. Gideon J. Pillow   32

Col. John V. Wright   43

Comdr. Henry Walke   61

First gunboat attack   63

U.S. gunboat *Taylor* (*Tyler*)   64

Col. James C. Tappan   72

Lt. Col. Tyree H. Bell   96

Capt. Alexander Bielaski   110

Battle of Belmont   128

Col. Benjamin F. Cheatham   141

Lt. Col. Augustus Wentz   151

Maj. Gen. Edward G. W. Butler   159

Reembarkation of Grant's force   167

Capt. James J. Dollins   176

Col. Henry Dougherty   181

MAPS

1. Cairo-Columbus Area, 1861   2

2. Major Operations of Grant's Command in Late 1861   54

3. Belmont, 1861   58

4. Union Approach   81

5. Deployment   85

6. Fight at the Cornfield   100

7. Capture of Camp Johnston   120

8. Confederate Counterattack   150

9. Confederate Pursuit   160

10. Union Withdrawal   169

PREFACE

I want to write the story of the battle of Belmont, sufficiently detailed to satisfy the Civil War student and to honor the subject yet with human interest enough to afford even the casual reader several hours of enjoyment. Belmont can be confusing. The first time I read an account closely was in 1987 in Philadelphia at the Pennsylvania Historical Society. It was John Seaton's description, and when I finished I felt quite mixed-up. The flow of action, the location, the characters needed to be straightened out for it to be intelligible to me. I hope I have done that in this study but not at the expense of the fervor and gunpowder that run through the sentences of Seaton and other participants.

Belmont, like all battles, is worthy of being shared. It places people we can admire, with whom we can identify, in an extreme situation. They must respond to life-threatening conflict. How they respond, how they behave, takes on significance for them, for their comrades, and for us. Hopes and dreams were dumped into shallow graves at Belmont. Blood and brains of complex men with high motives were splashed across dead leaves of the cottonwood that bright November day. But if we stand still and watch carefully, nobility, like a deer that has been observing us all along, will step forth from the thicket.

Today it is strangely quiet at Belmont. From the corner of one's mind comes a reminder that fifty years before the battle took place a great earthquake shook this very land apart, and the Mississippi River went crazy. Fifty years before, to the day, William Henry Harrison and Tecumseh had immortalized themselves at Tippecanoe. Many of these Belmont soldiers, blue and gray, knew that. They carried tradition in their knapsacks; their grandfathers' revolutionary war swords swung by their sides.

I hear soldiers' voices as I wander their unmarked field. Not one monument, not one tablet speaks for them. They do not ask much, these Belmont veterans. Just tell their story, the story of a violent, perhaps unpredictable, intersection of willful personalities at a town that was not a town; of practiced tactical formations going to hell in laughing underbrush; of a priest urging his flock to kill; of a drunk urging his men to place duty above self.

✳

Gideon Pillow led me to Belmont. I had wondered about this opening battle of the Army of Tennessee before, but curiosity only nudged me gently while Pillow came along and gave me a push. He had interested me for years, since I met him while doing a study of William J. Hardee. Whereas Hardee represented the quintessence of the professional soldier, Pillow represented something else. Both were Confederate patriots to the core, and both risked much, but fame eluded them. Had Hardee possessed Pillow's ability to arouse enthusiasm and impart a sense of urgency, his self-confidence, and his hunger for command and recognition, Hardee's legacy would have been quite different. On the other hand, had Gideon Pillow possessed Hardee's . . . But that is getting ahead of the story.

Chattanooga, Tennessee
May 1990

ACKNOWLEDGMENTS

At least nine studies of Belmont preceded mine. I built upon their work and I am obligated: Henry Walke (1877), Marcus J. Wright (1892), John Seaton (1906), William Mecklenburg Polk (1915), H. L. Kinnison (1921), Henry I. Kurtz (1963), James E. McGhee (1973), John Y. Simon (1981), and David E. Roth (1985).

Many others have contributed. Some I have been able to meet and have come to know. This has afforded me great pleasure. Others, whom I have not met, gladly and graciously helped me. There is a wonderful tradition of generous, sharing scholarship in Civil War research, and I have been a beneficiary of it for forty years.

Lynn N. Bock, an attorney in New Madrid, Missouri, more than once tramped Belmont peninsula with me, made my visits efficient and fun, and helped guide my investigation. Tom Arliskas of Plainfield, Illinois, welcomed me to the study of Belmont, his topic of special interest and research for twenty years. He read and constructively criticized my manuscript, as did my friend Nathan Lipscomb.

John Y. Simon, executive director of the Ulysses S. Grant Association, offered encouragement at every turn, led me to important sources, and introduced me to Bill Stoudt of Florissant, Missouri, who read part of the manuscript and helped me locate crucial sites on the battlefield.

Jere Ballentine of Dayton, Tennessee, unlocked the mysteries of word processing and listened dutifully to the charge of Walker's Legion on the ninth tee. E. Y. Chapin IV of Chattanooga was enthusiastic about reconstructing the Belmont battlefield graphically, came up with the idea of utilizing computer-assisted design, and gave hours of technical assistance.

Eric Rudolph, also of Chattanooga, enhanced the study with his interpretative maps and proved to be a diligent and generous coworker. Paula Wald did much to improve the manuscript in copyediting it for the University of North Carolina Press.

Bill Prince and Clara Swan went beyond the call of duty to make easily available the Wilder Collection at the University of Chattanooga and the history section of the Chattanooga Bi-Centennial Library.

I am indebted to the following individuals for their suggestions, assistance, and encouragement: Dr. James W. Livingood, Chattanooga; Patricia LaPointe, Memphis, Tennessee; Dr. Arthur W. Bergeron, Jr., Baton Rouge, Louisiana; Dr. Richard M. McMurry, Raleigh, North Carolina; Dr. Victor Hicken, Macomb, Illinois; Dr. Thomas P. Sweeney, Springfield, Missouri; Anne Armor, Sewanee, Tennessee; Charles L. Sullivan, Perkinson, Mississippi; Jerry Russell, Little Rock, Arkansas; Joseph J. Adler, Ridgecrest, California; Kathaleen S. Hughes, Chattanooga; the Rev. Larry J. Daniel, Memphis, Tennessee; Brent A. Cox, Milan, Tennessee; Dr. John Cain, Charleston, South Carolina; Dr. Anthony Hodges, Chattanooga; Clement Craven, New Madrid, Missouri; E. Cheryl Schnirring, Springfield, Illinois; Mrs. R. B. Jewell, Clinton, Kentucky; Lt. Col. Thomas E. Tappan, Jr., Memphis, Tennessee; Dr. W. Glenn Robertson, Fort Leavenworth, Kansas; Michael P. Musick, National Archives; Dr. Harold Moser, University of Tennessee at Knoxville; Dr. Tom Keiser, Manchester, Missouri; Dr. Richard J. Sommers, Carlisle, Pennsylvania; D'Arcy N. Hughes, Chattanooga; Dr. Frank Cooling, Washington, D.C.; Patricia L. Denault, Cambridge, Massachusetts; Capt. George E. Knapp, U.S. Army; Roy Morris, Jr., Chattanooga; James E. McGhee, Charleston, Missouri; and Dr. John McGlone, Paris, Tennessee.

For making their material available and for assistance of all sorts, I wish to thank the staffs of the Southern Historical Collection, University of North Carolina; Manuscript Division, William R. Perkins Library, Duke University; Division of Manuscripts, Library of Congress; Lincoln Collection and Manuscript Collection, Illinois State Historical Library; National Portrait Gallery; Missouri Historical Society; New York Historical Society; Robert W. Woodruff Library, Emory University; DuPont Library, University of the South; Louis A. Warren Lincoln Library; Princeton University Library; Special Collections, Virginia Tech Library; Massachusetts Historical Society; Cartographic and Military History branches, National Archives; Mississippi Department of Archives and History; University of Missouri–Kansas City Library; University of Missouri–Columbia Library; Sterling Library, Yale University; Arkansas Historical Commission; University of Arkansas Libraries; Naval Imaging Command; Allen County Public Library, Fort Wayne, Indiana; Newberry Library, Chicago, Illinois; Tennessee State Library and Archives; Mississippi Valley Collection, Memphis State University; Louisiana and Lower Mississippi Valley Collections, Louisiana State University Libraries; Memphis–Shelby County Public Library; Lupton Library, University of Tennessee at Chattanooga; U.S. Military History Institute, Carlisle Barracks, Pennsylvania; Historic New Orleans Collection; Chattanooga–Hamilton County Bi-Centennial Library; Western Reserve Historical Society; State Historical Society of Missouri; Howard Tilton Memorial Library, Tulane University; State Historical Society of Iowa; and Archives and Manuscript Department, Chicago Historical Society.

1

What I Want Is to Advance

An identifiable pattern of events leading to the battle of Belmont began
to emerge in late April 1861 when Federal soldiers occupied Cairo,
Illinois. Their presence in "this southernmost city in the free states"
underlined the strategic importance of the upper Mississippi and the
determination of the United States to control the river. As Union troops
transformed Cairo into a base of operations, the War Department purchased three steamboats and began converting them into timberclads.
Word of the gunboats and the troops at Cairo sent shivers down the
Mississippi. This show of military power by the Lincoln government
threatened the security of Arkansas and Tennessee, not to speak of
secessionist dreams for Kentucky and Missouri.

In early May, Gov. Isham G. Harris mobilized Tennessee and entered into a military league with the Confederacy. He placed the
armed forces of the state under her foremost military figure, Gideon J.
Pillow, and stationed him in Memphis, thus signaling "the supreme
importance" of the Mississippi River. Pillow set to work with vigor and
by midsummer had effectively organized much of Tennessee's manpower. Pillow believed Memphis and West Tennessee to be quite vul-
nerable, so he lavished human and financial resources upon the construction of river fortifications. As early as May 13, 1861, Pillow
advocated immediate occupation of Columbus, Kentucky, "a much
more favorable position for defending Tennessee as well as Western
Kentucky." Columbus dominated the Mississippi River flowing beneath its high "Iron Banks." Whoever held Columbus not only would
control the Mississippi but would be within striking distance of Padu-

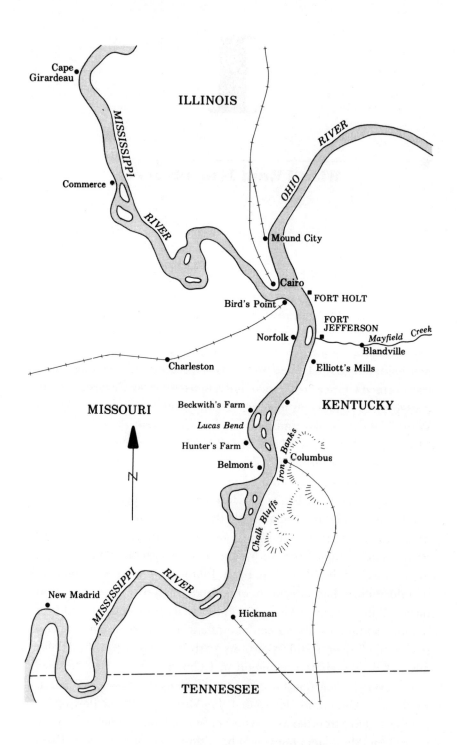

MAP 1. *Cairo-Columbus Area, 1861*

cah and Cairo. Pillow expected and feared the Federals would seize Columbus any day.[1]

Pillow was wrong about timing but correct about intent. The summer saw continuing concentration and organization by both sides. Leonidas Polk, bishop of Louisiana and a man much admired by Jefferson Davis, superseded Pillow when Tennessee's soldiers became Confederates in July. Polk had reluctantly agreed to assume command. He viewed it as a temporary measure, lasting until the arrival of his friend and former West Point roommate, Albert Sidney Johnston.

Polk's responsibility was the upper Mississippi; his authority, imprecisely defined, certainly improperly exercised, seemed limited. Within sixty days Polk's light-handed style of leadership had failed. August 1861 witnessed a collapse in Confederate effectiveness in southeastern Missouri. William J. Hardee and Pillow, through independent action and inaction, frittered away reasonable hope of success.[2]

Polk's counterpart in St. Louis, Maj. Gen. John C. Frémont, however, delighted in the exercise of command. Handicapped and frustrated in a hundred ways, he nevertheless sought offensive opportunities and aggressive commanders. Stung and frightened by Nathaniel Lyon's defeat at Wilson's Creek in August, Frémont ached to strike back at Sterling Price, but the threat posed by Hardee, Pillow, and M. Jeff Thompson in southeast Missouri held him back.

Over the summer Brig. Gen. Ulysses S. Grant had won Frémont's confidence with minor displays of competence and energy, and on August 28 Frémont rewarded him with the command of the District of Southeast Missouri. Frémont posted Grant at Cairo and defined his mission: clear southeast Missouri of rebel forces and occupy Columbus.[3]

Grant's mission seemed much easier when Pillow and Hardee abandoned southeast Missouri in September. Still, the dominant terrain feature of the area was a great swamp, five to twenty-five miles wide, extending from the Arkansas line northward to a point parallel with Cape Girardeau. This swamp offered shelter for Thompson and his mobile band of partisans, allowing them to move about southeastern Missouri with impunity. Thompson evaded determined pursuit but sought fights and conducted raids with a frequency embarrassing to the Union army and demoralizing to Union sympathizers. Thompson possessed a "combination of sense and bombast, of military shrewdness and personal buffoonery."[4]

Thompson "was a thorn that continually pricked, or threatened to prick, the sensitive Union flank, and he appeared to be covering Confederate detachments toward Price."[5] Frémont believed to the point of paranoia that Price, Thompson, and Polk worked in concert. Thus it became elemental to Frémont's Missouri strategy to cut communications between Columbus and Sterling Price. The possession of the little steamboat landing at Belmont, Missouri, would assure that. Grant dispatched units from Cape Girardeau and Bird's Point after Thompson, keeping him on the run, and once, with a 1,500-man detachment under Col. Joseph Plummer at Fredericktown, Grant managed to bloody Thompson's nose. But this would come in late October. Most of the fall Thompson rode loose in the counties west of the river like some nineteenth-century Baron Munchausen, annoying Grant greatly.[6]

In September, however, eyes shifted to bitterly divided and precariously neutral Kentucky. Both sides had been recruiting men and organizing units openly, but doing so "in gingerly fashion throughout the state, trying not to alienate." The August 1861 elections, however, brought a unionist legislature thanks to a boycott by secessionists. This "marked the beginning of the end of neutrality in Kentucky." Frémont poured oil on the fire by sending a force under Col. Gustav Waagner to occupy Belmont just across the river from Columbus. Waagner was to "keep possession of that place," scaring the wits out of pro-Southerners in southwestern Kentucky, and use it as a base to strike inland into Missouri against Thompson. Waagner captured Belmont on September 2. Meanwhile Federals demonstrated across the river from Paducah. These threats against Kentucky's strategic points "pulled the trigger in Polk's mind." He at last agreed with Pillow who had been pushing him for six weeks to react and seize Columbus. Pillow had been joined now by a chorus of citizens from the Jackson Purchase, "begging for intervention."[7]

Polk unleashed Pillow on September 3. Hickman, Kentucky, fell that night, Columbus the next day. It was a political blunder of the first order. The onus of "violation of neutrality" and "invasion" stuck to Polk like tar. The Kentucky legislature met on September 4, instantly "converted . . . from lukewarm to warlike unionism."[8] The Confederacy's first thought was to countermand Polk's action. Realists knew, however, that would be as futile as recalling a bullet once it had left the muzzle. Jefferson Davis agreed reluctantly that the "immense weight of military necessity" dictated such a course of action. He would spend the rest of his life justifying Polk's aggression.[9]

Grant arrived in Cairo to take command the day Columbus fell. Immediately he proposed a countermove, which Frémont approved. Grant gathered two regiments at Cairo and steamed up the Ohio River, seizing Paducah the morning of September 6, a magnificent show of offensive initiative.[10]

At the urging of Pillow, Polk made a belated attempt to drive Grant from Paducah, sending out Brig. Gen. Frank Cheatham from Columbus but only as far as Mayfield, Kentucky. Gen. Albert Sidney Johnston arrived, however, and believing Polk's forces overextended, aborted the effort.[11] In any case, Grant had discounted Polk's attempts to assume the offensive: "My own impression is that they are fortifying strongly and preparing to resist a formidable attack, and have but little idea of risking anything upon a forward movement."[12]

Thus Polk, at great cost in public opinion, preempted Grant and won the strategic prize of Columbus, effectively blocking the Mississippi, and Grant in turn preempted Polk with the capture of Paducah, gaining the Union still another splendid base of operations and assuring access to the Tennessee River that crisscrossed the heart of the South.

On September 8 the Federal gunboat *Lexington* dropped down the Mississippi from Cairo to Lucas Bend, just above the Iron Banks of Columbus. A brief exchange of cannon fire confirmed the power of the Confederate position on the bluffs, and the *Lexington* withdrew, abandoning the attempt to pass Polk's strong point. The following week Grant ordered a land reconnaissance down the Kentucky side of the Mississippi toward Columbus and also had Col. Henry Dougherty, supported by Comdr. Henry Walke's gunboats, lead a force from Bird's Point to within six miles of Belmont.

These probes began two months of similar missions, magnificent rehearsals for the coming strike against Belmont. Walke's gunboats learned about the river and the location and limitations of the enemy's heavy guns at Columbus.[13] The Union army, particularly the infantry, gained badly needed experience in maneuver. The Confederates, on the other hand, relied on the cavalry and their massive bluff batteries to meet these threats. Their infantry and field artillery for the most part remained immobile, employed in strengthening fortifications.[14]

Brig. Gen. Ulysses S. Grant (Library of Congress)

With each reconnaissance downriver Grant grew bolder. He pestered Frémont to turn him loose. "If it was discretionary with me with a little addition to my present force I would take Columbus."[15] His repeated requests went unanswered, and Grant despaired. "I am very sorry that I have not got a force to go south with, at least to Columbus, but the fates seem to be against any such thing. . . . What I want is to advance."[16] Frémont's reluctance to attack Columbus came from his preoccupation with the doings of Sterling Price in southwest Missouri. When Hardee and Pillow took their troops and crossed the Mississippi into Kentucky in September, threats from southeast Missouri became secondary. Frémont only worried that Polk, using Jeff Thompson's force as a screen, might transfer infantry back to southeast Missouri. From there they could march across southern Missouri to reinforce Sterling Price. Price was dangerous, and Frémont proceeded against him with excruciating caution. This caution, perceived in Washington as inexcusable timidity and ineptness, coupled with administrative and political gaffes, would bring him down. As October passed, Frémont's position grew more precarious. Finally Lincoln withdrew his support and decided to relieve him. The change of command would give Grant his opportunity.

2

Grant and McClernand

Ulysses S. Grant was hungry. Up until now his life had been high-lighted by a remarkable record of horsemanship at West Point, a strong showing as a quartermaster in the Mexican War, and a fortu-nate marriage into a St. Louis family of property and influence. Off-setting these advantages, however, were the abandonment of an army career, the succession of business failures, and the character-eroding necessity of favor grubbing. It would not have seemed unjust for a per-son in March 1861 to have believed Grant to be "a broken and disap-pointed man, for whom no one would have dreamed of predicting a brilliant future."[1]

Fort Sumter redeemed Grant. It helped, of course, that he had been a professional soldier. The citizens of Galena, Illinois, turned to him because they had no one else, and Grant responded eagerly, tossing off the small roles and small expectations that had squeezed him. Within six weeks he bounded from store clerk to colonel of the 21st Illinois. Fortunately Grant had caught the attention of Gov. Richard Yates and Rep. Elihu B. Washburne, "who were scraping the bottom of the barrel for officers to organize the unwieldy mass of Illinois volunteers."[2]

Grant understood volunteers, and he knew how to handle them, bet-ter, perhaps, than any regular officer in the Federal army. He knew how to toughen a regiment as well. When orders came for the 21st to move to Quincy, Illinois, in July, Grant chose not to move his men by rail but to have them march the ninety miles. Another July outing, this time against the camp of Missouri secessionist Col. Tom Harris, ended successfully when Harris withdrew at Grant's rapid and determined approach.[3]

Promotion to brigadier general came quickly. Grant got along with superiors, worked hard, and had strong political backing. But he did not inspire. Wearing a long beard, usually broken by a meerschaum pipe with a long curved stem hanging down from his mouth, he had "no gait, no station, no manner." But this "very ordinary sort of man" seemed to catch folks off guard; he fooled them. He would act first, then explain. His daring, persistence, and instinct for the kill remained concealed, however. The *Nashville Banner* on October 1 reported mistakenly that Brig. Gen. C. F. Smith had been sent to Paducah to replace Grant, "the cornstalk chap."[4]

Grant began to surround himself with exceptional staff. Instinctively he knew, or seemed to know, how to use them. John A. Rawlins, the young Douglas Democrat and Galena lawyer, would become indispensable to Grant the soldier and Grant the man. Of greater importance in the fall of 1861, perhaps, would be Maj. Joseph D. Webster, Grant's fifty-year-old chief of staff. Webster brought to Grant an unusual knowledge of the employment of artillery and an administrative ability that bordered on extraordinary. He would have Grant's ear at Belmont.

Grant's chief lieutenant in the fall of 1861, however, was John Alexander McClernand. During the spring and summer of 1861, McClernand was possibly the most important man in central Illinois, perhaps in Illinois itself. Abraham Lincoln seemed to think so.

This forty-nine-year-old Kentucky-born political adventurer, like his friend Lincoln, had educated himself. When an opportunity to study law came along McClernand took it. He spent a summer as a volunteer in the Black Hawk War and for a while tried his hand as a trader on the Ohio and the Mississippi. In 1835 he moved to Shawneetown, Illinois, where he established and edited the *Democrat*. Seven years in the Illinois House followed as he "attended a raucous and competitive school for politics." McClernand moved on to the U.S. House in 1843 and remained until 1851, verifying himself as an orthodox Jacksonian and Stephen Douglas's steady ally. His unquestioning support of Douglas cost him two elections, however, and for eight years McClernand, the "Grecian Orator," remained home in Illinois devoting himself to a booming law practice and to land speculation. He returned to Congress in 1859 thanks to creative redistricting.

At this point one might classify McClernand as a politician who had been "a member of the Democratic pack and always before had sought the safest path, free from controversy."[5] During 1859–61, however, two years so critical for the Democratic party (the "Democracy" in nineteenth-century terms) and for the nation, McClernand asserted himself, taking "his stand in the emergency without any of the vacillation for which he had been well known." He tried with all his might to hold the Democracy together. Jefferson Davis, among others, recognized this, and from the Senate Davis tried his best to rally support for McClernand. Compromise was McClernand's plea. He repudiated the abolitionists and, like Douglas, held out his hand to Southerners. "All government, all authority, all human life, is a compromise. Christianity itself is a compromise."

McClernand stood "on the edge of national importance" in 1860 as the Democracy turned to him for leadership. Some Southerners, however, seemed intent on pulling the party apart.[6] McClernand, always optimistic and full of energy, disregarded the voices of doom and in this year of crisis sought to become Speaker of the House. He continued to voice conciliation. "My convictions of public duty led me to do all in my power, throughout a period of near ten year Congressional service, to stay the impending casthophe [sic] as long as possible. In thus foregoing my habit of meeting danger, at the threshold, I thought it, in this instance, the wisest part."[7] McClernand came very close to winning the Speakership and "would have been elected if a small group of Democrats from the lower South had not refused to support him."

Voicing majority sentiment in Illinois, McClernand moved on during the winter of 1860–61 to oppose secession strongly, yet he reassured Southerners quietly. "Nobody . . . proposes to subjugate or invade a seceding state." By winter's end McClernand, reflecting Douglas's attitude, hardened his position. "If we become entangled with disunionism we will be lost as a party. . . . We must train the public mind to look upon disunion with horror." McClernand soon began to equate secession with radical revolution, "worse even than Red Republicanism! . . . worse than the Red Communists of France." "Treason" and "traitor" came more easily to his lips.[8]

The death of Douglas in April 1861 gave John McClernand an even greater opportunity for leadership. The Democracy looked to him to point the way for all those "whose hearts still held memories of the Little Giant as the greatest man since Andrew Jackson." McClernand

Brig. Gen. John A. McClernand (Library of Congress)

returned to Illinois at the request of Lincoln and picked up where Douglas had left off, pleading with the people of Illinois and the Midwest to wake up to the danger facing them. Especially in shaky southern Illinois McClernand did "a fine job counteracting proslavery and secessionist influence."

Rushing to Washington when he could, McClernand became the leader of the war Democrats strongly supporting Lincoln's program for rapidly arming the nation.[9] Then he would return to Illinois, helping Governor Yates round up volunteers to march from Springfield down to occupy Cairo. He crisscrossed southern Illinois, pulling along by the ear the popular but equivocal Democrat John A. Logan. McClernand aroused citizens, rallying thousands and Logan to the Union cause. With an extraordinary show of political persuasion and genius, he raised the McClernand Brigade from the most troublesome, the most dangerous area in the Midwest—southern Illinois or "Egypt." For "keeping Egypt right side up," Lincoln gave McClernand a commission as brigadier general, a token gesture for what he had accomplished and for accepting the responsibility entrusted to him.

Summer 1861 found McClernand as commander at Cairo busy readying his brigade. Always hyperactive, he widened his zone of venture, intercepting shipments of arms headed down the Mississippi and cutting off sources of supply for the rebels. No wonder Abraham Lincoln would make "it a point to take special care of him."[10]

McClernand's pre–Civil War life had a strong parallel in that of Lincoln, and his political convolution is reminiscent of Gideon Pillow, his fellow Jacksonian Democrat from Tennessee. Physically, he resembled neither. Almost six feet tall, thin, erect, dark skinned, "peaked in face and hooked in nose," McClernand seemed "fussy, irritable, and nervous, something fidgety about him." John Hay saw him as "a vain, irritable, overbearing, exacting man." His eyes demanded attention; his long, thin face concealed itself behind an "irregular growth of beard."[11]

John McClernand was ambitious. He had a "thirst for military renown" and "an extra-high opinion of himself." To Charles A. Dana he was "merely a smart man, quick, very active minded, but his judgment was not solid, and he looked after himself a good deal." Without a genuine sense of humor, McClernand gave play to a terrible temper, a sensitivity to slight, and a fondness for intrigue. He also had a "disdain for West Pointers" and the "trade-unionism of regular officers."

This touchy, dangerous, "old and intimate friend" of Lincoln required careful handling.[12] Grant was sufficiently perceptive to realize he commanded a powerful man hungry for national attention. It would be unrealistic, perhaps dangerous, to expect loyalty; it would be prudent to expect upstaging and insubordination. Grant's caution, his apprehensions became almost transparent in his overly correct relations with John McClernand.[13]

Naturally McClernand's aides consisted of trusted friends and good Democrats. Maj. Mason Brayman, for instance, handled his correspondence and supervised the rest of the staff. Former editor of the *Louisville Advertiser* and Democratic loyalist, Brayman could be counted on. An interesting addition to McClernand's staff was Lincoln's Polish friend Capt. Alexander Bielaski. A veteran of war against the Russians, Bielaski had immigrated to the United States and become a civil engineer in Illinois. Lincoln became one of his first American friends in 1837. Bielaski married in Illinois and began to raise his family. He moved to Washington in 1845 to work in the General Land Office. By 1853 he had become a principal draftsman with a good salary and a home within walking distance of the Capitol. When Lincoln became president he made a point of walking over to Bielaski's home in the evening, and the two would sit together on the front porch. Once war came, the fifty-year-old Bielaski offered Lincoln his services as a soldier. Lincoln appointed him aide-de-camp with the rank of captain.[14] So Bielaski resigned his "valuable situation in the Interior Department," sold his furniture, and moved his family to Springfield, going west to help Lincoln's friend John McClernand.[15]

3

Grant moved about the muddy streets of Cairo with care. Plank side-walks helped in spots, but "never otherwise than forlorn, Cairo is pre-eminently lugubrious during a mild rain. In dry weather, even glowing like a furnace, you may find amusement in the contemplation of the high water mark upon trees and houses." This tiny town of wooden houses dropped below the level of the rivers on either side, hiding itself behind a high stone levee infested with "very large rats." Charles Dickens, who visited Cairo in 1842, remembered "the hateful Missis-sippi, circling and eddying before it, and turning off upon its southern course a slimy monster hideous to behold; a hotbed of disease, an ugly sepulchre, a grave uncheered by any gleam of promise; such is dismal Cairo."[1]

Cairo remained "essentially a frontier town on the very borders of Secessia."[2] Rebel sympathizers infested the place. McClernand, as commandant, zealously monitored activities and "utterances" at the local "Beer Garden" and set secret watches for the Knights of the Golden Circle. Tennesseans had settled the area around Cairo, and virtually everyone in Egypt[3] thought of himself as a Jacksonian Demo-crat. The clamor for secession from Illinois had been stilled, but many people in these southern counties remained sullen. At least a company, perhaps a regiment, of citizens had crossed over to the Confederate side, John Logan's brother-in-law among them. Most people agreed with the South about slavery, and most rejected the notion of forceful coercion. But love of the union, as basic to Jacksonian Democracy as the coal floor under the state of Illinois, came first.[4]

Prosperity helped. Illinois was booming, its population having doubled during the past ten years. With pride Illinois flexed its muscles nationally: Lincoln and Douglas in 1858, the Republican National Convention in Chicago in 1860, two of the four presidential candidates, and now it was the home state of the president himself.

Secession, nevertheless, brought "deep grief." The previous March, Stephen A. Douglas would drop by a large home in Washington and spend the evening discussing the dangerous state of affairs with his trusted followers McClernand, Logan, and Philip Bond Fouke. Not only did these congressmen, the pro-Union, Douglas-Democrat triumvirate from central and southern Illinois, share the same political views, but they and their families shared the same home.[5]

People felt drawn to Phil Fouke because of his easy manner. He had a way of focusing on a person and making him or her feel important. Forty-three years old, son of prominent early settlers of southern Illinois, Fouke first thought he would be a civil engineer then at twenty-three turned newspaperman. Editing and publishing the *Belleville Advocate*, however, proved as unsatisfying as interviewing Charles Dickens. Welcomed by young editor Fouke and the good citizens of Belleville, Dickens had examined their proud new hotel with a "cynical expression" and had wondered what had led him to leave the comforts of St. Louis to explore Belleville, "the very heart of the bush and swamp."[6]

Phil Fouke switched to law. By 1846 he had a good practice in Belleville and had become prosecuting attorney for the Kaskaskia District. And, as seemed to be the case with young successful Illinois lawyers, he acquired an appetite for political life: he was elected to the Illinois House in 1851, followed by an unsuccessful bid for Congress in 1855. In 1859 Fouke won a seat in the House and went to Washington. His congressional career so far had been undistinguished, but convivial Phil Fouke knew everyone. Among the men whose company he enjoyed in Washington was Rep. John Vines Wright of Tennessee.[7]

When his friend John McClernand donned a brigadier general's uniform and set about recruiting an Illinois brigade, nothing would do but for Phil Fouke to join in. So Fouke came home and set to work. From the south-central part of the state he quickly raised ten companies of men who made up the 30th Illinois Volunteer Infantry. Fouke became their colonel.[8]

The farm boy privates from Laomi and Chester and Hutsonville who joined Colonel Fouke soon found themselves in Cairo in tents close to the river, exposed to the weather and to ordinary diseases against which they had little immunity. Measles raged in camp, and any form of serious illness seemed to mean death for the boys "who had not been much from home." Suicide, as well, was not a stranger in this dangerously unhealthy place.[9]

Fouke and the other regimental commanders knew what they must do. First the raw troops, filled with "home ideas," must learn with brutal suddenness what "superior authority" meant. It meant obeying orders and drill, drill, drill despite the "continuous rain and mud" or the "broiling sun." The troops were kept busy with dress parades at 5 P.M. daily, and frequent inspections. Pvt. David Poak complained about the third inspection one week: "We had our knapsacks on packed with everything we could get in them and had to take them off and open them out and then repack them again." They were forever on police duty or standing guard. Difficulties arose with the practice of Fouke's men firing their muskets "into the air" when relieved from watch. Artillery captain James Dresser had enough of this lunacy and went straight to brigade commander McClernand. A musket ball had just hit between two of Dresser's tents, and "day before yesterday while I was drilling my men a ball passed between me and the squad I was drilling."[10]

Privately, just out of sight of the troops, the officers of Logan's regiment, the 31st Illinois, drilled. Shouting commands with a respectful tone and demonstrating how to do the manual of arms was Pvt. Robert N. Pearson of Company K, a Mexican War veteran. Fellow veteran Lt. Col. John H. White, not John Logan, conducted the regimental drill while Private Pearson took care of teaching the officers their company drill.[11]

John White prepared the 31st to fight while Logan and Maj. Andrew J. Kuykendall, "a prominent Vienna Democrat," sought equipment and uniforms. Logan wrote letters to friends in Washington and Springfield and went about Illinois seeing the right people. John Logan called his men, most of whom were constituents he knew well, the "Dirty-first." These men of Centralia, Jefferson, Stonefort, and Pinckneyville in southern Illinois impressed Lieutenant Colonel White. It was "as fine a Regiment as in the United States." Company I, however, was different, mixed with men from outside Logan's district: some

Col. John A. Logan (Library of Congress)

from Chicago, some from Indiana, and one from Montreal. The large and popular 31st even attracted an independent cavalry company under Capt. James J. Dollins from Franklin County.[12]

"Black Jack" Logan was the heart and soul of the 31st and, excluding McClernand himself, the most important member of the Mc-

Clernand Brigade and of Grant's expeditionary force. With a complexion so swarthy that he could be mistaken for an Indian, this proud descendant of Robert Bruce was of striking appearance—powerful physically, with black eyes that glistened, "black oily hair, and a long drooping black oily mustache." Logan fought and swore and drank. He won Grant's heart with his ability to ride and to race. And he played the violin. One enduring word picture has him on a bench, a bottle of whiskey by his side, wearing nothing but his hat, blouse, and boots, playing the violin furiously for "darky roustabouts to dance." "The pride of Egypt" could tell a good story and talk and laugh all night. As a "stump speaker he had few equals"; he could sway men's convictions.[13]

Logan had been indicted twice as a young man for gambling, and he had chased runaway slaves and thundered off after horse thieves with legendary success. The Mexican War in which he served as a second lieutenant broadened his vision and whetted his ambition. He graduated from the University of Louisville in 1851 and was admitted to the Illinois bar in 1852. Politics naturally attracted him and, thanks to his father's "ready-made political organization," John Logan won and held a seat in the Illinois House during most of the 1850s. There he quickly displayed his "contentious spirit," becoming best known for his "vehement defense of the Fugitive Slave Act" and his bill to exclude free blacks from the state, the Logan Negro Law.

At the age of thirty-two, in 1858, he went to Congress as a free soil Democrat. His first speech in the House was so combative as to "disrupt proceedings," so infuriating to Republicans that a brawl nearly occurred on the floor. Logan would have liked nothing better. He "never hesitated" in his support of Stephen A. Douglas, and as a disciple of Douglas he became a trusted friend of McClernand. At the 1860 Democratic National Convention, however, Logan sympathized openly with the South and during the winter crisis of 1861 felt "ashamed to be a Northerner." He took a position as a peace Democrat, believing that secession "had law on its side." He quarreled bitterly with Douglas after the national election when the latter pledged Lincoln his support: "You have sold out the Democratic party, but, by God, you can't deliver it."

Logan went underground in the spring of 1861 and even obstructed the attempt to raise a regiment in Egypt. With his brother-in-law in

the Confederate army, it was widely believed that his name was being used for rebel recruiting purposes and that he would command
the men who left Illinois and ventured down to Tennessee. The situation was intolerable for him and his constituents, and he came "under
pressure throughout the state to end his silence." Logan apparently
reached his crisis when he decided to give a "spread-eagle" speech
for reenlistment to Grant's regiment at Camp Yates in June. McClernand's influence appears to have been decisive.

Lincoln and Illinois unionists were delighted with Logan's conver-
sion. And true to his word, Logan, silk hat, frock coat, and all, left
Washington in June, joined a Michigan regiment, and blasted away
at rebels in the battle of Bull Run. Grant knew Logan's popularity in
Egypt was "unbounded" now that "the very men who at first made it
necessary to guard the roads in southern Illinois became the defenders
of the Union."[14] Still there were many who doubted his sincerity and
distrusted him. Many always would. Critics, including George Thomas
and William T. Sherman, would charge that Logan was an opportun-
ist, a man capable of flipping from "Negrophobe to Negrophile," an
amateur, "theatrical" in appearance and action, a dangerous enemy of
the professional officer. Sherman would go on to say, however, that
Logan was "a brave, fierce fighter, full of the passion of war . . . perfect
in battle."

Grant had acquired in John A. Logan a powerhouse, a charismatic
leader of men who radiated a sense of alertness and anticipation, a
man who despised caution and indecisiveness, who hated "academic
soldiers," who "never did anything by halves."[15]

In sharp contrast to John Logan was the fifty-four-year-old colonel
of the 27th Illinois, Napoleon Bonaparte Buford. Attractive, refined,
well educated, Buford understood and appreciated the military establishment. He had attended West Point, graduating in 1827 with his
good friend Leonidas Polk, whom he admired very much. In Cairo in
the fall of 1861 their relationship was common gossip.[16]

After graduation from the academy, Napoleon Buford served as a
company grade officer in artillery and then went back and taught two
years at West Point. In 1835, however, Buford resigned from the army,
attended Harvard Law School, and for a short time taught natural and
experimental philosophy there. Then he became a civil engineer employed by his native state of Kentucky. In 1843 he moved to Rock Is-

Col. Napoleon B. Buford
(Chattanooga–Hamilton County Bicentennial Library)

land, Illinois, where he blended the enterprises of banker, merchant, and railroad enthusiast. Buford was one of the "originators" of the Rock Island Railroad and president of the Rock Island and Peoria. As a sideline he experimented in developing livestock, importing and widely exhibiting prize cattle. In 1861 he was caught with $200,000 invested in southern state bonds, which lost most of their value when war broke out. "Assigning his property to creditors," Buford raised the 27th Illinois.[17]

Buford had many powerful friends. Although a Democrat he had immediate access to Washington through his Republican friends, Salmon P. Chase and Orville Browning among them. In the spring of 1862, Secretary of War Edwin Stanton would even think of Buford as a possible commander of the Army of the Potomac.[18]

Grant did not impress Buford. "Grant has personal bravery but no capacity—was a very small man. Take the least and feeblest of the Circuit Judges of Illinois, and Grant was less than he." John Rawlins reciprocated: "Buford is a kind-hearted and affectionate old gentleman, entertaining views at variance with our republican institutions. . . . a weak and foolish old man." Surgeon John H. Brinton felt Buford to be a "fussy old gentleman, an old granny, but kind and amiable."[19]

The 27th came from the middle-western counties of Illinois.[20] Its ranks contained a number of Germans, including one young man whom Sen. Orville Browning had adopted and raised, Lt. William Shipley. Also in the regiment were the twenty-five-year-old farmer and observer Cpl. Edward W. Crippin and the captain of Company K, Lewis Hansback, a thirty-two-year-old schoolteacher. Napoleon Buford wanted the 27th to be a model regiment, and therefore he worked them hard, conducting much of the drill himself. After drill, in the old army style, Colonel Buford would invite one company then another to come by his quarters and sing patriotic and sacred songs, "melodious German and English songs," for him and Mrs. Buford.[21]

Incessant drill took its toll on the officers of the 27th. Although they took some pride, perhaps, in having a West Pointer for a colonel and having him drill them himself, enough was enough. Many of the officers and men became fed up with Buford and his martial airs. Three of his company commanders came forward and asked him to resign as colonel, "for which offense his majesty has seen fit to place them under arrest."[22]

Military proficiency came slowly, painfully. Many looked upon drill as foolishness and accepted discipline grudgingly. The veneer of the disciplined warrior was paper-thin, indeed. For personal disputes and civil crimes, "the lynch law of the West" often prevailed in the tent camps of Cairo.

Some of Grant's soldiers still wore civilian clothes as late as the end of October. At Bird's Point Col. Henry Dougherty's men of the 22d Illinois griped about their "kind of grey uniform." Capt. James C. Parrott of the 7th Iowa also complained, noting that the "Hawkeyes" looked "ragged as birds." Indeed, Pvt. Caleb Green of the 7th Iowa would go off to fight at Belmont "caparisoned like a city man of fashion." Affairs took a turn for the better in mid-October, however, when most of the 7th Iowa were issued a strange-looking dark blue jacket. They would still fuss about the issue, nevertheless, feeling they might be mistaken as Zouaves. "This regiment drew no overcoats. Rubber blankets and ponchos were not furnished to the troops at that time, so the men used their gray woolen blankets for both raincoats and overcoats." The "Suckers," Grant's Illinois troops, seemed to be receiving preferential treatment from the "shoulder strap officials."[23]

Perhaps Grant minimized the resentment, the rivalry, this Hawkeye regiment felt, but he knew too well the condition of his Cairo and Bird's Point troops. "The fact is when I sent troops to Paducah I selected the fullest Regiments and those best armed and equipped, leaving here the raw, unarmed and ragged."[24] The state of Illinois exerted itself to the limit to arm, feed, and train these volunteers who flowed into the army by thousands.

McClernand's men, thanks more to Frémont than anyone, had received their arms. Instead of the Springfields they wanted, however, they got the longer Austrian muskets, 2,000 of them, which first had to go to the Eagle Iron Works in Cincinnati to be "shorn of flint and frizzen, and supplied with cap locks." The "dangerous old musket . . . at every discharge 'kicked' in its recoil so vigorously that the soldiers cursed the day they made its acquaintance." The two flank companies of the 7th Iowa received Springfields with tape self-primers, while the rest got the modified "buck and ball" Springfield muskets. In any case, Grant's command was indifferently armed, and many, in some cases one-fourth, of the muskets in a company were to "choke and burst" at Belmont. Captain Bielaski, Lincoln's Polish friend on McClernand's staff, worried about the cavalry's not having lances. To strengthen his argument he provided McClernand with the number of light cavalry regiments using lances in the Austrian and French armies, noting that even the Cossacks actually were irregular cavalry lancers.[25]

Grant, concerned about the lack of proper arms, appealed to Governor Yates by letter and then made a trip to Springfield on October 21 for three days of meetings. A week later an investigating committee from the U.S. House showed up in Cairo and called Grant to testify about the equipment and arms needed by his command. Fouke and particularly McClernand strongly supported their commander and also actively solicited equipment and arms everywhere. Overcoats and haversacks by the thousands appeared on November 1 and were issued. More equipment was on its way. Cairo had clout.[26]

The men of Iowa at Bird's Point noticed that clout. Soldiers from the Sucker state "seemed to be treated a little better" than the Hawkeyes. Grant's 7th Iowa Regiment had been raised from the extreme north and south of the state, with a couple of companies representing central counties. The regimental band, the pride of the 7th, was from Muscatine. It was composed mostly of Germans, reflecting the high percentage of Germans in the regiment itself. Raised in July, armed in August, it "left for the front before it received uniforms or equipment." Indeed, the 7th was in the field at Ironton, Missouri, before they had their first opportunity to learn the manual of arms. They campaigned under Brig. Gen. Benjamin Prentiss in Missouri during September, then moved on to the Cairo area in October.[27]

Col. Jacob G. Lauman led the 7th. "A novice at war," this Burlington businessman possessed initiative and boundless enthusiasm. His men admired him and felt confident of his leadership in battle. Like John Logan, Lauman depended heavily upon his second in command. Lt. Col. Augustus Wentz had been born in Germany and immigrated to the United States. The outbreak of the Mexican War found him a young merchant in New York City, and he volunteered eagerly for the regular 2d U.S. Artillery as a private. Following the war he moved west, married nineteen-year-old Rebecka McMurty in Independence, Missouri, in 1852, and settled down in Davenport. He raised a company of Germans from Davenport in the spring of 1861, and with this three-month-old company he distinguished himself under Lyon at the battle of Wilson's Creek. Promotion came rapidly. By October Wentz was lieutenant colonel of the 7th Iowa.

The major of the 7th, Elliott W. Rice, had been promoted to corporal in July then to major later in the month. This twenty-six-year-old Oskaloosa lawyer had promising command qualities and a prominent older brother.[28]

Col. Jacob G. Lauman (Library of Congress)

Hard, monotonous drill sessions, relieved by an occasional game of horseshoes or a turn at trying to catch deer swimming in the river, could only last so long, however. Grant knew this, and he realized better than anyone he would have to fight these men soon or all the monotony and sacrifice of Cairo would be a waste. Often he sent small reconnoitering parties of infantry and cavalry into the Missouri and Kentucky countryside, partly to train his troops more realistically and partly for the "purpose of familiarizing the soldiers with the sensation of being in the 'enemys' country.'" Grant did a much better job of this than his counterpart in Columbus.

Now and then Grant would send a gunboat to "paddle down within shooting distance" of Polk's batteries on the Iron Banks. The sound of the gunboat's cannon could be heard back in Cairo, twenty miles away. The noise excited the men and made them "clamorous for a battle." "Burning with a valor as yet untried," soldiers of the Mc-Clernand Brigade "foolishly threatened to desert if something were not done to bring on the issue." [29]

4

—————————————————————————

Polk and Pillow

The Confederates at Columbus had an old man as their leader. "Old Granny" they called him.[1] And it was a point of embarrassment to have a divine, an ancient one at that, leading an army. When it came to fighting and the sterner stuff of war, what could a man expect?

Leonidas Polk looked like a major general, though—over six feet tall, straight, with hair and "side whiskers (a la militaire) precociously frosted," a remarkable nose, and a distinct voice suited for command. He laced conversation with revealing anecdote and "a dry vein of humor" that most thought "wonderfully charming," although one Yankee critic felt Polk's manner "somewhat flippant." The old general "was not altogether priest or soldier, and the admixture of the manners of both was not happy." Another Union soldier felt more strongly: "He was strutting in his uniform & yellow sash & impresses me as an insufferably vain, conceited old rebel cox comb whom I would like to know had met a traitor's death." A *New York Herald* correspondent, however, found Polk's company over several hours pleasant. "He is by no means an austere man . . . yet determination sits upon every lineament of his countenance, and firmness creeps out in every look and gesture."[2]

Admirers saw him as "dignified, firm and resolute, and with a heart wholly given to the cause." "Nothing mean or insincere could possibly be imputed to him." He was a man "whom noble men might love and meaner men might fear."[3]

Polk had been born to a prominent North Carolina family in 1806. His grandfather had distinguished himself fighting the British, and his father told the story of Tarleton's dragoons chasing him and his boy-hood friend Andrew Jackson down a Waxhaw, South Carolina, coun-try road. Polk's father had become a soldier, so it seemed destined that Leonidas Polk attend West Point. There he became Albert Sidney Johnston's roommate and friend for life. Cadet Polk startled Johnston, however, the rest of the cadet corps, and his family, when he was con-verted by the college chaplain and became overtly religious. The "first cadet ever to kneel during services in the Academy chapel," he made a profound impact upon underclassman Jefferson Davis who already admired him.

Polk graduated from West Point in 1827 and immediately began his theological preparation instead of entering the army. A highly success-ful ministry followed. In 1838 he was consecrated missionary bishop of the Southwest, a vast frontier diocese of the Episcopal church ex-tending from Alabama across the Mississippi to the Indian Territory. He attacked his charge. In the first six months of 1839 he traveled 5,000 miles, nearly all on horseback. In 1841 he became bishop of Louisiana. He owned a large sugar plantation named Leighton at Bayou Lafourche with about 400 slaves. He had the reputation of be-ing an enlightened master and married slaves in his home with cere-mony, but ultimately he failed as a manager and lost Leighton in 1854. It seemed he would not allow his duties as plantation owner to inter-fere with his obligations as bishop.[4]

A passionate defender of secession, Polk journeyed to Virginia in the early summer of 1861 to visit Louisiana troops. On the way he stopped off at Nashville and talked with Gov. Isham G. Harris. Harris asked Polk to call on President Davis while he was in Richmond and "im-press upon him 'the very great importance of effectively speeding up the defenses of the Mississippi Valley.' " Polk did see Davis and pre-sented the case of the western Confederates, adding that Albert Sidney Johnston would be a most welcome appointment. Davis turned the tables on Polk, however. Since Johnston was not yet available, would Polk himself accept a commission as major general and command the forces defending the Mississippi until Johnston arrived? Davis pressed him for an answer backed by delegations of men from the Mississippi Valley present in Richmond. Members of the cabinet also met with Polk and urged him to accept the president's offer. Polk debated with himself over a week. It was a wrenching decision; his letters to his wife

Maj. Gen. Leonidas Polk (Valentine Museum, Richmond, Virginia)

stand as evidence. In the end he accepted. Davis recalled he did so with reasons "beautifully and reverently" expressed. Polk wrote, "My heart is in it. . . . It seems to be a call of Providence."[5] Most of his fellow southern clergy disapproved, however, and his friend, Bishop Stephen Elliott, warned that he would be subjected to "the ordeals of all men who do unusual things."[6]

Thus there came to be at fortress Columbus a "curious flavor of medievalism in the appearance of this bishop at the head of an army"[7]—the first, according to historian John Fiske, since the bishop of Derry slain in 1690 at the battle of the Boyne.[8] Wags gleefully greeted Polk's statement, "I buckle the sword over the gown." Snickers of "fat bishoprics" and "warlike ecclesiastic" and "by command of the divine" abounded among his critics, then and since.

What had Jefferson Davis done in appointing a clergyman who had never seen battle and who, as an officer, had never given an order? Polk had received a soldier's education; he belonged to one of the most prominent extended families in the South; he was widely known and respected as an outstanding churchman and as the leader of a success- ful campaign to found the University of the South. He knew well the Mississippi Valley that he would command, its terrain, its people, and its leaders. Besides, Davis trusted Polk implicitly and believed him to be a natural leader, evenhanded in dealing with men. Davis knew it was a good appointment politically; militarily he hoped Polk would prove him right.

There did seem to be a sense of completeness about Leonidas Polk, a revealed value system. He would admit foul-ups and did not seem to brood. "He always thought of himself as a soldier," and "his air of command never left him." As bishop his leadership style had been to give subordinates "a great amount of freedom of action." "Make your- self felt rather than seen in your people's work. Always give them credit for what is done, never take it to yourself." "This great and good man was an elegant and noble gentleman," said a staff officer. "He was a strict disciplinarian, and required full service from his officers . . . ; but he was kind and just." "General Polk was a prince among men. . . . His character was beautiful in its simplicity and its strength."[9]

Polk's performance commanding the Western Department during the late summer and early fall disappointed his admirers. He bore re- sponsibility for the loss of the Confederate initiative in Missouri. His

seizure of Columbus appeared to have been a knee-jerk reaction, in-
flaming Kentucky. Then, after paying this enormous political price and
accepting the blame for aggression, he neglected to capture Paducah.
An impatient Southern public "could not understand why the army
did not move upon the enemy. He was sensitive of this and distrustful
of himself."

Was Polk only interested in conducting a holding action, focusing
exclusively on the defense of the Mississippi and hoping for a bloodless
solution in the West by establishing a massive, unassailable fortress?
Only an intimate friend like Bishop James Otey of Tennessee who visited Polk and talked late into the night would know "his earnest desire
and efforts to be relieved" of his command.

Between the professional officer and the volunteer officer corps,
however, Polk promised to be a bridge. Not handicapped by jealousy
and disdain for the profession and certainly not contemptuous and
distrustful of the volunteer, he could be appreciated by both. A well-
connected and knowledgeable Mississippi Valley citizen, Sam Tate,
remarked, "General Polk is a sensible man, and will do well if he had
proper cooperation." [10]

Proper cooperation, however, began with Polk's chief subordinate,
Brig. Gen. Gideon Johnson Pillow, a man of national reputation. Pillow had been instrumental in the nomination of Polk's uncle, James
K. Polk, as presidential candidate of the Democracy. He had also been
a major general, and one who had seen combat, having led troops to
victory in Mexico.

They were the same age, but Pillow looked "much younger." A
pleasant-looking man, with quick hazel eyes and animated features,
he appeared "rather the gentleman." Born of a propertied, well-con-
nected family with a tradition of being ferocious Indian fighters and
loyal Andrew Jackson lieutenants, Pillow had practiced criminal and
civil law. He was a good attorney with a strong practice in Columbia,
Tennessee, but law and the management of his farm Clifton Place
were not enough. His passions were land speculation and politics.
When one totals Pillow's real property in Tennessee, north Mississippi,
and along the Mississippi River in Arkansas, he emerges as one of the
largest landholders in the South and in 1860 perhaps the wealthiest
Tennessean. Unlike many of the South's great farm owners he had
access to capital in the East, particularly Pennsylvania. Ready capi-

tal helped him ride out cotton's peaks and valleys and enabled him to be a spokesman and leader for long-term improvements. Along the Mississippi, for instance, Pillow was personally responsible for the construction of miles of levees. As a highly successful capitalist he had much at stake when his native state assumed a warlike posture in 1861.[11]

Perhaps the beginning of Pillow's political career came in 1831. Gov. William Carroll appointed him at age twenty-five as district attorney general and soon thereafter inspector general of the Tennessee Militia. Pillow parlayed the latter post into a powerful base of support. Early he committed himself to the Democracy and to James K. Polk's political fortunes. Following Polk's death in 1849, he and J. Knox Walker, Polk's private secretary and nephew, became Polk's political heirs. In 1850 Pillow played a prominent leadership role in the pivotal Nashville Convention, helping defeat southern extremists. He also enjoyed a significant management role in Franklin Pierce's nomination in 1852, and Jefferson Davis believed Pillow "played a key role in securing Buchanan's nomination" in 1856. His attempts to gain the nomination for himself as vice president in 1852 and 1856 failed, as did his bid for a Senate seat in 1857.[12] Pillow in 1860, as an ally of compromiser John McClernand, tried valiantly to rally Tennessee behind Douglas and restore the shattered national Democratic party. He did not view the election of Lincoln as cause for secession himself but accepted the will of the majority of Tennesseans.[13]

The Mexican War had greatly broadened Pillow's national political base. His name became widely known, and he made allies of powerful leaders in the East, George Cadwalader and Franklin Pierce among them. His prominence would be tarnished, however, by the mishandling of his brigade at the battle of Cerro Gordo. Three courts of inquiry also blighted Pillow's military record—one for claiming responsibility for winning the battle of Contreras, another for "attempting to appropriate" a Mexican howitzer, and a third for insubordination. He was acquitted in each instance, but as Polk's tool, his self-promoting and disruptive antics so enraged Winfield Scott that they resulted in a shameful episode in which a popular and successful American military leader was relieved of command by the president at the moment of victory.[14]

The professional military establishment closed ranks behind Scott.

Brig. Gen. Gideon J. Pillow (Valentine Museum, Richmond, Virginia)

Their sarcasm knew no bounds. Sherman labeled Pillow "a man of vanity, conceit, ignorance, ambition, and want of truth." According to John Sedgwick, "The sentiment of the army will never acquit him." George McClellan denounced "his worse than puerile imbecility." Gordon Granger remembered, "I knew Gid Pillow in Mexico, and he always was an old fool." Lew Wallace thought he was "of a jealous nature, insubordinate, and quarrelsome." To the professional soldier, Pillow, with his lack of respect and antagonism toward the career officer, represented the epitome of the inept and unpredictable volunteer. They could not forgive his habit of undermining authority, "his record of conflict with his commander, flaunting of the military chain of command, and . . . staged press releases to snatch glory at the expense of others." Years later, in an unusually dispassionate assessment, Gen. Josiah Gorgas said, "He is a man of energy and ability, and, were he content to *serve*, would, I think, be very useful; but his great ambition leads him to seek commands to which his military status is hardly equal. To a General by whom he would be controlled he would be very useful."[15]

Grant shared the "openly bantered image" of Pillow "as a military buffoon." Pillow was "the one Confederate officer for whom Grant consistently and openly expressed personal contempt."[16] In a letter to his sister, Grant wrote, "I do not say he would shoot himself, ah, no! I am not so uncharitable as many who served under him in Mexico. I think, however, he might report himself wounded on the receipt of a very slight scratch, received hastily in any way, and might irritate the core until he convinced himself that he had been wounded by the enemy."[17]

The story about constructing fortifications backward at Camargo echoed in 1861 as Confederates began spreading tales of improper emplacements at Memphis with guns pointing away from the river. One Confederate observed that General Pillow "does more foolish things than any one I ever saw." Others noted his "squabbles with the other Generals," "his oily manner," and that he had the "courage and confidence of a fool."[18]

Missouri lieutenant governor Thomas C. Reynolds, a friend and political ally of Pillow's, remarked that his deployment of troops in southeastern Missouri in August 1861 was "so unskillful as almost to invite attack."[19] For the most part, however, the Tennesseans serving under him at Columbus felt as Lt. John Johnson:

He was always pleasant and approachable and indeed seemed to be fond of talking to the private soldiers, and he was withal a gallant old fellow, but had a good deal of egotism of an inoffensive sort. He loved to talk of himself and the great things he would do or had done, but was not arrogant or unkind to other people.

The soldiers all liked Gen. Pillow personally, although they did not have any great confidence in his military capacity.[20]

Gideon Pillow defies easy categorization. With the backing of his close friend, Isham G. Harris, Pillow built the manpower structure that would become the Army of Tennessee and infused it with his enthusiasm. Historian Richard McMurry acknowledges the contributions of Pillow and Harris but quite rightly points out that they pale when compared to the beginnings of the Army of Northern Virginia. Pillow's incompetence and his and Governor Harris's insistence on fortifying the Mississippi to the detriment of the rest of the state led to confusion, a "legacy of bitter personal feuding among the generals," and fatal strategy.[21]

Perhaps misguided, undoubtedly shrill, Pillow's was the most distinct demand for an offensive in the summer of 1861. He would suffer, demoted from major general of Tennessee's Provisional Army to Confederate brigadier while company grade officers under him in Mexico leaped ahead of him in 1861. With the blessing of that good Democrat Jefferson Davis, they held commands of greater responsibility and higher visibility. Pillow had more combat experience as a general officer than any other Confederate. Yet here he was in Columbus—the sword of the people of Tennessee sheathed in the scabbard of a cleric with the killer instincts of a sow.

Leonidas Polk knew Pillow, this self-obsessed man of enormous charm; he had known him and his family for thirty years. What was he to do? His senior officer, the man he must trust, he knew from reputation and experience to be a "reckless egotist," far more dangerous than any torpedo hidden in the waters of the Mississippi.

Leonidas Polk had a problem.

An English observer, a keen admirer of Polk, also saw trouble ahead. Pillow made no secret of his annoyance over not commanding all the Confederates at Columbus, "a position for which he is totally unfitted." The Tennessean's "vanity is not less conspicuous than it was in Mexico, and he is eternally carping at 'the bishop,' as he terms Polk." [22]

Maj. E. G. W. Butler, Jr., of the 11th Louisiana reported, "I see Genls. Polk and Pillow from time to time, they are both very polite to me allways; the army has no confidence in either of them." [23]

The Confederate army had a problem.

5

✳ ─── ✳

Columbus

Columbus, Kentucky, "Gibraltar of the Mississippi," lay low and flat on the east bank of the river. It boasted four brick buildings and "a population in its palmiest days of about one thousand." Towering above Columbus were spectacular bluffs, about 150 feet high. Those south of town were known to river people as the "Chalk Bluffs" because of their bright coffee color. Above town, defiantly facing north toward Cairo, sister bluffs a little higher than the Chalk Bluffs projected sharply into the Mississippi. These bluffs with their hint of iron caught the attention of explorers Marquette and Jolliet who named them the Iron Banks. The town eventually became the northern terminus of the Mobile and Ohio Railroad, which gave Columbus importance.[1] And, as was commonly known, its magnificent bluffs controlled the Mississippi, "a sort of shield to that Illinois sword lunging so far southward." It "was a near perfect place to post batteries," and "if properly fortified, no northern gunboat could pass."[2]

The Confederates believed that. Immediately they set about making Columbus the most heavily fortified point in North America. Down came the trees. A Confederate lamented, "The noble forest that beautifies our hill has been cut away, allowing our camp to look down on Columbus."[3] On the Iron Banks Polk's men constructed three tiers of batteries. First, fifteen feet above the river's edge, they built a water battery "composed of many 10-inch Columbiads and 11-inch howitzers." Midway up the bluffs came other batteries. At the top bristled cannon from a string of earthen forts. One featured the biggest gun in the Confederacy, a 128-pounder Whitworth rifled gun known as the "Lady Polk." About a mile north of town, "where the bluff jets out flush with the river," a shelf of land was cleared for still another battery position.[4]

Some 140 guns poked from embrasures. Any approaching enemy gunboat must confront this tremendous concentration of firepower with fire angles varying from plunging to waterline. Just beneath the surface of the river itself Confederate engineers suspended torpedoes, crude mines with wires attached for Yankee gunboats to touch and detonate. Another defensive feature was the great chain. It was "intended to stop the boats which should attempt to run past the fort until the land batteries could sink them." The chain extended across the river buoyed by a series of rafts. Its hundreds of iron links, weighing nineteen pounds apiece, were held in place by an anchor with seven-foot arms. This enormous, costly, imaginative, clumsy obstruction failed, snaring only a riverboat that drifted too close.[5] But the great chain symbolized the mind-set of Leonidas Polk, his absolute determination to defend the Mississippi.

The soldiers called the forts scattered across the top of the bluff "bull pen forts." Fifty to one hundred yards square, they had thick walls constructed from cornsacks filled with sand. A ditch ten feet deep and eight feet wide ran in a great crescent around the forts. In front of the ditch they cleared all undergrowth as well as trees. They sharpened the ends of the trees and laid them crisscrossed like matchsticks to form an abatis. The works, the ditches, and the forts extended four miles.

Polk had confidence that the guns would be well served. Brig. Gen. John Porter McCown would see to that—he had graduated from West Point, had long service in the artillery, had an excellent Mexican War combat record, and had seen action during the Seminole War. He had commanded, with some success, the Artillery Corps of Pillow's Provisional Tennessee Army. Two northern newspaper reporters met McCown in Columbus; he impressed them. "Every inch the soldier," reported the *St. Louis Republican.* "A veteran officer, burned by the sun in the performance of duty, nerved with the iron snarl of the bull terrier," recounted a New York journalist. Comparing McCown to Polk and Pillow, the reporter felt that surely McCown was the "fighting man of the staff."[6] Confederate insiders, however, had doubts. The lieutenant colonel of the 4th Tennessee discreetly summed up his view of the forty-six-year-old McCown: he was "an old dilapidated fellow with very little energy."[7]

McCown would supervise all of the artillery units, both heavy and light. He would also command the left of the Columbus defenses. Cheatham would command the right. To give defensive depth Polk ordered regular patrols north toward Fort Holt and established picket posts of company strength on the roads to Fort Holt and Blandville.[8]

Polk had the necessary manpower. Certainly he could have used more men, but at Columbus he did have an aggregate total of 17,230 with 16,307 present for duty on October 31. Polk divided his army into four Napoleonic divisions containing the customary infantry, cavalry, and artillery components. Pillow had the largest division—6,862 men in three brigades composed of nine regiments—while Cheatham (3,246), Col. John S. Bowen (3,165), and McCown (3,034) had two brigades apiece, each brigade composed of two regiments. Twelve of these twenty-one infantry regiments were from West Tennessee. An extreme shortage of engineering officers existed in Polk's command along with a drastically short supply of West Pointers.[9]

The Confederates looked like farmers playing soldier. "(I ought hardly to call them such, so rough, ill-clad and ununiformed did they appear) I may say there seems to be a vast field for improvement."[10] Their "clothes seemed old and some even ragged."[11]

As for arms, Jefferson Davis was hardly encouraging: "Get all the troops you can raise with their hunting rifles. They will make the best skirmishers if properly organized and trained."[12] By November 1861 the idea of equipping each soldier with breast and bowel armor plates had been abandoned but not the concept of individual weaponry. The well-armed Confederate brought a small arsenal from home. Lt. John McDonald of the 6th Tennessee appeared with a large knapsack loaded with rations, a double-barreled shotgun strapped across it, a rifle firing grooved minié bullets, a sword, a large knife, two pistols, and a hatchet. McDonald "had the rations to sustain his strength and the weapons to execute his will upon the enemy. His idea was to use his Minie at long range, then his shotgun, then his pistols; then, as the hostile lines came closer, to throw his tomahawk, and then, with sword in one hand and the big knife in the other, to wade in and dispatch ten traditional Yankees."[13]

Polk's men loved their knives. Similar to a bowie knife, steel tipped with both edges sharpened, they "were short as bayonets and broad as the old Highland broadsword."[14] Weapons this handy made for trouble. The Louisiana troops, particularly, demonstrated partiality for them as a device for the resolution of disputes. Lieutenant Favrot of the rowdy Dillon Guards had to shoot one of his men to break up a fight in which the Dillons were cutting up each other.[15]

Old army hand Gen. W. W. Mackall may have been right. "An army is an epitome of the world. . . . All that makes man at once so contemptible and so like a God."[16] The men did not feel much like God. One of the Louisiana privates put it this way: "We're left behind, a set of common laborers, working daily with the axe, the pick and the spade."[17] Bored soldiers, fated to drill and labor in war's backwash, accomplish odd things, such as felling a tree so that it killed a farmer's cow. That Kentucky farmer, whatever his motive, surrendered the cow to be basted with Louisiana sauces.[18]

From the countryside appeared "stout old country wagons of undoubted integrity, coming near the camp with apples, peaches, chicken, butter, etc.," but it seemed they all would "leak in the most unaccountable manner." Whiskey leaked from everywhere. Even down low along the Chalk Bluffs one could brush aside a handful of dirt and discover a spigot, behind it a barrel concealed in a hole dug in the bank. Polk would not stand for it, and Pillow, a teetotaler himself, agreed. So the "strictest martial law prevailed" in Columbus. When the provost caught two civilians selling whiskey, they were brought to the center of town and flogged for all to see.[19]

The conscientious confessed they could not stay clean, and they tired of the wind "whistling now through these old weather-beaten huts" on the top of the bluff.[20] Some like Lt. Charles Johnson, a young man with a medical degree who chose to be an infantry officer, sat on the bank, looked out over the Mississippi, thought of back home in West Feliciana Parish, and then returned to the pages of Francis Bacon.[21] Some chased the plentiful squirrels and gathered nuts by the basketful; some kept company with "the 'ladies' as the camp women are politely called"; others banded together and created minstrel shows.

There must be some sort of recreation indulged in occasionally to alleviate the general monotony. It is true, we have been abundantly supplied with such toys as the little boys like—axes, spades, wheelbarrows, cannon, and the like, and are permitted to play with them four hours each day—cutting down the pretty trees, digging out nice ditches, piling up beautiful dirt ridges, excavating the magnificent bluff, shaping the dirt and trees and things into batteries, poking guns away into all sorts of places, and so on. But this sort of play, though unmistakably healthful, is presided over by so many "speckled officers," and conducted in a style so mathematical, that most of the boys are tired of it and call it hard work. Consequently, whenever they have the chance, the boys engage in all sorts of athletic sports, some of which are harder than any work I ever saw. I may instance a certain herculean game of rolling a cannon ball at nine holes in the ground; foot-racing, wrestling, tree-climbing, etc.[22]

There was drill every day. On one special day the colonel wished to drill the regiment himself. Col. Samuel F. Marks, with his ten companies of the 11th Louisiana at "Present Arms," gave the order, "Stack Arms." An onlooker, who knew better, blushed for the colonel. "What a blunder this was." The Dillon Guards thought nothing about it, and "in an awkward and bungling manner," shouldered arms, marched forward, and stacked arms. However, Company F, the Continental Guards, sometimes called the Orleans Guards, stood fast. Their captain, John G. Fleming, looked stonily to the front.

"Captain Fleming, your men are not obeying my order!" said Colonel Marks. "Why not?"

"I don't know how to give the order, sir," the captain replied.

"Well, I'll have to teach them myself," said the colonel.

"That's just fine with me!" said the captain.

With that Colonel Marks, who was not a man to be trifled with, ordered the Continental Guards off the parade field and put Captain Fleming under arrest.

Lt. Thomas W. Peyton, who had instructed the Continental Guards, spoke to the colonel once the disastrous regimental drill concluded. "I am to blame, sir," he offered, explaining that he had taught the Continentals under no conditions to obey an improper order, and since the colonel's order was improper. . . . Colonel Marks blew up. The lieutenant thereupon offered the colonel his sword. Marks looked at the sword, looked at Lieutenant Peyton, then said, "I already have a good sword," and walked off. Somehow, in the mysterious manner that things resolved themselves in the 11th Louisiana, Captain Fleming returned to duty and things simmered down.[23]

The trouble was that Major Butler had been sick for nearly two months with measles. In July at Camp Moore, back in Tangipahoa Parish, Louisiana, no man could have been more unpopular than this sophisticated, wealthy, diplomat-turned-soldier, Edward George Washington Butler, Jr. He drilled the men incessantly, "though his youth as an officer was sometimes apparent." When the troops became reasonably proficient with small unit maneuvers, Butler taught the 11th how "to charge bayonets at double-quick with the 'Louisiana Shout,' and explained the object of the shout—his desire to see how nearly men in drill could come to the actual charge in battle." The major gradually won the respect of the men and by September perhaps could be considered "popular."[24]

Not that old Colonel Marks was not. This fifty-seven-year-old, battle-scarred veteran of the Seminole War had led the 3d Louisiana Volunteers in the Mexican War. And as a good New Orleans Democrat he served the Democracy as teller of the Louisiana Senate, postmaster of New Orleans, and auditor of the state party. In 1859 he even came close to winning the Democratic nomination for governor. Marks recruited the Continental, Catahoula, and Carroll Guards and interested Mrs. Tracey in giving and raising enough money to equip a company. To honor their benefactor, the men of this company, with her permission, took her maiden name themselves, becoming known as the Dillon Guards.

One would expect the Dillons to have been models of deportment, but such was not the case. The Dillons came to be known for using their knives on each other and for their drinking. In fact in August 1861 when they broke camp, the Dillons decided to celebrate leaving Camp Moore behind. They burned up the floors of their tents and pitched into the flames all the furniture they could find. Colonel Marks himself tried to stop this madness but could not, so he called out the sober half of the regiment to restore order. The next morning, as the 11th boarded the train for Columbus, half the Dillons had to be carried aboard. Trains in those days swayed, and two Dillons fell off, injuring one, killing the other. On the way up through Mississippi, the 11th embarrassed Colonel Marks again when soldiers broke into a whiskey store in Jackson and helped themselves, although no one in the town ever identified the company.[25]

Leonidas Polk knew many of these Louisiana troops. Major Butler's father was an old friend, as was Samuel Marks. This also was the regiment of the Barrows. Robert Hilliard Barrow, the lieutenant colonel, was a wealthy plantation owner—1,500 acres of land and 144 slaves. There were a dozen more Barrows and their relatives in the regiment. All were connected with former senator Alexander Barrow of West Feliciana Parish who was raised in Tennessee and with the prominent George Washington Barrow family of Nashville. Most of Polk's officers knew the dashing Batt Barrow, aide-de-camp of McCown; others knew Hilliard or Clifford or Capt. John Joor Barrow, commander of the Rosale Guards, the company named after the home of Mary Barrow, Robert's wife.[26]

It helped to be a Barrow; it helped almost as much to be a loyal Democrat—that is if one wanted to get ahead in Gideon Pillow's army. Democrats in camp at Columbus were more plentiful than squirrels—there were newspaper editors and congressmen and all sorts of functionaries. A number were officers, such as Col. Thomas J. Freeman of the 22d Tennessee. This hastily raised regiment admired Freeman's ability to speak, his wide reading, and his passion for the cause. Besides that, his grandfather had been a captain in the Revolution. So these men from West Tennessee (Carroll, Hardeman, and Dyer counties), with a few Kentuckians and Memphians thrown in, elected Freeman colonel.

A Baptist and a Mason, Freeman made his home in Trenton, Tennessee. As a young man he started off studying medicine then turned to law and practiced in West Tennessee. Following the Mexican War he switched political parties and rapidly gained favor with the leaders of the Tennessee Democracy, so much so that in 1856 he attended the Democratic National Convention as a delegate. He lacked military experience, but he could lead men and he could flatten complex issues and roll them out in terms that made sense.[27]

One should not come away with the impression, however, that Columbus was a convention of the southern wing of the Democracy. Here and there one could find a Whig: Capt. Dew Moore Wisdom, for instance. Back home in Purdy, Tennessee, twenty-four-year-old Wisdom edited the *Purdy Whig*. John Vines Wright, not wishing to leave anybody out, had convinced Wisdom to bury partisanship and join the 13th Tennessee. Wisdom was even put in command of a company.[28]

Everybody liked Col. John V. Wright. Some people remembered

Col. John V. Wright
(Chattanooga–Hamilton County Bicentennial Library)

that both he and Preston Smith, colonel of the 154th Senior Tennessee, had been arrested in Mexico by Gideon Pillow. But it did not amount to much, at least to John Wright. Pillow had let him off easy, not because he did not deserve punishment but because of the general's high regard for Wright's father.[29]

Wright had ample girth but energy aplenty. He brought the prestige of a veteran U.S. congressman to his work as well as an "easy and courteous manner" and a "seemingly inexhaustible fund of anecdotes and reminiscences." This loyal servant of the Democracy had been educated at the Universities of Virginia and Tennessee, vacillating between the study of medicine and law. Law and politics won out. At thirty-three, in the tradition of his revolutionary war grandfather, he had resigned from Congress and gone home to raise "Wright's Boys" in McNairy County. Wright never pretended to be a military leader and seems not to have had military aspirations, but West Tennesseans wanted John V. Wright to lead them.[30]

Happily for Wright he was ably seconded. Lt. Col. Alfred J. Vaughan had raised a company in Mississippi but had been unable to arm them. This cost him his command, so he volunteered for Wright's 13th. This able officer brought with him sound military schooling he had received at the Virginia Military Institute and the ability to excite subordinates.[31]

And so the fall passed. The Confederates grew stronger. They were short in cavalry, perhaps; the horses were good and they could have gotten more, but forage was terribly scarce. Pillow himself had tried to remedy the situation but ended up intercepting a supply of forage for a general named Bragg who had just organized a few cavalry units and now had to send them back home.

Soldiers worried about becoming sick. One regiment had almost 400 cases of measles. Chronic diarrhea downed hundreds as did respiratory ailments and infections of all sorts. Men were buried daily in the graveyard beside the camp on top of the bluffs. The infantry meanwhile built brick ovens, boarded up their shacks, and dug their ditches deeper and deeper. Around fires at night they watched goose bumps rise on their arms as they heard in the distance Col. Knox Walker's brass band serenade the officers at General Polk's headquarters. If only this waiting would end; if only they could have their fight with the Hessians.[32]

6

★ —————————————————————————— ★
Down the River to Look for a Fight

On November 2 Grant received this order from Frémont's headquarters in St. Louis:

> You are hereby directed to hold your whole command ready to march at an hour's notice, until further orders, and you will take particular care to be amply supplied with transportation and ammunition. You are also directed to make demonstrations with your troops along both sides of the river towards Charleston, Norfolk, and Blandville, and to keep your columns constantly moving back and forward against these places, without, however, attacking the enemy.[1]

Fresh orders from Frémont arrived the next day. Jeff Thompson had appeared with 3,000 men at Indian Ford on the St. Francis River twenty-five miles below Greenville, twenty miles west of Bloomfield. A force from Pilot Knob under Col. William P. Carlin had been sent to attack Thompson. Grant was to "send a force from Cape Girardeau and Bird's Point to assist Carlin in driving Thompson into Arkansas."[2]

Grant responded, directing Col. Richard J. Oglesby at Bird's Point to move his force by boat upstream to Commerce, Missouri. From there Oglesby would advance inland toward Sikeston. Col. Joseph Plummer at Cape Girardeau would coordinate with Oglesby by marching on Bloomfield. Their objective would be "to destroy" Thompson's force, but "the manner of doing it is left largely at your discretion, believing it better not to trammel you with instructions."[3]

On the morning of November 4, Oglesby landed at Commerce with a combined force of about 3,000 men. These troops, when added to Plummer's column, almost equal in size, which was advancing west from Cape Girardeau, represented a substantial commitment of Grant's 20,000 men. Thompson felt threatened by this "concerted movement to break up my command. Genl. Grant had become tired of having a force flying about his posts, that he could neither count nor locate."[4]

On Tuesday, November 5, Grant must have had second thoughts about having dispersed his forces so widely. A telegram reached him from Frémont "stating that the enemy was reenforcing Price's Army from Columbus by way of White River, and directing that the demonstration that had been ordered against Columbus, be immediately made."[5]

Despite the fact that Frémont's directive was "somewhat muddled and . . . based on faulty information," Grant swung into action with a flurry of orders as though he had long anticipated Frémont's order. To Brig. Gen. C. F. Smith at Paducah he wrote that he was "fitting out an expedition to menace Belmont, and will take all the force proper to spare from here—probably not more than 3,000 men. If you can make a demonstration towards Columbus at the same time with a portion of your command, it would probably keep the enemy from throwing over the river much more force than they now have there, and might enable me to drive those they now have out of Missouri."[6]

Smith had his men under way on November 6. His four infantry regiments with cavalry and artillery under Brig. Gen. Eleazer A. Paine advanced southwest to Milburn, Kentucky, while a supporting regiment from Col. W. L. Sanderson's Brigade marched south on the Mayfield Road toward Viola, securing Paine's left flank and substantiating this conspicuous threat against Columbus.[7]

Grant also alerted Oglesby about his Belmont intentions and ordered him to turn his column, now heading east through Sikeston toward Bloomfield, southeast toward New Madrid, "halting to communicate with me at Belmont from the nearest point on his road."[8] To insure that Oglesby received these instructions and to protect his column's left flank, Grant sent a duplicate order to Col. W. H. L. Wallace at Bird's Point. He directed Wallace to proceed with the 11th Illinois Infantry to Charleston, Missouri, to link up with Oglesby.[9] On the morning of November 6, Grant would activate still another column, instructing Col. John Cook at Fort Holt, Kentucky, to advance down the Kentucky side of the Mississippi with his regiment but to go no closer to Columbus than Elliott's Mills.[10] Thus on November 6 Grant would have seven columns of his command, about 15,000 men, simultaneously in motion, from Cape Girardeau to Paducah.

What about the Confederates? "Swamp Fox" Jeff Thompson was not at Indian Ford. With his small, raggedy, loosely organized force of Missourians he actually held Bloomfield, licking his wounds from an encounter on October 21 with Plummer at Fredericktown. Thompson worried that "the enemy columns that marched on Bloomfield would catch me between Negro Wool and St. Francis Swamps and crush me while Grant destroyed my camp."[11]

Union intelligence had Leonidas Polk dispatching streams of infantry across the Mississippi to assist Jeff Thompson or to reinforce Sterling Price.[12] On the contrary, Southern eyes turned east not west. Albert Sidney Johnston opposed sending troops to Thompson to "swell his ranks." Polk and Johnston both worried about a Federal advance from Paducah south toward Mayfield or Clarksville that might turn Polk's right flank and separate him from Johnston's army in Bowling Green. Such an advance "may at any moment demand all the force at your disposal." Indeed, Johnston wanted a full division, Pillow's Division, sent to Clarksville, but Polk protested and the two friends argued through dispatches. Polk asked if he might send Pillow in person to Bowling Green to explain fully. He and Pillow believed that stripping away 5,000 men would weaken Columbus so much that the town of Mayfield, Kentucky, which anchored Polk's right, would be jeopardized. The persuasive Pillow went to Bowling Green to explain their views, and Johnston listened but was not convinced. He sent Pillow back empty-handed to Columbus on November 5 with explicit instructions to send his division to Clarksville at once.[13] Pillow's men prepared to march to Clarksville on November 6, but wagons were in short supply, and as a result, they were directed to "pack up and cook one day's rations and be ready to march . . . by light in the morning" of November 7.[14]

November 6 in the South was a day of celebration, marking the election of Jefferson Davis as president of the Confederacy. It also was the day that Leonidas Polk sat at his desk and resigned his commission as major general. He reminded Davis that he had agreed to remain until Johnston took command in the West and "until the fortifications at

Fort Pillow and this very important point were completed. This has now been substantially accomplished."[15] Polk's thoughts must have wandered pleasurably to the prospect of returning to his duties and friends in the diocese of Louisiana, having fulfilled, for the most part successfully, his obligation as a soldier.

Grant, on the other hand, focused his attention on the moment—the expedition downstream. He summoned John McClernand to meet with him after ten o'clock on the night of November 5 and instructed him in the meantime to alert his brigade "to hold themselvs in readiness with two days rations in their haversacks and forty rounds of Ammunition in Cartridge box." He alerted Col. C. Carroll Marsh at Bird's Point to "have ready all able bodied men of the 22d Ill and 7th Iowa Vols. together with Taylor's Battery . . . and all the Cavalry at Bird's Point."[16]

Grant had acted boldly these first days in November. He had put in motion virtually his entire command, threatening not only the forces of Thompson and Polk but the towns of Bloomfield, Sikeston, Charleston, Belmont, Columbus, Milburn, Mayfield, and Clarksville. Certainly he had divided and exposed his forces audaciously but not recklessly. As they all deployed on November 6, it seemed quite reasonable to believe that the columns were large enough for the mission assigned and close enough for mutual support. Offensive options abounded. Grant just had to determine the proper timing and combinations to transform these options into opportunities.

For the Confederates these widespread simultaneous movements clouded Grant's objective. To organize an effective response would require a capable, unflappable Confederate commander receiving first-rate intelligence reports.

Bright sunshine greeted Grant's men on Wednesday morning, November 6. The camps at Cairo and Bird's Point came alive early with feverish activity as the regiments packed knapsacks, cooked rations, cleaned and recleaned weapons, and underwent careful inspections.[17]

Fouke's 30th and Logan's 31st Illinois marched down to the Cairo levee about three o'clock that afternoon and began filing over the stage planks onto the *Aleck Scott*, the largest of the private steamers Grant had under contract. Buford's 27th, the third regiment in McClernand's

Cairo Brigade, embarked on the *James Montgomery*. Captain Dollins's cavalry boarded either the *Rob Roy* or the *Chancellor*, and most of Grant's wagons went aboard the *Keystone State*. Before they embarked, however, McClernand sent a telegram to his friend George B. McClellan alerting him to the expedition.

About dusk the fleet left Cairo and steamed across the river to Bird's Point on the Missouri shore where Grant's large and luxurious *Belle Memphis*[18] took aboard Col. Henry Dougherty's 22d Illinois while Col. Jacob Lauman's 7th Iowa joined Buford's men on the *Montgomery*. Also boarding steamers at Bird's Point were Capt. Ezra Taylor's six-gun Chicago Light Battery and Delano's Adams County cavalry company, Lt. James K. Catlin commanding.[19]

The St. Louis *Daily Missouri Republican* reported that "more boats were taken than were absolutely necessary, in order to make the force appear more formidable than it was." Surgeon John H. Brinton disagreed. The "enterprise had been hastily undertaken" with inadequate river transportation. He could not get aboard "one ambulance or spring wagon of any description" and had to rely on two or three "road wagons, obtained from the quartermaster's train."[20]

All was ready and the sun was setting "robed in a blood red garment," noted Private Trueman of the 22d Illinois, when Grant came aboard the *Belle Memphis*.[21] Soon after dark Grant signaled to Commander Walke that the embarkation had been completed, and Walke eased the big black gunboat *Tyler*[22] into the main channel, closely followed by the *Lexington*. The *Keystone State* pulled into line behind the gunboats, beginning the grand procession of steamers, but everything came crashing to a halt as the *Chancellor* went aground. Grant had his pilot, Charles Scott, swing the *Belle Memphis* about so that she could take the *Chancellor* in tow. The big steamer pulled her free without great delay, and the fleet got under way again about 9 P.M.[23]

"'Where are we going on this dark night?' was asked by many yet remained unanswered as none but our great silent man knew." Wise troops on the transports watched the bows of the gunboats. "Up to that time we had not known whether we were going up the Ohio or down the Mississippi." When the *Tyler* turned downstream into the Mississippi it had an electrifying effect. "We have guessed our destination," thought Pvt. William Austin. Then the word began to spread, "We going to attack Columbus!" All along the crowded decks of

McClernand's ship, the *Aleck Scott*, one could see "soldiers cheering and waving their hats." [24]

As the transports pulled away leaving Cairo behind, strangely empty, the mood of the soldiers began to change to one of "utmost caution and quiet." "All lights had been extinguished. The steamers following us were equally dark." [25]

About 11 P.M. the *Tyler* pulled in close to the Kentucky shore and lay to for the night. Grant had chosen to land here, at the bottom tip of Island 1, the site of the old Fort Jefferson, eight miles below Cairo, eleven miles above Columbus. The rest of the flotilla tied up, and a strong guard was posted on shore.[26] Hardly had the little river fleet settled in before it was "approached by several men, apparently farmers, very curious about our numbers. No particular notice was taken of them." [27]

How could this be, given Grant's passion for secrecy, so pronounced that neither Walke, Dougherty, nor McClernand knew of his plans, although the latter two knew the expedition would be a demonstration of some sort? Grant hardly compromised the expedition by allowing strangers to sniff around. He probably hoped that they might be rebel scouts and that through them Polk might learn quickly of this landing, this feint on the Kentucky shore. Perhaps Polk would consider it the beginning of an attack against Columbus coming down the east side of the Mississippi from Fort Holt. Perhaps when Polk learned of Smith's two columns marching south from Paducah, Grant's presence would lend color to their movement, allowing it to be interpreted as part of a coordinated two- or three- or four-pronged attack on the Kentucky side of the river.[28]

Darkness pressed in on the transports. The "boys are all in glorious spirits and are singing, smoking and talking of storming batteries." [29] A lieutenant in Taylor's battery, Israel P. Rumsey, suffered the fate of every young officer's worst dream—in full uniform, in full sight of his men and his fellow officers, he fell over the side. Hilarity gave way to concern as the current washed him away. Lieutenant Rumsey fought the river, however, swam around the bow of the boat, and was hauled back on board.[30] Soldiers sought space to lie down and attempt to sleep, their weapons at their sides. Before his eyes closed, Private Trueman "cast my eyes above the tree tops and there I saw a cluster of stars, which instantly carried my mind back to my home." Some like Trueman slept well, but most found sleep fitful if not impossible.

Aboard the headquarters steamer *Belle Memphis*, officers from Dougherty's 22d crowded the cabin. Some slept, many talked beneath the dimmed lights of the chandeliers, discussing Columbus and what to expect when they attacked tomorrow. Grant and his staff sat around a table in the ladies cabin, distancing themselves from Dougherty's regimental officers. When they slept it was there in the cabin, in their chairs.[31]

About 2 A.M. that night as troops sought sleep and heavy darkness shrouded the *Belle Memphis*, Grant later reported, he received a message from Col. W. H. L. Wallace at Charleston, Missouri. Wallace "had learned from a reliable Union man that the enemy had been crossing troops from Columbus to Belmont the day before, for the purpose of following after and cutting off the forces under Colonel Oglesby."[32] According to Grant, the receipt of this message caused him to attack Belmont. He was motivated by two reasons—he sought to protect the exposed left flank of Oglesby's column moving toward Bloomfield and to prevent Polk from reinforcing Price or Thompson.[33] Grant also worried about his highly unstable volunteer force. These would-be soldiers and the men who led them, the McClernands and Logans and Doughertys, wanted a fight. That is why they had left home and enlisted. "I did not see how I could maintain discipline, or retain the confidence of my command, if we should return to Cairo without an effort to do something."[34]

Intelligence was sketchy. It would take boldness to act on the accumulated shreds of information, but Grant felt he had a good grasp of the general situation:

> He did know that there were strong defenses at Columbus, with some sort of a detachment at Belmont just across the river, but he did not know the exact strength of either. He also knew that Hickman, Ky., and New Madrid, Mo., were occupied by the enemy. He knew something of the movements of Jeff Thompson. It was suspected, at least by Department Headquarters, that Columbus was a point for detachment of reinforcements to Price and constituted a near-by support for Thompson.[35]

"It was an hour heavy with destiny for the United States. Grant faced a quick decision. The decision would show the kind of general he was; and on that would depend the future of the nation." Thus Kenneth P. Williams, relying on Grant's revised Belmont report, eloquently presented the standard, accepted interpretation of Grant's decision to at-tack Belmont. It was dramatic middle-of-the-night decisiveness, with a whiff of Napoleon's "three-o'clock-in-the-morning-courage."[36] But heady history sometimes is not fully accurate. John Simon allowed doubt to crack the door:

> No mention of the 2 A.M. message from Wallace appears in any USG account written after the battle; no contemporary documen-tary record has been found; and it is not listed in USG's register of letters received. It is not clear from USG's revised report dated Nov. 1 7 whether the message was verbal or written. . . . In private letters he revealed concern about his rank and command and a desire to engage the enemy in action. Throughout Sept., USG had exhibited an impatience to move downriver. In late Sept., he wrote that he would like to take Columbus but lacked sufficient forces. He stated that if he did not move quickly he probably could not do it at all.[37]

W. H. L. Wallace implied in a letter to his wife that the alarming report of Polk's troops crossing into Missouri was really just Grant blowing smoke. "The engagement was supposed to be necessary to protect our southwestern army in Missouri from overwhelming forces being rapidly consolidated against it."[38] James E. McGhee in "The Neophyte General: U. S. Grant and the Belmont Campaign" concurs. "Any supposed danger to Oglesby's column may have been just a pre-text, a convenient one to be sure, to initiate a battle."[39]

A recent Grant biographer, William S. McFeely, contends that "clearly he had already made the decision to attack when he left Cairo. . . . Grant had set out to fight . . . not to demonstrate."[40] Weight is lent to McFeely's position by a letter from Capt. Andrew H. Foote to Secretary of the Navy Gideon Welles and a speech made by John Rawlins to the Society of the Army of the Tennessee. Both suggest Grant set out from Cairo intending to attack whatever Confederate force was to be found at Belmont.[41]

It can be said with certainty, however, that Grant's decision and sub-sequent action were more than "an afterthought, growing out of what started as nothing more than a demonstration on Columbus," as his critic Stanley Horn maintained.[42] Henry I. Kurtz, another student of Belmont, believes that Grant "decided to stretch his orders" and attack. The idea had been "in the back of his mind all along."[43] John Simon agrees. "Knowing Polk's caution and believing Pillow to be a fool, Grant ran risks at Belmont which he would undoubtedly have considered too dangerous under other circumstances." He went "down the river to look for a fight—though just a little one."[44]

Grant's letters throughout the fall give example after example of "mounting impatience" and "impatience to strike."[45] Given Grant's personality, his itch to make something happen and to make a name for himself, it seems evident that he would attack—Belmont, probably; Columbus, perhaps.

The order to Oglesby to turn his column toward New Madrid and make contact at Belmont makes little sense, however, if Grant knew heavy Confederate units were crossing into Missouri from Columbus. The order would have had Oglesby marching smack into the Confederates. On the other hand it makes good sense if Grant planned all along to launch a major attack against Columbus. The *St. Louis Sunday Republican* indicated strongly that Grant intended doing so: "The programme was to attack and take the rebel camp at Belmont, opposite Columbus, from which point an attack was to be made on Columbus, in conjunction with a force that was sent from Paducah, and the Missouri expedition which . . . was to march down by Bloomfield."[46]

The *St. Louis Missouri Weekly Democrat* echoed a similar belief: "It was Gen. Grant's design to lead his troops on the Kentucky side, and threaten the enemy until Colonel Oglesby could reach Belmont, and co-operate in such movement as subsequent reconnaissance might dictate."[47]

Belmont presented few unknowns other than the size of the enemy force. And it is likely Grant believed Polk's force occupying Belmont or even in route through it would be smaller than his own. The Belmont strike had been well rehearsed in September and October by means of small forays from Bird's Point down to Hunter's Farm, even to the extent of combined operations.

The element of surprise belonged to Grant, especially if he attacked across the river on the Missouri side into the rear of the camp at Belmont. Thanks to the diversionary landing in Kentucky, Polk's scouts should have been bringing news of heavy troop movements on the east side of the Mississippi. Even if Polk had troops crossing the river to assist Thompson or Price, a chance Grant could not rule out, his strike

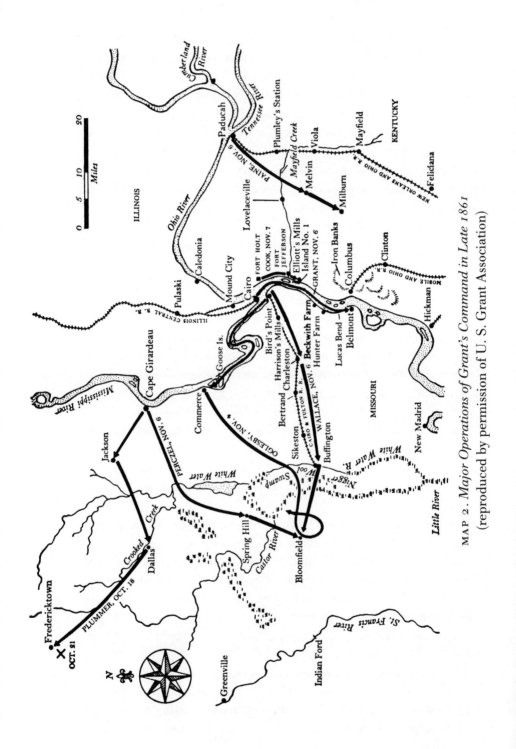

MAP 2. *Major Operations of Grant's Command in Late 1861*
(reproduced by permission of U. S. Grant Association)

against Belmont might well take them in the flank. The odds looked
good for a quick success. They would smash Thompson or whoever
was found in the camp at Belmont before Polk could wake up and send
help across the Mississippi. In any event, with Frémont being replaced
in St. Louis on November 2 and with the priorities of a new commander
less predictable than the movements of the enemy, Grant knew his time
had come. It might not come again.[48]

Sleepy telegraph operators kept their offices open late into the night at
Cairo and Fort Holt. "We expect to hear from below tonight."[49] Down
below, as Grant began preparing orders for the Belmont expeditionary
force, he realized that Colonel Plummer had not been told about the orders changing Oglesby's objective to Belmont. No longer could Plummer expect Oglesby's support. So Grant dispatched a warning: "This
will leave your command wholly unprotected from this quarter." Plummer's column, consisting now of the solitary 10th Iowa under Col.
Nicholas Perczel, had already taken Bloomfield, however, at noon on
November 6. Jeff Thompson's men were fleeing south, and Perczel
reported to Oglesby.

Oglesby, after great effort, had crossed Nigger-Wool Swamp and
was also closing on Bloomfield. The order to retrace his steps and turn
south to meet Grant at Belmont annoyed him. He wrote Grant on November 7, "I cannot recross the swamp here." Rather he would head
his force back east toward Buffington and Sikeston. To W. H. L. Wallace, Oglesby wrote that he could not go to Belmont or New Madrid
"except by leaving the Niger-Wool Swamp to my left. I would not cross
it again for a reputation. It is terrible."[50]

Grant did not know this. He believed Oglesby to be en route to Belmont. As he gathered himself for tomorrow's challenge, Grant could
inventory the disposition he had made of the troops of the District of
Southeast Missouri:

1. The Belmont Expedition (3,000+): moving at dawn downriver.
2. Oglesby's force from Commerce (4,000): closing on Belmont
   from vicinity of Bloomfield.
3. Plummer's Cape Girardeau column (3,000+): at or near
   Bloomfield, neutralizing Thompson and could hasten to Belmont
   if needed. (Unknown to Grant, all of Plummer's troops had

turned back to Cape Girardeau except for Perczel's 10th Iowa occupying Bloomfield.)

4. Wallace's half regiment (400): moving from Charleston to join Oglesby.
5. Cook (800): advancing south along the Mississippi from Fort Holt to Elliott's Mills.
6. Smith (3,000): Paine's force closing on Milburn.
7. Smith (800): Sanderson's 23d Indiana advancing on Viola.

These seven columns of troops, although dispersed widely, converged on Grant's two objectives, Belmont and M. Jeff Thompson. Every hour the net drew tighter.

While Grant took time out to write Plummer, Comdr. Henry Walke led the *Tyler* and *Lexington* downriver for a midnight scout. He did not encounter the enemy but found dense fog. The gunboats returned to the transport fleet at 3 A.M. and anchored. It was then Grant informed Walke of his assignment for the next morning.[51]

Orders began to flow from the ladies cabin of the *Belle Memphis* about the time Walke returned.

> The troops composing the present expedition from this place will move promptly at 6 o'clock this morning. The gunboats will take the advance, and be followed by the First Brigade, under command of Brig. Gen. John A. McClernand, composed of the troops from Cairo and Fort Holt. The Second Brigade, comprising the remainder of the troops of the expedition, commanded by Col. Henry Dougherty, will follow. The entire force will debark at the lowest point on the Missouri shore where a landing can be effected in security from the rebel batteries. The point of debarkation will be designated by Captain Walke, commanding naval forces.
>
> By Order of Brig. Gen. U. S. Grant
>
> John A. Rawlins
> Assistant Adjutant Genl[52]

At the first hint of dawn, noncommissioned officers went about the decks arousing sleeping soldiers. The men opened their haversacks and ate breakfast, using a portion of their cooked rations. About 6:30 A.M. the sun came up. "He appeared, . . . the morning of the battle, he seemed still bathed in blood. And everything seemed to indicate that there was a bloody struggle soon to be witnessed."[53]

At a given signal the fleet released lines attached to the Kentucky shore. There were the usual, perhaps inevitable, delays getting the transports under way and into line.[54] The gunboats went first, shepherding the steamers, their decks thick with troops. As they proceeded cautiously downstream, pilot Scott reported, "Grant came up to the pilot-house and asked how close we could land to Belmont on the Missouri shore, and to be out of sight of Columbus. I stated about three miles. Then he asked me about the road from where I could land to Belmont. On receiving my answer he ordered me to pick a landing and land where the balance of the boats could have room to tie up."[55]

Meanwhile the sun had risen higher. On the bow of the *Montgomery*, Cpl. William H. Onstot of the 27th Illinois appreciated the scene. "I thought it was one of the most beautiful mornings I ever saw. The Fleet composed of five noble steamers and two Gun Boates moving rapidly over the placid and beautiful Mississippi River was a sight not to be seen every day." Why are we here to fight, Onstot asked himself. For the Constitution, for Liberty, for "every thing dear to men" against a "treasonable horde."[56]

About 8 A.M. the first transport tied up on the Missouri shore. Walke's gunboats hovered out in the main channel. Pilot Scott had chosen a site called Hunter's Farm, a small steamboat landing close to the end of Lucas Bend, just out of sight, though not out of range, of the Columbus batteries. The riverbank at Hunter's Farm looked deserted except for a solitary black man sitting there as though he had been expecting them. Grant's medical director, young Philadelphian John Brinton, noticed the quiet scene and wrote that a "flock of geese settled in the river not far away" from his transport.[57]

While officers interrogated the black man and troops from the *Aleck Scott* poured ashore, "desultory" enemy musket fire came from behind a few trees on the bank. The fire was "returned from one side of the boat, while the men on the opposite side practiced at long range on the birds."[58]

The enemy disappeared, and Grant's men disembarked without further incident. Off-loading cannon slowed the process, but by 8:30 A.M. the infantry was ashore, at last.[59] Their officers formed them into ranks in "a sort of clearing in front of a cornfield, with wood roads, one lead-

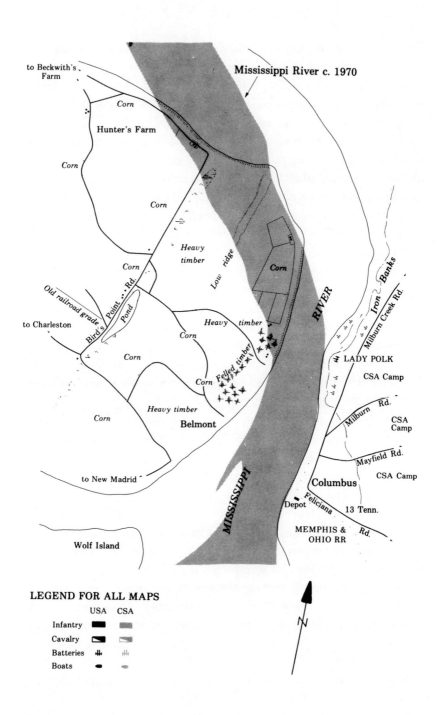

to Beckwith's
Farm

Corn

Hunter's Farm

Corn

Corn

*Heavy
timber*

Low ridge

Mississippi River c. 1970

Corn

Corn

Old railroad grade

Bird's Point Rd.

Pond

to Charleston

Heavy timber

RIVER

Iron Banks

Milburn Creek Rd.

LADY POLK

Corn

Corn

Corn

Corn

Felled timber

Heavy timber

Belmont

CSA Camp

Milburn Rd.

CSA
Camp

Mayfield Rd.

CSA Camp

to New Madrid

Columbus

Feliciana

Depot

13 Tenn.

MISSISSIPPI

MEMPHIS &
OHIO RR

Rd.

Wolf Island

LEGEND FOR ALL MAPS

	USA	CSA
Infantry		
Cavalry		
Batteries		
Boats		

N

MAP 3. *Belmont, 1861*

ing toward Belmont, and one off to the right." Behind them the soldiers could hear the Chicago Light Battery still coming ashore, drivers
shouting a "lively Hi, hi, hi" as they struggled with the horses dragging
the heavy guns up the steep bank.[60]

John Brinton felt detached observing the scene. He stretched and
looked about him. "The early autumnal morning was delightful; the
air fresh and invigorating, without being cold."[61] A laboring cannoneer
lifted his eyes from studying the soft sand of the landing. He heard shots
deep in the woods. The skirmishers were engaged.[62]

Walke

Comdr. Henry Walke had no illusions about engaging the Confederate forts, their guns massed, secure on the Iron Banks. This fifty-eight-year-old Virginian was a veteran not only of the Mexican War but of sea scraps in the Atlantic. He knew the *Tyler* and *Lexington* had the advantages of speed and maneuverability, but he also knew a lucky hit could send either drifting helpless downstream. But he had agreed that the gunboats would make a diversion for General Grant's landing force, and Henry Walke was not only a fighter but a man of his word.

With the infantry disembarkation at Hunter's Farm proceeding nicely, Walke left the transports and ventured downstream with the gunboats. Once the *Tyler* and *Lexington* turned Belmont Point they drew fire. It was 8:30 A.M. The gunboats then opened up and "threw their shot quite lively."[1] Samuel Vroom, the *Lexington*'s gunner, soon had the range for his thirty-two-pounders, but target identification was difficult. The best Comdr. Roger N. Stembel could do was point vaguely at orange splotches of fresh dirt on the sides of the bluff.

Walke leveled his glasses and watched the ripple of flashes seemingly dart from the land itself. The air on the river quaked to the echo of their bursts. While his guns blasted away in response, Walke made certain the Sebastian brothers, his pilots, kept the *Tyler* running in a rather tight circle. He did not bother to signal Stembel to do the same. The *Lexington*'s captain, veteran of several sorties against the Iron Banks himself, would copy instinctively the *Tyler*'s evasive maneuvers. It seemed, however, that range, not deflection, was the rebel gunners' problem. Consistently rebel shells from the Iron Banks passed high

Comdr. Henry Walke (Library of Congress)

over the two gunboats. The few rounds that fell short appeared to be coming from a field battery dead ahead on a high shelf of land.

Walke could easily pick out individual enemy projectiles as they screeched overhead. It seemed almost as if they had the transports as their targets. As he watched, he grew more and more alarmed for the safety of the transports and disengaged his two timberclads just before 9 A.M.[2]

The *Tyler* and *Lexington* returned to Hunter's Farm. The landing site seemed secure enough, out of range of the annoying light battery and out of sight (thanks to the heavy woods of Belmont Point) of the big guns on the bluffs. Nevertheless the Confederates kept up their "horrid music." Surgeon John Brinton heard a shot from a heavy Confederate gun, looked up, and traced its flight over the moored transports. Then came a second shell "gradually sinking as it came nearer. It seemed to me to be making a bee-line for my eyes, but fortunately changed its mind, and passing above my head, and apparently between our smoke pipes, buried itself in the dirt of the Missouri bank of the river."[3]

Walke would not risk this continued exposure of the transports. He ordered them to move upriver out of range of any gun at Columbus.

Soon the sound of small arms from the shore caught Walke's attention. It grew in intensity and prompted him to make a second sortie. Once again, the "magazine stewards, shell-passers, and powder-boys, were stationed at their different posts, ready to pass the ammunition from the ship's hold to the cannon's mouth."[4]

At a speed of about eight knots the vessels again rounded Belmont Point and opened fire. Repeating the tactics of their first run, the *Tyler* and *Lexington* drew even heavier enemy fire. Walke used every precaution, even having the lines and hawsers on deck coiled and stacked as an extra defensive layer for the boilers and machinery.[5]

Confederate private Henry Morton Stanley, atop the Iron Banks, observed how the gunboats "saucily bore down and engaged our batteries." "We novices delighted to hear the sound of so many cannon." Pvt. Stanley saw that it was a mismatch, however, as the gunboats could only offer a "few shots in return, but they were too harmless to do more than add to the charm of the excitement."[6] Commander Walke broke off the uneven engagement after twenty minutes. It "would have been too hazardous to have remained long under [the enemy's] fire with such frail vessels."[7]

First gunboat attack
(sketch by Henry Walke; U.S. Naval Historical Center)

Only six months earlier these "frail vessels" had been "powerful freight and passenger Ohio River steamboats." Comdr. John Rodgers had purchased three of the side-wheelers and, in a 100-day marvel of Yankee ingenuity and industry, had transformed these packets into the "nucleus of the Mississippi flotilla." The ironclads that were being constructed upriver would be ready for action shortly, but until then timberclad steamers would do battle with the heavy Confederate guns. Rodgers sheathed the decks and bulwarks of the *Tyler, Lexington,* and *Carondolet* with oak five inches thick, relocated coal bunkers to protect the boilers, and armed each boat with two thirty-two-pounders. The 575-ton *Tyler* got six eight-inch Dahlgren shell guns; the 448-ton *Lexington* got four. To crew the timberclads, the Navy Department had dispatched inland 500 experienced sailors who had been guarding Washington. These "tars," easterners from Boston and Philadelphia, gave Walke a sharp advantage.[8]

By noon the battle ashore raged, and Walke decided to try again. He knew Grant would welcome anything that might preoccupy the guns of Columbus. This attack would be different, however, and even more risky. Walke pushed the gunboats well beyond Belmont Point, about a quarter of a mile closer to the Confederate batteries. Then, with the "shots flying thickly around us," Walke and Stembel opened up with deafening broadsides. It appears they also fired several rounds, almost as an afterthought, across Belmont Point in the direction of Camp

U.S. gunboat Taylor *(*Tyler*)*
(drawing by F. Muller; U.S. Naval Historical Center)

Johnston. But their luck ran out. A solid shot struck the *Tyler*, crashing "obliquely through the side, deck, and scantling, . . . taking off the head of one man and injuring two others." It was "madness" to remain, so Henry Walke withdrew the two timberclads, "keeping up fire from stern guns till out of range."[9] He knew his primary mission was to cover the amphibious force. He had done what he promised.[10]

8

Turn Out! Turn Out!

Maj. Henry Winslow tapped on Polk's door. It was 2:10 A.M. Polk awakened and Winslow admitted a messenger. A dispatch from Jeff Thompson reported enemy columns converging on him at Bloomfield. At daybreak Winslow woke the sleeping general again. He told Polk Federal gunboats had appeared upriver. Scouts reported they were screening transports disembarking troops in "considerable force" on the Missouri shore.

Polk sent staff officers scurrying. An aide headed to the landing to direct the steamboat captains "to get up steam" and to hold themselves "in readiness for any emergency that might arise." Then the aide crossed the river on the *Charm*[1] to warn Camp Johnston. Simultaneously staff officers alerted Polk's division commanders and summoned Pillow to headquarters. Since Pillow's division was already formed and beginning its movement to Clarksville, Polk told Pillow to reverse the column, cross the river at once with four of his regiments, and take charge of the situation on the west bank.

After meeting with Pillow, Polk mounted and rode up to the forts on the bluffs, checking the readiness and alignment of the batteries. He ordered the balance of Pillow's division, together with those of Mc-Cown and Cheatham, to take position along the Columbus defensive perimeter. From the tent camp he could hear, "Turn out! Turn out!" Ammunition boxes were being broken open and cartridges distributed. A Louisianan later remembered his regiment was "called out and drawn up in line of battle expecting an attack from the enemy on this side too."[2]

Major Winslow meanwhile delivered Polk's warning to General McCown. He found McCown in the saddle, supervising the displacement of Capt. Richard A. Stewart's Pointe Coupee Battery. The battery of this Mexican War veteran moved forward along the riverbank to the prepared position "at the turn in the bend" where they could observe the gunboats and deliver direct fire if they came within range. To support Stewart's battery and to guard against an enemy advance down the Kentucky riverbank, McCown rushed forward Lt. Col. J. B. Kennedy's 5th Louisiana Infantry Battalion and a company from the 4th Tennessee. He posted them some four miles north of Columbus on the road leading to Elliott's Mills and Blandville. Three companies of Lt. Col. John Henry Miller's 1st Mississippi Cavalry Battalion screened Kennedy's troops and also picketed the roads east toward Milburn and Mayfield. In addition McCown sent Col. E. W. Gantt's 12th Arkansas Infantry toward Milburn. Quickly reports began to come in from these advanced units: "No enemy encountered."

Although greatly relieved, Polk still expected Grant's main thrust to come on the east side of the river against Columbus itself. The force threatening Tappan's outpost at Belmont must be a diversion, albeit a strong one.[3]

McCown and his Louisiana gunners could see the Federal gunboats easily enough and could tell "by the smoke that a larger number [of steamers] were hugging the Missouri shore, where they were invisible to us, owing to the thick woods across the river."[4] About 8:30 A.M. two pesky gunboats came around Lucas Bend to challenge McCown's guns.

McCown ordered Stewart to open fire. The first rounds were far short, and McCown helped adjust the elevation of the pieces. To their left they heard a welcome "whumph" as Capt. S. D. H. Hamilton's battery of siege guns joined in. Soon Maj. A. P. Stewart's heavy guns also began to fire. The Yankee gunboat commanders knew their business, however. Heavy smoke belched from their stacks as the two highly maneuverable side-wheelers began steering in circles. Now up from those black timberclads in the Mississippi came projectiles: shells striking against the bluff, airbursts near Stewart's battery, but no hits. Confederate gunnery proved equally poor, however. Some shells zoomed almost half a mile upstream beyond the transports at Hunter's Farm. So far, it was proving an innocent but grandly spectacular affair, a "spirited little artillery duel."

Suddenly one of the Pointe Coupee parrott guns "exploded in a thousand atoms." "Fragments of the gun flew in every direction." The blast killed two members of the gun crew and wounded another. One of those killed was a young Creole, Pvt. E. Madeline, who had just transferred in from the Watson Battery. Stunned, horrified, the rest of "Black Dick" Stewart's battery stopped firing.[5]

Below on the river the Yankee gunboats decided half an hour was long enough to be subjected to this heavy fire, so they uncoiled their circles and withdrew beyond Lucas Bend. Hamilton's and Stewart's heavy guns had the range, however, and they, supported now by the Lady Polk, kept firing.

Polk rode up and joined McCown. He watched the action through his field glasses and received McCown's report. He told McCown to be wary. He still believed the main attack could come on this side, probably in two columns: down the Mayfield Road and down the riverbank from old Fort Jefferson.[6] They discussed the dispositions made against enemy advances from Elliott's Mills and Milburn. Polk appeared satisfied, but he shook his head at the sight of Stewart's mangled battery.

Things were not going as he had expected. The Union fleet had popped up so quickly—from nowhere. And now they had landed men on the wrong side, the Missouri side, of the river. Was it a feint? If not, had he sent Pillow with sufficient men to relieve Tappan? Was this a situation he might turn to his advantage? Should he engage the enemy with superior force on the Belmont side before the attack on the Columbus side materialized? Perhaps the timing of the Federal attacks had gone awry. Nevertheless, when, or if, the attack came, the Columbus fortifications must not be so heavily committed across the river that they would be too weak to beat back the enemy. Polk turned his mount back toward Columbus. He would post himself on the riverbank, halfway between enemy threats.[7]

Gideon Pillow had been busy. Wednesday night, November 6, he had returned from his fruitless trip to see Albert Sidney Johnston. His troops had been up since dawn. Once they had breakfast, they formed into column and began the march eastward. Already their tents, baggage, and some ammunition had been loaded into wagons. The men themselves carried only essentials and a minimum of cartridges.

After going about a mile, "we were halted about 9:30 A.M. and held a good while, until we were tired of the waiting." Word came down the line to turn back and return to camp. Then they were ordered to proceed double-quick to the landing. Clanking and jangling they rushed back. Men would remember the hurried march to the river-bank, and they would recall how little ammunition they had. "I had only 7 cartridges and Polk Dillon just one." Many had only three.[8] Pillow's Tennesseans found the steamers *Charm*, *Prince*, and *Harry W. R. Hill* waiting at the landing with steam up.

Cpl. John G. Law, a preacher who had enlisted in the 154th Senior Tennessee Regiment, had left camp early that morning and walked down to the river landing. Law wanted to visit his mother who was a passenger on the *Prince*. She had come up to Columbus from Memphis once before, bringing with her a small cargo of clothes, wine, pickles, lemons, and other items. Sallie Gordon Law and her friends had gathered these items for the many sick soldiers at Columbus. This Thursday morning she had come up again and was having breakfast on the *Prince*. Capt. B. J. Butler of the *Prince* entered the cabin and in a grave voice announced, "Ladies, finish your breakfast, but the Yankees are landing their gunboats above." When she looked out the cabin window, Sallie Law saw the "wildest confusion" on the landing and in the streets of Columbus, soldiers of all ranks "running to and fro." From upriver she heard the roar of McCown's batteries and the gunboats. "The cannonading was sublimely grand."[9]

Lying beside the *Prince* was the *Charm*. Capt. William L. Trask had just finished unloading cargo when the landing became a scene of frenzy. Fortunate indeed were the Confederates that these two Yazoo River packets were at the landing. Also available that morning were the *Hill* and later in the day the *Kentucky* and the *Ingomar*. By 8:30 A.M. the 12th Tennessee began boarding one of the packets. They would be the first across.

At the head of the 12th rode their lieutenant colonel, Tyree H. Bell, a native Kentuckian but recently a Sumner County, Tennessee, farmer. Their colonel, Robert M. Russell, had brigade responsibilities today. Albert Fielder, a private in Company B, believed they were fortunate in their leaders. Colonel Russell had been a professional soldier and was, by far, the best trained of all the Confederate regimental commanders. This West Pointer had drilled them hard and took pride in how quickly his Gibson County farmers[10] took on the ways of real soldiers.[11]

Bell's 12th crossed the river and formed just beyond the steamboat landing at Belmont. During the next hour the *Prince, Charm,* and *Hill* crossed and recrossed the river ferrying three more of Pillow's Tennessee regiments. The *Charm* and *Prince* also brought over heavy boxes of ammunition. Soldiers unloaded them and piled them on the riverbank.[12]

Lt. Col. Daniel Beltzhoover sat in his tent at Belmont and picked up a pen and a sheet of stationery. It had been a nasty week, and he had found that it helped to air grievances privately, thereby avoiding the judgment, perhaps the alienation, of colleagues or running the risk of retribution. Beltzhoover prided himself on his professionalism.

This native of Maryland had been raised in Mississippi and attended West Point, class of 1847. There he had distinguished himself not as a horseman like Grant or as a cadet leader like Polk but as the organist at worship services in the chapel. He also liked poetry and composed verse. He could arrange music as well. Together with Bernard Bee, class of 1845, Beltzhoover had written "The Farewell to Mrs. General Scott." His service in the regular army consisted of duty with the 1st Regiment of Artillery from 1847 to 1855. He saw limited action in the Mexican War, mostly in Florida and California. He resigned from the army in 1855 to become professor of mathematics at Mount St. Mary's College, Emmitsburg, Maryland.

Beltzhoover early offered his services to Jefferson Davis. A more enticing offer, however, came from Col. Paul O. Hebert representing the state of Louisiana. Thus Beltzhoover became major of artillery in the Army of Louisiana, assistant adjutant general to Hebert, then to Brig. Gen. David E. Twiggs, then chief of staff of Twiggs's department, which included all of Louisiana and sections of Mississippi and Alabama. "While serving in this capacity he sent to the field the first twenty regiments of Louisiana troops."[13]

It is unclear how Beltzhoover was persuaded to leave his staff position and take command of a splendidly equipped artillery battery organized in New Orleans by Augustus C. Watson of Tensas Parish. Watson had recruited the sons of "well-known Creole families," the "finest young men of the city," and wanted the best artillery officer available. Watson's Battery compared favorably to the Washington Battery with its high proportion of "men of wealth and high standing with resplendent uniforms." Gus Watson equipped the battery himself at a cost of $40,000–$60,000. He bought six "splendid bronze pieces with carriages, caissons and appointments, completely made in New Orleans by Edmund J. Ivers." [14] Two of the brass guns were twelve-pounder howitzers, four were six-pounders. Watson also "collected the finest horses suited to the work to be found in the State," some 200 of them.

When Beltzhoover agreed to command the battery, the officers in place agreed to drop a rank. Watson himself wished to participate and enlisted as a private, albeit a most special one. This rich private Gus Watson had large holdings in the state along with his brother James and his brother-in-law George Hunt. The Watson brothers were well-known up and down the Mississippi for their poker skill. It appears that a common poker term of that day, "play it like the Watsons," came from their exploits at night aboard the steamboats. The men of the battery, to honor their benefactor, wore a "W" on their caps. The "Watsons," 150 cannoneers and 40 drivers strong, left New Orleans on August 13, still recruiting men as they journeyed upriver. They camped a month on the shore of Lake Bruin, six miles from St. Joseph in Tensas, the site of Gus Watson's plantation, Lakewood. They had believed the Confederate War Department planned to send them to Virginia, but Beltzhoover and the Watson Battery received orders for Memphis instead. [15]

The Watson Battery arrived in Memphis on September 18 and re-cruited even more men. Memphis Irishmen plugged holes in the ranks left after many of New Orleans's finest had "repudiated Watson and torn the initial W from their caps." Some of these men who quit were to fill the ranks of "Black Dick" Stewart's Pointe Coupee Battery. By the time they reached Columbus on October 1, the Watsons had tired of Beltzhoover as well as their make-believe private Gus Watson. In-deed, just before Belmont, forty privates from the battery presented a petition to General Polk himself. They wanted out of the Watson Battery. They blamed Beltzhoover mostly for his "rough and unfeel-ing treatment of them." [16] Matters worsened. A noncommissioned of-ficer expressed his "dissatisfaction" and openly quarreled with Beltzhoover. When the sergeant drew his dagger, Beltzhoover drew his sword. They fought, and the sergeant was "badly cut." Beltzhoover was placed under arrest "on account of charges brought against him by his own men." [17]

Angry and humiliated, Beltzhoover decided to spend some time Thursday morning writing a letter to a friend back in Natchez. He caught the smell of breakfast frying and heard the familiar morning sounds of the men of his battery, but his mood was sharp. He began: "I am thoroughly disgusted with the service. Gen. Polk acts more like a priest than a soldier. I don't meet a man once a month who knows anything about military. I have not seen a field officer who can drill a regiment, or a General who can review a brigade but McCown, who is an old artillery captain. We are still in Missouri, but expect orders to-day to join Bowen's brigade at Feliciana, Ky." [18]

Shouting interrupted Beltzhoover. Pvt. Tom Graham of Company A, 1st Mississippi Cavalry, had taken himself out early that morning foraging toward Hunter's Farm.[19] The two Mississippi cavalry companies used the place as a picket station. It was convenient since they picketed the Charleston Road and another small road bending north from Belmont toward the river and running on to Hunter's Farm. At daylight the cavalry pickets had returned to camp as usual, leaving just before the Federals landed. Tom Graham, however, had gone out again and happened to stumble onto Yankees disembarking. He was unobserved and raced back. "He rode into camp at full speed, hat in hand." [20]

Before he sealed his Natchez letter Beltzhoover added at the bottom: "P. S. Our pickets have just come in, bringing us the information that five steamers, with Federal troops, and two gunboats, are landing within two miles of us. We are all ordered under arms." [21]

The Confederate commander at Belmont, Col. James C. Tappan of the 13th Arkansas, had been absent, spending the night in Columbus. At the first alarm he raced down to the river and began searching for a skiff. Polk came down and joined him at the bank. Polk shared the intelligence he had received and told Tappan he would send Pillow over to help. In the meantime Tappan must see to the defense of Camp Johnston himself.

Tappan crossed over to Belmont at once. He sent the two Mississippi cavalry companies out toward Hunter's Farm to observe the

Col. James C. Tappan (courtesy Ivey S. Gladin)

enemy, then he recalled his own 13th Arkansas he had sent out earlier to cut trees.[22] In Camp Johnston "the long roll was beat and the cry 'fall in' 'fall in' sounded quick and sharp from every company street." Each man was issued twenty rounds of ammunition, which everyone thought would be plenty.

Tappan conferred with Beltzhoover and agreed that the six guns of the Watson Battery should be dispersed. They placed two guns in "an old field back of the camp," facing south, covering "the road that led round towards the river and extended up to my camp." This was the "back door" to Tappan's Camp Johnston. The other four guns Tappan ordered Beltzhoover to position commanding the road leading directly into the camp from Hunter's Farm.[23] Tappan spread out the 13th Arkansas: one company protected the two-gun section, two others supported the four-gun battery, while the remaining seven went into line of battle facing away from the river and to the right of the four guns.[24] The main portion of his regiment was in front of the tangle of felled trees. "Good idea enough," thought Pvt. Phil Stephenson of Company K, 13th Arkansas, "for the intention was for our men to use the fallen timber as bulwarks in case of having to fall back, and to depend upon it to retard the enemy's pursuit." Tappan completed his deployment by 8:45 A.M. and waited.[25]

The talented Beltzhoover looked upon the cosmopolitan Tappan as an equal intellectually, but even Tappan, like so many of the regimental commanders, seemed interested principally in establishing a public presence. A native middle Tennessean, Tappan had been afforded every opportunity. In a good-natured way men referred to him as "a perfect Chesterfield." Off to Phillips Academy in Exeter, New Hampshire, as a boy, he furthered his education at Yale College in the class of 1845 with Richard Taylor. Col. John C. Burch, Pillow's staff officer and political confidante, remembered Tappan as an upperclassman there. Following Yale Tappan read law in Mississippi then established a practice and his home in Helena, Arkansas. Tappan had married the niece of politician Aaron V. Brown of middle Tennessee, which connected him to Gideon Pillow by marriage and cemented him in the Democracy. By 1851 he was in the Arkansas House, and by 1861 he had served as judge and receiver of the federal land office at Helena. Tappan raised the 13th Arkansas easily in the southeastern part of the state and paid for much of their outfitting himself. He was wealthy, polished, affable, and courageous, but Dan Beltzhoover thought he looked about as silly as Gideon Pillow when he tried to drill his regiment.[26]

✳

Pillow arrived at Belmont about nine o'clock, perhaps as late as 9:15, with the first regiment of reinforcements, Bell's 12th Tennessee. Before Pillow established his line of battle he took three companies, each from a different regiment, and sent them out at once under command of Capt. F. Stith, adjutant of the 22d Tennessee, toward Hunter's Farm to engage and delay the enemy as long as possible.[27]

"I had no choice of position, nor time to make any reconnaissance,"[28] Pillow reported, but he set to work deploying his men. Regiment by regiment he called them out from the riverbank. "We were soon marched in double quick something less than a mile and formed into line of battle."[29] One student of Belmont contends that Pillow's deployment consisted of a "mere enlargement of that of Colonel Tappan."[30] Instead of accepting Tappan's line and extending it, however, Pillow made a critical change. He pulled Tappan back forty yards, which meant, when extended, the Confederate line no longer would run along the edge of the woods. Instead of having their backs to an open field, most of them, almost three full regiments, would be in the field itself. "Our position at this time was not an eligible one, as our force were mostly drawn up in the open field."[31]

Using the adjusted 13th Arkansas position as a base, Pillow placed Russell's 12th Tennessee under Bell in the woods on Tappan's right.[32] Bell had "a splendid position" as did Tappan. To Tappan's left Pillow put Freeman's 22d Tennessee, then Pickett's 21st, and finally Wright's 13th, which was bent back at an angle about thirty degrees to the left. The 21st had its left and left center echeloned in double ranks to the rear of the Watson Battery. The left companies of Tappan and the right ones of Freeman's 22d overlapped clumsily. At the left center of the line Pillow concentrated Beltzhoover's six guns, somewhat to the left front of Pickett's 21st, "commanding the main and probable road of Union advance."[33] It was generally believed by the Confederates that the only road leading from the enemy's landing site at Hunter's Farm to Belmont was "supposed to be on this side of a little lake that ran parallel with the river about a mile back."[34] The result was a short, somewhat cramped line of battle about 400 yards in length, running generally north to south across a wide cornfield. The axis of the line lay parallel to the river and some half mile west of Camp Johnston.[35]

Pillow's plan of defense appears passive: block the road upon which the enemy would be advancing on Camp Johnston, stand and receive the enemy's charge, and then, perhaps, in the back of Pillow's mind, countercharge with bayonets against a foe that had hurled himself against the line of battle and worn himself out. Such tactics would have worked against the Mexicans; also Gen. Henry Clinton's British infantry would have done it that way.[36]

Tyree Bell liked the position assigned the 12th. On the Confederate extreme right he had the advantage of cover, not only from the heavy woods but also from a ravine with a slight ridge in front. He did not overly concern himself with the enemy being able to make a lodgment in the small space between his right flank and the river. Tappan's 13th Arkansas also enjoyed the protection of the woods but worried about the three regiments extending the line to the south. Freeman's 22d and Pickett's 21st Tennessee lay entirely exposed in the cornfield. To their front and left Freeman's men could see a wooden fence crossing the field and behind it, some thirty to forty yards, the woods. To his rear Freeman had another fence and behind it a ravine. If posted there the 22d, and perhaps an additional regiment, would have been protected and concealed with good fields of fire. "The enemy would have been compelled to have approached my position through the open corn field for near 150 yards, perhaps farther, while we would have been comparatively defended."[37]

The six brass guns of the Watson Battery came next, pushed forward and insufficiently protected by infantry. On the far left and almost isolated was John V. Wright's 13th Tennessee. Wright's position was "an unfortunate one—in an open field."

It appears that Pillow placed Wright on the extreme left as a precautionary move: the regiment would serve as a potential flanking force and as a reserve to be recalled to the right if needed. To close the wide gap between the left of the 13th Tennessee and the river, Wright sent Company A under Capt. Matthew Rhea. Rhea was actually detached from the regiment and not only had the responsibility of sealing the gap between Company A and the rest of Wright's regiment but also was to control the New Madrid Road into Belmont. Pillow believed it to be of secondary importance since it was an unlikely avenue of approach.[38]

About forty-five minutes had passed since the skirmishers had been sent out. The troops waited in line of battle, facing west. Every few minutes a messenger would ride in from Capt. A. J. Bowles's Thompson Cavalry or Lt. Lafayette Jones's Bolivar Troop and advise Pillow of "the progress the enemy were making towards our line."[39]

Col. James Tappan was anxious. He remembered the payroll he had brought over from Columbus, so he galloped along the front of the line, stuffing "huge rolls of Confederate bank notes" into the hands of each of his captains. Pay off the men, he commanded. A few of Tappan's men from Arkansas kept breaking ranks and running off to find themselves a tree so they could fight "guerilla fashion." Their officers summoned them back, of course, and they returned "reluctantly" to the line of battle where the enemy would have a clear shot at them.[40]

Col. Ed Pickett was nervous too. He had no idea what to expect. He worried about being responsible for that Louisiana battery out to his left front. He did not like being out in the open field, but he admitted it would be an elegant position when the time came to "Charge Bayonet!" He went over in his mind regimental and battalion commands he might have to give, and he postured defiantly in his saddle, giving a cheery word to every man he encountered. Pickett knew his Irishmen would fight. They were like hounds pulling tight against their leashes right now.

Eight of his ten companies were Memphis Irishmen, and he, thanks to his relationship with Gideon Pillow, had been chosen to lead them. Firing volleys at approaching Yankees, however, would not be the same as firing at Whigs. As editor of the *Mississippi Free Trader* (Natchez) and the *Memphis Daily Appeal* he had earned his reputation as a political infighter, but he worried how those pugnacious qualities might translate on the field of battle. He thought back gratefully to his cadet days at the Kentucky Military Institute. They would sustain him.[41]

A final adjustment to the Confederate line of battle occurred when the companies of skirmishers under Captain Stith returned and rejoined their parent units. Back with them came the Mississippi cavalry. Pillow ordered Lieutenant Colonel Miller, who had crossed the river and reported for duty, to take command of all cavalry himself and post it "near the left wing."[42]

About 10 A.M. Major Winslow crossed the river and found General Pillow in front of the Confederate line of battle "returning from reconnoitering the enemy's position." The general, perhaps worried by the reports of enemy strength his cavalry kept bringing in, perhaps aware that he had no tactical reserve, asked Winslow to send over another regiment "to be held in reserve on the bank of the river and a section or two of artillery."[43]

Pillow was ready. His 3,000 troops were in position. He would contend later that he did not have time to make "satisfactory disposition for occupying the field left me" nor "time to make any reconnaissance."[44] Tappan maintained, on the other hand, they had nearly an hour after positioning the troops; Bell agreed.[45] He certainly had thirty minutes at least,[46] which would have been enough time to adjust the line but hardly enough to relocate the line of battle. Pillow did, however, change the dispositions made by Beltzhoover, who knew the ground and was, with the exception of McCown, the most experienced artillery officer under Polk's command. He also changed the alignment of the line of battle chosen by the local commander Tappan.

Pillow's deployment gave the Confederates the advantage of "good lateral and rear communications which facilitated control."[47] The right flank was well positioned; the left (13th Tennessee) was dangerously exposed and overextended; and the center lay in the open cornfield, facing heavy woods forty to eighty yards to its front through which Pillow expected the enemy to advance. As a soldier in the 22d put it, it was like he was "fighting a duel with his enemy behind a tree and he in the open field."[48]

Pillow did not take advantage of the acres of fallen trees around Camp Johnston forming an abatis that would break up any attacking formation. He ignored the defensive potential of sloughs and ravines running north to south, perpendicular to the enemy's line of advance. He allowed the enemy the heavy woods and took the open field. His critic Col. Thomas J. Freeman felt that "it would be very difficult to place our troops in a position where they would be more exposed to the fire of the enemy." Lt. Col. Marcus J. Wright, who came on the field later in the day, maintained, "There is no doubt that Pillow was unfortunate in his selection of a position for his line of battle." William M. Polk's questions remain unanswered, haunting the study of Belmont: having occupied Belmont two months, why did the Confederates not know the advantages of position; and if they did know, why did they not make use of them?[49]

The Confederates waited in the middle of the cornfield, facing to the front. But Gideon Pillow had left the back gate unlatched.

9

My Heart Kept Getting Higher and Higher

The infantry was ashore. They stood quietly, drawn up in line by regiments. They waited there at Hunter's Farm, backs to the river on a levee of sorts. With both hands grasping his rifle high near the stacking swivel, an introspective Private Trueman turned his head to the left, raised the visor of his cap, and glanced up. He noted the ominous morning sun, rising higher by the minute.[1] They waited. Napoleon Buford decided the occasion was fitting, so he moved his horse up close to the ranks of the 27th Illinois and gave them a rousing speech. "We are sufficient in number, are well armed, General Grant is our commander, but the Lord of Hosts is our leader and our guide."[2]

Young Surgeon Brinton came ashore, loaded with the paraphernalia of his profession. He found the roan stallion the quartermaster had provided and strapped his india rubbers and blankets to the saddle. He looked his charger in the eye, remarking to himself that the beast seemed "possessed of few virtues and many vices, like Byron's corsair." The roan had an ugly look that seemed to express a "marked unwillingness to suffer me to mount him." Several soldiers gladly came forward from the ranks to assist the encumbered surgeon. One soldier held the horse by the head, two shouldered against him so he would not turn around to bite, and one or two boosted up Brinton. At last "ensconced" in the saddle, the good doctor "felt confident of my position and certain that nothing short of an earthquake would unseat me. . . . I trotted fearlessly along lines of soldiers, when suddenly my horse gave an extraordinary sort of jump, forward one time, backward one time, then a sensation of vibratory unrest, and then *da capo*, one, two, three; and the more I said 'Whoa boy, be quiet,' and tried to stroke the horse's neck, the more he essayed this confounded buck jump. Then too, the more I tried to look unconcerned, the more the men laughed."

Out from the ranks stepped a deliverer. He steadied the roan. Then he reached over and took hold of Brinton's scabbard, holding it up so the surgeon could see. Somehow the tip of the scabbard had worked loose, "and the sharp point of the blade was pricking the rear hind leg of the animal at every step." Surgeon Brinton, in the presence of the enemy and before the eyes of 3,113 fellow Union soldiers, unbuckled his sword belt, removed it, and then rode on with dignity.[3]

Meanwhile Grant had sent for the pilot of the *Belle Memphis*, Charles M. Scott, and ordered him forward to show McClernand the road leading to Belmont. General McClernand and his staff rode down the road, far enough to feel oriented. Scott may have been helpful, but Capt. Adolphus Schwartz of the 2d Illinois Light Artillery, who had come along as a staff officer at McClernand's invitation, probably briefed McClernand. Schwartz knew the terrain, having participated in the August expedition to Belmont under Colonel Waagner.[4]

Grant himself did not accompany the party. Instead, because "no staff officer could be trusted with that duty," he took five companies from Dougherty's Bird's Point Brigade, two from the 7th Iowa, and three from the 22d Illinois and proceeded down a trail along the riverbank. He found a junction where a road from the south, the Bird's Point Road, intersected the trail.[5] There he halted the makeshift battalion and ordered the senior captain, John E. Detrich of Company I, 22d Illinois, to deploy the five companies in a dry slough. Detrich's battalion was to act as Grant's reserve and to "protect the transports and engage any forces of the enemy which might approach them."[6]

Detrich posted pickets and deployed his 350 men along the ravine facing east toward Belmont, then he looked about. It was a good defensive position, commanding the road junction and thus blocking a quick approach along the riverbank to the landing at Hunter's Farm. It also blocked any enemy flank movement from the river down the Bird's Point Road toward the rear of Grant's attacking force. Detrich observed that a drawback to the position was being so close and perhaps in view of the Iron Banks batteries.

In a few minutes Detrich and his men heard from almost a mile away to the south sounds of McClernand's and Dougherty's column marching east on the main road from Hunter's Farm to Belmont. In a few more minutes, solid shot began flying overhead. There would be "a puff, look out, a whizzing sound is heard." They ducked and dropped to the ground. At one point, a "ball comes screeching towards [us] and buries itself in a tree to our right." One man commented that "if they had shell it would be more disagreeable." Although it produced much noise, Confederate artillery fire from the Iron Banks was ineffective. Grant's reserve in the ravine could scarcely be seen, let alone hit, and the same was true for the Federal column advancing on Belmont. Although subjected to cannon fire off and on throughout the day, Detrich suffered no casualties until the time of reembarkation. Neither was he called forward all day although his command represented 25 percent of the strength of Dougherty's Brigade and 10 percent of Grant's infantry.[7]

Following his quick reconnaissance toward Belmont, McClernand released pilot Scott to the *Belle Memphis* and sent aides back to Hunter's Farm to order up his Cairo Brigade and Dougherty's Bird's Point Brigade.[8] Staff officers rode along the riverbank informing each unit commander of his place in the column. McClernand himself instructed Captain Dollins, commanding all Federal cavalry, to precede and screen the infantry column, "to scour the woods along the road to Belmont, and report to me from time to time."[9] The order of march was as follows: Dollins commanding his own and Delano's companies of cavalry, 27th Illinois, 30th Illinois, one section of artillery, 7th Iowa, two sections of artillery, 31st Illinois, and 22d Illinois. The infantry moved out with the order "Battalion, Forward March" at around 8:30 A.M.[10]

The column marched briskly to the south, passing down a farm lane running between two cornfields until they came to the road that led east to Belmont. Observant privates admired the "fine" cornfields. At this season, however, the corn had been harvested leaving only "field corn" and stripped stalks standing head high.[11]

The dew had almost burned off by now; in fact, the weather had turned out fine—sunny, with a hint of a breeze blowing upriver. It was indian summer, that most lovely time of the seasons. Depriving the men in heavy blue overcoats of the breath of wind, the road perversely began to turn away from the river. Trees closed over the soldiers'

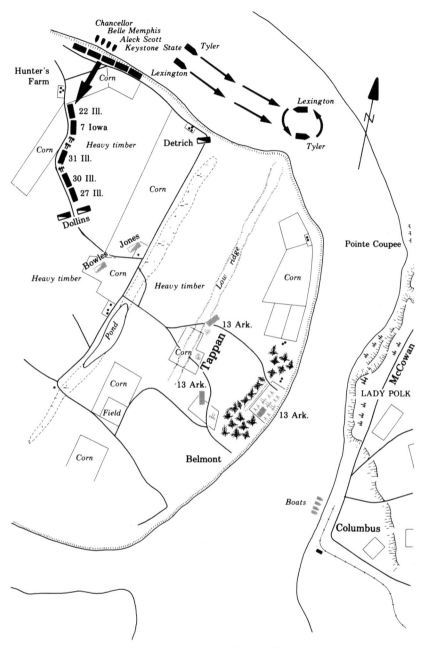

Chancellor
Belle Memphis
Aleck Scott
Keystone State

Tyler

Hunter's
Farm

Corn

Lexington

Lexington

Tyler

22 Ill.

7 Iowa

Heavy timber

Detrich

Corn

31 Ill.

30 Ill.

27 Ill.

Corn

Corn

Dollins

Jones

Bowles

Corn

Low ridge

Pointe Coupee

Heavy timber

Corn

Heavy timber

Corn

Pond

13 Ark.

Tappan

McCowan

Corn

Corn

13 Ark.

LADY POLK

Field

13 Ark.

Corn

Belmont

Boats

Columbus

MAP 4. *Union Approach*

heads. Between their straight trunks hovered a mugginess characteristic of river-bottom forests in the morning. The soil appeared rich, but
that seemed irrelevant in the thickness of this "forest of primeval
trees."[12] An occasional indigo bunting, frightened by the presence of
strangers, would burst through the heavy oaks, come to rest in a giant
buttonwood,[13] and stare at the soldiers in blue. The low ground that
flooded so often was marshy in spots, broken by sloughs and ravines of
varying lengths and depths, reminders of the cataclysmic New Madrid
earthquake. This day desperate men would stop to drink water trapped
in these ravines, taking "horrid mouthfuls . . . from the half stagnant
water of the slough or swamp, or back water."[14]

Ahead, crossing the Union line of advance, lay a major slough, "a
connected series of ponds" over a mile in length called Fish Lake on
some maps and unnamed on others. Although mostly dry, a quarter
mile or more of this great slough contained four feet of water.[15]

Beyond the great slough to the east, less than two miles ahead, lay
their objective: Belmont, "a name rather than a place," a steamboat
landing rather than a town, a low flat "formed by a bend in the river
and clothed with forest, partially cleared to make room for fields of
corn."[16] The widow Elizabeth Walker had been the chief citizen of the
Belmont peninsula the past twenty years, owning more than 300 acres
in partnership with several men. She farmed about half of the land and
operated a large wood yard, selling fuel to passing steamboats.[17]

Belmont attracted attention for its excellent river crossing and became the site of the Iron Banks Ferry.[18] Directly opposite the Belmont
steamboat landing was the depot of the Mobile and Ohio Railroad at
Columbus. Developers believed Belmont could become an important
railroad terminus.[19] A train could stop there and be loaded on the ferry
to be transported across the Mississippi to continue on its way to the
deep South using the tracks of the Mobile and Ohio. Indeed, an unfinished railroad bed just south of Hunter's Farm gave evidence of the
seriousness of investors.[20]

Two roads led into Belmont. The first, along which Grant's men
marched, swung inland from Hunter's Farm. At the point where it
intersected the Bird's Point Road that struck the line of march at a
right angle and ran north toward the river, it was almost a mile from
the water. From that intersection the Bird's Point Road led south then
west to Bird's Point and Charleston. The Hunter's Farm Road continued on past this junction, entering Belmont from the west. This is

the road that worried Pillow, on which he massed his artillery and infantry.

Another road, a meandering plank road south of the Hunter's Farm Road, also connected with the Bird's Point Road and the Charleston Road and eventually entered Belmont from the south, from the direction of New Madrid. Examination of the topography leads one to wonder if this plank road to the south had not been designed by an engineer on Grant's staff with the specific intent of providing the perfect means of envelopment: south along the Bird's Point Road, then east squeezing between easily defensible sloughs, then north toward the river again into Belmont's backdoor.[21]

A small log house with an outbuilding and a shed constituted Belmont. The "town" lay close to the river diagonally across from Columbus. "Immediately behind Belmont, and exactly opposite Columbus" at the ferry landing, was an open plateau of about "twenty acres surrounded by dense wood and thickets." And on this plateau or river flat was Camp Johnston, Polk's "camp of observation." The tents of the 13th Arkansas lay on the "plain" closest to Belmont; those of Beltzhoover's Watson Battery lay closer to the ferry landing. The campground, drill field, and tiny town were surrounded by a pole fence. On the riverbank and for several hundred yards inland the large trees had been cut down and positioned as an abatis to protect the camp from sudden attack from the river or from Hunter's Farm. "A good many big trees were on the ground, buttonwood trees they were, which had either fallen or had been cut down when the camp was formed. Their leaves, dried and withered, were yet on the bough." This crude abatis would break up any attacking formation. Besides, the partially cleared area provided additional security in that Camp Johnston and Belmont could be easily observed from the heights above Columbus.[22]

From Camp Johnston, if one looked carefully across the river, individuals could be seen distinctly in Columbus. The Mississippi was about 800 yards wide here. The river was low on Thursday, November 7, and continued to fall.[23] This meant the riverbanks rose sharply, sometimes as much as twenty-five feet from the water, leaving a narrow mud flat or shelf at their base. Between the riverbank and Camp Johnston, attempts had been made over the years to build a levee. In some places this running earthen mound rose fifteen feet.[24]

✳

The Union column pressed on. Occasional rebel shells would crash into the woods as the gunners on the Iron Banks sought the column, but Grant's men were concealed by the forest and they knew it. Confederate pickets, horsemen thin in number, appeared. They resisted Grant's advance lightly, apparently more interested in observing than fighting. Dollins's cavalry pushed them easily until they reached the great slough. At the point where the Hunter's Farm Road crossed the slough, it was broad and dry. In other places, particularly to the right or south where the water depth became four feet, it was impassable. Confederate resistance stiffened at the great slough, firing increased in intensity, and Dollins sent back word that he confronted more than enemy cavalry, but that he was still driving them.

Grant and McClernand consulted, and Grant gave permission to deploy the column. Dollins stayed to the Belmont side of the great slough skirmishing and serving as security for the deployment.

Union troops moved across the large cornfield and cabbage patch to a line of thick timber separating the cultivated field from the slough. They halted. Using this fringe of timber as cover, they deployed. The Federal column had come almost a mile from Hunter's Farm, and it was still about two miles from Belmont. Grant chose well. The position was protected; it was at the junction of the Hunter's Farm Road and the Bird's Point Road leading off to the south parallel to the great slough. Logan's 31st, the center regiment of Grant's line, "appeared at that time to be squarely astride the road to Belmont." It would be the axis of attack.[25]

The five infantry regiments went into line of battle with Dougherty's two on the left and McClernand's three on the right. From left to right, the order was: Hart's 22d, Lauman's 7th Iowa, Logan's 31st, Fouke's 30th, and Buford's 27th. Dollins's cavalry regrouped to the right of the 27th, while one artillery section took position in the cabbage patch, "in rear of and masked by the 31st Illinois." This section controlled the road junction. The other four guns were placed in the cornfield behind Dougherty's regiments.

On the extreme left of the Union line,[26] in the corner of another large cornfield, Surgeon Brinton found a log hut, the Bratcher cabin, where he established the field hospital.[27] He "seized all the water and put it under guard." He assigned surgeons to the hospital, sent the assistant surgeons forward with their regiments, and made certain that a receiv-

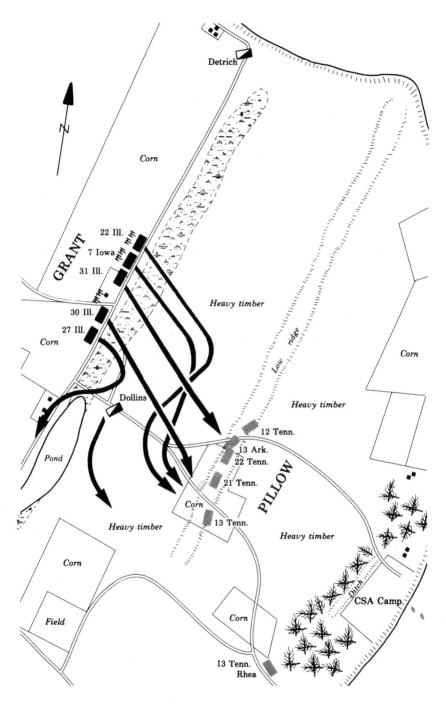

MAP 5. *Deployment*

ing unit was operative at the landing site. In the 7th Iowa bandmaster Thayer deployed his ten band members, one to the rear of each company, "to assist wounded to the rear and to assist the surgeon."[28]

Once the Cairo Brigade had been deployed, McClernand ordered forward two companies from each regiment as skirmishers "to seek out and develop the position of the enemy"—to "see the enemy."[29] It was 10 A.M.[30]

Across the slough started McClernand's skirmishers, "advancing in a regular and very extended line."[31] Spearheading McClernand's probing action on the far right was a platoon of Capt. William A. Schmitt's Company A, 27th Illinois. This was Buford's flank company under his best company commander. John Logan also put forward his two flank companies, A and K, under the experienced command of the indispensable Lieutenant Colonel White.[32] Even with White's direction, however, the attempts to "dress the line and present an even front" met with "not a little confusion." It seemed inevitable that the men would be "jammed in bunches."[33]

On the left side of the Union line was Dougherty's Bird's Point Brigade: the 22d Illinois (now commanded by Lt. Col. Harrison E. Hart) and Lauman's 7th Iowa.[34] The 7th, already diminished by the assignment of two companies to Detrich's boat guard, pushed out a heavy skirmish contingent of three companies. Grant was there on the left with Dougherty's Brigade.

"Colonel, advance your company of skirmishers," Grant ordered, turning to Hart. Hart saluted and instructed Capt. John Seaton of Company B to advance. He selected Seaton because, of the ten company commanders in the 22d, he "was the only captain who had paid any attention" to skirmisher drill. When Seaton inquired of Hart, "Colonel, shall I deploy by section, platoon, or company?" Grant intervened, telling Seaton himself, "Deploy your whole company, captain, to develop the line of the enemy." Grant then told Hart to order up another company and place it under Seaton's command as well to give Seaton backup.[35]

Seaton gathered his company and Company C that Hart had assigned. He addressed them all on the spot, explaining their mission and the formations to be used and reminding them about the enviable reputation the men of Illinois had won in the Mexican War. We shall "not shrink from our duty to uphold her honor and preserve the escutcheon unsullied." Seaton closed his appeal by telling the men if he, himself, "should show the white feather, shoot me dead in my tracks." The captain then sensibly ordered his men to take off their heavy coats and pile them. Many of the men rolled up their sleeves and made themselves as comfortable as possible.[36]

Grant probably considered Col. Henry Dougherty his best officer, certainly his most experienced. A native of North Carolina, Dougherty had come to Carlyle, Illinois, as a boy. His parents died when he was six, and he was "bound out" to farmers. He left this life when he could fend for himself and became an adventurer of sorts—trapping with a fur company in the Rockies at sixteen, joining the army at seventeen. Private Dougherty served in the 1st Dragoons under Col. Phil Kearny, an officer he observed and made his model. The Mexican War came, and the 1st Dragoons campaigned under Zachary Taylor and Winfield Scott, fighting in nine battles from Sacramento to the assault on Mexico City.

Dougherty won a name at the battle of Taos. He had been wounded in the leg and tried to find his way back to the regimental hospital by himself. He passed out and was found unconscious along the trail. After the doctor had dressed his wound and laid him aside, stretcher-bearers kept bringing in more bloody troopers. In the commotion, Dougherty took the opportunity to sneak out of the tent, steal a horse, and return to the fight. Afterward, the furious doctor reprimanded him before the men, which only sealed his reputation for having "fought like a madman." Dougherty spent three long weeks in bed following Taos. His injured leg would not be the only wound he would receive fighting in Mexico. Dougherty's Mexican War adventure closed with a dramatic shipwreck in 1848 at Brazos-Santiago.

He spent the rest of 1848 and nearly all of the next four years in the cavalry under Col. Edwin Sumner north of the Rio Grande fighting Navajos and Apaches. At age twenty-five, in 1852, Dougherty quit the army and settled down in Carlyle, Illinois. There he stayed except for the year he spent helping John C. Frémont explore the continent.

He volunteered again in April 1861. As a good war Democrat and ex-soldier in Carlyle, he raised a company, but Illinois would not accept it, so he joined up as a private under Capt. Sam Johnson, a Mexican War veteran he trusted. Before summer Johnson and the other men in the 22d Illinois Volunteers elected Dougherty colonel.

These men from southwest Illinois proved to be tough soldiers. Dougherty had drilled them hard and volunteered them for anything that smelled of action. They had gone into the battle of Charleston, Missouri, back in August like a horde of angry devils and broke up the rebels when they got close enough to fight hand-to-hand, Dougherty's way. Dougherty killed and captured Confederates himself at Charleston and took a musket ball for his trouble. He was popular and brave, and Grant had good reason to believe Dougherty was probably the best soldier he had brought downriver.[37]

Dougherty drew adventurers to him, like the would-be soldier mounted at his side, Pvt. Bill Travis—a privileged Virginian related to John Randolph, the Travis of Alamo fame, and even that rabid rebel Gov. Isham G. Harris. Son of an architect-scientist who could not manage money, Travis first tried his hand at being a cowboy on the prairie. Then sketching attracted him. He paid his way through Waveland Collegiate Institute in Indiana by giving drawing lessons. He joined up with the 12th Illinois and began to sketch army life and write some for *Harper's Weekly* and the *New York Times*. Henry Dougherty learned about him and invited him to join "his staff" as secretary.[38]

Along Grant's front, which ran about half a mile south down the Bird's Point Road, companies of infantry skirmishers moved forward across the slough and into the "labyrinth of wild wood."[39] They tried moving at the double-quick for a while, then slowed as the big trees and undergrowth sapped strength and disordered lines. "Not a little confusion followed the effort of officers and men to dress the line and present an even front, for in addition to the thick growth of timber the forest land was cut up in slashes by sloughs and ravines that made it impossible to maintain a perfect line."[40]

As they progressed they could hear drums in the distance, the "long roll" coming from the rebel camp. The advance became cautious. We "felt our way along." "We had learned the value of silence." Their senses sharpened, their throats tightened. Their feelings now were perhaps best summed up by Grant himself, explaining how he had felt moving up to the attack against Tom Harris's rebel camp back in July:

"My heart kept getting higher and higher until it felt to me as though it was in my throat."[41]

To the rear of the skirmish line, back on the Bird's Point Road, the main body of infantry and artillery waited and grew restless. These men with "bright new uniforms and ancient weapons" strained to hear sounds that would tell them what was going on. It was alarmingly quiet in the woods across the slough. "Few musket reports were only heard to break the stillness, for the gunboats and batteries had been resting for last half hour. The enemy's long roll is still heard." Sgt. John Wilcox of the 7th Iowa remembered, "All was silent for some time. . . . Many of our boys began to despond of having a fight."[42]

While the long skirmish line advanced east, two companies of rebel cavalry prowled the woods to the right front, therefore contact would be made first by the right of McClernand's line, Buford's 27th. The other four regiments would strike nothing but empty woods and ravines to their front for almost half a mile. As a result, gradually there came about a general change in the direction of advance obliquely to the right, to the southeast.

Schmitt's lead platoon, on the extreme right of Buford's 27th, encountered Confederate cavalry to their right, about 100 yards beyond the slough, and drew fire. They returned the fire, easily drove off the rebel horsemen, and continued on. After this initial contact, Buford stiffened and extended Schmitt's line by sending up the remainder of Company A. Still not satisfied with the number of troops forward, Buford now ordered his entire regiment over the slough in general support of Schmitt. After an advance of another 200 yards, Schmitt's company was struck again, this time by fire from a larger body of cavalry. One man fell wounded. Schmitt held his ground and formed his company into line, concentrated his fire, and drove off the enemy.

Buford had heard enough, he ordered the 27th forward at the double-quick. He dismounted and led the men himself, pushing companies ahead rapidly but cautioning against "becoming scattered and detached from the main body." Soon Buford's men began to see small groups of Confederate infantry in the thickets to their front and right. They exchanged shots, and the Confederates retired grudgingly.[43]

McClernand realized Buford's 27th had developed the enemy to his right, so he pushed Phil Fouke's 30th to the right front in support. Fouke's skirmishers passed through Buford's lines, allowing Schmitt's men to fall back upon Buford's line of battle for a rest.[44] McClernand next ordered Buford to move the 27th further to the right, and he placed Fouke with skirmishers out to Buford's left and positioned Logan's 31st to the left of Fouke, attempting to maintain the original alignment.[45] It was at this point that the call went back to the Bird's Point Road to bring up Taylor's Chicago Battery, but McClernand cautiously reconsidered and had his staff officer, Capt. Adolphus Schwartz, order Taylor to leave "a section of artillery to protect the road."[46]

In the center of the Union line (the left side of McClernand's Brigade), Logan's two companies of skirmishers had proceeded over half a mile. They had uncovered only small units of enemy infantry and were driving them, but Logan grew concerned about the growing volume of fire and the stiffening resistance, so he committed a third company, Capt. Ed McCook's Company I, to the skirmish line.[47]

On the far left, Seaton's 22d Illinois skirmishers advanced without opposition much farther than Buford's or Logan's. The men of Company B encountered large trees giving way to thick tangled woods with "the appearance of canebrake or close growth of willows." After advancing half a mile, they heard firing to their right; so had Grant and Dougherty. They changed the direction of attack for the Bird's Point Brigade sharply to the right, to the south.[48] They "advanced by a flank movement through almost impenetrable woods" toward the sound of the firing.[49]

With the field hospital established, John Brinton felt free to go to the front, so he followed the advancing line of regiments as best he could. He took along an orderly and his own prized bag of medical instruments. They met wounded skirmishers returning from the woods ahead and found several wounded men on the ground. Brinton would "arrest temporarily hemorrhages," send the wounded back to the field hospital, and move on. Then, suddenly, Brinton came upon a soldier "unhurt and armed" making his way to the rear. The surgeon demanded the soldier's name and unit and said, "You are a coward and are sulking, and I will report you." With that he left the man, who was still armed, and proceeded on his way. Some inner voice warned the doctor, though, and he looked back over his shoulder just in time to see the soldier taking aim. Brinton reacted quickly, drawing his pistol and snapping his horse sideways. His sudden movement surprised the soldier who leaped behind a tree and then slipped away into the forest.[50]

✷

The firing grew in intensity as the Union skirmish line began to encounter more Confederate infantry. Most of Grant's men remembered this heavy skirmishing beginning in dense timber with the enemy virtually hidden.[51] Fire discipline vanished—"Grant's men wasted a cartload of ammunition by firing blindly in the general direction of the enemy before they could see a single Confederate." It was this moment, when the infantry skirmishers of both armies came into contact, that Grant considered the beginning of the battle of Belmont: "The *Ball* may be said to have fairly opened."[52]

Slowly, but deliberately, Grant's troops "struggled forward" through the heavy forest thick with Confederate skirmishers. "We fought our way from tree to tree through the woods to Belmont, about 2½ miles, the enemy contesting every foot of ground."[53] "In places the ground was swampy, and between fighting, finding a road and waiting for the cannon to be dragged along the column, the march was far from easy."[54]

Grant's men pressed on, fighting sometimes by companies but more often by squads and individuals. Drill field precision formations broke down. Command, of course, passed to the lowest tactical unit, and the men's "nerves grew stronger" when they were told to "take trees and fight Indian fashion."[55]

For Taylor and his Chicago Battery the approach march was a nightmare. "The trees were so thick that we had to cut them down to allow the guns to pass" as they "moved on in the direction of the heaviest firing." "The march through this dense forest with plenty of underbrush and dead wood, was one of the most difficult I ever experienced, and I am astonished to say that we succeeded in getting the pieces through this wild country."[56]

Grant's regiments groped blindly for the enemy. Buford's 27th, as ordered by McClernand, had stopped its advance and moved off to the right "to feel the enemy and engage him if found in that direction."[57] Buford's move to the right disconnected the regiment from Grant's line and in effect created a wide gap in the right center.

Rushing through the timber, Col. Jacob Lauman of the 7th Iowa stopped still at the sound of heavy musketry coming from the right. He turned to his men who had not yet seen the enemy, raised his sword high, yelled, "There's fighting, boys," and led them west toward the sound of the firing.[58]

The decision "to march to the sound of the firing" sent the 22d Illinois and the 7th Iowa marching toward the blank space in the line vacated by Buford. Whether this decision was a spontaneous reaction by Lauman as he reported or the decision of brigade commander Dougherty or Grant himself is not certain. The result, however, was the entire left of Grant's army, Dougherty's Bird's Point Brigade, now began to move laterally, in "a somewhat complicated maneuver," *behind* the lines of the advancing Logan and Fouke.[59]

The Confederates steadily gave way before the Union advance. Although Captain Bowles's Mississippi cavalry and Pillow's infantry companies fought from favorable positions concealed in thickets and ravines, the rebel skirmishers were repeatedly outflanked and by-passed by Grant's superior numbers.[60] At eleven o'clock or somewhat earlier, all Confederate skirmishers had been driven back upon their main line of battle. Close behind came the regiments of Phil Fouke and John Logan.

10

Nothing out There but Yankees ✳

SECTOR 1

Alfred Fielder, a private in the Friendship Volunteers, Company B, 12th Tennessee, waited in ranks with the men from Gibson County. This forty-seven-year-old farmer could hear skirmishing plainly; it was drawing closer. "Every minute or so a runner would come in telling us the enemy were steadily advancing and . . . in great numbers."[1]

Fielder's regiment formed the Confederate right. To their left were the men from the 13th Arkansas and left of them was the 22d Tennessee, the center of Pillow's five regiments. There Capt. Robert Hancock Wood stood in line of battle with his men of Company B of the 22d. These men from Hardeman County called themselves the Hatchie Hunters. Wood, like Fielder, heard the forest to his front come alive with the sound of musketry and watched gray skirmishers empty out, falling back to the safety of the main line.

Soon two men came out of the woods carrying one of Tappan's Arkansas skirmishers "on a barrow made by joining their hands together under him & around his back. His face wore a ghastly expression & as they passed me he was gasping out complaints against his Lieutenant who he said had ordered him too far forward." His comrades laid him down next to the Tennesseans, and Wood, watching from the ranks, could see the man's torn throat. Wood thought he must help in some way, so he stepped away from the Hatchie Hunters to tend to the man. When the soldier from Arkansas died, it was Wood who closed his eyes, straightened his limbs, and laid his musket beside him.[2]

Confederate skirmishers now poured out of the woods, re-formed themselves into companies, and rejoined their regiments. Everything grew quiet. "It could not have been over a few minutes, but how interminable seemed that time. . . . Doubtless each felt distrustful of himself, as I did, for Battle was an ordeal the bravest man there had never tried . . . and no one could be certain how he would act. Then it was, curious things were done, and then it was memory and the senses registered the slightest sensations like sharpest photographs upon the mind. I well recall the smell of the crushed leaves and broken twigs and of the woods around us."

Back into the lines at the last second galloped a figure in black, the surgeon of the 13th Arkansas, sword in hand. Dr. Brooks, it seems, had turned over medical concerns to his assistant and "was in the thickest of the skirmishing from the start."

Then in a few minutes "the enemy were in sight fireing as they came. We were ordered to fire and such a roar of Cannon and sound of small arms never saluted my ears."[3] Almost two miles to the north Pvt. William Austin with Grant's "boat guard" heard the same frightening roar of cannon and the first volleys from the muskets.[4] On the bluffs above Columbus the noise "was most deafening."[5] Even at Mound City, Illinois, over twenty miles away, the noise of the fighting "could be plainly heard. . . . The roar of the battle profoundly agitated Colonel Morgan [commander of the 10th Illinois guarding gunboats under construction]. He nervously paced to and fro in front of his quarters. . . . The tears coursed down his cheeks as he exclaimed with disgust and grief. 'They are in the fight and we are carpet soldiers.' "[6]

The Federal skirmishers had done their job well, having developed the main Confederate line. Watching from the trees and firing off a round now and then, they maintained contact with the enemy until support came up. With Dougherty's Brigade shifting to the right behind McClernand's Brigade, Logan's 31st, Grant's largest regiment, now constituted the Union left. Directly ahead of Logan were Alfred Fielder's 12th Tennessee, the 13th Arkansas, and the right of the 22d Tennessee.

As he neared the Confederate position, Logan folded his three skirmisher companies back into his line of battle and gave Lieutenant Colonel White command of the companies on the left. Then the 31st advanced. White's left wing struck the left of the 12th Tennessee, strongly posted in a ravine. At a range of about 125 yards White opened fire in volleys. Tyree Bell's Confederates returned the fire, and after a time, White withdrew with casualties.

Simultaneously Logan's right wing came under heavy fire from Tappan's Arkansas troops. Two company commanders went down; Logan's horse was shot from under him, and a musket ball shattered the pistol on his hip. Logan commanded his men to drop to their stomachs and shoot from the ground. We "took cover from trees, logs and underbrush. Then we opened a fire on the enemy which was returned." Happily, the rebel volleys sailed through the trees above. Most of the shots from the 31st, however, were unaimed, just volume fire at an enemy 200–300 yards away hidden by intervening trees. Recognizing this, Grant ordered Logan to have his regiment cease firing to conserve ammunition.[7]

Grant sat on his horse behind Logan's prone riflemen. Surgeon Brinton found him there and rode up to report:

I could hear all around me the whiz of the bullets, and the dry pat as they cut through the dead leaves. At first I could not think what the noise was, but soon one fellow came unpleasantly near my ear, and as I saw and heard the dry leaves rip and fly, and saw the holes which were left, I then knew what it all meant. Then, too, men were hit near me and I began to feel uncomfortable; I felt as if I would like to ride away, but I knew it would never do to show fear, even if I was afraid, so I walked my horse over to where General Grant was, which drew upon me the kind of rebuke . . . that a doctor had no business there, and to get away. . . . In my heart . . . I am afraid I was afraid.[8]

Logan's position, Grant's left, was in danger, perhaps not so much from the volleys of the 13th Arkansas to the front but from even heavier fire coming from the 12th Tennessee that extended somewhat beyond Logan's left. McClernand corrected the situation with dispatch, moving the 31st to the left. Additionally he ordered up a section of the Chicago Battery to support Logan's movement and placed it under Logan's command.[9]

Fortunately for Logan, the 12th Tennessee, curling around his left flank, began to run low on ammunition. Bell decided to send a company, the Friendship Volunteers, to the rear to bring up cartridges.

Lt. Col. Tyree H. Bell (Tennessee State Library and Archives)

Fielder and the rest of his company went back 300–400 yards to find their ammunition wagon. They returned with cartridges but found that in the meantime the rest of the 12th had made a bayonet charge into the woods.[10] It seems General Pillow had learned first from Lieutenant Colonel Bell and then from other commanders that ammunition was growing short and had decided the time had come for a bayonet charge all along the Confederate line.

On the far right Bell's 12th Tennessee, bayonets fixed, crashed into the woods where Logan's men awaited them. The alignment of Bell's nine companies broke down from "the fallen timber, brush and unevenness of the ground," but nevertheless the 12th drove the enemy back "30 or 40 yards." Bell halted his men and began firing volleys into the woods. Logan's heavy fire, however, made their newly won position untenable, and Bell pulled back.[11]

James Tappan's regiment did not fare as well as Tyree Bell's. His 13th Arkansas had been blindly emptying volley after volley into the woods at an enemy "not visible to my regiment up to this time, being posted in the woods and distant some 150 or 200 yards." "Nothing out there but Yankees," recalled Pvt. Phil Stephenson. "We feel and hear the bullets about us, with their 'pang' or 'thud' or 'whiss,' and the air is getting distinctly hot. . . . We had old flint-locks . . . and hands and face and mouths soon get all begrimed with tearing open the cartridges with our teeth. Men were falling dead or wounded among us. . . . Their aim was good. It was rather a stolid monotonous affair at first, no shouting or moving around, just standing in our tracks and firing away at men we could not see. Rather an aimless sort of business one might think, only men were falling faster and faster about us! Every moment!"

When he received Pillow's order to charge, Tappan "thought that there was evidently a mistake as to the order, but on seeing Colonel Russell's regiment [Bell's 12th Tennessee] preparing to move, I ordered my regiment to charge." Private Stephenson saw it differently. "We ran out of ammunition! The twenty rounds were gone in a little while! And there we were! A pretty predicament! What then? We did the only thing we could do except to run! *We charged! charged bayonet!* (Although half our men had left their bayonets back in camp: not wanting to be bothered with them)."[12]

Before the battle of Belmont many officers believed as did Pillow that the issue on any battlefield was decided ultimately by a bayonet charge. That was how matters were settled in Mexico—with the moral force of cold steel.

Tappan's men charged, the enemy fell back before them, but after seventy yards they faltered, regrouped, charged again, halted, fired a few rounds into the dark woods, and fell back again. "I am satisfied that the enemy were at least 75 yards distant from us when we halted in the charge, while to have advanced farther in the charge, we would have been in danger from our battery on our left and of being flanked by the enemy, who were in force on our right." [13]

The fight in sector 1 continued after the repulse of the Confederate bayonet charge. Logan's men advanced "with a will and a yell" to the edge of the woods and beyond several times without much success. Twice Logan made determined attempts to flank Bell's right, but the 12th repulsed both. Beating back these Federal charges, however, gobbled up precious ammunition. Finally Bell's Tennesseans ran out. Efforts to bring up fresh supplies, such as those of Fielder's company, failed because "the only kind I got was the minie cartridge, a cartridge too small for the muskets used by my men. When the minie cartridges gave out we had to retreat." The 12th gave way first.

Lt. William Wallace McDowell of Company H fell back reluctantly. The former schoolteacher thought the charge through the woods might have broken through if the 12th had not become so disorganized. When the order to pull back came, McDowell determined to keep his men together and in good order. Company H retreated slowly but came under heavy fire, and McDowell fell wounded. [14]

With Bell's withdrawal and with Logan's men now lapping against his right flank, Tappan "gradually and in good order, without any confusion, retired through the timber recently cut down . . . to the bank of the river." Private Stephenson disagreed with his colonel. "A perilous business: for not only were we in danger of being run into the river, but there was that broad band of fallen timber in our rear, to impede our flight, break our lines, separate and demoralize our men! If we had had ammunition it would have been different, but as it was, we felt ourselves to be trapped! On we went, back towards the river, and soon all order was lost, of course! On, on, *back*, the yankees pressing us closer and closer, until the clearing around our Camp was reached and the river came in view."

During this pullback to the river, the 13th Arkansas suffered its heaviest losses. Pursuit by Logan's 31st Illinois, however, was slowed by a wide ravine and fallen trees, by fatigue, and by the firing of Tappan's orderly retreating Confederates. The battle in sector 1, the Logan-Bell-Tappan sector, had lasted an hour and a half. Logan's 31st had done very well. After a pause to "take breath," they prepared to attack Camp Johnston.[15]

SECTOR 2

Communication and control vanished in the forest. Two Iowa skirmisher companies crossed the great slough in good style and pushed forward about half a mile without encountering resistance. As they came upon a small cornfield in the woods, however, they began drifting and soon lost sight of each other. Capt. Ben Crabb's Company H pushed on, nevertheless. Just past the little cornfield Company H turned up rebel skirmishers "secreted in the woods." It was Lt. Matt Glass and ten men from Company B, 21st Tennessee. "They exchanged a few shots and Crabb's men dodged among the tall cornstalks to the farther end of the field." Pvt. John C. Temple was hit and killed here, the first from the 7th Iowa to die. Captain Crabb tried to flank the enemy on the edge of the cornfield, but the Confederates fell back through the trees. Encouraged, perhaps elated at driving the enemy, Crabb and his men pushed on by themselves. They came to the edge of a large cornfield and could see the retiring rebel skirmishers as they "disappeared beyond a long ridge in the middle." Crabb's men had just climbed over a pole fence in pursuit when a gray regimental line of battle arose from behind that ridge and fired a volley at them. Confederate cannon joined in. Crabb's men scrambled back to the safety of the woods.[16]

Soon Phil Fouke came up. He deployed the 30th Illinois into a line of battle some seventy-five yards deep in the woods and then tried to advance. When his men emerged into the open, they, like Crabb's skirmishers, made perfect targets for Beltzhoover's Louisiana cannoneers and the Tennessee infantry in the middle of the field. So Fouke quickly followed Ben Crabb's example and returned to the cover of the woods where he remained about thirty minutes, licking his wounds, "with

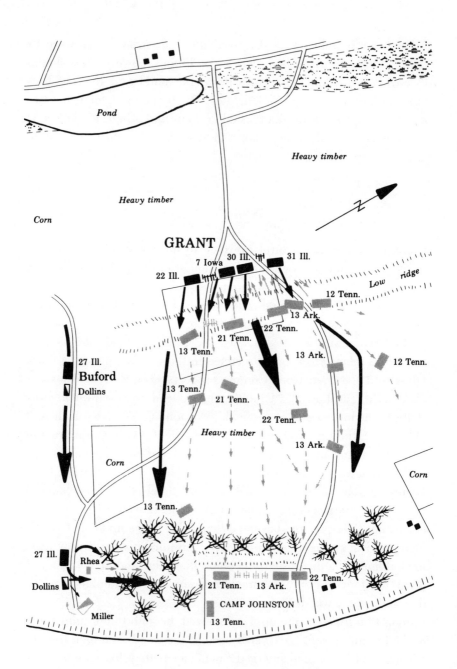

MAP 6. *Fight at the Cornfield*

enemy infantry to the front and a battery of artillery raking my lines."[17] Beltzhoover's cannon continued to blast away at Fouke, but for the most part, the fire, neutralized by the woods, proved ineffective, "simply scathing or shivering the trees."[18]

Meanwhile deeper in the woods, to the left rear of Logan, Dougherty's Second Brigade had changed its direction of advance sharply and now labored to the right or west. "We advanced by a flank movement to the right through almost impenetrable woods, climbing over felled trees and filing around tree-tops in the direction of the firing."[19] Dougherty passed to the rear of the 31st and the 30th and succeeded in bringing his troops up on their right. Lauman's 7th Iowa came up first and took position along the edge of the cornfield; Hart's 22d Illinois followed and began to form on the far right.

It was at this time that Seaton's company of skirmishers came hurrying along behind the Union line, moving to the right, seeking to rejoin their parent 22d Illinois. As they passed behind the 7th Iowa, an astonished Seaton saw it "swing back like the opening of a double gate and the Rebels wildly charging upon them." Companies of the 7th Iowa broke and ran past Seaton's column. With commendable initiative Captain Seaton faced Company B south and counterattacked. The shock stalled the rebel attack, the 7th Iowa rallied, and the combined Union force drove the Confederates out of the woods and back into the cornfield. Bandmaster Thayer of the 7th Iowa, furious at the loss of his band instruments when their position had been overrun, rejoiced when they retook the ground and recaptured "our instruments except one fife and drum head busted."[20]

With this rupture sealed, scattered clumps of Federals re-formed into a ragged line, reaching from the 31st Illinois on the extreme left to the 30th to the 7th Iowa to the 22d on the right. Jacob Lauman told the 7th Iowa "to fall on the ground" and allow the musket balls to pass over. "Crawl boys," Lauman now commanded, and the line inched forward. "When close enough to shoot with certainty, his command was: 'Up, boys, and fire.' Our first volley staggered them, then we loaded and fired at will."[21]

For a time the Federals remained relatively stationary, with short advances usually followed by short retreats, most less than 100 yards. While waiting for their artillery to come up and challenge Beltzhoover's Watson Battery, Grant's men contented themselves with shooting at rebels in the cornfield. Lt. Lemuel Adams of Company D, 22d Illinois, like many others, rested his rifle on the lower rail of a fence and fired away. "A storm of musketry raged along the whole line."[22]

John McClernand moved from regiment to regiment providing encouragement and leadership. He was largely responsible for stabilizing the Union line. He "was all the time in the front ranks, and his bravery and coolness are very highly spoken of." His body servant, William Stains, did his part, staying close by, "cheering the soldiers, and swearing that he would shoot the first man that showed the white feather."[23]

Dougherty's march to the right flank behind McClernand's Brigade had demonstrated "praiseworthy initiative" and may have saved Phil Fouke, outflanked and overmatched by Confederate infantry and by the Watson Battery on his right. Dougherty's action, nevertheless, did leave Logan alone and outnumbered and exposed on the left. And Dougherty's "march to the sound of the firing" did lead "to great confusion and mixing of units."[24]

The two Confederate regiments posted out in the cornfield, Pickett's 21st and Freeman's 22d Tennessee, attempted to return the deadly fire coming from the woods. At about 200 yards most of Pickett's men "kneeled and fired, some 7 rounds at them, with but little execution." Pickett himself, conspicuous up close in the line of battle, was establishing a name for gallantry.

When the 21st had "fired some seven or eight rounds," Pillow, "believing the firing to be ineffective, . . . ordered it to cease." Fortunate soldiers, like those in Robert Wood's Company B of the 22d, lay behind the ridge that ran through the field. There, sheltered, they loaded their weapons "as rapidly as possible & advanced up the ascent until they could see the enemy & then fired."[25] The Tennesseans tended to shoot high, however, since when they could see the enemy they saw only the upper part of their bodies. The Federals, on the other hand, probably because their targets stood in the open field, tended to shoot low.[26]

These tactics proved futile against an unseen enemy, however, so Pillow ordered Pickett's 21st "to fall back so as to draw the enemy out from the woods." But "the enemy would not follow."[27]

Pillow now rode up behind Freeman's 22d and asked a company

commander "if we could not charge and drive the rascals out." The captain replied that he thought so, but Colonel Freeman, who stood beside the captain, said nothing. Pillow then turned to Freeman himself and asked him. "I replied," said the colonel, "that I would charge if he ordered me to do it." Pillow thereupon gave the order and sent his staff riding along the line to insure all the regiments charged simultaneously.[28]

In Company I, 21st Tennessee, Capt. C. W. Frazer's men heard the command "Charge Bayonets!" With a great yell they charged at the double-quick, bayonets fixed. Across the open field they raced. From the woods in front of the 21st came a "withering volley which prostrated about forty of the men." Down went Lt. Jesse Tate; Pickett's own horse was struck in three or four places. With "shot falling like hail and whistling like the north wind," somehow Pickett's Tennesseans charged on and with "ranks sorely thinned" reached the edge of the wood. "As the men fell they cheered the others on to the charge."

They remained barely within the woods, "firing at the enemy as they showed themselves." Most of the time, however, they fired blindly. Then "a tremendous fire of musketry suddenly opened upon my line from the concealed enemy at very short distance." Where was the 22d on his right? Pickett could not see. Was he unsupported? "The fire of the enemy was one continuous roar." Pickett's men kneeled and continued to return the fire. His officers like Captains J. D. Layton of the Liberty Guards and Frazer, "disdaining to take advantage of the kneeling posture, stood by cheering their men and directing their fire." But their men shot at an enemy they could barely see, fifty or sixty yards deep in the woods. Pickett could not hold for long.[29]

Critical eyes were on Gideon Pillow, watching how he handled himself. To "establish a heroic presence" was essential for nineteenth-century combat leaders. Out of this fight would come an "unavoidable brand of approval or disapproval." Conspicuously mounted, surrounded by staff, uniformed with all the trappings, Pillow made a choice target. He had a reputation for bravery, and on this day at Belmont he exposed himself to enemy fire again and again. This display of courage, of "daring, personal bravery," won respect from the men in the line. Pillow hoped it would help sustain them.[30]

On Pickett's right came the charge of Freeman's 22d. From behind their protective ridge they advanced seventy-five yards across the cornfield, over a fence, and penetrated some fifty yards into the woods. The fence broke up Freeman's formation "and the men went into the woods in great disorder." Freeman rode into the woods behind his men and saw the enemy's line, "at least 75 or 100 yards from my own men, and in the midst of a forest of heavy Mississippi bottom timber." To his astonishment, Freeman heard one of his company commanders on the left shouting, "Retire! Retire!" "You are running into the fire of Pickett's men and the artillery." Freeman did not know if the order came from Pillow or not, but he could see it confused his men and countermanded it on the spot. "I ordered my men to go on and spurred my horse on." Once in the woods the 22d encountered "a most tremendous volley of musketry." They returned the fire, and the fight raged for a few minutes. Then came the order to retire, and Freeman's men pulled back. Captain Wood wrote, "The charge failed to drive our enemy from their hiding place in the woods & their incessant fire compelled us to fall back into the field." Freeman agreed with Wood that the concentrated enemy fire would have forced his regiment from the woods with or without the order to retire.[31]

Freeman was furious. It "was more like a plunge into the forest to ferret the enemy out and then drive him back. . . . I think the charge was ill-judged and almost impossible to have been executed with success."[32]

Freeman and Pickett came closer to success than they knew. The bayonet charge caused Phil Fouke's 30th to give ground and threw the 7th Iowa back in confusion. Seaton's timely arrival repaired the break in the 7th Iowa line and blunted Pillow's bold counterstroke. Nevertheless, it was a costly failure for the Confederates, in casualties and in morale. Safely back behind the shelter of the ridge volunteers in the 22d Tennessee ventured out to haul back wounded. Many of these daring Samaritans were shot down. Losses continued for the 22d as "balls of the enemy were falling thick as hail."[33]

While Captain Wood's company lay there, "a finely dressed officer came prancing up on a fine horse behind my company threatening to blow the brains" of any man who did not move back and re-form at a position he pointed out. Wood was aghast. He did not know the officer, he resented the way the man addressed his men, and he knew if his men moved to the position indicated it would "break the line of the regiment." As Wood and his men showed reluctance to obey, the officer drew his pistol to enforce his command. Wood then stood up, identified himself, and asked who the officer might be. By doing so he quickly discovered the officer was drunk. Wood told him to leave at once, and the man rode off. Wood learned later in the day that the interloper was not a line officer but the surgeon of the 13th Arkansas named Brooks.[34]

The position of the Confederates in the middle of the cornfield was intolerable. When Taylor's Chicago Battery succeeded in reaching the front and opened up on the Watson Battery and the Confederate infantry, the center of the Confederate line, the 21st and 22d Tennessee, gave way.

Captain Frazer blamed the retreat on Bell's 12th at the right end of the line. According to Frazer, the 12th came into the fight with only twelve rounds of ammunition and pulled back once it was gone. Frazer's Company I of the 21st found themselves "left alone," without artillery support and with bluecoats closing in from both sides. Only Layton's Liberty Guards and the hardy regimental color-bearer remained with them in the center of the field. Then the color-bearer who stood between the two companies decided enough was enough and "slowly walked away." Layton and Frazer and their men followed.

Dan Beltzhoover worried about the position of his guns and about his ammunition supply. The small-arms fire from the woods to his front grew in intensity. One venture by the Federals into the cornfield had been thrown back easily, but now the Tennesseans posted in the field were taking casualties; it was only a matter of time before they withdrew toward Camp Johnston or tried something desperate. He decided to do his part and continue shelling the enemy in the woods. His six brass pieces threw not only solid shot but also grapeshot into the trees. The Yankees still kept up the musket fire, and the Watsons went through their firing drills in a frenzy. One of the gunners lost his composure, however, and fired his piece while it was being loaded, striking Pvt. Clement Ory with the rammer-missile.[35] The fire of Beltzhoover's Watsons made a terrible roar. It kept the heads of Union soldiers down, but concealed seventy-five yards deep in the forest, they were safe and watched tame grapeshot strike the trees twenty feet over their heads and drop harmlessly at their feet like walnuts. Beltzhoover was "doing no damage whatsoever."[36]

It was 11:30 or 12 before a section of artillery came up in the center to help Fouke's and Dougherty's soldiers who were being pounded by the Watsons. The weary Chicago cannoneers, having fought their way through the forest, "halted, unlimbered, came into 'battery' and commenced firing." They had passed many wounded Illinois soldiers as they "plowed up the dirt" rushing to the front, and fear had long since "passed away, and what was left was a spirit of revenge."

Captain Schwartz positioned the guns just to the right of Fouke's 30th, in "point blank range" of the Watson Battery. Lt. Patrick White, commanding guns 3 and 4, told his men "to cover themselves the best they could and to fire low and to fire *direct* at their flash." Two more guns of the Chicago Light Battery, hurried forward by Schwartz, joined them in the nick of time, and "we had it hot and heavy for about half an hour." Fortunately for White's cannoneers, the Watson guns tended to shoot high, their shot and shell crashing into the trees. "After their discharge my men would shake the limbs and branches off themselves."[37]

For an agonizing interval the four Union guns found themselves 200 yards in front of their own infantry. Not that they should have been behind the infantry—such a tactic only would come late in the war with experienced and trusting unit commanders. But 200 yards in advance was like being alone! An infantry company from the 31st had been assigned to protect the Chicago Battery. They had joined the fight for a while, but the blistering artillery fire caused them to melt away. Lieutenant White sent Colonel Logan word that his infantry support had vanished. Logan very soon appeared with the delinquent company in tow and "exprest himself not in polite language commanding them not to leave me again."[38]

Fouke's infantry wanted to seize the Watson Battery themselves and with the help of Hart's 22d launched several attacks that were beaten back with loss. The men of the Watson Battery worked their guns "with fearful execution."[39]

The cannon fire grew so intense men could not hear and could hardly think. They could see, however, and Union soldiers watched their solid shot take the heads off rebel drivers.[40] They fired faster and even faster, their movements becoming automatic, dangerously reflexive. Lieutenant White wrote that gunner George Q. White "rushed in to sponge his gun. He thought when he herd the report of the other gun it was his, so just as he entered his [illegible] at the musel #4 pulled the trigger and he lost his right arm. I remember him holding up the stump saying, 'Oh Lieut., I can't help you.' I told him to get behind a tree and my intention was to care for him when I got through."[41]

A cheer went up. Through the smoke White's men saw the Watson Battery suddenly begin to "limber to the rear." One rebel gun, however, remained silent in battery.

What had happened? In his curiously abbreviated report of the battle, Beltzhoover merely states, "There we stood doing our best until the whole line retreated to the river." According to Pillow and Polk, Beltzhoover reported the Watson Battery out of ammunition, and Pillow ordered him to take the guns to the rear. Dan Beltzhoover had had a terrible time: his horse had been killed under him, his coat and hat were "literally riddled," and his sword had been "knocked all to pieces with minie balls." Troubles continued as the frightened team of horses of one gun ran off, dragging the limber with them and crushing the legs of Lt. C. P. Ball. Beltzhoover asked Pillow to send him some men to save the gun, but Pillow "thought it better to let the gun go, even if it should be ultimately lost, than to weaken the small force which then held in check the enemy's masses." Some later maintained that the infantry deserted the Watsons, so they had to withdraw.

In their hurry the Watsons forgot to spike the gun. A young boy dashed back. Virtually surrounded by advancing Yankees he reached the gun, jammed a file in the touchhole, and broke it off. Then he turned and ran for his life, ignoring calls on every side to surrender. He "made his escape without a scratch."[42]

After he had abandoned his prized gun, Dan Beltzhoover made his way back to Camp Johnston where he "formed into battery again, although I had no ammunition." Captain Schwartz saw the opportunity as the Watsons displaced to the rear. He now ordered up the four guns of the Chicago Battery to the "edge of the woods where the enemy had had their battery and opened again."[43]

The Chicago Battery believed their accurate and rapid fire had driven the Watsons from the field. Although Lauman's Iowa infantry disagreed, the "blue-jacketed Iowa 7th were the first to straddle their cannon," delirious with joy.[44]

Henry Dougherty came over and complimented the Chicago Battery. He told Lieutenant White that "he did not suppose a battery was ever placed under heavier fire than we were in the woods before we silenced their battery."[45]

The contributions of the Chicago Battery can hardly be exaggerated. Under unusually difficult circumstances presented by the terrain, they had reached the critical point at the critical time. They had outfought an opponent with superior firepower, and they now stood ready to shell Camp Johnston or to displace forward and form in battery wherever needed. Their mobility and efficiency so far at Belmont had been remarkable.

After the Watsons displaced to the rear, what remained of the Confederate center withdrew in orderly fashion to Camp Johnston. The 21st and 22d Tennessee would fall back, plant their colors, and rally; then under heavy fire they would abandon that position, fall back, and plant their colors again. Three hundred yards to the rear on a little rise at the edge of a field Pickett re-formed the 21st. There they fired three rounds at the enemy "advancing upon our lines in good order in double quick time with fixed bayonets." The Federals struck the 21st at the "front & left oblique." Captain Layton of the Liberty Guards continued to expose himself recklessly. He received a severe wound in his left side, knocking the sword from his hand, but he calmly bent over and picked it up, straightened himself, and continued to direct the fire of his men.

Some regiments found strong defensive positions behind their original line, some used the two ravines running behind and parallel to the original line of battle, but withdrawal was piecemeal and stands were temporary. The pounding from the Chicago Battery was frightful. "The enemy kept up a constant fire and drove us still farther back with the assistance of a battery." The center of Pillow's line had broken.[46]

SECTOR 3

On the bluffs above Columbus, Pvt. Henry Morton Stanley of the Dixie Greys, 6th Arkansas, listened to the firing across the river and strained to see. A "thick haze which settled over the woods" had obliterated the cornfields, and without these windows in the forest "we could not guess what was occurring."[47]

Equally hidden from such privileged Confederate spectators, from

Pillow's line of battle, and even from U. S. Grant and his four furiously engaged regiments was Napoleon Buford's column. Soon after Buford's skirmishers became engaged that morning, McClernand had halted the 27th Illinois and sent them off to the right, down the Bird's Point Road around the far end to the south of the long slough—around "the head of a pond" as McClernand put it. McClernand did so because the slough on the right of his line was "yet filled with water," four feet of it, for almost half a mile. As Buford sought to pass around, perhaps Dollins's cavalrymen, perhaps a local farmer, brought him intelligence that the Bird's Point Road on which he traveled parallel to and behind the slough would lead "to the rear of Belmont, and that by following it rapidly I would get into action at the right time and in the right place."[48]

The 27th marched south on the Bird's Point Road until the water in the slough ended and Buford knew he could cross easily. At this point, it seems, he made the decision to continue following the Bird's Point Road instead of turning left, crossing the slough, then moving back further left to close up on Grant's line and once again become the Union right. It was a decisive moment for a subordinate officer. Boldly assuming the consequences of the risk, Buford struck out south away from the sound of the firing, the men who needed his help, and his commanding officers who were counting on his regiment to extend the Federal line to the right.

Without doubt it made Buford more comfortable to have Alexander Bielaski along. Captain Bielaski, McClernand's staff officer, had left his commander and the rest of the staff back at the line of deployment. This was done with McClernand's blessing and at Buford's request. The two men rode at the head of Buford's column, and more than likely Bielaski encouraged Buford's decision. If their information was correct, this march would bring them to the flank and rear of the enemy, resulting in a classic envelopment, a grand maneuver, a decisive stroke.[49]

A quarter of a mile to the south, Bielaski and Buford found that the road divided. The right fork, the main road, led off to Charleston; the left, a crude plank road showing signs of infrequent use, led east in the direction of the river, perhaps to Belmont itself. Without hesitation they turned the column to the left. Soon after they turned onto the plank road, Buford and Bielaski began to encounter stragglers, not

Capt. Alexander Bielaski (Illinois State Historical Library)

only Federal but also Confederate, trying to slip the noose of battle. Then they had a happy surprise—out of a great cornfield on their left rode Capt. James Dollins at the head of his two companies of cavalry. Dollins put himself at Buford's disposal. Together they ventured down the plank road with Dollins's horsemen screening the column. At the edge of an old cornfield the road forked again. Dollins, Buford, and Bielaski conferred and quickly decided to take the left fork, to the

north, back toward the river. Acting without the knowledge of his superiors, dangerously separated from the main body, indeed, threatening to jeopardize Grant's entire mission, Buford ordered the 27th to
march on.

They advanced another mile, then Dollins reported sighting the
Confederate camp, a bright green flag flying at its center. As they came
closer they realized why they could see the camp so easily. The forest
had been leveled for a quarter of a mile around the camp, forming "an
almost impassable abatis of huge sycamore trees." Buford halted in
the woods on the edge of the abatis and formed his regiment into line
of battle. When he saw them ready, aligned on a quarter-mile front,
he waved his sword above his head and led the 27th forward into the
tangled timber.[50]

Directly ahead of Buford, between the 27th and the log houses of Belmont, were Capt. Matt Rhea and his eighty men of Company A, 13th
Tennessee, separated by half a mile from the rest of their regiment.
Rhea had been positioned there by Lt. Col. Alfred J. Vaughan, who
instructed him to guard the road leading down to the river behind Belmont. This was the road on which Beltzhoover had originally posted a
section of the Watson Battery. When Pillow deployed and consolidated the Watson Battery he ordered Col. John V. Wright of the 13th
to place a company there, in effect guarding the extreme left of the
Confederate line.[51]

It was simply a precaution, for Pillow believed the enemy would advance directly upon Camp Johnston from Hunter's Farm. He worried
far more about his right flank, the gap between the river and the 12th
Tennessee, than his left. In fact Pillow thought he might have placed
the 13th itself too far to the left and told Wright that "if the firing on
the right (which had already commenced) should continue for any
considerable time to move my regiment up to the right." So the 13th,
expecting to be at any moment called to the right, was deployed on
Pillow's far left, beyond Beltzhoover's battery, along an elevated portion of the same cornfield held by the 21st and 22d.[52]

There the 13th met the same fate as their comrades in the cornfield:
heavy musket fire from an enemy (22d Illinois and 7th Iowa) who
"could not be seen" in woods eighty yards to the front. Wright's men
"stood their ground, bravely defending their position, though the

killed and wounded were falling thick and fast on every side." Wright held for over an hour.[53]

Company C took the first casualty, Pvt. John P. Farrow. Then in Company G, the Gaines Invincibles, down went "Big Greasy," Pvt. James A. Mitchell, and "Blind Tiger," a Texan named W. C. Limburger who had asked to join up with this Fayette County company. Pvt. John W. Rogers died asking a messmate, kneeling beside him, to "tell my mother I died in discharging my duty; that was all I could do." Thirty-three servants were with the 13th, and a number of them got into the fight. One risked certain death in the open field when he saw "his young master fall and went into that storm of shot and shell and brought the body safely back."[54]

Lieutenant Colonel Vaughan's horse was shot from under him, then Colonel Wright's. When Wright fell, his knee twisted so painfully that he relinquished command to Vaughan. Vaughan remounted, helping himself to one of the Watson Battery's handsome animals. It had been harnessed to tow guns, but Vaughan cut it out of the team.[55]

Thirty-four-year-old Capt. Sam Latta commanded Company K of the 13th. Captain Latta and his Dyer Grays found themselves in the open, only fifty yards from the dense woods. "It was here for an hour our regiment maintained its ground amid a perfect hail of bullets from an enemy we could scarcely see—and lying flat upon the ground we returned their fire, with but little effect." To protect themselves "from the whistling bullets that swept over us" many of Latta's men gathered behind a small log in the field. "I verily believe that if we had stood erect, that not one half of us would have escaped."[56]

A bullet hit Latta and knocked him down. His leg felt paralyzed and he thought "my whole side was torn off." But he looked himself over and found no blood. "The ball struck upon the upper part of my pants, which I wear round my hips without suspenders. It struck upon the flap of my watch fob which was hanging over, and this had seven or eight thicknesses of cloth to penetrate. It glanced—cutting a piece out of the lining of the flap as nicely as if done with a knife. It just abraded the skin, but bruised severely—leaving a mark about the size of a dollar perfectly purple and is yet very sore."[57]

Three civilians, H. H. Falls and Arch Houston of Tennessee and Charles Roberts of Alabama, happened to be in Columbus the night before and convinced John Wright to take them across the Mississippi with the 13th to fight for the day. Roberts was killed in one of the first volleys, and Houston was wounded in the face by an exploding shell.[58]

About the time the 13th became hotly engaged in the cornfield, Wright heard behind him and to his left "a heavy fire of musketry" and knew Matt Rhea and his detached company had been attacked. Wright "immediately communicated this intelligence" to General Pillow. Half an hour later the ammunition of the 13th began to be exhausted. This too Wright reported.[59]

Pillow received Wright's message, delivered to him in person by Lieutenant Colonel Vaughan to emphasize the urgency, "that one battalion in his regiment had exhausted its ammunition." From the right Pillow had already received word from Bell that the 12th was out and from Beltzhoover that the Watson Battery could not continue to fire. It was at this point that Pillow ordered the bayonet charge by the entire line. Somehow the 13th never received Pillow's command. Thus in the Confederate bayonet charge across the cornfield the left flank of Pickett's 21st Tennessee went unsupported.[60]

Pillow watched the desperate charge fail and realized that he must order his men to pull back toward Camp Johnston. He sent Vaughan back to the 13th with his order. To leave their position in the line, however, entailed great danger. These men who had held and fought till their ammunition ran out[61] now had to cross the open field, making grand targets for Yankee marksmen. Many fell wounded as they retreated. Alfred Vaughan found a position 200 yards back, and here he raised the regimental colors and called on the men of the 13th to rally to them.[62]

By 2 P.M. Pillow's line had been abandoned. The retreat to Camp Johnston began in good order but deteriorated as panic set in and units lost their cohesion. A New Orleans gun had been left behind along with many dead and wounded. Four of Grant's guns now moved up to the elevation Beltzhoover had chosen for his own battery and faced east toward Camp Johnston. A target-rich scene greeted the gunners from Chicago. The range was very short; they could not miss. Grant's infantry was closing in too—Logan's 31st from the west, Buford's 27th from the south. It would require great luck, a desperate fight, and all the leadership and cunning Gideon Pillow possessed to save his men.

11

Pillow's line had collapsed. Furthermore the abortive bayonet charge had badly entangled companies in every regiment. Now retreat created even greater disorder. As the 12th Tennessee retired, musket fire from the 31st Illinois cut them down. Albert Fielder watched friends drop on either side and "felt the wind from a ball brush my left lock or whisker." Nevertheless most managed to get back into the fallen timber and dense woods north of Camp Johnston. The 21st and 22d in the center made temporary stands here and there in company strength, but these regiments also disintegrated as they retreated toward the safety of Camp Johnston. Most emptied into the drill field or "the plain" within the abatis surrounding the camp. There officers tried to re-form regimental lines of battle. On the bluffs across the river Pvt. John Bell Battle watched "with a spy glass and could see our men *running*. I saw one regiment run out of woods into a field and draw up in order of battle when a cannon (one of our own) was fired at them, when they would scatter and all run down to the river side and hide under the bank."[1]

As the 13th Tennessee on the left fell back, they found themselves under fire not only from Dougherty's pursuing 7th Iowa and 22d Illinois but also from the extreme left flank where Matt Rhea's Company A had been posted.[2] Company A had been overrun. Detached from the 13th earlier that morning, they had been left alone to confront Buford's enveloping 27th Illinois and Dollins's cavalry. Although Capt. William C. Burton, company commander, had been ill that morning, he had accompanied his men across the river. When they took up their position on the left flank of Colonel Wright's 13th, Burton tried to give commands, but his voice failed completely. He turned Company A over to Matthew Rhea and returned to the landing.[3]

Rhea first tried to halt the Federal advance using a company line of battle. Luckily, Company A caught Buford's men in the act of deploying into line of battle, and their first volley had shock effect—Buford's line wavered.

It was at this point that Alexander Bielaski appeared, it seemed everywhere along the line, "animating the men and assisting in forming the line," disregarding enemy fire, "urging us on to victory!" Suddenly a ball passed through Bielaski's hand, carrying away his sword hilt. Then another round struck his horse in the neck. The Polish captain dismounted and tied his horse to a tree. He grabbed a musket and fired several shots at the enemy, shouting to the men of the 27th to follow him. Then he swapped his musket for the national colors and continued on, leading the advance. With the 27th's flag in his hands, however, he made a conspicuous target. A bullet struck him in the head killing him instantly.

On came the men of the 27th determined to avenge Bielaski and meet the enemy "in his own position among fallen timbers." Rhea's fire became ineffective: "Every time we would fire on them, they would fall down, so we could not touch them, but when ever we would rise to fire they would shoot us down." Matt Rhea dispersed his eighty men among the fallen trees, yet despite the Confederates' excellent cover, weight of numbers quickly told as the 27th fanned out through the abatis.[4]

> While passing through the timber . . . , mounting over logs, and climbing through tree tops the companies became so badly scattered that they could not be formed again. In fact they were not formed again until they were paraded on their grounds in Cairo. Some of the officers tried hard to form their companies but they could not get their men together and finally had to give up trying. The Colonel had ordered us to shelter ourselves all we could behind logs and trees and the men were very willing to obey this command. Every man was now his own Captain and went into business after the old Indian fashion. Had they not done so, more of them would have been killed. When our men saw that they

were gaining ground they would advance and thus advance again.[5]

As they picked their way through the tangle, branches grabbed at muskets and tore at uniforms. Blindly they moved on, over and under the great trunks. At last they flushed out Company A. Matt Rhea and what remained of his company found themselves cut off and then surrounded. Rhea held tightly his grandfather's sword "worthily won" in the Revolution. He refused calls to surrender, "waved the grand old relic" above his head as though it were endowed with magical qualities, and fought on until he was killed. Well over half of Company A was captured.[6]

Buford's men soon cleared the fallen timber and broke into the open ground of Camp Johnston from the south and the west. "So our men now charged out on the open ground, fired, fell down, reloaded and fired again. But they were not yet ready to charge clear across the parade ground." Under fire from the 13th Tennessee and splinters of the 21st and 22d, Buford retreated back into the timber. "At this point we halted to 'take breath.' " Under cover of the woods the 27th regrouped and gathered their resolve before they set out once again at the double-quick across the parade field toward the Confederate tents.[7]

Dollins's cavalry covered Buford's attack. Some dismounted and assisted in dislodging Rhea's company, some guarded the road down which they had traveled, but most, including Dollins himself, watched the mouth of a defile leading along the river from Belmont. Soon a column of rebel horsemen appeared, led by Lt. Col. John Henry Miller.

Miller had rushed to get across the river and personally command his two companies at Camp Johnston, managing to arrive as Grant attacked Pillow's cornfield line. He reported to Pillow who told him to take his two companies of Mississippi cavalry and strengthen the extreme left flank. "Col. Miller, lead your men into action, Sir, and give the Yankees hell," Pillow said. Miller mounted his horse Arab saying, "That is the command I have been waiting and wishing to hear."[8]

A small man, Miller was almost fifty. He prided himself on being the grandson of Gen. Andrew Pickens of South Carolina. He had organized and trained the militia company in Pontotoc and for his efforts received a sword from the state of Mississippi. Unusually well educated with two degrees, this wealthy planter served in the state legislature and founded a local college. In 1848 he decided to enter the ministry and enrolled at the seminary at New Albany, Indiana. Miller received his license as a Presbyterian clergyman in 1850.

In the spring of 1861 the Reverend Miller quickly decided to support the Confederacy. Using his Pontotoc Dragoons as a nucleus, he added other companies to his command until it became the 1st Mississippi Cavalry Battalion. M. Jeff Thompson had complimented Miller's battalion for its work in August, and in October his Bolivar Troop, one of the two companies squeezing along this narrow passageway behind Belmont, had routed Illinois cavalry near Bird's Point.[9]

Miller and his men emerged from the river path and discovered Dollins to their front. Miller immediately ordered his companies into line. "I ordered 'Charge,' and 'charge' rang from a hundred voices." It is doubtful that the two lines of cavalry crashed into each other, nevertheless both claimed to have charged and routed the other. It appears they neutralized each other, although Miller's charge and subsequent maneuvers took him so far to the left that he would find his cavalry squadron cut off and ineffective.[10]

While the 27th attacked through the downed timbers, up came the 7th Iowa and 22d Illinois to form on Buford's left extending the Federal line in the woods fronting Camp Johnston. They too charged from the forest into the abatis but were driven back into the woods. The rebels "appeared to fight with a desperation not equalled any time before." From the edge of the woods Dougherty's men could see the enemy, some drawn up on the parade field behind the abatis, some strongly positioned "in a ravine surrounded by fallen timber in front of their camp." Waiting there in the edge of the woods the Union troops tried "to get breath and reform."

In the ranks, shoulder-to-shoulder, a soldier could hear someone humming a patriotic song; smell the cold leaves; breath in courage from comrades packed together in formation. Phil Fouke's 30th arrived and further extended the Union line east toward the river. It was not long before Logan came up too. He had pursued the 12th Tennessee and 13th Arkansas into the heavy timber east of Camp Johnston, but rather than continue on, he decided to move the 31st by the right flank and close the gap that had developed between him and Fouke. Logan formed his regiment in line of battle "on a high piece of ground overlooking the camp." Now all five of Grant's regiments ringed Camp Johnston and prepared to emerge from the sheltering woods.[11]

✳

From the heights of Columbus the Confederate artillery could see what was happening. Their comrades had been driven into Camp Johnston, and the Federals owned the forest, and no doubt, were forming to assault and finish off Pillow's men. At last it seemed safe to fire without hitting their own troops. So the Confederate heavy guns from across the river began to blast the forest. Across the Mississippi came shell, solid shot, and grapeshot, "literally mowing the tree tops where we were forming for another advance." "Fortunately their range was too high, the shell passing through the tops of the trees, and making a terrific racket." "The sound of a large shell is exactly like the sound of a saw in a saw mill cutting a piece of green timber." Surgeon Brinton's horse "stopped and shook all over."[12]

Although concealed by the woods and protected for the moment from the Columbus guns, success or failure for Grant's army hung in the balance. They must come out of the forest into the open. The Confederates in Camp Johnston must not be allowed time to reorganize. The advantage dearly won in the cornfield must be exploited. Ahead lay the abatis, not so thick on the west side of the camp as on the south but still a formidable obstacle. More dangerous than the abatis, however, would be crossing the "open plateau, immediately behind Belmont, and exactly opposite Columbus."[13]

As Dougherty's and McClernand's men prepared to charge across the parade field, "one section of Captain Taylor's battery of artillery emerged from the timber on the right and took position." These were Lt. Pat White's guns. "I was hard pressed to find my way through the thick timber and fallen trees but I managed to get through finally." Two more guns of the Chicago Light Battery, guided by Captain Schwartz, followed close behind. "Now we ran our pieces forward to the top of a little knoll that commanded the camp." Once Taylor's four guns had formed into battery they opened fire, "spreading consternation" in Camp Johnston. The range was point-blank—300 yards.[14]

Col. Jacob Lauman told the men of the 7th Iowa "to fall and let the battery play over us." The troops fought hard to maintain the tangled line of infantry as they climbed over and around and under sharp-pointed limbs and trunks. Sometimes they "crawled with their standards waving over them." Once through the abatis, however, order returned. When "close enough to shoot with certainty, the command was: 'up, boys, and fire.' Our first volley staggered them, then we loaded and fired at will. Volley after volley." Lauman waved his sword and led his men racing toward the acres of tents. Beside them ran the 22d. A ball struck Lauman's horse in the head, and he crashed to the ground heavily. Lauman got to his feet and saw just ahead the enemy colors waving. "Iowa Seventh, are you going to lose that flag?" The 7th responded with a rush, got to the flag first, and pulled it down.[15] Then Lt. William deHeuss of Company A took his company flag and planted it on top of one of the guns of the Watson Battery. Captains Sam McAdams of Company E and John Seaton of Company B, 22d Illinois, secured the remaining pieces. Colonel Dougherty immediately turned all of the captured guns over to Captain Taylor of the Chicago Battery. While Taylor's son tried to spike one of the Watson guns, "a wounded rebel raised up and fired at him." The shot missed, and young Taylor "ran him through before he could fire again." The fight near the flagpole at the south end of the camp "was awful."[16]

Federal infantry poured into Camp Johnston: the 7th Iowa and 22d Illinois from the front; Buford's 27th from the Union right and front; and the 30th and 31st from the left, led dramatically and bravely by McClernand, waving his hat at his men. They sent Pillow's rebels "skedunking from their den," "strewing the ground as they went with guns, coats, and canteens. Our brave troops followed them with shouts, pouring volley after volley into them." Grant's men "swarmed around the flagpole, cannon and tents 'like bees around an overturned hive.'"[17]

Dougherty's Brigade delivered the brunt of the attack, while McClernand's 30th and 31st had done the heaviest fighting at the cornfield. The appearance of Buford's 27th, however, crashing through the thick abatis on the south, broke the spine of Pillow's defense line at Camp Johnston.

It would be inaccurate to see Grant's attack as beautifully synchronized, as a model grand assault such as Gen. Edward Canby's on Fort Blakely at Mobile in 1865. Nevertheless Pillow's beleaguered troops believed the attacks coming at them from the front and from both flanks were simultaneous and delivered by overwhelming numbers.

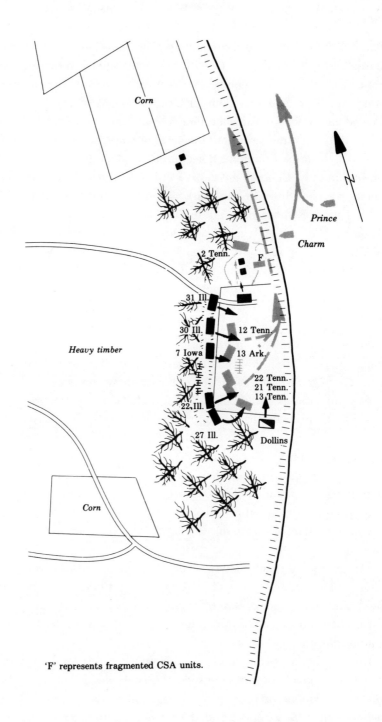

Corn

Prince
Charm

2 Tenn.
F

31 Ill.
30 Ill.   12 Tenn.
Heavy timber
7 Iowa   13 Ark.

22 Tenn.
21 Tenn.
13 Tenn.
22 Ill.

27 Ill.   Dollins

Corn

'F' represents fragmented CSA units.

MAP 7. *Capture of Camp Johnston*

The fall-back position of Camp Johnston proved disastrous, more of a trap than a defensive bastion.

Grant seems to have handled himself well. One observer reported him "swinging his sword above his head, . . . shouting himself hoarse." More characteristic would be Grant biographer Albert Richardson's view of Grant riding along with Maj. Joseph Webster, Capt. William Hillyer, and Capt. John Rawlins, "encouraging and rallying men from hiding places." Grant had unusual difficulty with his mount at Belmont; eventually the horse was hit in the stifle-joint and disabled. Hillyer[18] gave up his own mount to his commander, and Grant rode on leaving behind his saddle with his name on it.

Pillow also had a close call. His aide, Maj. Gustavus A. Henry, Jr., saw a Yankee take aim at the general and shouted a warning. General Pillow "spurred his horse & the fellow fired and down went my horse."[19]

With enemy infantry attacking from three sides and two sections of artillery blasting directly into their position, the Confederates abandoned their colors and their cannon.[20] As they fled north out of the tent camp and through lanes prepared in the abatis, they in effect were being flushed out into the waiting rifle sights of the 30th and 31st Illinois. They fled, running the gauntlet as "hundreds of muskets poured their deadly content."[21] "I felt as cool as though I was *shooting chickens*," said Cpl. Bill Onstot of Buford's 27th.[22] Hundreds of Grant's men, some from each regiment, took up the chase—a mob chasing a mob. This pursuit, such as it was, was led by Jacob Lauman.

Colonel Lauman was mounted again, probably securing another horse from the Watson Battery's fine collection, and took his place at the head of this mixed bag of Federals. They pursued Pillow's stampeded regiments a few hundred yards up the river road until they reached two wooden buildings on the riverbank. Here at the northern edge of Camp Johnston Confederate resistance suddenly and astonishingly stiffened. A wild Confederate counterattack came from the riverbank. Down went Lauman with a wound in his thigh; the Federal pursuit fizzled.

The timely arrival of Col. Knox Walker's 2d Tennessee from Columbus prevented the Federals from rounding up most of Pillow's troops. Its subsequent bayonet charge absorbed the impact of Lauman's attack, and it also struck or threatened the left flank of Logan's 31st advancing on the extreme left of the Federal line, thus deflecting Logan's attack to the south into Camp Johnston and away from the riverbank where Pillow's regiments hid demoralized.[23]

As Walker's troops were being ferried over by the *Prince* and *Harry W. R. Hill*, before the steamers could tie up at the Belmont landing, "many of the soldiers jumped from the boats and swam ashore, and the moment they got across rushed forward to fall with fury upon the enemy." Pillow met his friend Walker on the riverbank and urged him to buy some time by attacking "as promptly as possible to check the advance of the enemy's force." Walker carried out his orders. He formed a line of battle on the riverbank, adding to his regiment a number of men from the shattered 13th and 21st. Then Walker's reinforced 2d counterattacked "at the full run."[24]

Forty-three-year-old Joseph Knox Walker had been born in Maury County, Tennessee, the son of James and Jane Marie Polk Walker. A privileged young man, he attended Yale College, graduating in 1838. His classmate William F. Cooper confided to his diary in 1839 that Knox had "perhaps less genius [than another classmate], but decidedly more industry, besides he has a practical business kind of mind which will make him succeed any where."[25] Walker studied law and in the early 1840s shared a law practice in Columbia with his uncle James K. Polk and Pillow. When Polk became president in 1845, Walker went to Washington where for four years he served as his uncle's private secretary and lived in the White House. Walker's love of society, however, irritated his uncle. "In truth he is too fond of spending his time in fashionable & light society," the president wrote in his diary, "and does not give that close and systematic attention to business which is necessary to give himself reputation and high standing."[26]

At the end of Polk's term in 1849, Walker remained in Washington and tried his hand at banking. Then he moved to Memphis where he continued as a banker and practiced law. "He was conspicuous for his failure in the banking business, but was noted as a good lawyer and speaker."[27]

With the help of his brother Sam, Knox Walker recruited and outfitted the 2d Tennessee, also called Walker's Legion.[28] He had a good second in command, Lt. Col. William B. Ross, a natural soldier who until April 1861 had been a broker and merchant in Memphis. Walker also had recruited a few Mexican War veterans like Kentucky Irishman Dennigan of Company D.[29]

The 2d was a regiment of Memphis Irish. Walker's street soldiers who "swore allegiance to the Scarlet Woman" were particularly rowdy. Some observers believed the 2d had occasional mutinies; the men of the 2d called them friendly riots. They delighted in cardplaying and cockfighting. Their chaplain, Father Daly, celebrated mass in the morning, preached in the afternoon, and "settled the drunken rows" in the evening.[30] The 2d was noted for its glorious brass brand and its choristers; it was also noted for ingeniously combatting the order that stopped the whiskey ration.[31]

Knox Walker's sisters gave the 2d its flag; his daughter Sally considered herself "the daughter of my father's Regiment. . . . Memphis had a large Irish population; my father was their friend and counselor; in politics they followed his lead. So great was his influence with them, and their love for him, that Father Grace presented him with a pew for life in St. Patrick's Church, now the cathedral, though my father was an Episcopalian. The Irish had followed my father in politics and now they followed him in war."[32]

Walker's 750 Irish waded into the mass of Lauman's men and set them reeling. "Illivate your guns a little lower, boys," an Irishman yelled. Another in his excitement rammed down his first cartridge without biting off the end; as a result the trigger only clicked, so he poured in a second charge. "This time the gun and Dublin both went off."[33] There out in the open ground fighting grew savage with big knives flashing and rifles being used for clubs in hand-to-hand fighting. Some of the Iowa troops were "overpowered and threw down their arms." The Yankee pursuit had been stopped cold.[34]

Knox Walker's nephew, Lt. Jimmie Walker, lost his captain early in the attack and had to take over Company I himself. Twenty-two years old, the son of Memphis attorney Sam Walker, Jimmie "could dance the longest and laugh the merriest, and had always a kind word."[35] Leading his men out from the riverbank, Jimmie Walker was hit in the hip, the bullet penetrating the intestines. He pulled himself up on a log and kept giving orders to his company for about twenty minutes. Then, before he lost consciousness, he called to Lt. John Dagnan: "Fight, Daugues, fight or die! Don't let my men be taken prisoners."[36] Knox Walker "saw Jimmie who was just like my son dying," but directing the regiment was his duty and required all his attention, so he passed him by.[37]

The success of Walker's counterattack invigorated the Confederates scattered along the north end of Camp Johnston. Most, however, had fled further up the riverbank, away from the fighting, where Gideon Pillow was now trying desperately to bring them under control. The river pilot of the *Hill* tried to recall the scene for Samuel Clemens: "And here they came! tearing along, everybody for himself and Devil take the hindmost! and down under the bank they scrambled, and took shelter."[38] Those who remained at the edge of Camp Johnston tried to rally. Capt. Knox Walker, Col. Robert Russell, Maj. Francis M. Stewart, and Col. James Tappan did their best to organize them.[39]

Capt. Sam Latta brought what remained of his company of the 13th Tennessee up from under the bank and offered them to Colonel Tappan. Tappan asked Latta to place them in a ditch behind the levee, which was a good defilade position because the earth mound was about ten to fifteen feet high, but it had been built so close to the river that it provided little depth and thus could shelter only a few men. Tappan played an important leadership role here, but essentially he was dealing with broken units with broken morale.[40]

While the Confederates tried to develop a defensive line along the levee, Captain Schwartz, with the help of the Federal infantry, pulled four pieces of the captured Watson Battery north through the streets of the tent camp to a position where they could support Lauman's attack. Using mostly infantry to crew the guns,[41] Schwartz "formed in battery again on the open ground" and faced the guns north, aiming at Walker's charging Irish. The Watson guns, joined by a section from Taylor's Chicago Battery, opened fire. Canister from the beautiful brass guns cut cruel gashes in the ranks of the Irishmen; casualties dropped to the ground in squads.[42]

Having smashed Walker's regiment, Taylor and Schwartz turned the Watson guns on the fragile Confederate line strung between the abatis and the levee, "a little above the foot of the willow bar."[43] Fragments of rebel units hugged the levee. Capt. J. Welby Armstrong of the 2d linked thirty men of his Company A with the stubborn handful of twenty-five men that remained of Pickett's 21st Tennessee.[44] The fire was "murderous." To stand and shoot invited instant death. One Confederate who stood to replace his flint flipped back into the ditch with two holes in him. Behind the levee Capt. R. H. Wood of the 22d tried to fight on with a piece of his company as well as "a portion of the Harris Guards commanded by Lieut. Thurmond & a portion of

Capt. Marshall's company who then had no officers at their head." In the ditch Wood found an old soldier sitting, holding his company flag, "the bright folds lying in the dust. I told him to hoist the flag. . . . The old man gave me no answer but looked at me as if he would like to obey but was afraid." The old soldier was so frightened he could neither speak nor stand, so the resourceful Wood took the staff, stabbed it into the ground upright, and wrapped the man's fingers around it. "The old man sat in the ditch & held it up until we were driven over the bank."[45] Panic fed upon itself, and Tappan's makeshift force began to tumble over the riverbank. Once there they dared not look up. They were helpless as fish lying on the shore. "I felt no human power could save us & our whole command from capture or death."[46]

Men would remember a boy belonging to one of Tappan's Arkansas companies out in the river waving "two mimic flags one in each hand over his head" before he was shot down.[47] Many Confederates died at the riverbank, many fleeing, many manning the makeshift levee line. "I saw dead bodies lying under the bank and partly bathed in water." Bodies in gray bobbed in the river.[48] "Our men broke to pieces and fled in terror up the river bank. In going up the river they cowered under the bank and behind trees that had been cut down."[49]

Lieutenant Colonel Vaughan, on foot once again, went over the twelve-foot bank and managed to clamber aboard a flatboat. Once away from shore he yelled back to his tormentors, "Shoot this from under me if you can!"[50] Walker's Irish clung to the bank, humiliated. They spotted Capt. John Saffarans of Company I out in the river waist deep. "One of his men called, 'Captain, deer, are ye off for Memphis? If ye are, tell the ould woman the last ye saw ov me I was fighting, while ye were running away.'" Just then a ball struck Saffarans in the face.[51]

Meanwhile Lt. Pat White and the Chicago Battery had entered Camp Johnston. Drivers rounded up loose rebel horses and harnessed them to the guns, replacing their own that had been killed. By sections the battery moved north, some to help Taylor subdue the counterattack, some under McClernand's orders to look for targets of opportunity on the river.

First they fired a round or two into Columbus, just for the hell of it, then they discovered rebel steamers. They could see packets loaded with troops. The Chicago Battery and one of Beltzhoover's New Orleans guns "were firing round shot into their hulls with no effect. I [White] told the gunners to elevate their pieces and use shell. That had the desired effect."[52] "Our gunners made some splendid shots, and the splinters flew quite lively."[53] White's cannon fire ripped up the *Prince*, the *Hill*, and the *Charm*, tearing away chimneys, passing lengthwise through one main cabin, and crashing through two wheelhouses.[54] The steamers were close enough for the infantry to open fire also; "The splattering shot were like a hail storm."[55]

Near exhaustion the Chicago Battery nevertheless kept pounding away. One gun crew was down to four men. Gunner Sgt. William J. McCoy "threw himself down on the grass and said ' . . . I'm played out; I must rest if I am shot for it.' " Sgt. David Chase, the gun chief, took over and continued firing at the boats.[56] Then a rebel sniper firing from the cover of the abatis hit Chase, "so Frank Pond loaded while I sighted and fired."[57]

The steady, flexible, energetic work of the Federal artillery troops can scarcely be overemphasized. They broke up Walker's counterattack, they pinned down and demoralized any Confederates with fight left in them behind the riverbank, they blew holes in the transports bringing over fresh troops, and they even caused consternation among Polk's troops and boats trying to embark on the Columbus side. The casualties they inflicted and the confusion they created tilted the tables at Belmont.

For whatever reasons—perhaps the dulling effect of Walker's counterattack, the wounding of Lauman, the discovery of more alluring targets for the artillery, exhaustion, lack of ammunition, the pervasive conviction that the rebels had been thrashed and posed no threat, the desire to return to the captured camp and enjoy the nectar of victory, or that Grant was "afraid that [the Confederates] were trying to entice him on to some concealed batteries"[58]—Grant's pursuit stopped. Infantry activity on the riverbank degenerated into deadly skirmishing and sniper action with handfuls of diehard rebels who refused to join either the groups in gray surrendering or the herd bolting up the river.[59]

Pvt. Henry Stanley, Leonidas Polk, and the thousands of Confederates on the Kentucky shore watched in disbelief. Clearly they saw the enemy in Camp Johnston and Pillow's routed troops scattered and fleeing upstream. A lady standing beside Sallie Law said, "'Do look,

Mrs. Law, our boys are whipped; see how they are running.' But mother replied: 'No, they are not running, the poor fellow[s] are thirsty, and are going to the river to get water.' " [60]

Surgeon Brinton found one of the lost rebels, wounded and alone in the woods. He had been

> shot in the left arm, for he was supporting his elbow with his right hand. He was a tall fellow, in butternut brown trousers, and without a coat or hat. He was evidently suffering great pain, and the pain had produced a peculiar excited delirium. He noticed nothing which was transpiring around him, nor did he even seem to see our soldiers, but he kept steadily running up and down, forwards and backwards, by the side of a huge fallen tree, always turning exactly at the same point and retracing his steps to and fro, jumping over some bush at each tour. I watched him for some minutes with curiosity. [61]

About 2 P.M. firing ceased. An eerie lull, "a perfect quiet," came over the battlefield. Incredibly it would last almost thirty minutes. [62] Grant's army was celebrating.

The American flag rose to the top of the flagpole at Camp Johnston. Around it stood most of Grant's expeditionary force. "In the midst of it all, is heard one long, loud, continuous round of cheering as the Star-Spangled Banner is unfurled in the face of the foe, and defiantly supplants the mongrel colors." [63] John McClernand pushed his way to the center and called for three cheers. To the happy surprise of all, the band of Dougherty's 22d appeared with instruments in hand. McClernand brought them forward, and they circled the flagpole. They began to play the "Star-Spangled Banner," "Dixie," "Yankee Doodle," and other "soul-searching airs." The Yankees sang with "exuberance boundless," aiming their songs toward Columbus as though they were firing grapeshot. Capt. John Seaton found himself carried away emotionally. He mounted one of the Watson cannon and helped lead the singing. At the riverbank, men of the 21st Tennessee watched the flag being hoisted. All Col. Thomas Freeman's men could do was fire "upon it our last three cartridges." [64]

As the soldiers "cavorted and huzzaed," McClernand's political instincts surfaced, and he could not resist making "a spread-eagle speech." Others joined in. They "galloped about from one cluster of

Battle of Belmont (engraving from a drawing by William D. T. Travis;
Illinois State Historical Society)

men to another and at every halt delivered a short eulogy upon the Union cause." The soldiers "cheered themselves hoarse and the battle was soon turned into a Fourth of July orgy of bubbling eloquence." Each "eulogy on the Union cause was met with cheer and shouts."[65]

Everyone inspected the Confederate flag. It must have belonged to the Watson Battery, which boasted a heavy contingent of Irishmen, because the "cursed rag" was two-sided. On one side was the novel Confederate national design of three stripes and twelve stars; on the other a green silk field with the golden Harp of Erin.[66]

Then, to the mortification of their commander, jubilation and patriotism gave way to greed for the spoils of war. "Our men laid down their arms and commenced rummaging the tents to pick up trophies. Some of the officers were little better than the privates."[67] They "were in search of a bite, and commenced plundering the camp."[68] Many exchanged their muskets. "They pulled trunks out of the tents and looted them, loading themselves with small arms, baggage and even horses." They marveled at an artillery officer's belongings (probably Beltzhoover's), "which could not have been valued at less than $500." They helped themselves "to the untouched breakfast, which seemed to have been especially prepared for them."[69]

While individual soldiers pillaged Camp Johnston, others worked to salvage valuable military property. The camp was a wreck: "Fragments of wagon, horses and men lay scattered." "Around their cannon the dead and dying lay in heaps."[70] Captain Schwartz sent back to the great slough for a caisson to bring up ammunition. He would use the caisson to help haul off the equipment and the Watson guns. He ordered soldiers to gather rebel horses running panic-stricken through the streets of the camp. He harnessed the few that soldiers brought in to the guns, but they were not enough, so he ordered infantry to help. After, they dragged two pieces a short distance, the soldiers quit, "too tired and worn out, partly feeling too victorious and safe."[71]

Surgeon Brinton also did fine work under hard circumstances and managed to see that nearly all wounded were returned to the field hospital at the Bratcher cabin. Some of the officers made the journey atop caissons. Brinton dumped out the contents of the few ammunition wagons and packed them with the many injured enlisted men. From the field hospital nearly all of these wounded went back on wagons to the transports. Jacob Lauman came along later. He had hailed Ezra

Taylor as he went by and managed to be placed aboard a cannon for his trip to the rear.[72]

The joy of the Union troops in Camp Johnston knew no bounds. A "carnival spirit prevailed." They shouted and cheered, compared trophies, and went about "shaking hands and congratulating one another." These men, who six hours before scarcely knew the sound of a volley, looked about at their comrades, their faces black as coal miners from biting cartridges. They felt like veterans; they *were* veterans![73]

They may have become bloodied veterans, but Grant knew they were no longer a fighting force. His soldiers had become "demoralized from their victory."[74] Efforts to have the men abandon their loot and re-form proved futile.

To regain control Grant ordered Camp Johnston burned immediately. Field grade officers carried torches and set the fires themselves. Flames made short work of what remained of the tents, belongings, and equipment of the Watson Battery and the 13th Arkansas.[75]

Confederates later believed rampaging Yankees had bayoneted sick and wounded members of the 13th in their tents. "Not only this, they set fire to the tents, used as hospitals." Many were "consumed by flames." Sick and wounded Confederates confined in the tent camp could scarcely have been in a worse location. They were exposed almost as much as men in line of battle. Furthermore it seems probable that in the Federals' haste to fire the camp, wounded men in the tents may have gone unnoticed. When later found by their comrades, these wounded men who burned to death would have certainly given the appearance of having been murdered in their tents. Even Brig. Gen. Frank Cheatham would use this as a rallying cry to infuriate Confederates waiting on the Columbus bank.[76]

Beyond the abatis, down below the riverbank, Confederate soldiers worked their way north along the river, away from their burning camp and the Federal gunfire. The Mississippi was low, fortunately, creating a narrow shelf of deep mud that hid them, thus saving them. They waded through the water and clinging mud and slithered with difficulty over great logs on the bank. Tappan's men from Arkansas had placed them there, deliberately, to break up any column of Yankee raiders sneaking along under the bank to surprise them in their beds.

The jammed mob of men, panic-stricken, fought their way along, "expecting every minute that the enemy would advance up the river and fire from the overhanging bank down upon us."[77]

A hundred yards or so past the north end of Camp Johnston, Captain Wood climbed to the top of the bank and looked down.

Here was a scene of confusion such as I had never witnessed before. One man, in his haste to get across the river, pulled off his boots & socks & rolled up his pants to wade it. He waded in to his chin & looked wistfully across, then turned & crawled upon the bank. I found on the bank a large crowd, a good many of our own regiment. . . . Col Freeman had (as I afterwards learned) given up all as lost & taken passage for Columbus, a step many would have taken if they had the opportunity, (though he did very wrong to desert his command at such a time). It was however a time of general panic. . . . General Pillow with his whole suit partook of the general panic & rushed madly to the water's edge (as I am informed by reliable men who witnessed it.)[78]

The weight of testimony from witnesses, however, refutes the substance of Captain Wood's information about Pillow.[79] Although it is quite likely the general dashed to the riverbank and fled along it after Camp Johnston was overrun, he seems to have bounced back and worked hard to rally his scattered regiments. "We saw the old hero stand exposed to grape and bullet beg his men to stand when hope was gone and hundreds of our brave boys had fallen. He rode in front all day at Belmont and the raging thunder of artillery did not alarm him."[80] That he had lost control of his command there is no doubt, and Leonidas Polk later would make a curious and uncharacteristic remark, replete with innuendo: "Of General Pillow's personal bearing on the field I have spoken in my official report of the battle in such terms as the information brought me at the time warranted. I am not concerned to reopen the question as to the justness of the opinion then expressed."[81]

Could the Confederates be rallied and reorganize? Could they return and renew the fight? Could Pillow revive them? It seemed doubtful. With six chewed-up regiments scattered and frightened, could or should Polk redeem Pillow's defeat by committing more regiments? If so, how many more?

On the other hand, Camp Johnston's faithful abatis, now reversed, might work once again in the Confederates' favor. The high riverbank offered protection against Yankee firepower, at least for the moment. The strip of forest beginning at the northern edge of the camp that stretched along the river up to a point of land jutting into the Mississippi could cover reorganization and reinforcement. And then there were all those boxes of ammunition, "a good supply," lying below and on top of the riverbank. If only Grant would allow them time; if only a glimmer of hope, of confidence, would revive them.[82]

12

Fighting the Same Ground over Again

Leonidas Polk paced the riverbank. He would stop and listen carefully, then he would pace again. All seemed silent behind him. The multitude of soldiers lining the bluffs watched the forest across the river intently. Beside him two infantry regiments, a thousand men, stood quietly in ranks, checking and rechecking their gear and their weapons. The 15th Tennessee and the 11th Louisiana were Polk's reserve. He had stationed them, as he had stationed himself, at the Columbus landing, midway between the outer works of Columbus and the fighting at Camp Johnston. His officers watched him. What would he do? Whom would he order over? When?

Polk could see with his own eyes the outcome of Pillow's fight at the cornfield. Confederates began to stream back into the open field around Camp Johnston. Slowly, with agonizing slowness it seemed, some began to re-form. Many others ran on, fleeing down to the river. The bank itself seemed to be turning gray with stragglers. It was shortly after 11 A.M.

How many men confronted Pillow over there? He had reported an attacking enemy with three times his own numbers, a "very large force."[1] Polk had already sent more ammunition, Knox Walker's regiment, and two field batteries.[2] Nevertheless, disaster stared back at him.

Polk decided, although "with great reluctance," to commit his reserve. He ordered Col. Samuel Marks to take his 11th Louisiana across. He had faith in these Louisiana troops and in the veteran Marks. As the 11th began boarding the *Charm*, Polk decided to send the 15th Tennessee along. Then he sent an aide off to the right sector of the Columbus works to find Brigadier General Cheatham. Have Cheatham, he instructed the aide, come to the riverbank immediately and bring his First Brigade with him. Thus Polk committed his reserve and set about replacing it. In the process, however, he weakened seriously the force manning the Columbus defenses.[3]

As the 11th Louisiana embarked, Polk took Marks aside and told him to land upriver from Camp Johnston, near the point jutting out into the Mississippi, use the woods there to cover his movement, and then strike the enemy in the flank.[4]

Polk probably had doubts about the 15th Tennessee. Although regarded as a Shelby County regiment, it was made up of troops from different areas, thus lacking the homogeneity of a usual regiment. The Madrid Bend Guards came from Lake County; the Washington Rifles, formerly a militia company, was "composed entirely of foreign born citizens in Memphis." Company G, led by Capt. Thorndike Brooks, contained ardent secessionists from Williamson County, Illinois. Among them was Logan's brother-in-law, Capt. Hilbert B. "Hibe" Cunningham. On their way south to join Frank Cheatham at Union City, Tennessee, Brooks and his men had picked up enough Kentucky recruits, mostly from the Paducah area, to make up a company. Cheatham assigned the company to Col. Charles M. Carroll's 15th Tennessee.

Carroll, a onetime militia officer and assistant Memphis postmaster, son of one of Tennessee's most powerful and popular governors, great nephew of Richard Montgomery of Quebec fame, had failed in command. Three weeks earlier, he had been court-martialed for "conduct prejudicial to good order and discipline," found guilty, and reprimanded.[5]

The men of the 15th turned to Polk and asked for Maj. Robert C. Tyler, an assistant quartermaster on Cheatham's staff, to lead them. They got him, and Tyler in return got a second star on his collar. Polk was curious, even concerned, about the choice. Rumors surrounded Lieutenant Colonel Tyler. He was "of San Juan fame," some said. Most thought he was certainly William Walker's filibustering associate. No one seemed to know much about him, however, and Tyler revealed little himself. For all Polk knew, his real name might not have been Tyler at all.[6]

Tyler loaded his men on the *Hill* in good order. At the last second three strangers climbed aboard—three privates from the 5th Tennessee hoping to get into the battle. The men of the 15th welcomed them and took it as a good omen when they discovered one's name was also Robert Tyler! The *Hill*, crammed with Tyler's 15th, cast off. Capt. Tom H. Newell steered for Belmont. To the men aboard it appeared he "wanted to land at the burning camp, in front of the enemy."[7] As they neared shore, the men of the 15th could see soldiers in blue among the scraggly trees on the willow bar. Without hesitating, Tyler's Tennesseans opened fire with muskets from the three decks. Then they saw more Yankees rolling forward a field piece from Camp Johnston, positioning it at the top of the riverbank. The gun crew shifted the cannon till it aimed at the *Hill* and rammed home a charge. The "federal gunners directed shots at the hull to sink her."[8] Close in to the bank Newell gave his boat "a broad sheer to starboard," and using the bank itself as partial cover, raced upriver.[9] "The steamer, as soon as the cannon opened upon her, steamed rapidly up the river to a point where all but her Texas and chimneys were protected by the bluff banks from the balls which were sent as thick as hail after her tearing away a chimney & a portion of her wheel house."[10]

Tyler's men realized what they had done. Those desperate fellows out on the willow bar they had fired upon had been comrades in arms, Confederates wearing dark, almost blue, blouses, seeking shelter from the Yankees.[11] The *Hill* proceeded upriver about 400 yards to the "upper landing," a spot directly opposite the Iron Banks. There the men disembarked, and Tyler had company commanders take them into the shelter of the woods and deploy into a defensive alignment. The 15th would wait there until their brigade commander, Colonel Marks, arrived.[12]

By 11:30 the *Charm* had taken aboard all of the 11th Louisiana. More ammunition was carried on as well, and for good measure Polk added a company of cavalry, Capt. William F. Taylor's Memphis Light Dragoons of Logwood's Tennessee Cavalry Battalion. Loading Taylor's horses unfortunately went slowly, "causing some delay."[13] Captain Trask released the *Charm*'s lines and proceeded across the Mississippi. He watched the Missouri shore closely, but he and his chief mate kept jerking their heads, glancing upstream at Belmont Point. Who knew when the gunboats might reappear? If they came, "nothing in the world could have saved us."[14] Before the *Charm* reached midstream, enemy field pieces opened fire from the parade field of Camp Johnston. From the upper deck the Dillon Guards were appalled at the chaos on shore. They saw Beltzhoover's New Orleans guns in Yankee hands, saw them reversed and "turned on the Tennesseans" and now on the *Charm* itself.[15] Captain Trask changed the *Charm*'s course and "under a heavy fire" made for shore about 400 yards upriver from the battery. He, too, kept "as close in shore as possible" to interpose the riverbank between the *Charm* and the enemy cannon to increase drastically the gunners' angle of fire.

The upper landing should have been a good site, protected by woods.[16] Rather than a happy welcome, however, "we found the landing obstructed by our disorganized forces, who endeavored to board and take possession of our boat, and at the same time crying: 'Don't land!' 'Don't land!' 'We are whipped!' 'Go back!' &c."[17]

"The moment looked dark," but Colonel Marks would have none of it. He ordered the 11th to fix bayonets. Then six of his companies, each like a Greek phalanx, came down the stage planks forcing the rabble aside. The mob on the bank grew, however, almost geometrically it seemed. Major Winslow of Polk's staff tried to help. Commands, even pleas, failed, so Winslow pushed his horse to the front of the mass, drew his saber, and "applied it." Nevertheless, neither Winslow's saber nor Marks's bayonets could stem the panic. The mob "made a rush on our boat," said Captain Trask, "and forced me to give the order to back the boat from the landing, leaving my stage planks on the river bank." Marks yelled out to Capt. John Austin of the Cannon Guards to take charge of the four companies remaining on board and land them higher up the bank. Trask cast off, and the *Charm* steamed 200 yards still further upriver. Trask found a spot that suited him and told Austin to have the men "jump from the guards of the boat when she touched the bank," which they did. At last, at just after 11:30 A.M., the 11th Louisiana was ashore.[18]

Without stage planks and with a mob still trying to board the *Charm* like a swarm of pirates, Trask backed off again.[19] What should he do? On board he still had the Memphis Light Dragoons and their horses. Back out into the Mississippi went the *Charm*, but luckily Trask met the *Kentucky* whose captain allowed him to borrow stage planks. Trask then returned to the Missouri shore and managed finally to land Taylor's cavalry company.[20]

The 11th meanwhile regrouped in the woods amid cries from Pillow's staff (one recent Louisiana civilian called them "Pillow's order-lies") who "begged us for 'God's sake' to hurry up." Lt. Col. Dan Beltzhoover cheered when he saw Marks's companies coming ashore. He had been badgering, begging, Gideon Pillow to attack to retrieve his lost battery. Now Beltzhoover's hopes revived. "Hurrah! I see the Louisianans, my battery is safe." Beltzhoover turned to what remained of his cannoneers and had them form as a company in rear of the 11th.

When all his men had landed, Marks moved the 11th forward and joined Tyler's Tennesseans. Pillow rode up and told Marks to take command of both regiments, thus giving Lt. Col. Robert H. Barrow immediate command of the 11th Louisiana. Pillow gave Marks the same order as Polk had: "to lead the advance in double-quick time through the woods and to the enemy's rear, and to attack him with vigor." He would support this attack on Grant's rear, Pillow assured him, with another attack made by the regiments now rallying on the riverbank under Col. Robert Russell. To guide Marks would be Capt. "Red" Jackson, another battery commander without a battery. Jackson's battery had not been able to cross over from Columbus, but he had nevertheless made it across earlier in the day and gone to Gideon Pillow volunteering to help.[21]

The 11th moved deeper into the woods. Capt. John J. Barrow of the Rosale Guards doubtless liked the idea of his cousin Bob commanding the regiment. He and the rest of the regiment must have been curious about the men who had joined the 11th for the day: two Tennessee cavalrymen, one with his arm in a sling and a knife in his free hand. Every step must have hurt Pvt. Albert K. Graham who only the night before had been injured in a train derailment outside Columbus. The crash had dislocated his shoulder and friends took him to Dr. John Forbes, surgeon of the 13th Tennessee, who snapped it back into place. The other man, Pvt. William H. Gailor, had disobeyed his company commander and slipped away from the Shelby Light Dragoons.[22]

For about fifteen minutes Red Jackson led the 11th and 15th west into the forest. They traveled almost a mile, far enough to avoid those cannon blasting away on the river and to be behind Camp Johnston and to Grant's rear. Then they flanked south toward the open ground of Belmont. Ironically the 11th and 15th had assumed almost the identical position and angle of attack used by the 31st Illinois four hours earlier.

Red Jackson called Barrow and Marks to the head of the column. He showed them, out to the left, a group of soldiers in formation. They were in the open, in a cornfield, but "partially hid from our view by an intervening rise of ground. They displayed or had amongst them a Confederate flag."[23] To the right Jackson pointed to another indistinct body of troops. Colonel Marks took precautions. He told Barrow and Tyler to have their regiments change formation from column into line of battle and prepare to fire. Suddenly, the soldiers seen to their right shouted, "For God's sake, don't fire on us; we are friends." Marks was cautious, skeptical, but passed the order to stand fast and wait. He felt he must be certain before he acted, so he sent down the line for Maj. "Eddy" Butler. Go to the edge of the woods, Marks told Butler, and find out which regiment was on the right.[24]

Butler reached the wood line and saw the regiment in the field. They seemed to be dressed in blue, but he could not be sure so he stepped into the field, bent low, and ran a few yards forward to a rail fence. The enemy! He turned and raced back to the forest, but they had spotted him. A dozen or more rifles fired at once. Butler stopped, stiffened, and fell into the shade of the trees.[25]

Back on the Kentucky side, Frank Cheatham rode down the steep road from the top of the bluff to the steamboat landing and reported to Polk. Strung out behind him in a long column came the First Brigade under Col. Preston Smith: the 154th Senior Tennessee Regiment under Lt. Col. Marcus J. Wright, Lt. Col. Andrew K. Blythe's 1st Mississippi Battalion, and a field battery from the Second Brigade under Capt. Melancthon Smith.[26]

Across the river the situation had worsened. Camp Johnston was burning. Beaten Confederates packed the Missouri shore. Federal batteries had been brought "close up to the river bank, and opened a brisk cannonade upon [the] troops and the steamers detailed to transport the command across the river."[27] The steamers at the Columbus landing made splendid targets at a range of 800 yards. The *Charm* took hit after hit, "one ball, in passing through the boiler deck, tore off several splinters, one of which prostrated one of the pilots, Mr. Clayton, stunning him severely." Captain Trask[28] backed the *Charm* away from the landing to a safer mooring upriver. Polk, however, had seen enough and suspended embarking his infantry. It would be slaughter to pack them aboard the steamers and send them over now, like ordering them to march at slow-time across a rifle range.[29]

Perhaps Frank Cheatham could do something about that milling mass of humanity across the river, rally them, organize them so they could hit back, or at least move them out of reach of the Yankees. So Polk ordered him across with instructions to try "to rally and take command of the portions of regiments within sight on the shore, and to support the flank movement ordered through Colonel Marks."[30] Cheatham and his staff rushed to board Captain Butler's small steamer *Prince*, which had been busy ferrying ammunition and wounded. Cheatham stopped. He remembered Melancthon Smith's field battery and sent a staff officer back to suggest to Polk that he bring up the battery to the riverbank. From there Smith could try to knock out the enemy battery on the opposite shore, suppress its fire, or at least divert the attention of its gunners.[31]

Polk, it appears, immediately followed Cheatham's suggestion and sent for the field guns. Melancthon Smith rushed forward, went into battery, and opened fire with his twelve-pounders. "A very spirited cannon duel forthwith commenced." From atop the Iron Banks, Maj. Alexander P. Stewart's heavy guns joined in, but Stewart elevated his guns, targeting the burning camp and the Federals beginning to form on the parade ground "in plain view." The Lady Polk sent a huge shell crashing into the drill field. The "cross-fire of the fixed and field batteries" quickly had its effect: the Yankee battery on the Missouri bank limbered up and sought cover, the blue infantry column faced left and moved off to the west into the woods at the double-quick, and "the enemies shouts of triumph from Tappan's camp ceased." Once "the field of battle was in full view," Polk's guns dominated the action and made Belmont untenable. Ironically, "they . . . aided Grant in a way, driving his disorganized men from the camp and thus making it possible to bring them under some semblance of control."[32]

Cheatham and his staff set across the Mississippi on the *Prince*. The packet seemed to recoil and rock from explosions as the opposing field batteries discovered each other. The men on board flinched and ducked inadvertently, but the enemy cannon had no interest in them. The voyage seemed interminable to Frank Cheatham, as if some great unseen clock suspended in the clouds governed affairs. He could not

Col. Benjamin F. Cheatham (Tennessee State Library and Archives)

wait for the *Prince* to touch shore. "He stuck spurs in his horse and jumped him out of the boat before it had landed. . . . The fore feet of his horse struck the bank, but his hind feet went into the water." A shout was raised when the Tennesseans caught sight of him. As he rode up the bank they gathered to him in hundreds. Cheatham told them "to follow him, and he would lead them to h–ll or to victory."[33]

This quick-tempered horseman and farmer from Nashville stood five feet, eleven inches, tall, with dark brown hair, a moustache, blue eyes, and an expressive face. Most considered him an attractive man, but Cheatham had guarded his bachelorhood for forty-one years. His emblem was his pipe. He owned many, and one was constantly in his mouth, even in combat. He was "known to be addicted to strong drink," and he had a fighter's reputation, won through fistfights with toughs in his command.

He and his family were strong, influential Democrats. As a result Cheatham, like Pillow, had the opportunity to become an officer in the Tennessee Militia at an early age. As a junior officer he fought with distinction in the Mexican War under the popular Whig, William B. Campbell, colonel of the 1st Tennessee Volunteers. Then in 1847, at the age of twenty-seven, Cheatham returned home and raised a regiment, becoming their colonel. Back to Mexico he hurried, arriving in time to help with Scott's attack on Mexico City. For a while in Mexico Cheatham commanded not only his regiment but also another from Tennessee and one from Indiana as well. "I have had command of a Brigade so long, that I believe I could stand the elevation [to Brigadier General] without any great shock to my delicate nerves."

Following the Mexican War Cheatham headed off to the California goldfields with some of the men of his regiment. He did not find gold himself but ran a hotel and became a conspicuous leader in the Democratic party of California. He returned to Tennessee in the 1850s and resumed farming. He was an outstanding, innovative farmer, winning awards and recognition for his willingness to experiment. He joined the Provisional Tennessee Army in May 1861, and many regarded him as its most capable general officer. In September Jefferson Davis wrote Polk, "You have in Genl Cheatham a brave and zealous officer who will lead a column and fully cooperate with other commanders with whom he may happen to do duty."[34]

Once ashore Frank Cheatham set to work. He found that Pillow had already formed a mixed group of men, about a regiment in size. Most were troops of the 13th Arkansas, 13th Tennessee, and 2d Tennessee. With the exception of a couple of companies under Maj. Francis M. Stewart, the 21st and 22d Tennessee seemed leaderless and wrecked. What was left of Tyree Bell's 12th offered little encouragement. Cheatham and his staff, greatly aided by Col. James Tappan, "with the assistance of others of less note went to work & in a short time . . . had formed a considerable army of the disorganized fragments."[35] They seemed "anxious to again confront the enemy." Capt. Robert Wood and some men of Company B, 22d Tennessee, who he had managed to hold together joined Cheatham's formation. Wood and other officers busied themselves "distributing cartridges—getting our men & everybody else's in a line." Cheatham had plenty of fresh ammunition passed out along the line, and then, just off the riverbank, he formed the Confederates in a double line of battle, the 13th Arkansas in front, the 2d and 13th Tennessee behind. Companies from the other regiments filled in, with Tyree Bell and a piece of his 12th on the right. Pillow, Tappan, and Knox Walker played conspicuous leadership roles in the reorganization.[36]

This reconditioned force of Confederates, probably 1,000–1,500 in strength, re-formed in a large column and followed Cheatham directly inland through the woods, southwest from the Mississippi. After advancing about 500 yards the head of the column came upon fifty mounted men. Cheatham himself rode forward with an orderly to investigate.

"What cavalry is that?" Cheatham asked.

"Illinois cavalry, sir," responded an officer in blue.

"Oh, Illinois cavalry! All right; just stand where you are."

Cheatham turned and rode away, noticing beyond the cavalry a large line of battle consisting of two infantry regiments. The enemy infantry saw him too but thought little of it since he seemed "one of them."[37] Cheatham returned to his flanking column and quickly, using the cover of a dry slough, deployed them into the line of battle rehearsed on the riverbank. Tappan's 13th Arkansas would be his base regiment, the others forming either on Tappan's flanks or to the rear.

The Confederates moved forward to the attack and, when within range, exchanged volleys with the enemy for about fifteen minutes. Pvt. David Vollmer of Company K, 2d Tennessee, shouted along the line that he personally was going to capture the colors waving to their front or he would die in the attempt. The colors he saw were those of the 7th Iowa.[38]

Then Cheatham ordered, "Charge Bayonets!" Cheatham led the charge himself. He eyes lit up with the excitement of a fight. One Confederate wrote, "We charged the enemy under his and Col. Tappan's lead in a glorious style. They stood our fire well for 15 to 20 minutes (our men frequently lying upon the ground and firing). They were finely dressed and well armed and fought with coolness and desperation."[39]

The Yankees fought with the support of a section of the Watson Battery posted in the open on high ground. When Cheatham's men broke out of the trees these cannons opened on them. A portion of Knox Walker's 2d was blown apart. Capt. J. Welby Armstrong, "a large fine-looking Englishman," leading the Sons of Erin (Company G) with his cap atop his sword, was hit and seemed to explode before his men's eyes.[40] The chunk of the 12th that Bell still commanded had had enough and sought shelter in the fallen timber.[41]

But most charged on. Vollmer and his friend Sgt. Dennis Lynch got ahead of the rest of Company K in their dash for the Iowa stars and stripes. Vollmer jammed his bayonet into the Yankee color-bearer, grabbed the flag, and waved it over his head for the rest of the bloodied 2d to see. Suddenly a shower of musketry struck both Vollmer and Lynch, and they were killed.[42]

The Federals standing in the cornfield where many of the Confederates had stood that morning made fine targets themselves, however. They began to crumple and fall at an alarming rate. Bodies clad in blue lay "as thick as stumps in a new field." The Confederate line of battle soon overlapped the enemy's, and volleys of musket fire inflicted heavy loss. After Cheatham ordered the bayonet charge, it was carried out with a great shout and with determination.[43] Albert Fielder of the 12th Tennessee remembered that when they were "ordered to charge, a yell was raised and we charged to within full range of our guns and down we fell and at it we were shooting as fast as we could load and fire[,] one not waiting for another and the Louisiana Reg having flanked them still further down the River[.] [T]he enemy were exposed to a cross fire which soon caused them to retreat."[44]

The Federal line began to break. Two men named Hunt, one from the 13th Arkansas and the other from the 2d Tennessee, rushed forward and recaptured one of the Watson guns. The Yankees had tried at first to pull away their prize, but seeing the Confederates closing in, they cut the horses loose so they might escape themselves. The Hunts hardly had time to celebrate before Dan Beltzhoover and the Watsons came up to reclaim their piece. To Beltzhoover's dismay, the Yankees had spiked it.[45]

Colonel Marks's column meanwhile, having deployed in line of battle, tried to mount its attack. But both the 11th Louisiana and the 15th Tennessee maneuvered clumsily. Companies became entangled, their sense of direction destroyed by the forest. Marks, convinced that the enemy was trying to flank him both on the left and the right, divided his brigade, trying to get it "in a position to front the enemy each way." Colonel Tyler's right companies popped up on the left of his regiment; Colonel Barrow's horse went down, killed by confused Louisiana troops.[46] About this time a Yankee counterattack, compact and aggressive, struck them. Massed musketry and cannon fire roared into their ranks. "Everybody waded in on his own account and acted the general for himself."[47] Capt. Red Jackson went down, painfully wounded, as did Pvt. Bill Gailor, the adventurous Tennessee cavalryman who had joined up with the Dillons. Lt. Robert J. Alexander of the Cannon Guards, after coming all the way back from Virginia so that he might serve as an officer in the 11th, fell dead.[48]

Pvt. Phil Stephenson of the 13th Arkansas, who had joined up with Marks's column, reported,

> We had scarcely taken position, when looking diagonally across the clearing, backward toward the river, I saw the blue line of the enemy, not a hundred yards off. Nay the nearest end of their line much closer! We had got almost in their rear and they had to run the gauntlet of our fire in order to retreat! Simultaneously with that look of mine, there came a blast of fire . . . full in our faces, a horizontal sheet of flame and bullets that took my breath away! They had seen us first and had got the drop on us! Never shall I forget the sensation of that moment! . . . Something hit me in the side and I fell on my face, stunned and breathless. The din was so

deafening around me and I myself so dazed I know not how long
I lay there. I was certain I was shot. But after a while, reaching my
hand around and feeling carefully, I could discover no blood. . . .
I never knew what struck me, whether a splinter or limb from a
tree, a spent ball or what, but it disabled me for the day.

Both of Marks's regiments had been badly shaken by this musket
fire and by cannister from Taylor's guns. They tried to return the Yankee volleys, and the 11th Louisiana attempted a bayonet charge, but
the 15th had had enough. Tyler's troops began to fall back toward the
river.[49]

The two regiments of Marks's command swung apart, like a double-
sided gate. Through this gate came the enemy at the double-quick,
four abreast.[50] They seemed intent, however, to return to their boats
and to escape the musket fire on their right flank and rear from Cheatham's troops. "They could not take the time to attend to us," said one
of Marks's men.[51] One Yankee regiment went by in good order, then
another. They were ignoring the 11th Louisiana! Positioned there on
the enemy flank, Marks and his troops finally came to their senses and
realized their good fortune. Instead of being cut off and virtually surrounded as they had thought, they had a position on the retreating
enemy's flank. They started firing at will. It had turned into an ambush, a turkey shoot.[52]

13

Surrounded! Surrounded!

Propped up against a tree and pale from a wound in his chest sat Pvt. Henry I. Smith, Company B, 7th Iowa. Beside him sat a bleeding rebel. Without a word the two men watched soldiers race up and down the streets of Camp Johnston, torches in their hands, touching sides of tents. The canvas would smolder, darken, and then burst into flame. Out toward the parade field, away from the heat of destruction, they saw McClernand's and Dougherty's men gather, almost reluctantly it seemed, and begin processing themselves once again into company and regimental entities. The Federals still wished to savor their victory and to rest, but officers prodded them into line. The march back to the boats was beginning.[1]

The battle of Belmont was over. Grant's men had smashed the rebels in the defensive position of their choice. They had driven them into and out of their fortified camp. The Stars and Stripes flew over Camp Johnston while the rebel banner, a rank curiosity, drooped across a captured caisson.

And then, as though the burning camp itself had been a graphic command, came a blast from atop the Columbus bluffs. A large projectile, like a "lamp post," hurdled the Mississippi and crashed into the parade field. Dirt flew. The round ricocheted over the massed troops and broke into the forest, thrashing about like some crazed beast. Grant's horse panicked and pawed the air with its hooves.

The Lady Polk had said hello. Gun after gun joined in. "The shells fell among us thick and fast," said one Federal soldier. Another reported "hearing the castings which held the shot together passing over." Grant's captured New Orleans battery on the riverbank withdrew and made off into the woods. Quickly, without elaborate instruction, the infantry now fell into formation. "I caused my colors (then riddled with balls) to be planted," Phil Fouke said, "my drums to beat, and rallied my regiment."[2] Grant's men quickly marched by the flank, at the double-quick, off Camp Johnston's parade field, past the abatis, into the trees. Once safe in the forest, enduring the furious but futile enemy barrage became fun. The soldiers laughed at the "deluge of shots," which, for the most part, "passed high above the heads of the national troops, doing little or no damage." John Brinton remembered that "a great shell struck the top of the tree under which we were standing, and cut all of the upper part of it squarely off, and down it fell, point foremost; I remember it all most distinctly how that stem of the tree looked as it struck the ground perpendicularly."[3]

Up to Grant rode Lieutenant Pittman of Company F, 30th Illinois. He reported heavy Confederate reinforcements crossing the river.[4] Simultaneously Brinton "saw the pipes of two steamers going up the river. I thought to myself, 'These cannot be our gunboats,' and so rode up to General Grant and pointed them out to him. He could not at first credit these as the enemy's transports until I drew his attention to their course, as shown by the direction of the motion of their pipes."[5]

Grant saw them—two transports "black—or gray—with soldiers from boiler-deck to roof."[6] He gave the order to form the regiments in a column and move out toward Hunter's Farm.[7]

Adolphus Schwartz and Ezra Taylor were determined the six New Orleans guns would be taken back to Cairo. Using enemy horses, even unhitching their own from the caissons, they got four of the captured pieces under way. Schwartz wanted the others, however, and "begged every Company of Infantry passing me, to drag them along." Some of the infantry tried to pull the heavy pieces, but only for a while. The men tired easily and were far more worried about getting themselves back to the boats. Rebel prisoners seem to have been handled casually, remaining in the custody of the regiment that captured them and moved along under guard with the main body.[8]

Grant's column began their march toward the steamboat landing about 2 P.M. McClernand's Brigade led: Logan, then Fouke, then Buford. Dougherty's Brigade followed: Hart, then Lauman. It was a broken, irregular, clumsy formation. Lt. Pat White put it plainly: "We were demoralized. Officers would call to their men to fall in but the men would pay no attention. Every man was trying to save himself, some would throw down their arms and part of a regiment would take one rout and the other part start another way."[9]

Then the rebels appeared, "on our right, in the direction of the river." Despite having seen the steamers crossing with reinforcements, the presence of Confederates in organized force seems to have astonished the Federals. Only an hour before, Pillow's regiments had been driven from the field, routed, broken beyond repair. Their reorganization and rejuvenation had taken place quietly, quickly, while concealed in the heavy woods of Belmont Point. Apparently Grant's strike force, beginning with Grant himself, had utterly discounted the ability of the Confederates to resume the fight. They had taught the rebels a sharp lesson, and all that remained, they believed, was to gather up trophies and march back to the boats.[10]

The rebels attacked with a shout. Surprised first by the rebels' appearance and then by their sudden, aggressive counterattack, the part of Grant's column closest to the river, the 7th Iowa and 22d Illinois with a fraction of the 27th, scrambled to confront the enemy with a line of battle. These regiments formed "in considerable confusion; some were tired out, and some did not care much about further fighting. Here the volunteer spirit showed itself; they had done their day's work, and wanted to go home."[11]

The Union troops exchanged volleys with the enemy, but the rebels pressed their attack with the advantages of number and position. Dougherty's men began to fall at an alarming rate. He could use help. Where was Buford and the main body of the 27th?

The right of Dougherty's line of battle, the 7th Iowa, found itself a beleaguered rear guard. "We are flanked," rang out along the line. "They're surrounding us," others began to cry. Lt. Col. Augustus Wentz steadied his men. With a heavy German accent he shouted, "Remember how the 1st Iowa held at Springfield—equal them!" A musket ball, however, knocked Wentz from his horse. His men tried to carry him off, but he pushed them away. "Let me alone, boys. I want to die on the battlefield."[12]

Dougherty's line gave ground and began to crumble. The Confederates broke through and encircled the right half of the line, the 7th Iowa. A member of the 7th Iowa reported, "All the Illinois troops had

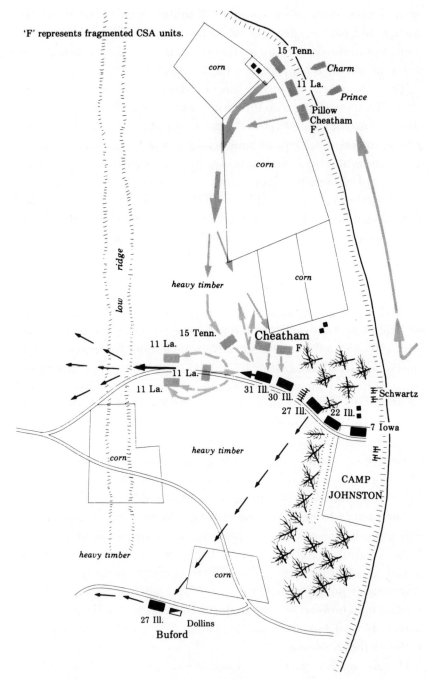

'F' represents fragmented CSA units.

corn

15 Tenn.

Charm

11 La.

Prince

Pillow
Cheatham
F

corn

corn

low ridge

heavy timber

corn

15 Tenn.

Cheatham
F

11 La.

11 La.

11 La.

31 Ill.

30 Ill.

Schwartz

27 Ill.

22 Ill.

7 Iowa

heavy timber

corn

CAMP
JOHNSTON

heavy timber

corn

27 Ill.

Dollins

Buford

MAP 8. *Confederate Counterattack*

Lt. Col. Augustus Wentz
(Illinois State Historical Library)

left us or were leaving, except the Twenty-second Illinois." With Lauman gone and Wentz down, Maj. Elliott W. Rice, already wounded himself, took command of the 7th. He rallied a large portion and, placing himself at their head, attempted to break out. Somehow Rice, with a grand display of personal leadership, disengaged most of the 7th Iowa and saved them from capture. Under constant fire, they raced through the woods, trying to reconnect themselves to Grant's retreating column. Rice's mount was "pierced with 20 bullets, his sword scabbard shot in two and his sword belt shot away." He tried to keep his men together in units large enough to defend themselves and ignored rebel shouts of "surrender!" that rang out all around.[13]

At the same time that Dougherty's Brigade began to engage the lines of rebels attacking Grant's right flank, more Confederates turned up. Facing the head of Grant's column, indeed astride the road to the steamers and safety, was "a considerable body, in regular order." A Federal soldier reported that they "advanced from the woods, into the opening on our left" and "in front of us as we were then marching, facing toward our boats." "In fact we had changed fronts, they had the ground we occupied in the morning." This new Confederate line of battle attacked "and poured a galding fire into our ranks." With this attack from the rear, and hearing the heavy firing from Dougherty's fight on the right, cries rang out among the Illinois soldiers, "Surrounded! Surrounded!" Men reported seeing rebel cavalry behind them along the edge of the river.[14] Eyes turned to Grant. "I announced that we had cut our way in and could cut our way out just as well, it seemed a new revelation to officers and soldiers."[15]

McClernand also seems to have responded well. He saw some slightly elevated ground and directed Logan to place a battery there and open fire on the enemy line of battle. Logan had Captain Taylor go into "battery upon a commanding plateau without any natural protection and we opened a heavy fire upon them, thus cutting our way through the ranks of the astonished enemy." Firing "with great spirit and effect" Taylor's Chicago Battery "opened on them with double shot on top of conster. They could not stand that, so their lines broke; then we limbered up and pushed on and I remember unlimbering again to give them another discharge when a staff officer called on me to hasten and get out."[16]

✳

Once the artillery had blown an opening in the enemy line Mc-Clernand told Logan and the 31st to "cut their way through them." Black Jack Logan did just that. "I took my flag, and told Capt. McCook to carry it at the head of the column, and die with it in his hands." With a flourish of his hat, Logan waved his men forward, shouting to the 31st to close ranks and "follow the flag and myself."[17]

Logan spearheaded the breakout. He "ordered his flag in front of his regiment, prepared to force his way in the same direction, if necessary. Moving on, he was followed by the whole force except the . . . 27th and Dollins and Delano."[18] "Logan's personal presence cheered us on there, and with double shotted canister I think we cut a row through them, and we went through them pretty quick."[19] After one good volley by Logan's men, perhaps two, the hole Taylor's guns had made in the Confederate line of battle split wide open, much in the manner in which the 7th Iowa parted earlier in the day at the cornfield. Rebels melted into the forest on the left and right of the Federal column. The enemy thrown back to the right, toward the river, appeared to be broken and in confusion. Logan's 31st with the help of Taylor's guns had cleared the passage.[20]

A wounded Iowa soldier, captured by the Confederates, watched Logan's breakthrough. It came as rebel officers were "parlaying as to what to do with us who were wounded. Col. Logan's regiment, with himself in command, came charging through and drove them back." They "came along in double quick time, four abreast and in good order." An Arkansas soldier would remark later that the Union column attacked "in good order, which was done, well done. There bravery alone accomplished the feat."[21]

Logan recaptured some Union wounded. He had them picked up and placed in a wagon drawn by four mules. The wagon with its cargo of pain began "a run through cornfields and woods to the boat, avoiding the roads." The 31st continued on through the woods, virtually unmolested. Most of them drifted to the west toward the Hunter's Farm Road.[22]

"Driving the enemy back on either side, we moved on, occasionally exchanging shots with straggling parties." Although enemy fire from the flanks was comparatively light immediately following the breakout, it was dangerous. Logan had his pistol shattered at his side and a horse shot under him. A rebel musket ball "took out a dot of flesh" from his hand. John McClernand's horse received three wounds and

McClernand himself had two shots hit his holster. Another struck the cylinder of his pistol and broke it. A company grade officer beside McClernand went down, and William Stains, McClernand's body servant, dismounted and offered the wounded man his horse. He eased the man up into the saddle, but then, out of the woods, a Confederate rode up to take the captain prisoner. Stains "drew his revolver and put a ball through the rebel's head, scattering his brains over the horse's neck." [23]

Phil Fouke struggled to keep the column closed up, but Taylor's guns traveled with his regiment, which slowed him considerably. Fouke had taken great care to safeguard these guns, dividing his companies with some before, some behind. [24]

Fouke could hear to his rear the firefight between Dougherty and the rebels attacking from the river, but he knew he had all he could handle, just getting through the woods. His men could see enemy to the left and right in the woods. These rebels fired at the passing column sporadically, and for the most part, ineffectively, but the volume of their fire was increasing.

Moving cannon through the woods proved extremely difficult. The pieces got caught in the trunks of the trees or in the undergrowth or would get stuck in low places, and the gunners, drivers, and Fouke's infantry would have "to push and pull." Eventually Ezra Taylor gave up trying to have soldiers drag the captured cannon. Then the captured horses pulling one New Orleans piece "gave out," and Taylor had to leave the gun behind. One by one he was losing his brass prizes. [25]

Suddenly, the 30th received "a galling fire" from the left. Three balls struck Fouke's saddle, one slashing the crupper in two. One of his mounts went down, then the next. The 30th returned three volleys and rushed on deeper into the forest, abandoning one New Orleans gun. Fouke wanted to maintain contact with Logan's regiment at all costs. [26]

Grant's loosely connected column fragmented. Although Logan and Fouke remained in visual contact, the two regiments broke through the woods toward the Hunter's Farm Road not in tandem but on a two-regiment front. The gap had widened between Fouke and Dougherty's Brigade so that contact was lost, and Fouke's men felt they "covered the rear in the retreat." [27] It should be noted, however, that these disjointed movements of the Federals confused the enemy as well, especially Marks's 11th Louisiana blocking force, and in effect, may have protected the column from greater loss.[28]

Once Grant reached the road to Hunter's Farm, he rode ahead to find his reserve. The five companies could screen the retiring infantry and give them time to regroup at the landing. To his disgust, his reserve had vanished. Their commander, Captain Detrich, had heard the battlefield bedlam, shouts of victory, and music from the direction of the camp and guessed what had happened. Then he heard the Confederate steamers crossing. The pickets he sent out reported rebels in force in the woods between him and Belmont Point. Detrich, a company grade officer on his own, believed the enemy intended a sweeping movement south toward the field hospital and then west toward Hunter's Farm, bypassing his force altogether. To defend the steamers and the landing, his primary responsibility, he therefore ordered his five companies to retire to the landing itself. There he deployed them. By the time Grant arrived at the landing, however, Detrich had taken his men aboard the *Belle Memphis* where they were useless to Grant.[29]

The reserve was snug and safe. Logan's men were coming raggedly down the road to the landing. The 30th was also approaching. Taylor's artillerymen, at last, reached the Hunter's Farm Road. To their dismay, however, they found the way so clogged with infantry that they had to force their passage.[30] But what about Dougherty's Brigade and Buford?

Disaster had befallen Dougherty. Overrun by Cheatham's attack, his brigade now retreated in disorder past rebel units and individuals, hidden among the trees waiting in ambush. "The enemy flanked both sides and poured upon us a raking, galling fire for half a mile." "Men fell in every direction like leaves in autumn." Confederates reported: "As they were passing our forces we riddled them badly." At places in the woods fifteen to twenty bodies could be found, "all in a heap." The 22d Illinois suffered many casualties, but the 7th Iowa, continuously "subjected to enfilading fire," was shot to pieces—all their field officers dead or wounded. Their loss was extraordinarily high, with an unusually large killed-to-wounded ratio (1.25 killed to 2 wounded).[31]

Surgeon Brinton's expedient of using ammunition wagons for the wounded failed during the breakout phase of Belmont. The number of wounded was overwhelming, and the pressure of the enemy too great. Bandmaster Thayer tried to save one man from the enemy "by holding on to the end board of the wagon and letting him lay across my arms, carrying him in that way about two miles to the boats. It was a four mule team and was hurriedly driven through the woods, over stumps and sticks, without roads." Stumbling along, a wounded Capt. James C. Parrott, who would later command the 7th Iowa, "had to hang on to my [Thayer's] coat tail to keep up."[52]

Fortunately Colonel Lauman had been sent on ahead atop one of Taylor's cannon. The wounded Lauman heard the noise of fighting behind him and quickly realized the seriousness of the situation. He ordered the cannoneers to halt and had a mount brought to him. Then with the aid of brigade commander Dougherty he remounted.

Dougherty had helped extricate most of the 22d. Once the advance elements of the regiment neared the landing, Dougherty told Lt. Col. Harrison Hart to take them directly aboard the *Belle Memphis*. Meanwhile Dougherty himself, accompanied by his secretary Bill Travis, would ride back into the woods "to fetch up the rear of the brigade." Thus they came upon Colonel Lauman.

As Lauman righted himself in the saddle with Dougherty and Travis by his side, a volley of musket shots rang out. Dougherty was hit. One bullet struck his shoulder, another his elbow, then still another shattered his ankle. In the melee and confusion that followed, Lauman got away, but Dougherty was left behind, with Bill Travis kneeling beside him.[33]

Despite the assertion of Grant and others that "there was no hasty retreat or running away,"[34] the retreat from Camp Johnston had degenerated into a rout.[35] "To say the least, there was much confusion"; "Something approaching panic struck the Union army."[36] Even the march of Logan's "Dirty-first," the lead regiment, "at first was slow in order, but became more and more uncontrollable, until, all was in a mass of confusion, Artillery, Cavalry, Infantry—horsemen and all were in a state of confusion mixed and intermixed—dropping guns, coats, blankets . . . on their flight."[37]

The Chicago Battery tried to stop and "make a stand, but after we had halted the battery, could not stop the infantry, so away we went again."[38] "Many of the prisoners had escaped and our men were falling fast."[39]

Exhaustion took its toll in every regiment. One soldier reported, "I was so exhausted at the close of the battle that I could scarcely walk. . . . I passed many poor fellows on the way who I fear never reached the boats."[40] "Most of those who fell on the backward march were abandoned."[41]

"This retreat was the worst of all. It was there our noble fellows were killed. They were surrounded & each man had to fight his own way back."[42] It seemed no matter which way they turned in the forest they would encounter more Confederates.[43] They could not see the enemy until they fell upon them.[44]

Although they both were wounded themselves, Pvts. John Knight and Dave Wallace of Company E, 7th Iowa, struggled to carry back John's brother William who had been hit in the knee. They had gone almost half a mile when the rebels closed in. They placed William carefully under a big tree and went on. But Wallace soon grew too weak to continue, and he dropped. Only John reached the transports.[45]

William Austin of the 22d believed he survived only because he "ran rapidly in a zig zag manner to dodge balls."[46] A Confederate wrote, "It so happened that the *dogs* had to pass the whole length of this Regt. [11th Louisiana] and received their fire, and it was then that they were shot down like deer."[47] "We mowed them down like grass in the retreat."[48]

Now it was our turn. We outflanked them in the retreat—and the slaughter on their side was terrible. The noble Dyer Grays [13th Tennessee] did most admirably. The retreat was through the open woods. We stood behind the trees and shot them down. I saw them fall in my direction. I killed no one nor did I try but directed and encouraged my men. We took many prisoners. I took one with my own hand. I headed him off, ran upon him with my sword, seized him by the neck & ordered him to surrender, which he did without a struggle. The poor fellow was worried & frightened to death. Frank Sampson took twelve. He got in front of them with his gun . . . made them halt and lie down. I have a trophy in the shape of a nice comfortable militaire overcoat. In their retreat they threw away everything.[49]

Several Confederates mention, however, that Leonidas Polk himself intervened and halted the slaughter, saying it was "too cruel to shoot fellows who were running for their lives."[50]

The 700 men in Logan's regiment had all arrived on the Missouri shore with a coat and blanket. "Not more than about 50 brought any back."[51] "It was a second 'manassas' rout—the road was strewn with overcoats, blankets, haversacks, guns, cartridges, boxes, coats, caps, etc. . . . Every fence corner had a knapsack or a gun in it; the cornfields were covered with them."[52] Rebels looking to swap weapons found a "quantity of firearms of every description, from the flint-lock musket to the fine Colt's revolving rifle." "I have eaten from Grant's mess chest, which was one of the things he had to drop in his flight. It was plainly marked, 'U.S.G.' "[53]

Surgeon John Brinton watched with admiration as Logan's 31st led the breakout. He rode forward with the column toward the boats but heard a cry and turned in the saddle. There on the ground by a rail fence, lay a Confederate officer. The man called out to Brinton, asking him, "if you are a gentleman," to please stop and help him. "Urgent as the position of affairs was, I could not resist his appeal. I dismounted, knelt down by him, examined him, and found that he had been shot through the liver, and was rapidly sinking. He told me that his name was Butler, 'Major Butler of Louisiana.' "

As he examined Butler, John Brinton learned about Butler's diplomatic service in Berlin and about his mother's family in Clarke County, Virginia. He also learned of Butler's mother's friendship for Mrs. George McClellan, Brinton's aunt.

> He asked me how long he could live. I answered, "but a very short time." He then said to me: "Please send a message to my father,—by the first flag of truce,—tell him how you found me,—and tell him, too, that I died as behooved me, at the head of my men." I did all I could for him, stimulating him from my flask. He was very grateful and said, "Oh, Doctor, I wish I had met you before this." He begged me to remain with him, and when I told him that our troops were on their way to their boats, he offered to protect me while he lived, if I would only stay. I assured him that his own people would find him, and that I must go. So I mounted and reluctantly left him on the ground.[54]

Brinton rode into the woods. Almost immediately he encountered rebels, a large number of them, and they aimed their weapons at him.

Maj. Gen. Edward G. W. Butler
(Historic New Orleans Collection Museum/Research Center)

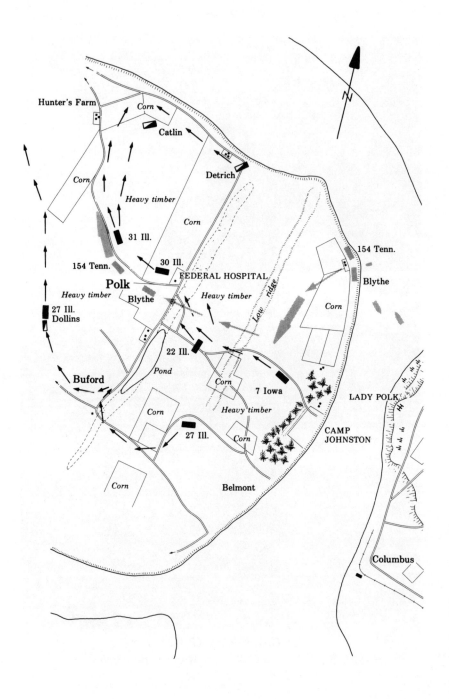

MAP 9. *Confederate Pursuit*

His civilian overcoat saved him as he waved at them "in a deprecatory, and at the same time authoritative sort of a way." When they hesitantly lowered their muskets, Brinton turned his horse, dug his spurs into its side, "and dashed through a dogwood thicket, and was out of their sight in half the time I have taken to write the last line."[55]

Brinton became disoriented in his flight. He crossed a portion of the morning's battlefield and found himself alone with "only the dead and wounded." He rode on and came out on the bank of the river. There he found two old black men who helped him because he was "one of Massa Linkum's sojers." They showed him that he was *below* Belmont and then drew him a map on the ground. Brinton went on his way west "trying to keep a general direction parallel to the Mississippi River."[56] Eventually, after he had crossed the bed of an unfinished railroad, he ran into Dollins's cavalry company, also lost. They journeyed on together blindly, along side an impassable slough between them and the river. They finally discovered a place to cross the swamp and soon came upon "a poor log house." There Brinton found "the mistress of the little cabin or farm house I had occupied as a hospital early in the morning." The woman had appreciated Brinton's efforts then to protect her property, and "bitter rebel as she was," she repaid him now, telling her young son to guide the lost Federals to safety, which he did.[57]

What had become of Napoleon Buford and the 27th? When Grant ordered a return to the boats, the 27th formed and began to march at the rear of McClernand's Brigade, the connecting regiment with Dougherty's command. Cheatham's attack closely followed by Marks's blocking action disrupted the column. Soon reports came to McClernand that the column had been broken and that Buford's regiment, or most of it, had disappeared. Perplexed and furious, McClernand sent staff officer Maj. Mason Brayman looking for Buford and Dollins. When Brayman reported back empty-handed, McClernand went out himself, twice. But Buford had marched off west toward the sinking sun.[58]

A small part of the 27th, about 20 percent, had gone into line of battle, joining Dougherty's Brigade in its fight against Cheatham. The remainder, however, under Buford himself, saw the enemy ahead and rather than follow the counterattack of Logan and Fouke "sought to find a new route to return." Without orders, indeed contrary to orders, and without notifying his superior, Buford struck out south through the woods away from the firing and then west "guided by the descending sun" toward Hunter's Farm. Presently the 27th struck the great slough. Buford, "recognizing the position," swung the regiment's line of march further to the south around the obstacle. He found the road that he and Bielaski had used that morning and continued on.[59]

Incredibly Confederates would contend they did not know of this road so close to Camp Johnston. A few days after the battle Capt. W. D. Pickett, an engineering officer, and Capt. Josiah S. White of the Tennessee Mounted Rifles returned to the battlefield and explored. To their astonishment they found "a new road which had been cut through to a point about midway of the lake, heretofore considered an impassable lagoon, we found to be fordable. The enemy crossed their artillery and infantry of the right wing here and thus securing to themselves an avenue of retreat of which our generals, and the troops who had occupied the ground for months, were profoundly ignorant."[60]

Pickett and White believed that this ford "must have been shown them by someone very familiar with the ground." Suspicion pointed toward a local farmer who was found dead on the battlefield.[61]

When the 27th crossed the great slough, Buford turned right or north and proceeded along the Bird's Point Road almost to the jump-off point for the attack that morning. He halted his column, however, when he heard heavy firing ahead, between them and the transports. Deeming it "prudent to keep back, and move parallel with the river," Buford decided to turn the column west again, "in rear of the farms on Lucas Bend."

Sometimes marching through the woods, sometimes using a railroad cut, sometimes using "wood roads," the 27th made its way west, parallel to the river. The trek was an ordeal, frightening and fatiguing for all but tortuous for the wounded. Those with more serious injuries and those too weak to continue were held up on horses by comrades marching along beside them. A few died as they were carried along, and their bodies were left in the woods miles from the landing and the battlefield.

To add to the misery Walke's gunboats opened fire from the river.

Many of the naval shells carried into the forest and fell among Buford's men "which happily did us no injury."[62] When he was above Hunter's Farm and believed the firing to the north to have subsided, Buford changed direction again, this time heading the column "blindly" for the river. When the 27th reached the water about three miles upstream from Hunter's Farm, the sun had set. It was growing dark. The transports and the gunboats had gone.[63]

Napoleon Buford told his men they must continue on up the banks of the Mississippi, perhaps march all night, possibly all the way to Bird's Point. Those mounted gave up their horses to the wounded who had marched along on foot, and the weary column set out once again.

Afterward Buford's men would feel proud of their long march, fortunate not to have been cut off. "First on the field, last to retire," they would say. "The way of retreat between him and the boats was closed, and he was obliged to find another route. . . . Our Sagacious Col. as he has proved himself to be in this day's fight, marched around the Bayou some three miles above where our boats lay. Thereby escaping the terrible fire to which the balance of our forces were exposed."[64]

Although McClernand and Grant had restrained criticism of Buford in their Belmont reports, John Rawlins bluntly denounced his action in a letter to congressman Elihu Washburne.

> His disobedience of positive orders given him on the field of the Battle of Belmont came near losing to the country his entire Regiment which was saved from such fate by the fire from our gun boats driving him off of the main road, and thereby avoiding meeting the enemy. Had he obeyed the orders given him by both Generals Grant and McClernand he would have helped defeat the enemy in the fight coming out of Belmont, saved the lives of many gallant men &.embarked his Regiment with the other troops, before reinforcements for the enemy could have crossed from Columbus. As it was, it was the merest accident he was saved.[65]

A sergeant in the 27th spoke for his regiment, McClernand's Brigade, and perhaps Grant's expeditionary force when he commented on their retreat from Belmont. "Our brigade is in a most scattered condition. We are not yet veterans only recruits after all."[66]

14

✳ ——————————————————————— ✳

A Perfect Storm of Death

Leonidas Polk must have felt the compelling impatience about him in the eyes of Blythe's Mississippians and Smith's Tennesseans. He had already committed half of his infantry to the fight; Frank Cheatham was gone, disappearing into the forest across the river. Now Polk determined to risk Columbus itself. He would cross over himself, taking along Cheatham's fresh infantry units under Smith and Blythe.

What prompted his decision? Perhaps it was the burning of Camp Johnston; perhaps Pillow's desperate requests for reinforcement brought by Captain Butler on the *Prince*. Polk never explained, but having become "satisfied the attack on Columbus for some reason had failed," he moved decisively.[1] First, he sent orders to McCown to release two regiments from the trench lines and hurry them down to reconstitute a reserve. Then he directed Col. Preston Smith commanding the troops now on the riverbank to cross. Smith's Brigade, the 154th Senior Tennessee Regiment and Blythe's 1st Mississippi Battalion, pressed toward the boats. "One wild shout went up from a thousand throats at the prospect of meeting the enemy."[2]

There would be less risk in crossing now. Melancthon Smith had silenced the Yankee field battery on the Missouri bank. It had displaced and moved off, for the moment at any rate. One of Smith's West Tennesseans reassured Polk about the lost New Orleans battery. "'All right, General, we will have those guns turned in the other direction in a few minutes.' 'Yes,' he said, 'You must retake that battery.'"

Polk recalled the *Charm* from her temporary haven upstream, bringing her down "near the foot of the bluff and alongside the *Ken-*

164

tucky." He sent Smith's two regiments aboard the packets and added Capt. Josiah White's company of Tennessee cavalry, supervising the loading himself. To Polk's exasperation, however, as Captain Trask cast off and backed away from the bank the *Charm* went "hard aground." Polk and the men of the brigade could only wait and watch. Trask hailed the *Prince*, and she maneuvered up close, tossed lines aboard, and towed the *Charm* free. But all this took precious time.[3]

Once across the river Polk met a crowd on the shore, "the remnant of the drooping force," and spoke "cheering words" to them. Then he conferred with Cheatham and Pillow. Cheatham, pleased with the success of his counterattack, had halted the pursuit at the Bird's Point Road and ridden back to the steamboat landing to receive Polk's orders.[4] He reported that the assortment of regiments he commanded "were tired and pursued them [the Federals] only in squads." He welcomed the sight of "my 154th."[5]

Without hesitation Polk directed Cheatham to continue the pursuit, "to press the enemy to his boats," using not only Smith's fresh brigade but "the whole force."[6] Cheatham ordered Preston Smith through the woods at the double-quick after the retreating enemy. Smith's first regiment, the large 154th under Lt. Col. Marcus J. Wright, advanced through the woods at Belmont Point toward the road to Hunter's Farm. Smith accompanied the 154th, sending back a staff officer, Maj. F. H. McNairy, to hurry forward Blythe.[7]

There seems to have been another halt and a general regrouping of the Confederates at the Federal field hospital at the intersection of the Bird's Point Road and the road leading to Hunter's Farm. "Here we found a yard full of knapsacks, arms, ammunition, blankets, overcoats, mess-chest, horses, wagons, and dead and wounded men, with surgeons engaged in the appropriate duties of their profession."[8]

The 11th Louisiana, which had failed to block Grant's retreat but had inflicted heavy losses on the enemy as they passed, had "hotly pursued" through the woods for half a mile, had become disorganized, and had been halted and recalled by Colonel Marks. The 11th waited near the Bird's Point Road as did a mixed band of pursuers, fragments of Marks's and Cheatham's counterattacking columns. They had dwindled in number and determination, and they welcomed the arrival of Polk with Preston Smith's fresh brigade and two Tennessee cavalry companies.[9]

Uncertain what would await them, Polk proceeded warily along the road to Hunter's Farm. He knew the head of the pursuing column already marched within range of Grant's gunboats, and he expected Grant, despite evidence of precipitate retreat, to have taken up a defensive position. A perimeter of fire would likely be encountered, perhaps from uncommitted enemy units. Therefore Polk tried not to be clumsily predictable. On the spot he planned a rather elaborate envelopment. He ordered Smith's two regiments to continue up the road but to swing well south of the landing itself. Once past the landing and upriver from the transports, Smith would then, "facing by the rear rank," surround the enemy at the landing, "preventing them returning to the woods." As the other troops came up they would be fed in to reinforce the encirclement.[10]

Smith led the column forward with Capt. Ed Fitzgerald's Company F of the 154th ahead as skirmishers.[11] On the road Fitzgerald brushed aside intermittent fire from straggling parties, and his men "found large quantities of baggage scattered in the road, indicating that our pursuit had been very close." They passed exhausted and wounded Federals and came upon two of Beltzhoover's guns, carefully spiked by the enemy.

When the pursuing column reached the lane that turned off toward the steamboat landing, Smith could see, off in the distance to the right front, chimneys of three Yankee transports. Out in the river he saw, darkened by the setting sun, two "black monsters" belching smoke. Preston Smith became anxious. He sensed the enemy might be "about to move off." He therefore divided his column into two wings, sending Marcus Wright and half of the 154th angling to the right toward the riverbank while Cheatham led the other half of the regiment and some of Blythe's Mississippians farther down the road to a point above the landing. When Smith believed the extended line of his brigade was directly opposite the landing, "I gave the order to charge."[12]

Three hundred yards out from the landing, Lieutenant Colonel Wright, commanding the 154th, "saw an officer waving his sword and urging his men aboard. The front file of my command drew their guns to fire, but I at once ordered them to shoulder, as I knew their firing would draw a fire on my command."[13] Wright wished to approach even closer, using to the fullest the concealment offered by thick cornstalks. Perhaps surprise could be achieved. Wright deployed his com-

Reembarkation of Grant's force
(sketch by Henry Walke; U.S. Naval Historical Center)

panies of the 154th into line and moved forward on a broad front. He quickly saw, however, Yankees "hurrying on board," so he ordered his men to fire. Firing at the transports on the run, they crossed the corn-field to the bank of the river. From above the landing Preston Smith and Frank Cheatham with the balance of the brigade also "charged down on the retreating boats."[14]

Aiding Smith's Brigade in the attack was Col. Robert Tyler with several companies of the 15th Tennessee. Part of Marks's 11th Loui-siana and miscellaneous companies from five other regiments also took part. The fighting at the landing, however, was done essentially by the 154th.

Cheatham posted his men along the bank and told them to drop to their knees. "We loaded and fired on our knees and on our backs, under the shelter of a rail fence." The fire from these assorted Confed-erates armed with "Minnie & Sharp's rifles" was terrific. The Confederates were convinced they slew a multitude of Yankees: they expected "bodies piled upon the decks to the depth of three or four feet"; "gutters . . . filled with torrents of blood[;] . . . decks so slippery that men could scarcely stand." Pilots who approached the wheel were "shot down as fast as they appeared."[15]

Polk, observing the sunset fight at the Hunter's Farm landing,[16] believed that "under this galling fire," the enemy "cut his lines and retreated from the shore, many of his soldiers being driven overboard by the rush of those behind them."[17] Pillow reported that the Confederate fire "was so hot and destructive that the troops . . . rushed to the opposite side of the boats and had to be forced back by the bayonet to prevent capsizing."[18]

Miller's cavalry participated as well. They dismounted, attacked through the cornfield alongside Smith's infantry, and lined the riverbank firing at the transports. Thus far at Belmont the four Confederate cavalry companies had made an insignificant contribution. The activity of the two Mississippi companies in the morning had been minimal. The addition of Taylor's company of Tennesseans about 1 P.M. seems to have gone unnoticed by those who conducted and reported the Confederate counterattacks. There is evidence, however, that Taylor and perhaps Miller's companies played an active but uninspired role in the pursuit of the fleeing Federals to the Bird's Point Road. Their very presence, however, frightened the retreating Federals. White's company arrived on the field in midafternoon accompanying Smith's Brigade but served as Polk's escort and "took little part."[19]

Another opportunity for Confederate cavalry occurred at dusk, after the fight at the landing. Cheatham ordered Captain White to take his Tennessee Mounted Rifles and "proceed down the lake and look after a body of the enemy who were supposed to have retired in that direction." It was too late. Buford and his orphan 27th had crossed through the woods to the riverbank. Captain White lamely reported to Cheatham the following morning that he had proceeded as directed and captured eight prisoners.[20]

The Confederates attacking the landing, contrary to Union reports, had no artillery. Capt. Marsh Polk's field battery was on its way, but darkness intervened and the Union fleet sailed before it reached the landing.[21] Confederates believed that if "we had had a battery of artillery we could have taken the boats without trouble." Thus when the

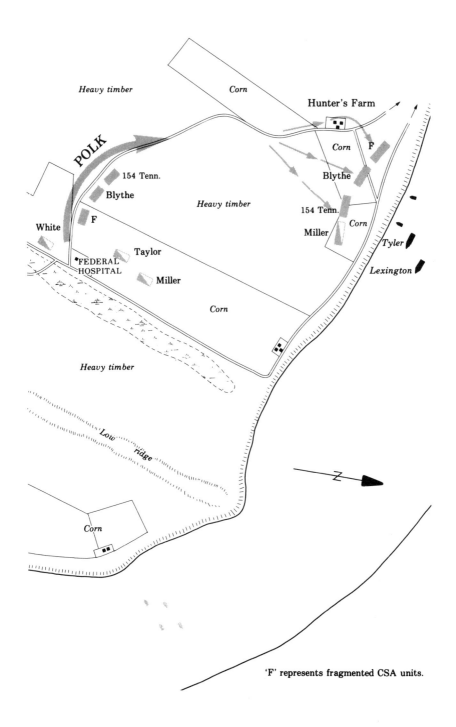

Heavy timber

Corn

Hunter's Farm

POLK

154 Tenn.

Blythe

F

Corn

F

Blythe

White

Heavy timber

154 Tenn.

Corn

Miller

Taylor

FEDERAL
HOSPITAL

Miller

Tyler

Lexington

Corn

Heavy timber

Low ridge

Corn

N

'F' represents fragmented CSA units.

MAP 10. *Union Withdrawal*

Chicago Battery on board the transports and the gunboats began to fire, the Confederates "had no means of reply." A Tennessean reported, "Seeing that we could not reach them with our muskets we were ordered to fall back, the shell plowing up the field in every direction, and we dodged them behind the trees and still kept retiring. . . . The Lincolnites knew our direction and their range was very accurate."[22] The rebel infantry hugged the ground or fled into the woods, and the gunboats' frightening salvos "passed high over our heads as a wood was intervening and they did not know exactly where we were."[23]

✻

Polk had been too slow. Grant had the luxury of at least half an hour, perhaps closer to an hour, to load his troops.[24] To cover the embarkation Grant wanted to use his reserve, Detrich's battalion, but gave up the idea when he realized he must retrieve them from the transport and then reassemble them.[25] A private in the 22d Illinois arrived at the landing and reported to Grant that the rebels were closing in. Grant responded that "it is no use, the infantry won't come off the boats and the gunboats must cover our retreat."[26]

McClernand seems to have done more than his commander. He alerted Commander Walke to the rebel approach and had him bring the transports down to the landing prepared to embark troops. Disappointed at not finding Detrich's boat guard in position, McClernand halted the embarkation of Delano's cavalry company and sent them back to the cornfields at Hunter's Farm "to watch the enemy."[27] Someone, probably Captain Schwartz, who was riding with McClernand, ordered Lt. Pat White of the Chicago Battery to put two guns in a defensive position on the bank. He managed to place one. According to White, "Lieut. Barrett came up from the boat and said run the gun aboard. I called out, 'don't stir that gun yet.' Well, when all was aboard except this gun, the enemy came for us with a yell, so we gave them its contents and then ran it aboard and then used two guns on them from the bow of the boat."[28]

White himself boarded with difficulty. His horse had to be "pulled down the river bank on its haunches and dragged across the stage plank." The other guns, including two New Orleans cannon, went aboard "as quick as anything I ever saw." "We slid our guns lively. I tell you."[29] Pilot Scott disagreed: "Owing to the cowardice or traitorism of the captain of one of the steamers, this [loading of the guns] detained us, as instead of keeping his boat still so as to get the guns aboard, he would keep backing and going ahead so that it was impossible to bring them aboard. At length John A. Logan stepped up to him, and, putting a pistol to his ear, threatened to shoot him if the vessel was not held still."[30]

Confusion and nervousness reigned at the landing. "Certain it is, that the men rushed pell mell on board of the boats." "We reached the boat, and the colonels and officers tried every means to rally their men, without success." Pvt. Lindorf Ozburn barely made it: "We rushed for the boat, (I was riding) the boats commenced shoving off. I tried to rush my horse on but, the staging was dropping off the bank. I left my horse and took to my heels, and got aboard." "The gunboats was all that saved us from being shot like hogs."[31]

The rebels seemed to burst from the cornfield, hidden by corn "so tall and thick as to cut off view even of men on horseback."[32] Musket fire erupted not only from there but from the woods and all along the bank. Federal soldiers on the bank and on the decks of the steamers shouted the alarm. Deck hands struggled to secure stage planks and swung axes high above their heads chopping frantically at hawsers. McClernand, Schwartz, and quartermaster Capt. Reuben Hatch came aboard the *Chancellor*. Grant remained on top of the bank for a last look, then turned his mount toward the *Belle Memphis*.

> The captain of a boat that had just pushed out, but had not started, recognized me and ordered the engineer not to start the engine; he then had a plank run out for me.[33] My horse seemed to take in the situation. There was no path down the ["perpendicular"] bank. . . . My horse put its fore feet over the bank without hesitation or urging, and, with his hind feet well under him, slid down the bank and trotted aboard the boat, twelve or fifteen feet away, over a single gang-plank.[34]

Grant went from the deck to the "texas,"[35] on the top deck of the *Belle Memphis*. He found the captain's quarters and stretched out on a sofa.

The steamers backed off. Soldiers on deck could see the enemy all along the shore. They also could see there on the landing survivors of Dougherty's Brigade, begging to be taken aboard. Pvt. John W. Pierson, Company C, 7th Iowa, "arrived in time to see our boats pulling away leaving myself and others on the bank with the enemy."[36] Also abandoned were many of the wounded, most of them men who had been hit after the capture of Camp Johnston and could not keep up on the retreat.

The *Belle Memphis* had a terrible time. Her stern became tangled with a "wrack heap,"[37] and her pilot had to go ahead on one wheel, go back on the other, then back on both wheels until she worked free. Of course this furious but seemingly futile performance disconcerted the soldiers aboard who would report later that "the engineer lost his head" and that "not less than four pilots were killed on her." Private Austin, Company A, 22d Illinois, could not believe that the boat was headed downstream into the teeth of the Columbus defenses. He looked up at the pilothouse and could not see anyone there, so up he went himself to discover if the pilot had been injured. He had not.[38]

In freeing herself from the wrack heap, the *Memphis* had drifted downstream, not only scaring silly the infantry on board but blocking the line of fire of the *Lexington*. Walke had moved the gunboats down-river to avoid the transports and to achieve a good angle of fire. Now his plan was frustrated by the contortions of the *Belle Memphis*. Nevertheless, displaying a coolness that appalled infantrymen, the *Lexington*'s captain, Comdr. Roger Stembel, called out to the soldiers on the deck to lie down. They did. "At that moment, the best music of the day set in." The *Lexington* and the *Tyler* opened fire. First they used their bow guns, shooting at an oblique angle, then as the "*Memphis* sheered out and went ahead," Walke's gunboats opened up with their heaviest guns at the enemy on the bank.[39] "Our boats being in good position we opened fire with our grape, cannister and 5 second shells, and completely routed them we learn with great slaughter. After silencing the enemy, we continued our fire with the broadside guns throwing shell on the Banks ahead with bow gun to protect the Transports and throwing shell from the stern gun upon the enemy's ground so long as we were in reach."[40] They "poured a perfect storm of death into the rebel masses . . . , whole ranks mowed down by a broadside."[41] Some of the rebels tried hiding behind a wagon stacked high with hay, but "the gunboats nocked [sic] it to splinters."[42]

Grant heard the enemy bullets striking the ship. Then he heard the noise of the *Memphis*'s engines and the blasts from the gunboats. He got up from the sofa and went out on deck. There he watched a furious firefight.

Five Federal sources including Walke mention they fought against Confederate artillery on the bank, placed there "to cut off the retreat." None mention Confederate cannon firing, but four sources agree that the Federals blasted a cannon to smithereens as it came into battery. "The Rebel gunner was just about to pull the lanyard when shell from the gunboat burst directly under the carriage of the gun throwing all high into the air. The rebel gunner and several others were killed, the carriage demolished and while in the air it exploded."[43]

To add to the Confederates' woes Ezra Taylor and his men on the *Chancellor* decided they could help. So, from the bows of the transports at least two of the Chicago guns began to fire grapeshot and solid shot. They found firing from the deck so effective that they "used one of the captured pieces and it *done* well."[44] They aimed at the lane between the cornfields "through which we had just retreated." It was "full of secesh."[45] In a remarkable and much-admired feat of gunnery, Sgt. William J. McCoy aimed his gun at a building on shore with a tall chimney. The ball knocked the chimney down.[46]

Then the infantry joined in. Logan's and Fouke's men kneeled on the hurricane deck of the *Aleck Scott*, propped their rifles on the rails, and fired away. Aboard the *Memphis* remnants of the 7th Iowa and 22d Illinois fired with a vengeance. Sheets of bullets and shell poured from the five vessels. The firing continued "with terrible effect" and "with great spirit" as the steamboats drew off upriver. Grant's flotilla had "cleared the coast."[47]

With the Mississippi so low that November day, Grant would remember the riverbanks being "higher than the heads of men standing on the upper decks." The rebels generally fired high and, although they "well peppered" the superstructures and smokestacks of the steamers, particularly the *Belle Memphis*, they inflicted few casualties.[48] Others, however, reported that "a good many were shot on the boats and our cabins were riddled with minnie balls."[49] A wounded Iowa soldier remembered "balls literally riddled the upper works of the boats where the wounded lay in windrows on the cabin floor. There being scarcely any one on board [the *Memphis*] but the wounded, there was no resistance offered save by a few who were slightly wounded. The fire was so fierce that it was impossible to even cut the lines and get underway. There we lay until the gun boats came to our rescue, and gave them a broadside which put them to flight."[50]

It had been a furious firefight, replete with thousands of rounds, bursting shells, and deafening explosions. However, like many twilight battles, the senses deceived. It is unlikely that any Federal or Confederate lost his life during the reembarkation fight. Cheatham and Wright had their men firing prone from the bank and then withdrew when the naval guns opened up. No one was killed in the 154th, the 1st Mississippi Battalion, or the cavalry. Confederate fire, like Federal, was noisy but not deadly. The fight probably resulted in a total of twenty-five wounded from both sides.

Later, safely en route upstream, Grant returned to his sofa in the captain's cabin. He saw that a rebel bullet had pierced the wall of the cabin and gone all the way through the sofa itself. Grant found it "lodged in the foot."[51]

While Grant examined his sofa and contemplated his mortality, Surgeon Brinton ventured up to the texas to visit the captain of the *Belle Memphis*. Brinton later recalled that they uncorked a bottle of "champagne" and that he had "tasted many a glass of wine since, but never one which tasted better than did the fictitious champagne of that evening." Although it was an "occasion to rejoice at our narrow escape," the cabins of the transports were crowded with wounded—at least 100 men "in all stages of mutilation." Two surgeons worked hard to alleviate their distress. Out on the decks exhausted troops threw themselves down to rest, thought to themselves about the sounds of battle still humming in their ears, and immediately fell off to sleep.[52]

Walke's gunboats, following behind the flotilla, overtook the *Chancellor* which had lagged behind the other transports and then turned back. John McClernand was frantic about Buford's 27th. He directed Walke to turn back to look for men on the riverbank above Hunter's Farm. Still not satisfied, McClernand ordered the *Chancellor* to land. He would go ashore and look for them himself.

The moment the bow of the *Chancellor* touched land and McClernand stepped off, "Lt. H. A. Rust, adjutant of the 27th Illinois, hastened up and announced the approach of the 27th and Dollins cavalry." McClernand, Hatch, and Schwartz rode down the bank and met

Buford and the advance elements of his regiment. McClernand ordered Buford to take them aboard the *Chancellor* at once. Continuing on down the bank they met Dollins and sent him and his command up the bank to board the *Chancellor*. Still further down the bank, near Beckwith's Landing, they came upon the remainder of the 27th with prisoners in tow. McClernand hailed Walke and asked him to take them aboard the *Tyler*. Walke turned the bow of the *Tyler* to shore and picked them up. Stembel and the *Lexington* stood off while all this transpired, securing the embarkation. It was about six o'clock.[53]

Grant's fleet steamed slowly upstream toward Cairo. The Mississippi, which had been changing colors since dawn, now wore black. Soldiers on the transports felt the emptiness of the darkness. "Nobody knew where his regiment was, or what had become of the rest." Wounded men crowded the staterooms and cabins. Capt. John Seaton remembered the "solemn trip" back home. In the main cabin officers "very glibly" recounted the adventures of the day. Grant sat by himself and "said not a word but to the waiter. . . . We thought he was hard-hearted, cold, and indifferent, but it was only the difference between a *real* soldier and amateur soldiers."[54]

Aboard the *Tyler* surgeons tended the wounds of Buford's men. Walke's crew paid special attention to the Belmont casualties, "furnishing them with their own hammocks and bedding."[55] The *Rob Roy* came downstream to greet Grant's fleet. As the *Belle Memphis* was steaming past, a correspondent aboard the *Rob Roy* hailed Grant, "who came out on deck and yelled over about the victory his men had just won."[56] Grant also shouted across the water to the captain of the *Rob Roy* to continue downstream, meet Walke, and remove the wounded and prisoners from the *Tyler*. Walke should then remain anchored at Island 1 until he heard that Colonel Cook and his 7th Illinois had returned safely to Fort Holt from their reconnaissance toward Columbus.[57]

It was a triumphant return. Happy salutes of congratulation were fired from Fort Holt, Bird's Point, and Fort Prentiss. When the fleet reached Cairo about 9:30 that night, "the entire city . . . was illuminated in honor of our victory at Belmont." The high levee surrounding the town was "thronged with people," as were the streets.

Grant left the *Memphis* and made his way through the crowded streets to his headquarters. Immediately he wired news of the battle to

Capt. James J. Dollins
(Illinois State Historical Library)

St. Louis.[58] Once the wounded had been unloaded carefully and carried off to hospitals, the steamers with Bird's Point regiments crossed the river again and anchored about midnight. It took a while to offload the artillery, but all was complete by 2 A.M., and the weary men of the Chicago Battery were soon fast asleep.[59]

15

Pumpkins in a Cornfield

Confederate surgeon Lunsford Yandell picked his way across the battlefield, guiding his horse cautiously in the moonlight to avoid stepping on bodies. "The wounded men groaned and moaned, yelled and shrieked with pain. I had opium, brandy, and water, with which I alleviated their torture, and poor creatures, they were exceedingly grateful."[1] Yandell remained out until 2 A.M. tending to the wounded. A battalion of the 4th Tennessee helped him. Portions of the woods had caught fire during the afternoon. The Confederates succeeded in putting out most of the fires, but "numbers of their dead were badly burnt and mutilated."[2] Fortunately for the wounded left out overnight, it did not rain, nor was it cold.[3]

Dawn came. Under flag of truce Yankees and rebels worked side by side to undo what they had done. "It was a most horrible sight to contemplate."[4] The "blue coats" were "laying thicker over that cornfield than ever I had seen pumpkins in a cornfield."[5] "I wish the war would close. Such scenes . . . are sickening, and this destruction of life so useless." Lt. W. Y. C. Hume, an artillery officer who lived to see many bloody battlefields, vividly remembered the large number of enemy dead.[6] Dead and wounded lay everywhere: under logs where they had crawled to die, beside the pole fence, out in the cornfield. They found one who had decided "to take a smoke . . . in a sitting position, against a tree, dead, with his pipe in one hand, his knife in the other, and his tobacco on his breast."[7] "All over the Battlefield they lay in close proximity to each other. Some torn asunder by cannon balls, some with frightful wounds. . . . Some were killed outright with musket balls through the temples or forehead, others with limbs torn off suffering the most torturing agonies."[8]

The Confederates buried their dead across the river in Kentucky, close to camp. They wrapped comrades in blankets and laid them in trenches, by company. A priest read prayers, and three volleys were fired. "The Federals buried theirs hastily, without coffins or blankets; in one instance lay 41 clad, just as they fell, in a single long trench and covering them with earth to the depth of about two feet." "The scene of throwing the rigid bodies, crusted with blood and dirt, into a shallow ditch, the heavy fall of the sod on the mass being accompanied by rude jest and laughter" startled men's sensibilities.[9]

Confederates had looted the bodies. "They were very well cleaned in death. I never saw one single fellow unless he had his legs shot off [who] had his pants and shoes. . . . It was mostly done by Irish soldiers."[10]

Rebecka Wentz found her husband Augustus in the cornfield. "His body was divested of all his clothing except shirt and drawers, as was the case with many others of our dead; buttons were found wrenched off and pockets turned inside out."[11] She gave a "low agonizing cry" and fell "prostrate upon his body." A Confederate who watched remarked, "I'd given ten thousand dollars to recall that man to life."[12] Capt. McHenry Brooks of Buford's 27th found his brother dead, "a minie ball through his head." He buried him apart from the others and put a slab at the head of his grave. Then "sitting down beside his mother's son, wept like a child."[13] His brother was a rebel, surgeon of the 13th Arkansas.[14]

Polk's men tried to search the three or four square miles for wounded as. fast and as thoroughly as they could. "A wounded man, with both legs nearly shot off, was found in the woods, singing the Star-spangled Banner; but for this circumstance the surgeons say they would not have discovered him."[15] Federals, restricted by flag of truce, could only look in obvious places.[16] "An old Missouri farmer, whose slaves had gone back with the Federals," wandered the battlefield. He suddenly came upon Col. John Logan "and abused him in the most vehement and bitter language, I ever heard, calling him 'a d—— nigger thief,' etc. But, under a flag of truce and unarmed, all the Colonel could do was to take it; but his eyes flashed, and I felt sure that if he ever met that old farmer again under different conditions he would repay him with interest for the abuse."[17]

Some wounded Yankees were carried to the riverbank on stretchers or on "blankets fastened to poles and muskets."[18] Most, however, like

Pvt. Caleb Green of the 7th Iowa, were brought by wagon. "Regardless of fractures," regardless of their injuries, they were "dumped into a wagon and seated between the outstretched legs of a comrade behind me—the method adopted in packing all of us." The wagon jolted along, the "torture most exquisite." [19]

The *Charm* and *Prince* ferried over wounded, Confederate and Federal, late into the night on November 7. The Confederates fared better, of course, although the wait seemed endless. Capt. J. D. Layton, wounded in the side by a musket ball, remained with the Liberty Guards, as he had all day, until "he saw the last man properly cared for at night." Wounded rebels had to smile as they looked up and saw a captured Yankee flag flying jauntily from the jackstay of Captain Trask's *Charm*. [20]

One Confederate officer brought back injured from the battlefield was Maj. Eddy Butler. Polk ordered that he be taken to his headquarters, a frame house in the middle of Columbus. When Polk and his staff returned, Butler had regained consciousness. His voice "took on a new ring." The two men "seemed to exchange character." Polk's face revealed "pain and suffering," Butler's "triumph." Butler said, "I did not recklessly go in advance of my men till it became necessary; and my only regret is, that I cannot live to be of some service to my country." Polk was "entirely overcome." He took Butler's hand and said "in broken tones, . . . 'Your father shall know all.' " Polk returned to sit by Butler's pallet during the night, and the bishop gave Butler a final blessing as he died early in the morning. On November 9 Polk wrote his friend E. G. W. Butler, Sr., "I return you the dead body of your gallant son. He fell as a Butler ought to fall in the discharge of his duty." The body, wrapped in a Confederate flag, was sent downriver by steamer. [21]

The hospital in Columbus, of course, was overwhelmed. Surgeons set up tents nearby, but still the wounded came from across the river —over 400 Confederates and 100 Federals. Surgeon R. W. Mitchell of the 13th Tennessee reported 101 wounded Federal prisoners, all of whom suffered from gunshot wounds except one who had a saber slash across his back. In desperation Confederate infantrymen had to be assigned as nurses. Pvt. Aaron C. Harper found himself on such duty, having to care for Yankees as well as his comrades. "I felt that it was my duty to treat them as I would our own men." Federal pris-

Col. Henry Dougherty
(drawing by William D. T. Travis; Illinois State Historical Library)

oner Caleb Green reported that the rebels "treated our wounded prisoners as well as they could. They even took some of their own sick off the beds to make room for our wounded. . . . I had fallen among gentlemen, whom to describe as humane, would but inadequately convey even a faint idea of their kindness, tenderness and affectionate warmth."[22]

Mrs. Sallie Law made Henry Dougherty her special project. With one leg amputated and compound fractures of the shoulder and forearm, Dougherty was near death. She nursed him and fed him lemonade with a spoon. Then she went to General Polk and convinced him to agree to a special flag of truce so that Mrs. Dougherty might be brought through the lines from Bird's Point.[23]

Many Federals, however, complained of Confederate neglect. Surgeon Brinton felt "little attention had been paid during their stay in Columbus." "The dressing of wounds and operations performed reflected but slight credit on the enemy's surgeons."[24] Several Confederates, on the other hand, charged that the two captured Federal surgeons refused to help out, even with their own wounded.[25]

The morning after the battle Lt. Lemuel Adams, 22d Illinois, stiff and hurting, discovered he could get about pretty well, so he walked around the "old hotel building used for a hospital. . . . There was a large pile of legs and arms in the yard, mostly from the wounded rebels. . . . There was a large crowd on the street, many had come up from Memphis and were shipping their dead friends home."[26]

Among the many other Memphis visitors, Dr. Creighton of Beale Street arrived, bringing with him fourteen doctors he had gathered.[27] After emergency treatment at the Columbus military hospital, nearly all of the Confederates, especially the more seriously wounded, were shipped down to Memphis. Civilian leaders there had wired Polk that they had "made every preparation for all wounded you have."[28]

The *Hill* transported the first sixty patients to Memphis on November 8; then came more on the *Kentucky*, the *Yazoo*, and the *Bracelet*. The city cried out for volunteers, funds, and old linens. The new Overton Hotel was "thrown open" for the wounded. "It was a splendid building and had only a short time been finished, the marble steps and rich tapestry contrasted sharply in the dazzling gas light with ghastly faces and tattered clothes. We found beds—real beds, imagine our astonishment, prepared for us and after a warm . . . soupe [sic] I feel [sic] asleep."[29]

The Memphis City Hospital, staffed mostly by the sisters of St. Agnes Academy, accepted many of the wounded; Sallie Law's Southern Mothers Home took others. Mrs. Frank Newsom, the widow of a doctor, heard of the need for nurses and journeyed to Memphis, bringing her servants and surgical supplies. Susan Kirby Smith, whose husband served in Jackson's Battery and whose son was in Preston Smith's 154th, also volunteered. "It was appalling to behold the mangled and disfigured bodies. . . . It was a new era in our lives."[30]

Memphians watched with great curiosity as the *Ingomar* brought down a different load of men—Yankee prisoners. Over 100 of them marched under guard down Main Street to Mosby's Cotton Shed where they remained for weeks. John Pierson remembered the slippery, cold rock floor "in an old slave pen." Several of these men from the 7th Iowa were never exchanged, going on to the horrors of Andersonville and gaining their freedom only in April 1865. Two of the 7th Iowa prisoners would die in Macon, Georgia; two in Annapolis, Maryland.[31]

✳

Grant returned to Cairo the night of November 7 with over 200 wounded; another 125 would follow within the week. Those Grant brought back had been wounded in the early and middle phases of the battle. They had been brought to the log house on the Bird's Point Road where they had their wounds dressed. Amputations were performed at the cabin with the aid of chloroform. Once they had been treated at the log cabin, the Federal wounded were carried on wagons to the transports.

Upon arrival at Cairo about half of the wounded were dispersed to regimental hospitals. The more seriously injured either entered the General Hospital (the Brick Hospital) at Cairo or were sent to the military hospital in Mound City. The latter occupied a block of brick stores and was becoming known as one of the best hospitals in the United States. It was staffed by the Sisters of the Holy Cross from Indianapolis. These nuns also operated the Brick Hospital. The sudden rush of casualties, however, overtaxed these medical facilities and their personnel. Calls for aid and even offers to pay went out. The Sisters of Mercy responded positively, as did women throughout Illinois and "certain members of the Sanitary Commission."[32]

The nurses received mixed reviews. Mother Mary A. Bickerdyke at Cairo would become legendary. Lt. Lemuel Adams testified, "I have seen her sit all night by the cot of a sick and dying soldier, she never seemed to tire, and could do more work than any two nurses I ever saw and she saw that every one had attention and no special favors shown."[33] The Sisters of Mercy, on the other hand, "were a poor lot," according to Adams. "One of them was rather tall and slim, she would come around, roll up her eyes, count her beads and inquire how we felt, but done little to relieve anyone; the boys called her 'Sister Shanghai.'"[34] The Sisters of the Holy Cross fared better. Everyone respected their superior, Mother Angela Gillespie. Grant considered her "a woman of rare charm of manner, unusual ability and exceptional executive talents."[35] Some complained about the Catholic sisters' proselytizing, and Grant had to have McClernand stop John Logan from calling the medical director of the hospital a "brute," but for the most part the Union wounded received good-to-excellent medical treatment.[36]

Some of the wounded were nursed by wives. Capt. William A. Looney of Logan's 31st remained in Cairo to recuperate, nursed by his wife, but his severe shoulder wound would not heal. Finally he was sent home where he suffered for months, "never again fit for duty."[37] This brush with death, this "having seen the elephant," rattled the composure of the bravest. "For 2 or 3 weeks after this affair," said Lt. Pat White, "when I would here [sic] a shot fired I would shiver all over."[38]

Grant lost between 320 and 400 wounded, over 100 of whom fell into Confederate hands; more than 100 were captured unwounded; and about 90 were killed, for a total loss of about 550, perhaps 600, men.[39]

Reconstructed from twenty official reports, newspaper lists, and miscellaneous sources, the following are the casualties suffered by the respective Union regiments:

7th Iowa (512): 31 killed, 77 wounded, 114 missing[40]
22d Illinois (562): 31 k, 78 w, 37 m
27th Illinois (720): 11 k, 47 w, 27 m
30th Illinois (522): 9 k, 27 w, 8 m
31st Illinois (610): 10 k, 63 w, 18 m
Cavalry and artillery: 2 k, 11 w, 1 m
Walke's command: 1 k, 3 w

Grant had bloodied his command. His loss amounted to about 12 percent of the Belmont expeditionary force and 16 percent of those engaged. Dougherty's Bird's Point Brigade with only fifteen companies engaged suffered two-thirds of the total casualties with only one-fourth of Grant's troops.

The Confederates lost more: 105 killed, 419 wounded, and 117 missing.[41] The total number of Polk's troops engaged has been accepted generally at about 5,000. Forces taking part in the late-morning fight between Pillow and Grant were roughly equal in number: about 2,500 Federals and fewer than 3,000 Confederates.[42] Three regiments with a total of 1,500 Confederates joined the fighting in piecemeal fashion from noon until three o'clock. Preston Smith's pursuing column of the 154th and Blythe's 1st Mississippi Battalion (about 1,000) became only lightly engaged.

Regimental numbers and losses for the Confederates have been obtained from similar sources as used for the Federals. For some commands such as the elusive 15th Tennessee, however, numbers require interpretation.[43] Confederate casualties include:

Staff: 3 w
13th Arkansas: 12 k, 45 w, 23 m
11th Louisiana: 13 k, 43 w
Blythe's 1st Mississippi Battalion: 1 w
2d Tennessee: 18 k, 63 w, 33 m
12th Tennessee: (633): 12 k, 46 w
13th Tennessee: (400): 28 k, 75 w, 46 m[44]
15th Tennessee: 10 k, 10 w, [45]
21st Tennessee: 13 k, 62 w, 5 m
22d Tennessee: 10 k, 67 w, 9 m
154th Senior Tennessee: 13 w
Watson Battery: 2 k, 4 w, 1 m
Pointe Coupee Battery: 2 k, 1 w
Cavalry: 1 w

Bragging rights about captured and destroyed material went to Grant's men. They burned Camp Johnston and with it all tents and equipment of the Watson Battery and the 13th Arkansas. The following week Colonel Tappan had friends in Memphis conduct fundraisers to help reequip his regiment.[46] Beltzhoover's men lost their cherished "Jeff Davis" piece and a six-pounder; their four remaining guns had been spiked. The enemy captured twenty of their fine artillery horses with all their expensive harness.[47] One Arkansas officer lost a magnificent cream-colored Arabian stallion with a white flowing mane "given by a lady." It became the subject of prolonged, serious, but futile negotiations. Among the many Confederate horses killed was Lt. Col. John Miller's horse Arab.[48]

Grant lost his bay horse that had cost $140. In addition he left behind "my fine saddle and bridle and the common one," his mess chest, and his gold pen. The morning after the battle Captain Trask of the *Charm* used Grant's bay to ride over the battlefield, then he wrote letters to friends using Grant's pen.[49] "A handsome iron-framed cot" of John McClernand's fell into enemy hands, as well as his field desk with dispatches and an inkstand inscribed with his name.[50] Surgeon Brinton lost a set of surgical instruments that he treasured.[51]

The Confederates captured two of the Chicago Battery's caissons, a wagon, some horses, and several mules. To Polk's delight they also brought in about 1,000 rifles. Col. Thomas Freeman wired ordnance officer Col. W. R. Hunt, "Had a hard fight. Got plenty of arms now. You need not send me any more."[52]

The Confederates "returned Yankee clad with the spoils of the battlefield, everybody had a trophy."[53] It seemed hundreds had seized blue overcoats.[54] The Reverend John G. Law took one that he much admired and, "with the trophy on my back," reported to the *Prince* to relieve his mother's worries about his safety. Sallie Law welcomed him: "'John, take off that coat! I would not be seen with such a thing on my back.' General Cheatham who was present laughed heartily, and said, 'Why madam, I have a fine Yankee overcoat myself in which I expect to keep warm this winter.'" Despite Cheatham's intercession, Mrs. Law would not be reconciled. "In deference to her wish," Law decided to "hang the coat on the wall and stick to gray."[55]

Perhaps Pvt. John Cooper best summed up Belmont's bloody exchange. He reported to Col. Phil Fouke on November 10 that he had been wounded and had lost his rifle, revolver, overcoat, blanket, and knapsack but that he had captured a rebel horse and delivered him to the quartermaster.[56]

Early Friday morning, November 8, Grant dispatched the *Belle Memphis* downstream with a flag of truce and a letter to Polk carried by Major Webster. Lieutenant Colonel Hart and a burial party of infantry went along as well as sixty-four "sick and wounded" Confederate prisoners whom Grant offered to release "unconditionally." A steamer bearing Polk's staff officer, Capt. Edward Blake, met the *Memphis*. Webster handed Blake Grant's message, and Blake allowed the burial party to go ashore and begin its work. The wounded Confederates remained on board, however, while Polk wired Richmond for instructions. Captain Blake returned to the *Memphis* late in the afternoon and told Webster that Polk had been authorized to accept the prisoners. In return thirteen badly wounded Federals whom General Cheatham had found on the field that morning and brought aboard the *Memphis* were released.[57]

Negotiations resumed on November 12 when Polk wrote Grant stating that he had received authority to exchange more prisoners. He offered to turn over the remainder of the Federal wounded (105) held in Columbus.[58] The next day the *Aleck Scott* went down from Cairo with

104 Confederate prisoners. The *Scott* and the *Prince* met just below Lucas Bend at 10 A.M. The two boats were lashed together in the middle of the river, their "uneasy wheels keeping sufficient motion to prevent a backward drift downstream." The Confederate party included, among others, Polk, Cheatham, McCown, Lt. Col. Hiram Tilman of the 21st Tennessee, Capt. A. B. Gray of Polk's staff, and Captains Haywood and Ballentine of Logwood's Tennessee Cavalry Battalion. The Federal party consisted of Grant, Logan, Grant's quartermaster Capt. Reuben Hatch, Judge Sidney Breese, former Democratic senator from Illinois,[59] and others. There were also three ladies on each boat.[60]

Grant and Polk talked at length. Much of their discussion centered about technicalities of exchange, but Polk thought Grant "looked rather grave . . . like a man who was not at his ease." Polk managed, however, to get "a smile out of him and then got on well enough." Important to Polk's agenda was some understanding between them regarding "the principles on which I thought the war should be conducted; denounced all barbarity, vandalism, plundering, and all that, and got him to say that he would join in putting it down. I was favorably impressed with him; he is undoubtedly a man of much force. We have now exchanged five or six flags, and he grows more civil and respectful every time."[61]

The Confederate and Federal officers meanwhile "mingled and drank champagne together." "It was an odd sight to see the Federals and Rebels mingling together promiscuously, smoking and drinking and laughing as though we were all the best of friends." Grant released enough prisoners to bring his total to 124; Polk released 114 and later told Grant that he would choose by lot ten unwounded prisoners imprisoned in Memphis to make up the difference. He also released Grant's servant.[62]

The *Prince* and *Aleck Scott* pulled apart, and the parties on deck waved good-bye with hats and handkerchiefs. It had been "altogether a most delightful time, . . . conducted on both sides in the most chivalric and high-toned style."[63]

More meetings would follow during November. Federal and Confederate leaders would drink and dine aboard each other's steamers and seemed to extend themselves to make these "flags" socially enjoyable. Cheatham, "an ardent follower of the turf, discovered symptoms of a like weakness in General Grant," and the two talked horses whenever possible. Cheatham proposed a "grand international horse-race on the Missouri shore" as a substitute to continued fighting. "Grant laughingly answered, he wished it might be so." Grant asked for a souvenir from Cheatham, and Cheatham gave him his knife so that he might cut a button from his coat. Cheatham would later complain, however, that Grant left a hole in his uniform the size of a "silver half dollar."[64]

Polk and Buford were old friends. At one luncheon Buford proposed the toast: "'George Washington, the Father of his Country.' General Polk, with a merry twinkle in his eye, quickly added: 'And the first Rebel!' The Federal officers, caught in their own trap, gracefully acknowledged it by drinking the amended toast."[65] Sadly Polk declined Buford's earnest entreaty, "even on the score of our friendship," to release more of the prisoners from his regiment. Polk refused and still had 100 Federal prisoners after all the exchanges.[66] Polk said of Buford, "He is as good a fellow as ever lived, and most devotedly my friend—a true Christian—a true soldier—and a gentleman every inch of him."[67]

This meeting with Buford occurred on November 15th. The boats had met higher upriver, and Buford asked Polk to come under his protection to Cairo and spend the night in his quarters.[68] Polk refused, of course, but even the thought of such behavior would perish that winter, and these half dozen interludes on the river would prove to be the indian summer of the American Civil War. The *Nashville Banner* offered perspective: "We wouldn't be surprised to hear of a nice little picnic among all hands if it were summer, and the days grow too hot for fighting."[69]

16

★ ———————————————————— ★

A Glorious Repulse

Citizens of Memphis awoke on the morning of November 8 to the shocking headline of a bloody battle near Columbus. Three thousand Memphians were up there in Polk's army. "Scarcely was there a human being amid our vast population of forty thousand persons, who had not a brother, father, husband, son, or at least a friend among them."[1]

Before ten o'clock a crowd had gathered at the telegraph office. "What's the news? What's the news?" Nothing official came through beyond Thursday night's notification of the fighting. It had ended with an ominous "our losses were heavy." Individual messages began to come over the wire: "I was spared; so were Ira and Robinson. Jeff has thigh shattered."

"Anxious minds could learn no more." Some relief came, however, with an extra issue published by the *Daily Appeal* late that morning. It contained a soldier's letter and fragments of information obtained from passengers just off the "down train from Columbus." The Confederates had won. There was no question about that. But the phrases "acres of dead" and "slaughtered at every step" frightened everyone. "Some whispered that perhaps we had not heard the worst." By late evening realists in Memphis took charge and called a public meeting that was heavily attended. Preparations must be made to receive the wounded.

With tortuous slowness more details began to come in, giving comprehensible shape to the glory and the horror that was Belmont.[2] Gideon Pillow wired his wife the night of the battle: "I fought 4 regts against 9 for 4 hours without help. . . . We drove enemy back three times; his greatly superior numbers overpowered my command. I rallied it repeatedly, and ultimately got reinforcements, drove them from the field and pursued them five miles into their boats."[3]

Memphians learned of Polk's congratulatory order to his troops. He told them on November 8 that Belmont would prove a "lesson" to the enemy. "We can and we will be free." He took the opportunity to remind them and the South of "the favoring providence of Almighty God by which the hearts of our troops were made strong in the day of battle. Confiding in the justice of our cause, we have felt we could put our trust in His protection and defense, and He has given us the victory."[4]

By Sunday, November 10, boatloads of wounded had arrived in Memphis. The city began to realize the extent of her loss. The *Nashville Banner* reported, "Memphis today is like Rachel mourning for her children."[5] Schools closed. Men and women lined the riverbank. "At midnight," Sally Walker Boone remembered, "we would hear a dirge; we would go to the window and listen, with bated breath and blanched faces in fear that the procession coming down the street from the Mississippi and Ohio RR depot would stop at *our* house. What fervant [sic] prayers of thanksgiving we would offer when it passed."[6]

In the Sam Walker home, in a room just off the main hall, a dying Lt. Jimmie Walker, an arm around each parent, was propped up on his pallet to receive last rites from Bishop James Otey.[7] Sharp losses in his uncle's regiment, the 2d Tennessee, as well as in the 21st and the 154th, all Memphis regiments, had "brought great grief to the city."[8] Belmont and Memphis seemed irrevocably entwined. "Later on in the war I was near larger battles, where we were defeated and where the loss was greater, but Belmont was ever our battle; there the Memphis soldiers fought, there Memphis soldiers died."[9]

Across the South, however, newspapers and the public in general greeted Belmont as a "glorious victory," a "complete triumph of Southern valor," a "glorious repulse," and a field "consecrated . . . by the blood of martyrs to Southern liberty." It "more than compensates for the reverse at Port Royal. The insolent invaders have again been driven back."[10] Albert Sidney Johnston declared, "The 7th of November will fill a bright gap in our military annals, and be remembered with gratitude by the sons and daughters of the South." Jefferson

Davis sent "sincere thanks for the glorious contribution you have just made to our common cause."[11] The Confederate Congress rushed through a resolution congratulating Polk, Pillow, and Cheatham for having "converted what at first threatened so much disaster into a triumphant victory."[12]

Poems and songs followed, lionizing the Confederates of Belmont. "The Belmont Quick Step," for instance, appeared within a month.[13] Yet, not all Southerners were so sure of the victory. One week after the battle, the *Memphis Argus*, perhaps still angered over the "inexplicable embargo" placed on the telegraph by Polk,[14] observed that instead of being a great victory, Belmont was a demonstration of the "disgraceful ineptitude" of Leonidas Polk. It quoted the *Daily Appeal*'s remark that the "whole affair looks very much like a surprise."[15] Surgeon Yandell sadly noted in a letter that "it was Providence or mere chance which defeated the enemy at Bellmont. Our generals proved themselves incompetent, and our men showed they were not invincible."[16]

In any event the South could not long savor its "victory" at Belmont. The election of Jefferson Davis on November 6 had diminished it. Then on November 8 came two significant events that swept Belmont from the headlines: the capture of Port Royal by Admiral DuPont and General Sherman with the greatest fleet "ever to have been gathered under the U.S. flag" and the momentous Trent Affair that inflamed British and French public opinion and brought the United States close to war with the two great powers. Mary Chestnut added perspective: "Pillow has had a victory—away off somewhere. First he lost, then he was being reinforced. Faraway news—I care not for it."[17]

A near calamity struck Columbus on November 11. The monster gun Lady Polk exploded, killing her crew and several observing officers. Leonidas Polk himself escaped, apparently because he happened to be standing directly behind the gun. Still he was severely stunned and found that he could not carry out his duties, so he turned over the command of the First Division, Western Department, to Gideon Pillow.

Pillow rang the fire bell. On November 13 he sent dispatches to Governor Harris, Gov. John J. Pettus of Mississippi, and the military commander at Memphis stating that the enemy was gathering before Columbus in enormous numbers.[18] "The entire militia of the west end of the State should be called out," he wrote Harris. "I anticipate being

entirely surrounded."[19] Something close to hysteria gripped Columbus. The movement of Pillow's division to Clarksville, Tennessee, repeatedly ordered by Johnston, was countermanded. Despite skepticism
on the part of some of Pillow's men who suspected this was "another
of the Genl's *blows*," work on fortress Columbus proceeded at a furious pace, "day and night."[20] Pillow announced to the South, "We will
hold this place and fight to the end." A distraught political leader Sam
Tate wrote from Memphis on November 30, "His daily sensational
dispatches keep the country in alarm and commotion. . . . No one here
has the slightest confidence in Pillow's judgment or ability, and if the
important command of defending this river is to be left to him, we feel
perfectly in the enemy's power. . . . [The battle of Belmont] has not in
the least changed public opinion about Pillow."[21]

December 1861 would see Polk back in command, but Pillow, a
subordinate once again, fretted and chafed and finally exploded. After
Christmas he resigned and went home to Columbia, Tennessee, cast-
ing blame for his action on Polk's usurpation of authority that "in-
fringed on that of the President of the Confederacy" and on Polk's
conduct of the battle of Belmont.[22] This comedy of one man desperately seeking the command held by another who wished with equal
desperation to be relieved of it rivals fiction. If Pillow's actions and
attitude had not been so self-destructive, so harmful to men of good-
will, and so detrimental to the cause he loved, one might, with a
snicker, dismiss the man and the episode as Grant did.[23]

Polk was not the only general with a feisty subordinate. The morning
after he returned from Belmont, John McClernand dashed off a letter
to George B. McClellan reporting the victory.[24] McClernand then held
a review of his brigade and moved from regiment to regiment giving
speeches of congratulations and gratitude. He pointed out that they
had driven the enemy two miles back into their camp, destroyed it,
then faced about and "fighting the same ground over again, you drove
them a second time."[25]

Grant also thanked the men of both brigades and Walke's command
that morning for having "sustained the honor of the American Union."
He said that "it has been his fortune to have been in all the Battles
fought in Mexico, by Genls. Scott and Taylor, save *Buena-Vista*, and

never saw one more hotly contested, or where troops behaved with more gallantry."[26]

The evening of November 8 Grant wrote his father, Jesse R. Grant. As with many letters of public figures, it appears to have been intended for publication.[27] Grant sketched the battle, carefully explaining that the "object of the expedition" was not to attack Columbus but "to prevent the enemy from sending a force into Missouri to cut off troops I had sent there for a special purpose, and to prevent reinforcing Price." He believed his losses would total 250, but "taking into account the object of the expedition the victory was most complete."[28] Grant "far understated" his losses and justified his Belmont strike as a preventive measure to keep Polk from reinforcing Price. Furthermore, he claimed that Belmont kept Polk from cutting off Oglesby's expedition he had sent to chase Thompson.[29] To Brig. Gen. C. F. Smith in Paducah, Grant wired on November 7: "We drove the Rebels completely from Belmont, burned their tents, & carried off their artillery, for want of horses to draw them, we had to leave all but two pieces on the field. The victory was complete. Our loss is not far from 250 Killed, wounded, & missing. The Rebel loss must have been from five to six hundred including 130 prisoners brought from the field."[30]

Grant's official report of Belmont came on November 10. It expanded somewhat his November 8 letter to Jesse Grant and raised the number of Federal casualties from 250 to almost 400. This report, however, is not the one that appears in the *Official Records*. That report, dated November 17, 1861, according to John A. Rawlins, was actually written in 1864.[31] Compared to the first report, the revised report, defensive in nature, is heavily documented with communications. It is in this revised report that the mysterious 2 A.M. message from W. H. L. Wallace that Grant claimed "determined me to attack" appears.[32]

In seeming contradiction to the confidence he expressed, Grant, on the night of November 7 and the morning of November 8, pulled back the units he had deployed in Missouri and Kentucky. An Illinois soldier wrote, "Well, Grant got whipped at Belmont, and that scared him so that he countermanded all our orders and took all the troops back to their old stations by forced marches."[33] He recalled Oglesby's expedition from Bloomfield and sent Colonel Marsh from Bird's Point to meet him, telling him, "Keep the RR transportation with you well guarded to avoid against the possibility of having your retreat cut off."[34] Colonel Cook's probe down the east side of the Mississippi was also recalled. Lt. Leroy R. Waller reported, "Your order for the retreat of the 7th & 28th Infantry to Island No 1 has been complied with & will make fort holt at 12 o'clock." Colonel Plummer commanding at Cape Girardeau worried about the 17th Illinois he had sent south to help Oglesby. On the morning of November 8 Plummer wrote to Col. L. F. Ross of the 17th Illinois that he had just talked with Commander Walke and learned "that our forces at Belmont were badly defeated yesterday afternoon." He told Ross to hasten back. Watch out "if they [the enemy] come out from Belmont to cut you off."[35]

Other mutterings of uncertainty or of discontent could be heard. Colonel Wallace wrote his wife, "He [Grant] had not the courage to refuse to fight. The advantages were all against him & any permanent or substantial good an utter impossibility under the circumstances. I see that he & his friends call it a victory, but if such be victory, God save us from defeat. True, it demonstrated the courage and fighting qualities of our men, but it cost too much."[36]

Captain Foote criticized Grant sharply for failure to communicate with him and for not alerting Walke and Stembel "until, at the last minute, he directed them to convoy the transports."[37] Some felt Grant had "proved that he was wholly incapable of command."[38] Charles Wills confided to his diary:

> Grant says that he achieved a victory and accomplished the object of his expedition. It may be so (the latter part of it) but almost everyone here doubts the story. He says his object was to threaten Columbus, to keep them from sending reinforcements to Price. Well he has threatened them, had a fight, and why they can't send reinforcements now as well as before, is more than I know. I never will believe that it was necessary to sacrifice two as good regiments as there were in the West, to accomplish all that I can see has been done this time.[39]

An embittered survivor of the 7th Iowa reported that on November 11 when the regiment formed for parade one company had only 11 men, another only 15. "General Grant tries to make out that there were about 150 or 175 men lost on our side. I'll stake my life that we lost not less than 500."[40]

Although Southern public opinion revealed some uncertainty about Belmont, it appeared unanimous compared to that in the North. Historian John Fiske believed the North viewed Belmont as a defeat, and it became a "theme of angry sarcasm."[41] "The withdrawal seemed an ignominious flight to many disappointed union critics upon whom the heavy union losses . . . had a most depressing effect."[42] "The country at large . . . regarded Grant with mistrust and looked upon the battle as at best a glorious misfortune."[43]

At three o'clock the night after the battle, the correspondent tor the *St. Louis Sunday Republican* wired from Cairo, "We have met the enemy and they are not ours." Later that morning the *St. Louis Missouri Weekly Democrat* admitted, "There is no disguising the fact that we were defeated, and badly too." The *Chicago Tribune* agreed, speaking of the "disastrous termination of the Cairo expedition to Columbus. . . . Our troops have suffered a bad defeat." The editor of the *Louisville Daily Journal* criticized his colleagues, some of whom "have gone so far as to proclaim it a rout." "Belmont was a defeat for the union forces, and barely escaped being a disaster. It cost many good lives and resulted in very little, or nothing." "There were not a few at the time who believed that Gen. Fremont ought to have treated Gen. Grant in the way Paine was treated by Gen. Smith.[44] In later years and with riper experience, Gen. Grant would have expected as much." The *Illinois State Journal* bitterly expressed the hope "that in future expeditions generals of the North would have a more worthy object in mind than a bloody fight."[45]

Iowa was in a fury. The *Keokuk Gate City* and the *Burlington Hawk-Eye* lashed out against the Illinois press for "neglect of the merits" of the Iowa troops and against Grant for his bungling of the expedition: "Generals Grant and McClernand, at the battle of Belmont, were never nearer the rebel battery than the Hospital, one and a half miles distant."[46] Governor Kirkwood and Republican Senator James Harlan joined in, stating that the Iowa troops had no confidence in Grant and that the excessive casualty rate "was due to carelessness or inability of General Grant and he should not be continued in his command. At Belmont he committed an egregious and unpardonable military blunder, which resulted in almost annihilating an Iowa regiment."[47]

To add to Grant's chagrin, Lincoln wrote to McClernand three days after Belmont congratulating McClernand on the victory: "You have done honor to yourselves and the flag. . . . Please give my respect and thanks to all."[48] Indeed, it seems that whatever credit could be dispensed immediately after the battle went to McClernand. "Grant bungled and McClernand saved the day."[49]

These attacks stung. Charges that Belmont had been "unnecessary, barren of results" not only bothered Grant at the time but twenty years later would cause him, the undisputed hero of the Union, to continue to defend and justify.[50] Gradually, however, the views of the press softened regarding the Belmont strike. Grant, McClernand, and their political friends insisted that Polk's troops had every intention of reinforcing Price, but "the reception they got from the Egyptians of the Sucker State prevented it."[51] Targeted by Grant and his friends was the *Chicago Tribune*, "whose editorials had shown a 'determination to embarrass and disparage our army.'"[52] The soldiers themselves were infuriated by "editorials so malignant."[53] The veterans of Belmont felt they had been victimized by "one of the most wanton and damaging falsehoods that ever blistered a tongue."[54]

Within weeks, however, creative journalists came to regard Belmont as "one of the most signal and brilliant [battles] since Buena Vista."[55] The *New York Herald* proclaimed Belmont a victory "as clear as ever warriors gained." An extraordinary view of Grant and McClernand as warriors emerged, with Grant "swinging his sword above his head shouting himself hoarse in the thickest of the fire and of McClernand setting his boys an example of heroism by plunging headlong into the rebel ranks and making himself a road of blood."[56] Grant himself believed that "the Battle of Belmont, as time passes, proves to have been a greater success than Gen. McClernand or myself at first thought. The enemies loss proves to be greater and the effect upon the Southern mind more saddening."[57]

Grant and Polk would reflect about Belmont and its implications during a cold and wet December. Small river adventures broke the monotony, but both sides concentrated on building their strength. Columbus grew more and more formidable although Polk abandoned the encampment at Belmont. Grant, whose command was enlarged to include the mouths of the Cumberland and Tennessee rivers, kept pressure on Columbus—so much pressure that Polk and Pillow continued to resist Johnston's demands for some of their troops at Forts Henry and Donelson.

One might suggest that his bloody near-success at Belmont led Grant to try his second amphibious adventure, the success of which is exceeded only in legend. And, with beautiful irony, mighty Columbus would fall in March 1862 without being attacked. Polk would surrender the high bluffs with their magnificent fortifications so dearly bought with Southern treasure and begin a demoralizing march south to Shiloh.

17

It Will Not Do to Smile in Triumph

Any attempt to assess what occurred at Belmont is fraught with peril. It is tempting to end the narrative as the reassuring levees of Cairo come into view.

One student of Belmont has compared Grant to the young Napoleon in his first Piedmont campaign, poorly served by ill-disciplined troops. This is misleading and unfair. The 8,000 American civilians who tried their best to fight as soldiers at Belmont did so with astonishing valor. Standing in a line of battle ready to receive and return the fire of an enemy armed with rifled muskets required the icy discipline of the veteran. The physical and psychological exhaustion of maneuvering and fighting for nine hours in Belmont's dense, tangled woods would have challenged Caesar's best. The horror of confronting cannon fire for the first time has overwhelmed men of courage and conviction before and since. "Whatever other comment may be made," said William Preston Johnston, Albert Sidney Johnston's son and biographer, years later, "or lesson learned from it, [Belmont's] story is highly honorable to the individual courage, tenacity and intelligence of the American soldier."[1]

Were these brave men of the Mississippi Valley, Federal and Confederate, well served by their commanders? "There was no generalship displayed on either side," reported the New Orleans *Daily Picayune* a week later.[2] Perhaps this is true.

Leonidas Polk certainly relied too heavily on his second in command, whom he suspected of incompetence. He sent Pillow to meet the emergency on the Missouri bank and kept McCown, his highest-ranking professional, on the east bank. This can be justified, but it was a mistake. Also, despite his elaborate refutation in the *Official Records*, Polk appears to have been slow in sending reinforcements to Pillow's aid. Perhaps this was fortunate. If they had appeared at Camp Johnston in the piecemeal fashion in which they were dispatched, they would have had to fight their way through demoralized comrades to meet onrushing Federals, flushed with success and supported by field artillery. They would have met the fate of Walker's 2d Tennessee and ended up hiding under the muddy bank.

There was careless, almost criminal, neglect of Belmont's defenses. Polk, not Pillow, bears responsibility for this. The likely avenues of approach should have been studied and elementary defensive precautions taken. The western road leading up to the rear of Belmont should have been well guarded, if not utilized for a counterstroke. Polk should have rehearsed, in his own mind at least, the possibility of a surprise attack in force on the Missouri bank. That he was surprised tactically by Grant's landing goes without question. That he was surprised further by the speed of Grant's assault and by the appearance of Union field artillery is also evident.

Polk's ten companies of cavalry were improperly used. If they had been posted well out on the roads east of Columbus toward Milburn and north toward Elliott's Mills, they could have provided early necessary intelligence and security. A daytime patrol, if not an entire company or both companies for that matter, at Hunter's Farm would have allowed Camp Johnston some defense in depth and, properly handled, could have slowed and wearied Grant's column and perhaps forced an earlier deployment. Polk was not well served by having his senior cavalry commander on the west bank, Capt. Frank Montgomery, absent on leave.

Polk's field artillery, except for the intervention of Melancthon Smith's battery at Cheatham's suggestion, also played an inconsequential role. Polk did attempt early to send two batteries to reinforce Pillow, but incredibly they were prevented from landing by the loss of stage planks. Had they arrived with Walker's infantry, they might have retrieved defeat, yet it is likely they would have been improperly positioned by Pillow and knocked out by the well-served Union field guns.

Critics have pointed out that Polk was confused by Grant's landing on the Kentucky shore the previous night, by information about an enemy advance from Paducah, and by reports of columns converging against Thompson. However, he did hold to the belief that Columbus was Grant's real objective too long. Then he reacted to the threat against Camp Johnston by dividing his force. Why defend Camp Johnston at all? Why not abandon the tents and bring Tappan and Beltzhoover to Columbus?

Polk did behave with great caution. His slowness in responding to the Belmont threat is understandable, however. He had expected and had prepared for an attack on the Kentucky side. His opponent's true course seemed obvious, and he feared he was being deceived by a feint at Belmont. The stakes were high. But Polk lacked boldness; moreover, he lacked the driving compulsion to seek out and destroy the enemy. He had the opportunity and the strength at hand to counterattack and cut off Grant's escape, but he let his chance slip away.

It is less easy to comprehend why Polk, once he came ashore with Smith's Brigade and took command in person, did not press Grant to the boats. The Federal embarkation could have been made quite costly. Caution again prevailed, it appears. Why did Polk fail to send his four companies of cavalry to sweep the area north of the battlefield for surviving Federals?

Although Polk claims credit, with the support of Marks, for planning the heavy Confederate counterattack and blocking action, the first three regiments he sent over, including that of Marks, tried their best to land at Camp Johnston and join the fight there instead of landing with an aim to flank the enemy and cut them off from their transports. Ironically, effective Union artillery and musket fire chased the Confederates to their true course. One should point out as well that Polk benefited from the good fortune of having four steamers tied up at Columbus the morning of November 7.

Belmont should have been Gideon Pillow's kind of fight. An amateurish but aggressive Confederate commander might have led his five regiments blindly into the forest at once to grapple with the enemy, trusting in the great bowie knives of his infantry, confident of a fallback position at Camp Johnston. On the other hand, a defensiveminded amateur might have positioned his raw volunteers along the sloughs crisscrossing the Belmont peninsula. He would have used the woods to his advantage, not abandoned them to the enemy. He might have agreed with the hasty dispositions of Tappan and secured the roads with cannon and rested his flanks on the abatis. Certainly he would have picketed the road leading into Belmont from the west.

Pillow did none of these. Rather he resorted to the burlesque of sta-

tioning men in the cornfield, receiving Grant's fire, and then launch-
ing an all-or-nothing bayonet charge against an enemy concealed and
protected by timber. Such reckless tactics threw away lives, surrendered advantage of position, and defied the common sense of the men
Pillow commanded. Grant could have wished for nothing better.

Pillow should be credited with attempts to rally his men at Camp
Johnston, only to have his formations blown away by Taylor's guns and
Buford's flank attack. He tried again at the riverbank and, assisted by
Cheatham, succeeded in organizing remnants of his force into a group
capable of counterattack. Pillow fought bravely himself and, despite
the knowing looks exchanged by his colleagues, somehow managed to
perpetuate the charade of military prowess, at least among many Tennessee volunteers. But Grant knew better. The tooth fairy gave him
Pillow.

What about other Confederate leaders? John McCown handled his
wide responsibilities to Polk's satisfaction, but with the exception of
posting infantry on the Columbus roads with dispatch and directing
the artillery fire from the Iron Banks, his role was essentially passive.
Frank Cheatham, on the other hand, shined at Belmont. He won
Polk's confidence.[3] He demonstrated initiative and proved himself
to be cooperative and energetic—a fighter and a leader. His most effective act may have been recommending Smith's battery be brought
into play.

Three Confederate colonels acted as brigade commanders at Belmont: Preston Smith, Knox Walker, and Robert Russell. None distinguished himself. Smith and Walker essentially fought with their own
regiments, while Russell's role cannot be reconstructed from the data
available. It seems the services of these three were wasted in a battle
fought at the regimental and company level. One wonders about the
shadowy figure of Russell. With the strongest military credentials of
any Confederate colonel, he should have contributed significantly.

Of the other colonels, James Tappan displayed combat leadership,
as did Ed Pickett. Samuel Marks and Robert Tyler did not excel. Their
maneuvering was clumsy, poorly coordinated; their crucial blocking
action failed. John V. Wright and Thomas Freeman demonstrated neither skill nor leadership. Mexican War veteran Andrew K. Blythe and
his battalion, part of Smith's reinforcing brigade, seem not to have
been a factor at all.

Among the lieutenant colonels, Alfred Vaughan handled the 13th

Tennessee well in a most difficult situation; Marcus J. Wright showed promise. John Miller, Robert Barrow, and Tyree Bell did not distinguish themselves. Dan Beltzhoover's failure may have cost the Confederates victory. His immobile Watson Battery might as well have been siege guns. A field battery that does not maneuver in a fluid battle is a contradiction in terms. Beltzhoover's lack of ammunition remains a grand mystery, but responsibility for such grand neglect does not.

✳

Grant's subordinates performed better. Captains Ezra Taylor and Adolphus Schwartz contributed significantly. Their opportune and decisive handling of the Federal guns contributed largely to Grant's success. This became known rather widely. W. H. L. Wallace wrote after the battle, "To him [Taylor] & his admirable company more than to any other cause we are indebted for saving our broken forces at Belmont from utter destruction."[4] Much could be expected from them in the future. Dollins's handling of the cavalry seemed uninspired but adequate, particularly in the approach march phase. Without the continuing leadership of a wounded Maj. Elliott Rice, the 7th Iowa might have been destroyed during the Federal retreat. Lt. Col. Harrison Hart, working under the close supervision of Henry Dougherty, seems to have handled his regimental responsibilities effectively. John White and Augustus Wentz performed well.

Among the colonels, dependable Phil Fouke seemed ready to fight, appearing when and where Grant wanted him. Jacob Lauman excelled. He stood out for initiative and eagerness to fight. He aggressively handled the 7th Iowa, a regiment weakened by Grant's assignments. They played a major role in each phase of Belmont, receiving the brunt of counterattacks by Pickett and Freeman in the cornfield, by Walker at Camp Johnston, and by Cheatham as they prepared to return. Grant determined they should be the last regiment out, and for this they paid a horrible price. Using good amateur instincts, Lauman, not Grant or Dougherty, it seems caused the Bird's Point Brigade to swing to the right and fill the gap in McClernand's attacking line at the fight for the cornfield.

John Logan emerged from Belmont as a hero. He fought his regiment well and provided critical leadership during the breakout. The "Dirty-first" returned to Hunter's Farm bloodied but intact. They, if required, could have continued the fight.

Napoleon Buford's role is controversial. His flank attack in the morning was not decisive; Taylor's Chicago Battery provided the decisive element. But Buford's dramatic march and assault, probably encouraged by Alexander Bielaski, shattered any hope of a Confederate stand at Camp Johnston and insured Pillow's defeat. Buford's independence of thought and action deserves to be noted.

John Rawlins, however, charged that Buford jeopardized the retreat by "his disobedience of positive orders." It appears from thinly disguised anger in Grant's and McClernand's battle reports that Buford, in the march back to the boats, was ordered to take his place in the column and failed to do so, lunging off to the west on his private escape route, leaving Dougherty's Brigade to its fate.

Buford's highly independent action may have saved the 27th many casualties, but it must have disconcerted the plans of his superiors. One wonders, however, if Buford's presence in the fight against Cheatham and in the breakout column might have led to an even greater disaster than befell Dougherty's Brigade. Yet it must be conceded that without Buford, Grant lacked the strength to defeat the counterattacking Confederates. Furthermore Buford endangered his regiment by wandering about in the swamps and deep woods, and a good number were captured anyway. One can only imagine the consequence if he had been pursued aggressively. His action in the retreat to the boats appears insubordinate, contemptuous of McClernand, and reckless in the extreme.

Grant seems to have been well served by his brigade commanders. Of course John McClernand should not have lost his head and played master of ceremonies at Camp Johnston, but it would be hard to imagine politician-soldiers McClernand, Fouke, and Logan behaving otherwise. McClernand had difficulty holding his brigade together, certainly, thanks to the terrain and Buford's adventures, but he was visible as a leader. He, more than Grant, seemed responsible for direction of the artillery. He certainly displayed initiative and responsibility when he ordered Walke's gunboats to turn back and retrieve the 27th. Otherwise Buford and his men might still be wandering the banks of the Mississippi. McClernand cooperated well with Grant on the battlefield. In all, his performance held promise for the future.

Grant's best combat officer, Henry Dougherty, kept the Bird's Point Brigade at the point of action all day. They fought well until smashed by Cheatham's counterattack. Dougherty handled himself with customary bravery according to Grant who was beside him much of the battle. Dougherty worked closely with Ezra Taylor in support of his battery, and it was his men who led the frontal assault at Camp Johnston, capturing the Watson guns. After returning to Hunter's Farm, however, Dougherty made the responsible but costly decision to turn back and assist the 7th Iowa. The wounds he thus received destroyed his usefulness, depriving the Union of one of its most promising soldiers.

Comdr. Henry Walke played an important role at Belmont. He provided continuous protection for the transports and the landing site. He and Commander Stembel steamed forward with their timberclads and engaged McCown's batteries three times, diverting attention from Grant's infantry to some extent. Where Walke failed at Belmont was his overriding concern for the safety of the fleet. When enemy guns began to score hits on the gunboats, Walke withdrew. Although he had fulfilled Grant's orders, Walke had not gone far enough. His *Naval Scenes* implies that he realized this, rather limply explaining how he tried to fire over Belmont Point into Camp Johnston.

A daring naval commander would have rounded Belmont Point and run past the guns of the Iron Banks. The reward might have justified the risk. Walke could have stopped and probably destroyed the *Charm* and the *Hill* with their deckloads of reinforcements, not only interdicting the battlefield but also dealing out a calamity. To such a suggestion, Walke would have probably responded, with warmth and logic, that such a course would have been suicidal. If Walke had been daring, however, Grant might have won a stunning victory. Even allowing for Walker's 2d Tennessee coming ashore, no effective Confederate counterattack could have been mounted, despite the best efforts of Frank Cheatham. Holding the camp, the artillery, and the riverbank, Grant's five regiments would have bagged Pillow and six regiments.

What about Ulysses S. Grant? He deserved credit for badly scaring Polk, for stirring up dust all over southeastern Missouri and southwestern Kentucky with converging columns of less than 20,000 men, and for jabbing the Confederates at Belmont. One must admire Grant's speed: first Paducah, then Belmont, next Donelson. One must admire the distracting tactic, be it design or accident, of tying up noisily on the Kentucky shore at night, then by day attacking across the river. Grant might be compared to his Chicago Battery—mobile and opportunistic, crashing through where field guns were not expected, and once within range, blasting away furiously.

When Grant decided to attack Belmont, he did so swiftly and with the courage to keep his own counsel. Although this resulted in charges that Grant was being secretive, with McClernand second in command it appears to have been a wise course. Grant's army kept focused on their objective, with little wasted motion. He made excellent use of the volunteer leadership of McClernand, Logan, Fouke, and Lauman, applying a minimum of direction once the regiments had been deployed. He let his citizen soldiers fight it out themselves. He took the responsibility; he took the risk of failure.

The discovery of an audacious general who would go looking for a fight downriver delighted Lincoln. Belmont brought Grant's name forward at a time of reorganization of the army. A student of war however, might be doubtful. Had not Grant "technically disobeyed orders, . . . initiated the attack without instructions?"[5] It was a "shoe-string operation," characterized by vagueness, certainly not a study in "sound planning and organization." Brashness, courage, simplicity of concept, sloppiness of execution might produce marvels against a Pillow, but what might happen against an enemy whose idea of counterattack went beyond bugles and bayonets? Was not the maneuvering of Grant's army as it closed on Camp Johnston so clumsy and ill coordinated that it appeared comical? The lack of a ready reserve might have been fine at Belmont where Grant pushed everything forward except a five-company boat guard to achieve maximum velocity in his attack, but it violated military common sense. Why did he keep his most experienced subordinates Dougherty and Walke in ignorance of his plans? Why did he give Dougherty only six hours' notice that he would command a brigade instead of his regiment? Why did he further weaken Dougherty's undersized brigade? Indeed why did he go into battle with such imbalanced units? Why did he allow his command to drift to the right on their approach and fail to have infantry secure the riverbank as they advanced? Why deploy so early? Surely heavy skirmish lines would have been as effective, and certainly they would have been less tiring. Once his infantry had passed through Camp Johnston, why did he not rush all of his artillery to the riverbank and beat off the Confederate transports? Why did he underestimate, with great irony, the ability of the enemy to counterstrike, using the river as its ally?

Why did he allow Walke to act so independently when intervention by the gunboats might have spelled total victory? Why did he allow his men their demoralizing celebration in Camp Johnston and ignore Pillow's beaten army that lay at his feet?

It seems obvious in the comfort of hindsight that Grant's objective was wrong. Of course it should have been Pillow's force, not Camp Johnston. Even so, a splendid victory could have been achieved had he not mismanaged so badly the consolidation phase of the attack. He violated a fundamental principle of offensive warfare by failing to pass through the objective and secure it before ending the attack.

Perhaps he should have created more of a reserve, maybe of regimental strength, and kept at least a section of his artillery with it. Aligned there at the great slough, this reserve would have given pursuing Confederates a deadly reception and easily covered the reembarkation. On the other hand, without all of his artillery at the front and with five less companies of infantry, Grant might not have broken Pillow's line of battle, and his attack on Camp Johnston might have been beaten off. Of all criticisms that have been made of Grant's conduct at Belmont, the most common but the least convincing is his failure to establish a proper reserve. He did establish a reserve at the Bird's Point Road, halfway between the landing and Belmont. To dismiss Detrich's five companies as a boat guard rather than a reserve seems nitpicking. Grant should be faulted instead, it seems, for forgetting or failing to utilize this reserve.

Of course Grant should have kept closer control of Walke's gunboats, Dollins's cavalry, and Buford's wandering regiment. He had displayed "the nervous ineptitude of the tyro," but, after all, it was 1861.

One tends to forget whom Grant commanded at Belmont. He led not a seasoned Army of the Cumberland, but 3,000 combat-naive recruits over whom he could exercise only a minimum of control. He had had six months' experience with these western individualists, and he had seen some of them in action in Mexico. He believed the way to make them into soldiers was to fight them.

Grant gained experience at Belmont. He made mistakes and took risks and got away with it. He discovered that rather vague objectives, if kept to himself, could be translated by quick decision into opportunities. He found out that victory, if not controlled, could be quite "as demoralizing on troops as defeat."[6] He learned he could not be everywhere at once and direct an army by himself. Amphibious operations,

an enigma to most army commanders, now would find a skilled prac-
titioner in Grant. More than any other Civil War military figure, he
came to appreciate and apply the doctrine of combined arms. Belmont
was his primer.

He had done well; he would do better.

One might suggest that bloody Belmont changed Ulysses Grant. He,
like Jacob, had wrestled with a god. The terror, the personal danger,
the life-and-death proportions of this risk he had taken left him
strengthened. This mystical Belmont experience rewarded him with a
changed name, a clean slate, a kind of recognition of himself.

✳

The argument about who won the battle of Belmont has never been
resolved. Democrats sarcastically hung this dead chicken around
Grant's neck in 1868; it would be brought back out as late as 1886.
Fair-minded Northerners would admit Belmont "cost many good lives
and resulted in very little, or nothing."[7] Some might quibble and say
the "expedition was a failure, the battle a success."[8]

For the Democracy it was a suicidal bloodletting. Arrayed against
each other were four members of the House (McClernand, Wright,
Fouke, and Logan), numerous state and local functionaries, editors,
and the party's president-maker, Pillow. Divisions within the party certainly existed before, but now Jacksonian disciples of southern Illinois
had killed Jacksonian heirs of West Tennessee. There could be no
turning back.

Polk's Confederates won the battlefield at Belmont. They should
have. With advantage of position and overwhelming numerical supe-
riority, Polk and his men should have punished Grant's impudent
foray and relegated this untried Union general and his clique of
Democratic subordinates to the backwash of the Civil War. Instead
they allowed Grant to execute his hit-and-run play. If Polk had inter-
cepted Grant and pinched off his expeditionary force, the tone and the
tempo of river warfare in the West might have been quite different.
Instead the ponderous Confederate response at Belmont encouraged
Grant and audacious downriver campaigning.

Although many Union officers and men, especially the Iowans,
viewed bloody Belmont "as a blunder and poor generalship," Yankee
confidence increased vastly. "The enemy were well armed and fought
bravely," a Union soldier wrote, "but are no match for us, man to

man."[9] "The boys are not the least discouraged and they all want to go back and try it again."[10]

When Confederates finally learned the actual size of Grant's expeditionary force, their morale sagged. Southern patriots doubted the competence of Pillow and Polk. They began to doubt themselves. The enemy had beaten them on their own ground, one-on-one, then slugged their way back through fresh Confederate reinforcements to their boats. Perhaps these Yankees had been handpicked regulars! Certainly the men of West Tennessee had fought "not the Dutch, not the offal and scum of the streets," but frontiersmen, western men.[11]

A cocky John Logan tried to sum up his feelings about the outcome: "If this were a Confederate victory, there could scarcely be too many of them."[12] The *Ohio State Journal* could not resist: "Indeed we are at a loss how to characterize the affair; it was not a success; nor was it a failure. . . . It will not do to smile in triumph, nor will it answer to weep in dismay; the only feasible procedure is to draw one corner of the mouth upward and the other down."[13]

Belmont broke the quiet along the Kentucky-Tennessee front. It demonstrated clearly the importance of Columbus. As long as Polk held the Iron Banks, he controlled the Mississippi, and the capture of Memphis or Vicksburg must wait.

Both sides realized this. What would they do? Grant's raid had alarmed the South, especially the appearance of gunboats shepherding steamboats with deckloads of infantry and artillery. "The terror inspired by the blow from the Naval Expedition" sped efforts to shore up fragile defenses.[14] Polk reflected this fear and dug in deeper and deeper; he requested more men and guns. He became more and more reluctant to heed the calls of Johnston for manpower. Therefore, in a strategic sense, Belmont served as a diversion, perhaps a crucial diversion, for Grant's attack on Fort Henry and Fort Donelson. Ironically, instead of blocking reinforcement of Price, as Grant hoped, Belmont may have blocked reinforcement of Johnston's river forts, which would prove vastly more significant.

The Federals got smart. They kept up enough demonstrations against Columbus that winter to scare the wits out of Pillow and Polk, and meanwhile Grant and Henry Halleck probed for a weak spot in Albert Sidney Johnston's 500-mile line.

APPENDIX 1

Organization of Forces at the Battle of Belmont

Grant's Expeditionary Command,
District of Southeast Missouri
November 6–7, 1861
Maj. Gen. Ulysses S. Grant

MCCLERNAND'S BRIGADE
Brig. Gen. John A. McClernand

27th Illinois   Col. Napoleon B. Buford
30th Illinois   Col. Philip B. Fouke
31st Illinois   Col. John A. Logan

DOUGHERTY'S BRIGADE
Col. Henry Dougherty

7th Iowa   Col. Jacob G. Lauman
22d Illinois   Lt. Col. Harrison E. Hart

CAVALRY

Dollins's Company   Capt. James J. Dollins
Delano's Adams County Company   Lt. James K. Catlin

ARTILLERY

Chicago Light Battery   Capt. Ezra Taylor

GUNBOATS

USS *Lexington*   Comdr. Roger N. Stembel
USS *Tyler*   Comdr. Henry Walke

STEAMERS

Aleck Scott   Capt. Robert A. Reilly
Chancellor
Keystone State
Belle Memphis   Captain Turner
  Pilot Charles M. Scott
James Montgomery
Rob Roy

COOPERATING UNITS SUBJECT TO GRANT'S COMMAND
(in motion on November 6, 1861)

From Bird's Point toward Bloomfield
Col. W. H. L. Wallace
11th Illinois (minus one battalion)   Col. W. H. L. Wallace

From Bird's Point toward St. Francis River via Commerce

OGLESBY'S BRIGADE
Col. Richard J. Oglesby

INFANTRY

10th Iowa (from Fifth Brigade at Cape Girardeau)	Col. Nicholas Perczel
8th Illinois	Lt. Col. Frank L. Rhoads
11th Illinois (one batallion)	Lt. Col. P. E. G. Ransom
18th Illinois	Col. Michael K. Lawler
29th Illinois	Col. James Reardon

CAVALRY

Langen's Company	Lt. Ferdinand Hansen
Pfaff's Company	Capt. Ernest Pfaff
Noleman's Centralia Company	Lt. Samuel P. Tufts

ARTILLERY

Schwartz's Battery (one section)   Lt. George C. Gumbart
Campbell's Battery (one section)

From Cape Girardeau toward Bloomfield
PLUMMER'S BRIGADE
Col. Joseph B. Plummer

11th Missouri   Col. Joseph B. Plummer
17th Illinois   Col. Leonard F. Ross

From Cape Giradreau toward Charleston

20th Illinois   Col. C. Carroll Marsh

From Fort Holt, Kentucky
(demonstrating against Columbus)
COOK'S BRIGADE
Col. John Cook

7th Illinois   Col. John Cook
28th Illinois

From Paducah
(demonstrating against Columbus in concert with Grant)
Brig. Gen. C. F. Smith

FIRST BRIGADE
Brig. Gen. Eleazer A. Paine

9th Illinois
12th Illinois
40th Illinois
41st Illinois

CAVALRY

Thielemann's Dragoons   Capt. Christian Thielemann

ARTILLERY

Buell's Battery

SECOND BRIGADE

23d Indiana   Col. W. L. Sanderson

COOPERATING UNIT NOT SUBJECT TO GRANT'S COMMAND
From Ironton toward St. Francis River

38th Illinois   Col. W. P. Carlin

First Division, Western Department
November 7, 1861
Maj. Gen. Leonidas Polk

CAMP OF OBSERVATION AT BELMONT, 8 A.M.
Col. James C. Tappan

13th Arkansas   Col. James C. Tappan
1st Mississippi Calvary Battalion   Lt. Col. John H. Miller
Watson Battery   Lt. Col. Daniel Beltzhoover

REINFORCEMENTS BROUGHT BY PILLOW
Brig. Gen. Gideon J. Pillow

12th Tennessee   Col. Robert M. Russell
                  Lt. Col. Tyree H. Bell
13th Tennessee   Col. John V. Wright
                  Lt. Col. Alfred J. Vaughan

21st Tennessee   Col. Edward Pickett, Jr.
22d Tennessee   Col. Thomas J. Freeman

UNITS DISPATCHED TO REINFORCE PILLOW

INFANTRY

11th Louisiana	Col. Samuel F. Marks
	Lt. Col. Robert H. Barrow
1st Mississippi Battalion	Lt. Col. Andrew K. Blythe
2d Tennessee	Col. J. Knox Walker
	Lt. Col. William B. Ross
15th Tennessee	Col. Charles M. Carroll
	Lt. Col. Robert C. Tyler
154th Senior Tennessee	Col. Preston Smith
	Lt. Col. Marcus J. Wright

CAVALRY

Logwood's Tennessee Battalion (−) Lt. Col. Thomas H. Logwood

STEAMBOATS

Charm	Capt. William L. Trask
Harry W. R. Hill	Capt. Tom H. Newell
Ingomar	Capt. Joe D. Clark
Kentucky	Capt. Billy Priest
Prince	Capt. B. J. Butler

ARTILLERY FIRING FROM KENTUCKY SHORE

Bankhead's Tennessee Battery	Capt. Smith P. Bankhead
Hamilton's Tennessee Seige Battery	Capt. S. D. H. Hamilton
Jackson's Light Battery	Lt. William W. Carnes
Pointe Coupee Battery	Capt. Richard A. Stewart
Smith's Mississippi Light Battery	Capt. Melancthon Smith
Stewart's Heavy Battery	Maj. Alexander P. Stewart

UNITS IN RESERVE IN OR NEAR COLUMBUS

INFANTRY

6th Arkansas	Col. Richard Lyon
10th Arkansas	Col. Thomas D. Merrick
12th Arkansas	Col. E. W. Gantt
7th Kentucky	Col. Charles Wickcliffe
12th Louisiana	Col. Thomas M. Scott

21st Louisiana (5th Louisiana Battalion)	Lt. Col. J. B. Kennedy
9th Mississippi	Col. John M. Bradley
22d Mississippi	Col. D. W. C. Bonham
25th Mississippi	Lt. Col. Edward F. McGehee
1st Missouri	Col. Lucius L. Rich
4th Tennessee	Col. Rufus P. Neely
5th Tennessee	Col. William E. Travis
6th Tennessee	Col. William H. Stephens
9th Tennessee	Col. Henry L. Douglass
33d Tennessee	Col. Alexander W. Campbell

ARTILLERY

Hudson's Mississippi Battery	Capt. Clement L. Hudson
Polk's Light Battery	Capt. Marshall T. Polk
Williams's Tennessee Battery	Lt. Thomas F. Tobin

CAVALRY

6th Tennessee Battalion	Lt. Col. Thomas H. Logwood
Neely's Company	Capt. James J. Neely
Haywood's Company	Capt. Robert W. Haywood
Hill's Company	Capt. Charles H. Hill
Ballentine's Company	Capt. Charles J. G. Ballentine
1st Mississippi Battalion	Lt. Col. John H. Miller
Thompson Company	Capt. A. J. Bowles
Bolivar Troop	Lt. Lafayette Jones
Hudson's Company	Capt. C. S. Hudson
Klein's Company	Captain Klein
Cole's Company	Capt. Warren Cole

APPENDIX 2
Beyond Belmont

ADAMS, 2D LT. LEMUEL, 22D ILLINOIS, would be promoted to first lieutenant in January 1862 but resign in November because of wounds received and return to Greenville, Illinois, where he would become postmaster.

AUSTIN, PVT. WILLIAM MONTGOMERY, 22D ILLINOIS, would be promoted to sergeant and die of wounds received at Chickamauga.

BARROW, CAPT. JOHN J., 11TH LOUISIANA, would be wounded at Shiloh and return home to manage his plantations.

BARROW, LT. COL. ROBERT H., 11TH LOUISIANA, would fight with the 11th Louisiana at Shiloh, leave the army in May 1863, and spend the balance of the war in prison and at home.

BELL, LT. COL. TYREE H., 12TH TENNESSEE, would command the 12th Tennessee at Shiloh, receive rapid promotion, and become an able brigade commander under Forrest.

BELTZHOOVER, LT. COL. DANIEL M., WATSON BATTERY, would be appointed chief of artillery and be complimented by Johnston on the field at Shiloh. Never promoted, however, he would see service at Vicksburg and defend Mobile at the end of the war. A schoolteacher, he would die of yellow fever in Mobile in 1870.

BLYTHE, LT. COL. ANDREW K., 1ST MISSISSIPPI BATTALION, would be killed at the head of his Mississippi infantry at Shiloh by the guns of Adolphus Schwartz.

BUFORD, COL. NAPOLEON B., 27TH ILLINOIS, would rise to brevet major general and see action at Island 10, Corinth, and Vicksburg. Shelved as a combat officer, he would prove to be an able administrator of the District of Arkansas.

BUTLER, CAPT. B. J., STEAMER *PRINCE*, would leave the river to become a major of commissary on Cheatham's staff.

CARROLL, COL. CHARLES M., 15TH TENNESSEE, would not be reelected as colonel and would serve out the war as a captain on Forrest's staff.

CASH, PVT. PATRICK BOGGAN, 13TH TENNESSEE, would be killed at Murfreesboro.

CHEATHAM, BRIG. GEN. FRANK, SECOND DIVISION, would rise to lieutenant general and corps commander in the Army of Tennessee.

CRIPPIN, CPL. EDWARD W., 27TH ILLINOIS, would die of wounds received at Missionary Ridge.

CROWLEY, PVT. JOHN, 11TH LOUISIANA, lost his right arm at Belmont. Five months later at Shiloh a shell would tear off his remaining arm.

DELANO, CAPT. STERLING P., DELANO'S ADAMS COUNTY CAVALRY, would be accidentally shot and killed in April 1862.

DOLLINS, CAPT. JAMES J., DOLLINS'S CAVALRY, would serve Grant well as a cavalry officer, then return home in 1862 and raise and command the 81st Illinois Infantry. He would be killed leading the assault on Fort Pemberton in 1863.

DOUGHERTY, COL. HENRY, BIRD'S POINT BRIGADE, would attempt unsuccessfully to return to command. He served until May 1863 as post commander at Paducah, continually embroiled in controversy. He died in 1868 from his Belmont wounds.

FOUKE, COL. PHILIP B., 30TH ILLINOIS, would be attacked within a week by hungry creditors who would attempt to sell his home in Belleville. These "shilocks," Fouke wrote, "threatened to throw them ["his orphaned children" tended by his mother] into the streets." Fouke resigned from the army in 1862 and returned to Congress. He established a successful law practice in Washington, and when he died in 1876, President Grant and a number of U.S. senators acted as his pallbearers.

FRAZER, CAPT. CHARLES W., 21ST TENNESSEE, survived two wounds and two years in prison to become a lawyer in Memphis.

FREEMAN, COL. THOMAS J., 22D TENNESSEE, would be wounded severely at Shiloh. After his recovery he would serve competently as a cavalry officer under Forrest.

GRANT, BRIG. GEN. ULYSSES S., DISTRICT OF SOUTHEAST MISSOURI, would bring his family to join him in Cairo, at the expense of his long beard, which his wife did not fancy. Grant's eyes began to turn toward Donelson and fame.

HANSBACK, CAPT. LEWIS, 27TH ILLINOIS, would move to Kansas and practice law, eventually becoming a Republican member of Congress.

HART, LT. COL. HARRISON E., 22D ILLINOIS, would become ill of typhoid soon after Belmont and die at his home in Alton, Illinois, in July 1862.

JACKSON, CAPT. WILLIAM H., JACKSON'S LIGHT BATTERY, would rise rapidly in rank to command a division of cavalry under Forrest.

KNIGHT, PVT. WILLIAM, JR., 7TH IOWA, would die unexpectedly in a Cairo hospital after his exchange.

LAUMAN, COL. JACOB G., 7TH IOWA, would command a brigade under C. F. Smith at Donelson and become a brigadier by spring. He led a brigade at Shiloh and a division at Vicksburg. His division would suffer terrible casualties in Sherman's move against Jackson, Mississippi, and Lauman would be relieved and sit out the remainder of the war.

LOGAN, COL. JOHN A., 31ST ILLINOIS, would perform well as brigade, division, and corps commander under Grant and Sherman. He became "perhaps the Union's premier civilian combat general." In the postwar period he would continue his tempestuous, high-profile political career in the House and Senate, but as a Radical Republican.

LOGWOOD, LT. COL. THOMAS H., LOGWOOD'S TENNESSEE CAVALRY BATTALION, would become the able colonel of the 16th Tennessee Cavalry under Forrest.

MCCLERNAND, BRIG. GEN. JOHN A., FIRST BRIGADE, CAIRO FORCE, would rise to corps commander and astonish everyone with his ability to raise troops. He would break with Grant in 1863 at Vicksburg and break with Logan in 1866–67 when Logan blocked his appointment as ambassador to Mexico.

MCCOOK, CAPT. EDWIN S., 31ST ILLINOIS, would be wounded at Donelson but recover, suffer two more wounds, and rise to colonel.

MCCOWN, BRIG. GEN. JOHN P., THIRD DIVISION, DEPARTMENT OF THE WEST, would hold various commands of minor importance along the Mississippi for a year, then, following Murfreesboro, run afoul of Braxton Bragg.

MARKS, COL. SAMUEL F., 11TH LOUISIANA, would be wounded at Shiloh and watch his regiment dwindle to a handful and his officers face conscription. He would die in poverty in 1871.

MILLER, LT. COL. JOHN H., 1ST MISSISSIPPI CAVALRY BATTALION, would excel at Shiloh, but on a Sunday in March 1863 as he rode to church to preach, he would be waylaid and murdered by two of Fielding Hurst's Tennessee Federals. They made off with $60, a watch, a pair of glasses, a silk hat, a sermon, and a set of artificial teeth.

ODUM, ADDISON, CIVILIAN WHO REPLACED HIS BROTHER MARTIN, 31ST ILLINOIS, would switch to the 15th Illinois Cavalry but would be discharged in April 1863 because of disability. In 1887 he was a blacksmith in Benton, Illinois.

OGLESBY, COL. RICHARD J., 8TH ILLINOIS, would become a division commander in the XVI Corps, resign, and become governor of Illinois.

ONSTOT, CPL. WILLIAM H., 27TH ILLINOIS, would rise to sergeant and eventually 1st sergeant.

OZBURN, PVT. LINDORF, 31ST ILLINOIS, would become colonel of the "Dirty-first" following Fort Donelson and the death of Colonel White. When the new Illinois constitution and Lincoln's Emancipation Proclamation caused consternation among his troops in the fall of 1862, Ozburn tried to end the unrest by arresting officers and enlisted men. Unrest in the 31st and his terrible fall from a horse resulted in Ozburn's resignation in 1864. At a farewell banquet, one of his men who still held a grudge hit him in the head with a weight and killed him.

PAINE, BRIG. GEN. ELEAZER A., FIRST BRIGADE, PADUCAH FORCE, would become a division commander in the Army of Mississippi but spend most of the war guarding the Louisville and Nashville Railroad.

PARROTT, CAPT. JAMES A., 7TH IOWA, would command the 7th Iowa at Shiloh and would be brevetted brigadier general by war's end.

PILLOW, BRIG. GEN. GIDEON J., FIRST DIVISION, DEPARTMENT OF THE WEST, would leave the army in disgrace after Donelson, then return and perform in a highly questionable manner at Murfreesboro. He would end the war contributing positively in the Conscript Bureau.

PLUMMER, COL. JOSEPH B., 11TH MISSOURI, would command a division in the Island 10 campaign and die of exposure at Corinth in 1862.

POLK, MAJ. GEN. LEONIDAS, FIRST DIVISION, DEPARTMENT OF THE WEST, would become a mainstay corps commander of the Army of Tennessee and be killed at Pine Mountain in 1864.

RICE, MAJ. ELLIOTT W., 7TH IOWA, would command the 7th Iowa on crutches at Donelson, fight at Shiloh under W. H. L. Wallace, move up to brigade commander, and as a brigadier general, wounded seven times during the war, lead a brigade under Logan in the final campaign of the war in the Carolinas.

ROSS, LT. COL. WILLIAM B., 2D TENNESSEE, would be mortally wounded at Murfreesboro.

RUSSELL, COL. ROBERT M., 12TH TENNESSEE, would be conspicious at Shiloh commanding a brigade that suffered terrible loss. In 1863 he would raise and command the 20th Tennessee Cavalry under Forrest.

SCHWARTZ, CAPT. ADOLPHUS, 2D ILLINOIS ARTILLERY, would become lieutenant colonel and chief of staff of McClernand's XIII Corps.

SMITH, PVT. HENRY I., 7TH IOWA, would recover from his Belmont wound, become a veteran sergeant, and write the history of his regiment.

SMITH, COL. PRESTON, 154TH SENIOR TENNESSEE, would be wounded at Shiloh but rise rapidly in rank. He would be killed as a division commander under Polk at Chickamauga.

STANLEY, PVT. HENRY M., 6TH ARKANSAS, would be captured at Shiloh, go over to the enemy but leave them in turn, and end up a legendary journalist and explorer.

STEPHENSON, PVT. PHILLIP D., 13TH ARKANSAS, would fight in every major battle of the Army of Tennessee and become a Presbyterian minister in Trenton, Tennessee, looking out upon Col. Robert M. Russell in his congregation.

TAPPAN, COL. MAMES C., 13TH ARKANSAS, would command a brigade under Sterling Price and remain west of the Mississippi. In 1885 he would become a member of the Board of Visitors for West Point.

TAYLOR, CAPT. EZRA, CHICAGO LIGHT BATTERY, would fight at Shiloh and Vicksburg and become first Sherman's then James McPherson's chief of artillery. He would be wounded severely at Dallas in the summer of 1864 and would be brevetted brigadier general the following March.

TAYLOR, CAPT. WILLIAM F., MEMPHIS LIGHT DRAGOONS, would become an outstanding cavalry officer under Forrest and a grocer in postwar Memphis.

TRASK, CAPT. WILLIAM L., STEAMER *CHARM*, would find himself in the fall of 1862 done with river adventures and adjutant of a battalion of sharpshooters from the 11th and 13th Louisiana infantry regiments. He is credited with capturing Gen. W. H. Lytle at Perryville. He remained with the Army of Tennessee, fighting at Murfreesboro and Atlanta. In postwar Memphis he became a cotton factor, then "river reporter" for the *Memphis Avalanche*, and then editor of the *Memphis Public Ledger*.

TRAVIS, PVT. WILLIAM D. T., 22D ILLINOIS, would stay by Dougherty's side until May 1863 when he deserted. He rejoined the army and had his name cleared by Gen. Alexander McCook. He served as a nurse until November 1863 when he was discharged for chronic diarrhea. After the war he would gain a reputation in the East as a lecturer, painter, poet, and farmer.

TYLER, LT. COL. ROBERT C., 15TH TENNESSEE, would command the 15th Tennessee at Shiloh and become brigadier general in 1864. He would lose a leg at Missionary Ridge and would be the last Confederate general killed, defending West Point, Georgia, with a band of convalescents and militia.

VAUGHAN, LT. COL. ALFRED J., JR., 13TH TENNESSEE, would become an able brigade commander under Cheatham, fighting in every battle of the Army of Tennessee until losing his foot at Vining Station in 1864.

WALKE, COMDR. HENRY, GUNBOAT *TYLER*, would serve conspicuously at Donelson, at Island 10, and throughout the remainder of the war, ending his career as an admiral. He would provide not only accounts of Belmont in *Battles and Leaders* and in his *Naval Scenes* but magnificent etchings as well.

WALKER, COL. J. KNOX, 2D TENNESSEE, would vow, after the death of his nephew Jimmie, that "none of my relatives shall ever serve with me again."

He would lead the 2d Tennessee at Shiloh and Corinth, but exposure broke his health and he returned to Memphis under a "parole of honor." He died in Memphis during the summer of 1863.

WALLACE, COL. WILLIAM HARVEY LAMB, 11TH ILLINOIS, would be killed at Shiloh, commanding a division.

WENTZ, REBECKA MCMURTY, WIFE OF LT. COL. AUGUSTUS WENTZ, 7TH IOWA, would marry again in 1865, 1872, and in 1892, bury all four husbands, and die in California in the twentieth century.

WHITE, LT. COL. JOHN H., 31ST ILLINOIS, would be killed at Donelson.

WHITE, 2D LT. PATRICK H., CHICAGO LIGHT BATTERY, would be captain of the Chicago Mercantile Battery and win the medal of honor at Vicksburg when he "carried with others, by hand, a cannon up to and fired it through an embrasure of the enemy's works."

WISDOM, CAPT. DEW M., 13TH TENNESSEE, would be severely wounded twice.

WRIGHT, COL. JOHN V., 13TH TENNESSEE, would leave the army after Belmont and serve the remainder of the war as a member of the Confederate Congress.

WRIGHT, LT. COL. MARCUS J., 154TH SENIOR TENNESSEE, would rise to brigadier general and after the war become an indispensable chronicler of the Army of Tennessee.

NOTES

ABBREVIATIONS

AGO   Adjutant General's Office.

CHS   Chicago Historical Society. Chicago, Ill.

CSA   Confederate States of America.

CV   *Confederate Veteran.*

DU   Duke University. William R. Perkins Library. Durham, N.C.

EU   Emory University. Robert W. Woodruff Library. Atlanta, Ga.

FC   Filson Club. Louisville, Ky.

HL   Huntington Library. San Marino, Calif.

HNO   Historic New Orleans Collection. New Orleans, La.

HSP   Historical Society of Pennsylvania. Philadelphia, Pa.

ISHL   Illinois State Historical Library. Springfield, Ill.

LSA   Louisiana State Archives. Baton Rouge, La.

LSU   Louisiana and Lower Mississippi Valley Collections. Louisiana
       State University Libraries. Baton Rouge, La.

MDAH   Mississippi Department of Archives and History. Jackson, Miss.

MHS   Massachusetts Historical Society. Boston, Mass.

MSR   Military Service Record.

NARS   National Archives and Record Service. Washington, D.C.

NYHS   New-York Historical Society. New York, N.Y.

OR   U.S. Government. *The War of the Rebellion: A Compilation of the
       Official Records of the Union and Confederate Armies.* 128 vols.
       Washington, 1880–1901. (Unless otherwise indicated, all
       volumes cited throughout notes are from series 1.)

PU   Princeton University Library. Princeton, N.J.

SHC   Southern Historical Collection. University of North Carolina.
       Chapel Hill, N.C.

SIU   Southern Illinois University. Morris Library. Carbondale, Ill.

TSLA   Tennessee State Library and Archives. Nashville, Tenn.

UAL   University of Arkansas Libraries. Fayetteville, Ark.

UAMS   University of Arkansas for Medical Sciences Library. Little Rock, Ark.

UCLA   University of California at Los Angeles. Los Angeles, Calif.

UMKC   University of Missouri–Kansas City. Western Historical Collection. Kansas City, Mo.

UNSO   University of the South. DuPont Library. Sewanee, Tenn.

USAMHI   U.S. Army Military History Institute. Carlisle, Pa.

USMA   U.S. Military Academy Archives. West Point, N.Y.

CHAPTER 1

1. Horn, *Army of Tennessee*, p. 48; Cooling, *Forts Henry and Donelson*, p. 11; G. J. Pillow to Gov. Beriah Magoffin, May 13, 1861, Harris Papers,TSLA; McPherson, *Battle Cry of Freedom*, pp. 295–296.

2. Acknowledging Columbus as the best defensive position on the river north of Vicksburg, Harris cautioned Pillow "don't violate the neutrality of Kentucky," amending his stricture with permission to attack if Union troops appeared in Columbus itself. "Forbearant conciliation is the true policy." I. G. Harris to G. J. Pillow, June 12, 20, 1861, I. G. Harris to J. Davis, July 2, 1861, Harris Papers, TSLA; Horn, *Army of Tennessee*, pp. 49–51; Parks, *Polk*, pp. 187–95; Lindsley, *Annals*, p. 23; Peter Franklin Walker, "Building a Tennessee Army," p. 107; Mullen, "Turning of Columbus," pp. 214–30.

3. Coulter, *Civil War*, pp. 110–16; Simon, *Papers of Ulysses S. Grant*, 2:151n–52n.

4. The young, keen-eyed Kentucky surgeon Lunsford P. Yandell, Jr., wrote to his sister Sally describing Thompson as a "'slopsided, stoop-shouldered, hatchet-faced, hook-nosed' man who rode a 'circus-looking horse' and whose constant companion was an Indian dressed in ceremonial regalia and armed with a 'tommehawk and scalping knife.'" L. P. Yandell, Jr., to Sally Yandell, Sept. 14, 1861, in Baird, "No Sunday," p. 320; Evans, *Confederate Military History*, 9:67–68; *Daily Missouri Republican*, (St. Louis) Oct. 10, 1861.

5. Kinnison ms., SHC.

6. Thompson Reminiscences, SHC; U. S. Grant to John Cunningham Kelton, Aug. 16, 1861, de Coppet Collection, PU; Kinnison ms., SHC; *OR*, 3:206–26, 235–36; Catton, *Terrible Swift Sword*, pp. 38–39, 43, 67; Grant, *Memoirs*, 1:261; Monaghan, *Swamp Fox*, pp. 30–40.

7. Eaton, *Confederacy*, pp. 34–35; McFeely, *Grant*, p. 91; *OR*, 3:142–43;

McPherson, *Battle Cry of Freedom*, p. 295, 295n; G. J. Pillow to L. Polk, Aug. 28, 1861, Snyder Collection, UMKC; G. J. Pillow to L. P. Walker, Sept. 1, 1861, CSA Papers, DU; Catton, *Grant*, p. 42; Coulter, *Civil War*, p. 110; Stickles, *Buckner*, p. 87; Williams, *Lincoln Finds a General*, 3:53, 55; Hall Allen, *Center of Conflict*, pp. 22–27.

8. McPherson, *Battle Cry of Freedom*, p. 296.

9. Harrison, *Civil War in Kentucky*, p. 12; Connelly, *Army of the Heartland*, p. 53; Sept. 2–19, 1861, entries, Edenton Diary, TSLA; E. G. W. Butler, Jr., to Frances Parke Lewis Butler, Sept. 27, 1861, Butler Family Papers, HNO; Davis, *Rise and Fall*, 1:387–89, 391, 393–96; Catton, *Terrible Swift Sword*, p. 38.

10. Western Department, Telegrams, NARS; Grant, *Memoirs*, 1:264–67; Simon, *Papers of Ulysses S. Grant*, 2:190, 192n; Hall Allen, *Center of Conflict*, pp. 22–27; E. B. Long, "Ulysses S. Grant for Today," in David L. Wilson and Simon, *Ulysses S. Grant*, p. 14.

11. Solomon Scrapbook, DU.

12. *OR*, 3:197–215.

13. Walke came to agree with his superior, Capt. A. H. Foote, and his colleague, Comdr. W. D. Porter, about the feasibility and "necessity" of attacking Polk "with a combined army and naval force." Conger, *Rise of U. S. Grant*, pp. 82–84; U.S. Government, *Union and Confederate Navies*, 22:430.

14. Eddy, *Patriotism*, 1:170; Simon, *Papers of Ulysses S. Grant*, 2:306, 3:27; *OR*, 3:142–43, 168–69, 197–200, 480–81; U.S. Government, *Civil War Chronology*, 1:28; R. J. Oglesby to U. S. Grant, Sept. 16, 1861, District of Southeast Missouri, Letters Received, NARS; *Daily Missouri Republican* (St. Louis), Sept. 30, 1861; U.S. Government, *Union and Confederate Navies*, 22:389; Williams, *Lincoln Finds a General*, 3:53–55; Connelly, *Army of the Heartland*, p. 103; *Nashville Banner*, Nov. 26, 1861.

15. *OR*, 3:168–69.

16. U. S. Grant to Julia Grant, Oct. 20, 1861, in Simon, *Papers of Ulysses S. Grant*, 3:63–64; U. S. Grant to Mary Frances Grant, Oct. 25, 1861, de Coppet Collection, PU; Catton, *Terrible Swift Sword*, p. 67; Fiske, *Mississippi Valley*, p. 44; U. S. Grant to John C. Frémont, Sept. 12, 1861, in Simon, *Papers of Ulysses S. Grant*, 2:241–42; *OR*, 3:149; Conger, *Rise of U. S. Grant*, pp. 82–83; U.S. Government, *Union and Confederate Navies*, 22:430.

CHAPTER 2

1. Fiske, *Mississippi Valley*, p. 43; Eddy, *Patriotism*, 1:178–79; McFeely, *Grant*, pp. 45–90; Chetlain, *Recollections*, p. 93.

2. McPherson, *Battle Cry of Freedom*, p. 296.

3. Williams, *Lincoln Finds a General*, 3:20; McPherson, *Battle Cry of Freedom*, p. 395. By the middle of May, Grant's regiment needed to be reenlisted. Grant felt he could not make an effective appeal himself, so he wisely recruited

two Illinois congressmen, two war Democrats. John A. McClernand spoke to the men with patriotic eloquence, but it was John A. Logan from the southern part of the state, "Egypt," who roused the regiment with a highly emotional plea that brought the 21st "almost to a man into Federal service for three years."

4. McFeely, *Grant*, pp. 2, 73, 76–90; Catton, *Grant*, p. 3; Brinton, *Memoirs*, pp. 37–38; Catton, *Never Call Retreat*, p. 298; *Nashville Banner*, Oct. 1, 1861.

5. Dell, *Lincoln*, p. 74.

6. Longacre, "Congressman Becomes General," p. 30; U.S. Government, *Biographical Directory*, p. 1523; Hicken, "From Vandalia to Vicksburg," pp. 23, 32–76.

7. McClernand, Autobiography, CHS.

8. *Chicago Daily Tribune*, Jan. 21, 1861; Potter, *Impending Crisis*, pp. 388–390; Dell, *Lincoln*, p. 75; Johanssen, *Douglas*, pp. 855, 862; Hicken, "House Speakership Struggle," pp. 120–25; Sandburg, *Lincoln*, 2:109–10, 114; Dell, *Lincoln*, pp. 38–39.

9. Thomas and Hyman, *Stanton*, p. 265; Liddell Hart, *Sherman*, p. 128; "McClernand," Schwartz Collection, and "Biography of McClernand," Wallace Papers, ISHL.

10. "McClernand," Schwartz Collection, ISHL; Carter, *Final Fortress*, pp. 85–86.

11. Dee Alexander Brown, *Grierson's Raid*, p. 106; Hicken, "From Vandalia to Vicksburg," pp. 4, 37, 122–23, 285; Longacre, "Congressman Becomes General," p. 30; "Biography of McClernand," Wallace Papers, ISHL; Milton, *Eve of Conflict*, pp. 405, 407, 431; Lewis, *Sherman*, p. 260; Carter, *Final Fortress*, p. 42.

12. Sandburg, *Lincoln*, 2:109–10, 114; McCartney, *Grant and His Generals*, p. 237; Sword, *Shiloh*, p. 36; Hicken, "From Vandalia to Vicksburg," pp. 122–40; Liddell Hart, *Sherman*, p. 128; Longacre, "Congressman Becomes General," p. 30; Catton, *This Hallowed Ground*, p. 196; Simon, "McClernand," p. 456.

13. Grant to McClernand, Oct. 21, 1861: "I am suddenly called to St. Louis and shall leave this evening by special train. In my absence the command of the District is in your hands. I am satisfied that it could not be in better."

McClernand to Grant, Oct. 21, 1861: "I acknowledge the obligation imposed by the confidence which you are pleased to repose in me. While I cannot expect to equal, or even approximate the merit of your military administration, you may rest assured that I will do all in my power to justify your expectations of me and to insure success." Simon, *Papers of Ulysses S. Grant*, 3:67, 67n.

14. Mark E. Neely, Jr., director of the Louis A. Warren Lincoln Library and Museum, after examining Lincoln's letters regarding Bielaski and his daughters Rosie and Agnes found in Basler, Pratt, and Dunlaps's *Collected Works of Abraham Lincoln*, and noting that no Bielaski letters appear in the Lincoln Papers at the Library of Congress, believes that the relationship was

not close, indeed probably remote. "Lincoln tended not to be guarded in such letters, but he always chose his words carefully. If the man had been a good or close friend, he'd [Lincoln] have said so. And if Bielaski had been his friend since 1845, Lincoln probably wouldn't have said, 'I knew [him] in Illinois, more than twenty years ago.' The reason Lincoln gives for the favor is Bielaski's patriotic martyrdom and not one of a more personal nature." Mark E. Neely, Jr., to author, Sept. 1, 1989. Nevertheless, the story of their friendship persists. "Forgotten Likeness," p. 15.

15. James Grant Wilson, *Sketches*, pp. 30, 83; Bailache-Brayman Family Papers, ISHL; Rawlings, "Polish Exiles in Illinois," pp. 97–98; J. A. McClernand to Mrs. A. Bielaski, Nov. 8, 1861, McClernand Papers, ISHL; Levene, "Illinois Catholics," p. 18; Mrs. Alexander Bielaski Pension Application, NARS; "Forgotten Likeness," p. 15; J. A. McClernand to Gov. Richard Yates, Yates Papers, ISHL; A. Lincoln to Simeon Cameron, Aug. 10, 1861, A. Lincoln to Salmon P. Chase, Mar. 11, 1864, in Basler, Pratt, and Dunlaps, *Works of Abraham Lincoln*, 4:480, 5:230.

CHAPTER 3

1. Mark Twain described the river differently: "The Mississippi is a just and equitable river; it never tumbles one man's farm overboard without building a new farm just like it for that man's neighbor. This keeps down hard feelings." Roth, "Civil War at the Confluence," p. 13; Twain, *Life on the Mississippi*, p. 203.

2. Brinton, *Memoirs*, pp. 49–53; *Daily Missouri Republican* (St. Louis), Nov. 7, 1861; John Alexander Logan, *Volunteer Soldier*, pp. 109–15; Crippin, "Diary"; McPherson, *Battle Cry of Freedom*, p. 392; Hall Allen, *Center of Conflict*, pp. 14–15.

Over a century later Cairo, although it still "bills itself as the 'Gateway to the South,'" finds itself plagued with economic and racial problems and appears to an observer as "a town gasping for air." Wade, "Prospects for Cairo."

3. This area of southern Illinois gained its name when the people were spared from the widespread crop failures occurring around them in the early part of the nineteenth century. They had grain and people came to them to be fed. The area is dotted with towns named Thebes and Karnak underlining the tradition. A less charitable interpretation might be that Egypt had a biblical reputation for backwardness.

4. Hicken, *Illinois*. For a discussion of these perilous and adventurous times in Egypt, see Erwin, *Williamson County*; for McClernand's counter subversive measures in Cairo, see McClernand Papers, ISHL.

5. Mrs. John Alexander Logan, "Illinois," p. 234.

6. Snyder, "Charles Dickens," pp. 10–12.

7. U.S. Government, *Biographical Directory*, p. 1177; *Journal of the Illinois*

Historical Society 5:66, 17:503; Nebelsick, *History of Belleville*, p. 40; P. B. Fouke to William T. Avery, July 26, 1862, Gordon and Avery Papers, TSLA; Dell, *Lincoln*, p. 44; Bateman, *Illinois*, pp. 174–75.

8. Eddy, *Patriotism*, 2:145–46; Illinois AGO, *Report*, 2:503–38.

9. John Alexander Logan, *Volunteer Soldier*, pp. 109–25; Adams, "Memoirs," ISHL; Brinton, *Memoirs*, pp. 60–64; Crippin, "Diary."

10. John Alexander Logan, *Volunteer Soldier*, pp. 115–30; D. W. Poak to S. J. Poak, Oct. 30, 1861, Poak Papers, ISHL; Capt. J. M. Dresser to J. A. McClernand, Nov. 8, 1861, McClernand Papers, ISHL.

11. Morris, Kuykendall, and Harwell, *31st Regiment*, pp. 19–20.

12. Illinois AGO, *Report*, 2:539–73; Morris, Kuykendall, and Harwell, *31st Regiment*, pp. 9, 12–15; Hicken, *Illinois*, p. 20; Eddy, *Patriotism*, 2:148–49; James P. Jones, *"Black Jack,"* pp. 106–7; J. H. White to family, Nov. 3, 1861, USAMHI.

13. James P. Jones, *"Black Jack,"* pp. 6–11, 14–35; Castel, "Black Jack Logan," pp. 4–6; George W. Smith, *Southern Illinois*, 1:327; John Alexander Logan, *Volunteer Soldier*, pp. 40, 59–62; Milton, *Eve of Conflict*, p. 431; Dawson, *Logan*, p. 45–61; Eisenschimml, *Fitz John Porter*, p. 257; Sandburg, *Lincoln*, 1:334; Eidson, "Logan," pp. 1, 5–6, 11.

14. James P. Jones, *"Black Jack,"* pp. 11, 14, 46, 55–123; Warner, *Generals in Blue*, pp. 281–83; U.S. Government, *Biographical Directory*, p. 1472; John Alexander Logan, *Volunteer Soldier*, pp. 59–71; Castel, "Black Jack Logan," pp. 4–6; Johanssen, *Douglas*, pp. 661, 721, 862; Eidson, "Logan," pp. 5–16; Milton, *Eve of Conflict*, pp. 431, 520, 565, 565n; Dell, *Lincoln*, pp. 33, 34, 57, 59; Simon, *Papers of Ulysses S. Grant*, 3:102n; Grant, *Memoirs*, 1:244, 246; Sewell, "Loyalty," pp. 16–19.

15. John W. Allen, *Legends*, pp. 28–29; Brinkman, "They Wronged John A. Logan," p. 159; Warner, *Generals in Blue*, pp. 281–83; Williams, *Lincoln Finds a General*, 5:75; Castel, "Black Jack Logan," pp. 4, 6, 45; McCartney, *Grant and His Generals*, pp. 101–2, 104; Liddell Hart, *Sherman*, pp. 255, 285; Shanks, *Recollections*, pp. 307, 308, 311; James P. Jones, *"Black Jack,"* pp. 87–117.

16. W. H. Onstot to Lizzie Onstot, Oct. 27, 1861, Onstot Papers, ISHL; Mary Ann G. Buford to Dr. W. M. Polk, Feb. 19, 1864, Polk Papers, UNSO.

17. James Grant Wilson, *Sketches*, pp. 21–22; Warner, *Generals in Blue*, pp. 53–54; Bateman, *Illinois*, p. 65; Sears, "Sears," pp. 309, 311.

18. Thomas and Hyman, *Stanton*, p. 189.

19. John Rawlins to Elihu B. Washburne, n.d., in Simon, *Papers of Ulysses S. Grant*, 7:302n; Browning, *Diary*, 1:591; Brinton, *Memoirs*, p. 56.

20. A letter from a Private Trueman to Elizabeth Simpson is one of the finest and most reliable accounts of the 27th Illinois and of Belmont. Trueman, however, remains a mystery. He does not show up in the muster rolls of the 27th, nor does he seem to have a military service record, nor does he appear in pension application files or U.S. Army enlistment papers. Perhaps he signed

the letter using a name other than his own, or perhaps he belonged to or is listed in another regiment. There is little doubt, however, about the authenticity of Trueman's battle observations or of the map he drew on the back of the letter. Private Trueman to Elizabeth Simpson, Nov. 11, 1861, Simpson Letters, ISHL.

21. Illinois AGO, *Report*, 2:389–416; Crippin, "Diary," pp. 220–21; Browning, *Diary*, 1:508; U.S. Government, *Biographical Directory*, p. 1261; Jansen Reminiscences, ISHL.

22. Crippin, "Diary," p. 230.

23. Brinton, *Memoirs*, pp. 49–55; Henry I. Smith, *Seventh Iowa*, p. 9; Adams, "Memoirs," ISHL; Ingersoll, *Iowa*, p. 128; Upham, "Iowa," pp. 37, 39.

24. *OR*, 3:528.

25. J. A. McClernand to N. B. Buford, n.d., McClernand Papers, ISHL; Morris, Kuykendall, and Harwell, *31st Regiment*, pp. 19, 22; Henry I. Smith, *Seventh Iowa*, p. 6; Upham, "Iowa," p. 22; *OR*, 3:287, 289; Ingersoll, *Iowa*, p. 128; Seaton, "Belmont," p. 318; A. Bielaski to J. A. McClernand, Oct. 30, 1861, McClernand Papers, ISHL.

26. Simon, *Papers of Ulysses S. Grant*, 3:70–76; Crippin, "Diary," p. 231.

27. Ingersoll, *Iowa*, pp. 128–30; Leonard Brown, *American Patriotism*, pp. 164–66; Henry I. Smith, *Seventh Iowa*, pp. 15–19; Iowa AGO, *Report*, pp. 80–81; Upham, "Iowa," pp. 22, 37, 39; Iowa AGO, *Roster and Record*, 2:911, 922–23.

28. Warner, *Generals in Blue*, pp. 275–76, 399–400; Stuart, *Iowa Colonels*; Henry I. Smith, *Seventh Iowa*, pp. 18–22; *Burlington* (Iowa) *Hawk-Eye*, Apr. 18, 1862, quoted in Throne, "Lauman," p. 273; Peter Wilson to father, Mar. 11, 1862, in *Iowa Journal of History and Politics* 40 (July 1942): 280; Briggs, "Enlistment of Iowa Troops," pp. 334–37; Byers, *Iowa*, p. 82; Rebecka McMurty Roberts Pension Application, NARS; Iowa AGO, *Roster and Record*, 2:921.

29. D. W. Poak to S. J. Poak, Poak Papers, ISHL; Adams, "Memoirs," ISHL; Seaton, "Belmont," p. 307; *Weekly Missouri Democrat* (St. Louis), Nov. 19, 1861; Grant, *Memoirs*, 1:269.

CHAPTER 4

1. In years the fifty-five-year-old Polk was hardly an old man, but he was considered "old" because the Civil War was a young man's fight; young soldiers were commanded by young generals. To be sure there were a dozen generals born in the eighteenth century, but all except Samuel Cooper faded away. Even forty-eight-year-old St. John R. Liddell wrote home, depressed "to think that I must be getting to *look* old." St. John R. Liddell to Mary M. Liddell, Feb. 18, 1863, Liddell Family Papers, LSU.

2. *New York Herald* clipping, n.d., Solomon Scrapbook, DU; Parks, *Polk*,

pp. 115–17; Brinton, *Memoirs*, p. 57; *Nashville Banner*, Nov. 13, 1861; *Daily Missouri Republican* (St. Louis), Sept. 29, 1861; W. H. L. Wallace to Ann Wallace, Nov. 14, 1861, Wallace-Dickey Papers, ISHL; Rennolds, *Henry County Commands*, p. 28; Stevenson, *Thirteen Months*, p. 77.

3. Keating, *Memphis*, 1:498; McIlvaine, "Polk," pp. 375, 379; Perry, *American Episcopal Church*, 2:563.

4. Polk, *Polk*, 1:17–65; Roland, *Johnston*, p. 15; Parks, *Polk*, pp. 36–44, 115–116; *Journal of Southern History* 15:19; McIlvaine, "Polk," pp. 375, 379.

5. Polk, *Polk*, 1:359.

6. Parks, *Polk*, pp. 168–70, 539; *OR*, 4:522, 539; L. Polk to Frances D. Polk, June 10, 19, 22, 1861, Polk Papers, UNSO; L. Polk to Rev. Stephen Elliott, June 20, 1861, J. Davis to W. M. Polk, Dec. 15, 1879, Polk Papers, SHC; Polk, *Polk*, 1:358–59; Horn, *Army of Tennessee*, p. 49; Rev. W. Meade to L. Polk, Nov. 15, 1861, Rev. Stephen Elliott to L. Polk, Aug. 6, 1861, Polk Papers, UNSO; William Mercer Green, *Otey*, p. 99.

7. Fiske, *Mississippi Valley*, pp. 40–41.

8. Although it was not possible to substantiate Fiske's statement, record was found of John Margetson, bishop of Armagh, who met his end during the siege of Limerick in 1691.

9. Parks, *Polk*, pp. 115–16; Spence, "Polk," p. 373.

10. William Mercer Green, *Otey*, p. 93; Keating, *Memphis*, 1:498; *OR*, 4:396; Joseph Jones to Frances D. Polk, Mar. 26, 1870, Polk Papers, UNSO.

11. *New York Herald* clipping, fall 1861, Solomon Scrapbook, DU; *Nashville Banner*, Nov. 13, 1861; Stevenson, *Thirteen Months*, p. 63; U.S. Government, 1860 Census, Maury County, Tennessee; Erickson, "Hunting for Cotton," p. 497; Pillow Letters, HSP; Livingston, *Sketches*, 1:691–92.

12. Adding to the gall of Pillow's defeat by Andrew Johnson were three articles appearing in the *Nashville Banner* authored by Simon B. Buckner. They were "masterpieces of gibes, ridicule, irony and sarcasm." Why Albert Sidney Johnston entrusted these two enemies with the fate of Fort Donelson, when it was common knowledge they could never be expected to cooperate, challenges one's imagination. Stickles, *Buckner*, pp. 40–41; Hamilton, *Fort Donelson*, p. 48.

13. G. J. Pillow to Dixon J. Allen, Aug. 5, 1831, CSA Papers, DU; Graf, *Papers of Andrew Johnson*, 3:615n; J. H. Otey to G. J. Pillow, June 7, 1841, Dreer Collection, HSP; Pillow, *Speech*; Pillow Papers, MHS; Bell, "Pillow," p. 13; Jefferson Davis note, Nov. 11, 1856, in Crist, *Papers of Jefferson Davis*, 6:514–15; Stonesifer, "Pillow," pp. 340–43.

14. Livingston, *Sketches*, 1:692–716; Justin H. Smith, *War with Mexico*, 2:56–57, 151–214, 437n; Frost, *Mexican War*, pp. 78–79; Pillow Correspondence, NYHS; Hogan, "Lonely Grave"; Lewis, *Captain Sam Grant*, p. 164; *Memphis Daily Enquirer*, June 4, 1847; *American Eagle* (Vera Cruz, Mex.), May 5, 1847.

15. Bell, "Pillow," pp. 13–14, 19; Shanks, *Recollections*, p. 274; Eckenrode,

McClellan, p. 20; Smith, *War with Mexico*, 2:377, 437n; Lew Wallace, "Capture of Ft. Donelson," 401; Jan. 31, 1864, entry, in Gorgas, *Civil War Diary*.

16. Cooling, "Pillow," 3:862–63; Catton, *Grant Moves South*, p. 34.

17. Sandburg, *Lincoln*, 1:466. When Grant met with Simon B. Buckner following the surrender of Fort Donelson, he asked about Pillow. "Where is he now?" "Gone," Buckner responded. "He thought you'd rather get hold of him than any other man in the Southern Confederacy." "Oh," replied Grant, "if I had got him I'd let him go again. He will do us more good commanding you fellows." "This made us both laugh, for we remembered Pillow in the Mexican War," Buckner thought. McFeely, *Grant*, p. 102.

18. L. P. Yandell, Jr., to L. P. Yandell, Sr., Dec. 15, 1861, Yandell Family Papers, FC; John F. Henry to mother, Oct. 31, 1861, Henry Papers, SHC; Montgomery, *Reminiscences*, p. 61.

19. T. C. Reynolds to W. J. Hardee, Aug. 25, 1861, Hardee Papers, HL.

20. Johnson, "Reminiscences," TSLA.

21. McMurry, *Two Great Rebel Armies*, pp. 78–86.

22. *Battlefields of the South*, p. 121.

23. E. G. W. Butler, Jr., to Frances Parke Lewis Butler, Sept. 27, 1861, Butler Family Papers, HNO.

CHAPTER 5

1. On April 22, 1861, one week after the attack on Fort Sumter, the Mobile and Ohio opened for traffic at Columbus. Roth, "Civil War at the Confluence," p. 7.

2. Catton, *This Hallowed Ground*, p. 70; Long, "The Paducah Affair," p. 255.

3. *New Orleans Daily Crescent*, Oct. 24, 1861.

4. Frank Moore, *Rebellion Record*, 5:223–26; Rosser, "Battle," p. 33; Stevenson, *Thirteen Months*, pp. 65–66; Mullen, "Turning of Columbus," p. 218; James L. Nichols, *Confederate Engineers*, p. 51; Hall Allen, *Center of Conflict*, pp. 19–20.

5. Pillow had positioned a similar chain at Fort Pillow in July, and although it was swept downstream, he did not lose faith and convinced Polk to try it again. Irreverent enlisted men called it "Pillow's Trot Line." Stevenson, *Thirteen Months*, pp. 59, 66; Simon, *Papers of Ulysses S. Grant*, 3:55; *CV* 34:221; Hall Allen, *Center of Conflict*, p. 19.

6. *Daily Missouri Republican* (St. Louis), Sept. 29, 1861; *New York Herald* clipping, n.d., Solomon Scrapbook, DU.

7. John F. Henry to mother, Oct. 31, 1861, Henry Papers, SHC.

8. In January 1862 Polk would add a further defensive refinement, planting mines "out in the roads." Stevenson, *Thirteen Months*, p. 65; July 21, 1861–July 28, 1863, entries, Harper Diary, USAMHI; Frank Moore, *Rebel-*

lion Record, 5:223–26; *OR*, 3:343; Nov. 2, 3, 1861, entries, Dillon Diary, in personal collection of Mrs. N. E. Ward, Prescott, Ark.; Walke, "Gun-boats," p. 360.

9. Memphis citizens poured out in support of the war effort, eventually supplying fifty companies of troops, about 5,000 men out of a population, black and white, of some 23,000. No city of its size "furnished so large a proportion of the adult male inhabitants to the armies of the South." Young, *Memphis*, p. 337; *OR*, 53:730, 723.

10. *New York Herald* clipping, n.d., Solomon Scrapbook, DU.

11. *Daily Missouri Republican* (St. Louis), Sept. 29, 1861.

12. J. Davis to L. Polk, Sept. 2, 1861, Polk Papers, UNSO.

13. Lindsley, *Annals*, pp. 207–8.

14. W. W. Searcy to E. H. East, Jr., Apr. 30, 1861, Confederate Collection, TSLA.

15. Winters, *Civil War in Louisiana*, pp. 23–24.

16. W. W. Mackall to wife, June 7, 1864, Mackall Papers, SHC.

17. *New Orleans Daily Crescent*, Oct. 14, 21, 1861.

18. Ibid., Sept. 26, 1861.

19. Ibid., Oct. 21, 1861.

20. R. H. Wood to Mary Wood, Nov. 25, 1861, Wood Letters, TSLA.

21. C. J. Johnson to Lou Johnson, Nov. 17, 1861, Johnson Letters, LSU.

22. *New Orleans Daily Crescent*, Oct. 29, 1861.

23. Ibid., fall 1861.

24. Ibid., Nov. 2, 11, 1861; Johnson Letters, LSU.

25. Conrad, *Louisiana Biography*, 1:549; Frank L. Richardson to father, Sept. 4, 1861, Richardson Letters, EU; Winters, *Civil War in Louisiana*, pp. 23–24; *Louisiana Genealogical Register* 17:62; *CV* 1:172; *Louisiana Historical Quarterly* 25:680, 1039; Sword, *Shiloh*, p. 454; Johnson Letters, LSU.

26. Arthur W. Bergeron, Jr., *Louisiana Confederate Military Units*, pp. 98–99; Evans, *Confederate Military History*, 10:337–38; Floyd, *Barrow Family*, pp. 17, 35–37, 40–61.

27. Speer, *Sketches*, pp. 194–96; Lindsley, *Annals*, p. 309; Caldwell, *Bench and Bar*, pp. 309–11.

28. Lufkin, "Divided Loyalties," p. 175.

29. John Vines Wright, Speech, Apr. 13, 1907, Wright Scrapbooks, SHC.

30. Wakelyn, *Biographical Directory*, p. 499; U.S. Government, *Biographical Directory*, p. 2047; Evans, *Confederate Military History*, 10:797–98; Wright, *Tennessee in the War*, p. 99; Speer, *Sketches*, pp. 97–99, 524–26; Vaughan, *Thirteenth Regiment*, pp. 83–84.

31. A. J. Vaughan to Elliott Danforth, Confederate Collection, TSLA; Evans, *Confederate Military History*, 10:337–39; Warner, *Generals in Gray*, pp. 315–316; Sword, *Shiloh*, p. 196.

32. *New York Herald* clipping, n.d., Solomon Scrapbook, DU; *OR*, 4:503, 533; E. G. W. Butler, Jr., to Frances Parke Lewis Butler, Sept. 27, 1861, Butler

Family Papers, HNO; Oct. and Nov. entries, Dillon Diary, in personal collection of Mrs. N. E. Ward, Prescott, Ark.; *New Orleans Daily Crescent*, Oct. 21, 29, 1861; *Nashville Banner*, Sept. 26, 1861.

CHAPTER 6

1. *OR*, 3:267.

2. Ibid., 268.

3. U. S. Grant to R. J. Oglesby, Nov. 2, 1861, in Simon, *Papers of Ulysses S. Grant*, 3:105, 105n; Fiske, *Mississippi Valley*, p. 46; Kinnison ms., SHC.

4. Thompson Reminiscences, SHC.

5. This telegram, so crucial to the campaign, has never been found. Grant scholar John Y. Simon thinks it is "more than odd that this telegram was not officially mentioned until 1865, four years after the battle," when Grant's staff submitted a revised report of the battle of Belmont. He feels the telegram "was extrapolated by Grant's staff from the nature of the orders Grant wrote that day and the next; in any case it is almost surely nonexistent." On the other hand, W. C. C., the correspondent in Cairo for the *Louisville Journal*, wrote a week following the battle of Belmont: "I was shown a letter in Gen. Grant's quarters to-day from Assistant Adjutant-General McKeever directing him to move only against Belmont and avoid Columbus." Then there is McKeever's statement, "Genl. Grant did not follow his instructions. No orders were given to attack Belmont or Columbus." Further speculation is futile, and the most balanced view is that of John Simon: "Because of the contradictory nature of the sources, it appears impossible to reconcile the divergent interpretations of USG's motives in attacking Belmont. A close look at the documentary evidence, however, casts such doubt on the alleged telegram of Nov. 5 and the message of 2 A.M., Nov. 7, as to suggest that no satisfactory explanation can be found by examining the orders of USG's superiors or the actions of his opponents. The answer must be found in USG himself, and no simple answer will do." Simon, "Grant at Belmont," p. 163; Frank Moore, *Rebellion Record*, 3:288; *OR*, 3:268, 53:507; Simon, *Papers of Ulysses S. Grant*, 3:152n; *Louisville Daily Journal*, Nov. 15, 1861.

6. *OR*, 3:273. It is interesting to note that even Confederate officers knew four days after the battle of Belmont that the Federals "had heard the bulk of the [Confederate] army had moved off to the interior leaving an inconsiderable garrison in Columbus. A simultaneous attack was to be made on both sides of the river." R. H. Wood to Mary Wood, Nov. 10, 1861, Wood Letters, TSLA.

7. Brig. Gen. C. F. Smith to U. S. Grant, Nov. 6, 1861, District of Southeast Missouri, Letters Received, NARS.

8. *OR*, 3:269. Kenneth P. Williams goes to great pains to explain why Grant changed Oglesby's direction of march and ordered Oglesby to contact him "at Belmont," all the while maintaining that Grant did not set out from Cairo with

the intention of attacking Belmont. Williams, *Lincoln Finds a General*, 3:81–83.

9. Grant, Letters Sent, NARS; Kinnison ms., SHC.

10. Simon, *Papers of Ulysses S. Grant*, 3:121–22.

11. Thompson Reminiscences, SHC.

12. An interesting comment, though of uncertain reliability, comes from Charles M. Scott, the Irish pilot of the *Belle Memphis*: "On the second day after our return from Commerce [transporting Oglesby's command], Capt. Curry, the federal scout, reported that there was one [Confederate] regiment on the Belmont side of the river and that two or three others were under orders to cross the river next day and take the Cape Girardeau road to where it crossed the road from Commerce to Bloomfield." Such a move, of course, would have struck Oglesby's column in the flank and rear, so, according to Scott, this intelligence caused Grant to gather the five largest steamers to carry his troops immediately against Belmont and to wire Smith in Paducah to co-operate with a demonstration. *St. Louis Daily Missouri Republican*, Jan. 16, 1886.

Soldiers in the 22d Illinois watched a Confederate deserter, a German named William Alle, come into camp at Bird's Point and enlist with Grant's blessing. After Belmont they learned that Alle had come to Grant and told him of overhearing Confederate officers discussing how they would move across the Mississippi and help Sterling Price. They knew the Yankees in Cairo were "afraid to come down here." Grant told Alle to "keep complete silence" and find himself a place in the ranks of the 22d. Jansen Reminiscences, ISHL.

13. L. Polk to A. S. Johnston, Nov. 4, 1861, Leonidas Polk MSR, NARS; *OR*, 4:491, 513–17, 554.

14. Nov. 6, 1861, entries, Fielder Diary and Firth Diary, TSLA.

15. *OR*, 4:522.

16. Initially Grant had asked McClernand to ready one regiment but changed his mind later in the day and expanded the order to include all three of McClernand's infantry regiments and a cavalry company. U. S. Grant to J. A. McClernand, Nov. 5, 1861, Special Order 1496, McClernand Papers, ISHL; Simon, *Papers of Ulysses S. Grant*, 3:113, 115; *OR*, 3:296.

17. Crippin, "Diary," p. 231; Nov. 6, 1861 entry, Austin Diary, ISHL. Pilot Charles M. Scott wrote in a newspaper article in 1886 that he had discovered a plot to inform Polk of the Belmont strike and told Grant. Grant, puffing on his pipe, handled the situation calmly. Scott's accounts, however, are to be taken with extreme caution.

18. This steamer appears in accounts with the names *Belle Memphis, Memphis,* and *Belle of Memphis* used interchangeably.

19. *OR*, 3:283; *Daily Missouri Republican* (St. Louis), Nov. 9, 1861; Crippin, "Diary," p. 231; *Chicago Daily Tribune*, Nov. 11, 1861; Williams, *Lincoln Finds a General*, 3:90.

20. *Daily Missouri Republican* (St. Louis), Nov. 9, 1861; U.S. Government, *Medical and Surgical History*, 1 (appendix): 19.

21. Private Trueman to Elizabeth Simpson, Nov. 14, 1861, Simpson Letters, ISHL.

22. The *Taylor* transformed its name as well as its hull in the heat of 1861, using the less objectionable *Tyler*. Walke would slip from time to time and refer to his boat as the *Taylor* nevertheless.

23. Private Trueman to Elizabeth Simpson, Nov. 1861, Simpson Letters, ISHL; Nov. 6, 1861, entry, Austin Diary, ISHL; *OR*, 3:296.

24. L. Ozburn to Diza Ozburn, Nov. 10, 1861, Ozburn Letters, ISHL; Nov. 6, 1861, entry, Austin Diary, ISHL; *Daily Missouri Republican* (St. Louis), Nov. 10, 1861; *OR*, 3:278.

25. *Weekly Missouri Democrat* (St. Louis), Nov. 19, 1861; Jansen Reminiscences, ISHL.

26. Eleazer Paine's Brigade camped on Mayfield Creek that night, about eight miles east of Grant. Although Grant had pickets out, there appears to have been no effort to communicate with Paine's force.

27. *Daily Missouri Republican* (St. Louis), Nov. 15, 1861, Jan. 16, 1886; Walke, *Naval Scenes*, p. 33; Schwartz, Report, CHS; Grant, *Memoirs*, 1:271; Morris, Kuykendall, and Harwell, *31st Regiment*, p. 22; *OR*, 3:269, 275, 278; U.S. Government, *Medical and Surgical History*, 1 (Appendix): 18; Seaton, "Belmont," p. 308; Nov. 6, 1861, entry, Austin Diary, ISHL; Odum, "Reminiscences," ISHL.

28. Morris, Kuykendall, and Harwell, *31st Regiment*, p. 22; Marshall-Cornwall, *Grant*, p. 40; Robert Underwood Johnson amd Buel, *Battles and Leaders*, 1:360; *OR*, 3:269; U.S. Government, *Medical and Surgical History*, 1 (appendix): 18.

29. Nov. 6, 1861, entry, Austin Diary, ISHL.

30. *Reunions of Taylor's Battery*, p. 26.

31. Albert D. Richardson, *Grant*, p. 197; Seaton, "Belmont," p. 308; *OR*, 3:269.

32. Grant scholar John Simon emphasizes that the "authenticity of this message [from W. H. L. Wallace] must be viewed with deep suspicion." Simon, "Grant at Belmont," p. 165; *OR*, 3:269.

33. *OR*, 3:269; Grant, *Memoirs*, 1:271–72; Kurtz, "Belmont," p. 20; Parks, *Polk*, p. 190.

34. "Our soldiers and officers, from inactivity, had become clamorous for a battle," reported the *Weekly Missouri Democrat* (St. Louis), Nov. 19, 1861. Grant, *Memoirs*, 1:271.

35. Kinnison ms., SHC.

36. Williams, *Lincoln Finds a General*, 3:81.

37. Simon, *Papers of Ulysses S. Grant*, 3:150, 151.

38. Isabel Wallace, *Wallace*, p. 141.

39. McGhee, "Neophyte General," p. 480.

40. McFeely, *Grant*, p. 92.

41. Simon, *Papers of Ulysses S. Grant*, 3:151n.

42. Horn, *Army of Tennessee*, p. 64.

43. Kurtz, "Belmont," p. 19.

44. Simon, "Grant at Belmont," p. 164.

45. Ibid., p. 165.

46. *St. Louis Sunday Republican*, Nov. 10, 1861.

47. *Weekly Missouri Democrat* (St. Louis), Nov. 13, 1861. Capt. John Seaton, Company B, 22d Illinois, and others felt even after the landing later at Lucas Bend that they would be switching back to the Kentucky shore to attack Columbus at any moment. Seaton, "Belmont," p. 309. Even the *Memphis Avalanche* reported three days after the battle that it was "well understood" that the Federals planned to take Camp Johnston and erect fortifications "while seventeen regiments" attacked Columbus on the Kentucky side. *Memphis Avalanche*, Nov. 10, 1861.

48. Hicken, *Illinois*, p. 20; *Weekly Missouri Democrat* (St. Louis), Nov. 19, 1861; Albert D. Richardson, *Grant*, p. 197; Tom Arliskas to author, Nov. 28, 1988; *Frank Leslie's Illustrated Newspaper*, Nov. 1861, p. 195; *OR*, 3:237, 268–69, 22:397; Grant, *Memoirs*, 1:271; U. S. Grant to Julia Grant, Oct. 20, 1861, U. S. Grant to Jesse Root Grant, Nov. 8, 1861, in Simon, *Papers of Ulysses S. Grant*, 3:63–64, 137–38; Isabel Wallace, *Wallace*, p. 141; Badeau, *Grant*, 1:13–21; Catton, *Grant Moves South*, pp. 72–83; McGhee, "Neophyte General," pp. 468–72; Kurtz, "Belmont," pp. 19–20; Conger, *Rise of U. S. Grant*, p. 85; Kinnison ms., SHC; Marshall-Cornwall, *Grant*, pp. 38–40; *Daily Missouri Republican* (St. Louis), Nov. 9, 1861.

49. John J. Mudd to Telegraph Operator, Cairo, Ill., Nov. 6, 1861, McClernand Papers, ISHL.

50. U. S. Grant to J. B. Plummer, Nov. 7, 1861, in Simon, *Papers of Ulysses S. Grant*, 3:127; N. Perczel to R. Oglesby, Nov. 6, 1861, R. Oglesby to U. S. Grant, Nov. 6, 7, 1861, R. Oglesby to W. H. L. Wallace, Nov. 7, 1861, Oglesby Papers, ISHL.

51. Robert Underwood Johnson and Buel, *Battles and Leaders*, 1:360; Williams, *Lincoln Finds a General*, 3:83; U.S. Government, *Union and Confederate Navies*, 22:399–402. Capt. Andrew H. Foote, commanding the gunboat fleet and Walke's superior, expressed his displeasure to Gideon Welles about being the victim of Grant's secrecy. Grant had assured him that he would be informed "whenever any attack was made requiring the cooperation of the gunboats." Foote did not learn of the Belmont strike until after it had been completed.

52. McClernand Papers, ISHL; Union Battle Reports, NARS. This order organizing the expeditionary force was hand delivered by Rawlins and according to Dougherty was the first he knew of commanding the Second Brigade. *OR*, 3:270, 291.

53. Private Trueman to Elizabeth Simpson, Nov. 11, 1861, Simpson Letters, ISHL; Seaton, "Belmont," p. 309.

54. A *Chicago Journal* correspondent felt this delay destroyed Grant's design "to reach Belmont just before day light." Greeley, *American Conflict*, 1:595n.

55. *Daily Missouri Republican* (St. Louis), Jan. 16, 1886.

56. W. H. Onstot to Lizzie Onstot, Nov. 16, 1861, Onstot Papers, ISHL.

57. *OR*, 3:275; John A. McClernand, Report, CHS; *St. Louis Sunday Republican*, Nov. 10, 1861; *Daily Missouri Republican* (St. Louis), Nov. 14, 1861; Walke, *Naval Scenes*, pp. 38–39; "Biography of McClernand," Wallace Papers, ISHL; Brinton, *Memoirs*, p. 88.

58. "Biography of McClernand," Wallace Papers, ISHL; Brinton, *Memoirs*, p. 88.

59. Schwartz, Report, CHS.

60. Nov. 7, 1861, entry, Austin Diary, ISHL; U.S. Government, *Union and Confederate Navies*, 22:400–402; *OR*, 3:278; Brinton, *Memoirs*, p. 73; *Chicago Daily Tribune*, Nov. 11, 1861; White, "Diary," p. 646.

61. Brinton, *Memoirs*, p. 73.

62. White, "Diary," p. 646.

CHAPTER 7

1. Brinton, *Memoirs*, p. 76.

2. Walke, *Naval Scenes*, pp. 38–39; *OR*, 3:275–76; *New Orleans Daily Crescent*, Nov. 13, 1861.

3. Brinton saw the place in the bank where the second round hit and dispatched "two darkies" to dig it out. He paid $1.00 for the trophy, a "round conical shell about eighteen inches long filled with lead." Unhappily, safely back in Cairo, the ugly and extremely heavy curiosity became "an elephant on my hands." A correspondent aboard the *Aleck Scott* watched the same shot hit the bank three-quarters of a mile beyond the landing. According to Mr. Reeder, clerk of the *Scott*, the projectile dug into the earth ten feet. Brinton, *Memoirs*, p. 71; *St. Louis Sunday Republican*, Nov. 10, 1861; *Weekly Missouri Democrat* (St. Louis), Nov. 19, 1861.

4. Frank Moore, *Rebellion Record*, 5:224.

5. Ibid.; U.S. Government, *Union and Confederate Navies*, 22:400–402; Walke, "Gun-boats," p. 361.

6. Stanley, *Autobiography*, p. 175.

7. Walke, "Gun-boats," p. 361.

8. Boynton, *Navy*, 1:501; Eads, "Recollections," p. 338n; *OR*, 3:359; Scharf, *Confederate States Navy*, pp. 241–42; Gosnell, *Guns on Western Waters*, pp. 15–16; Walke, "Gun-boats," pp. 358–59; U.S. Government, *Union and Confederate Navies*, 23:395.

9. U.S. Government, *Union and Confederate Navies*, 22:400–402; *OR*, 3:276; *St. Louis Sunday Republican*, Nov. 10, 1861; J. B. Battle to Flora B. Turley, Nov. 9, 1861, in Rosser, "Battle," p. 33.

10. Henry Walke would become defensive about his performance at Belmont and after the war would contend that his report to Foote on November 9 contained inaccuracies. He said his second and third attacks were made in the afternoon rather than late morning and noon. Also he abandoned his station

in the middle of the river and returned to the landing only when he "perceived the firing stopped at Belmont." In any case, the *Cincinnati Daily Commercial* wrote that "the gunboats could not prevent the rebels from crossing below Belmont, as they could not pass their batteries at the town." Walke also reported firing over Belmont Point at the Confederate steamers bringing reinforcements, which drove the rebel commanders "to land their troops lower down; which was the very thing we desired to accomplish." According to Walke, captured rebels told him cannon fire from the gunboats cut holes in the hulls of transports as they crossed the river.

These disingenuous retorts by Walke are unsubstantiated in other accounts of the battle. The Confederates feared that the gunboats would intervene at any moment while their troops were being ferried across the river, but the gunboats remained tucked out of sight behind the point. The transports landed reinforcements not "lower down" but higher up, almost on Belmont Point itself. Walke, *Naval Scenes*, pp. 35–38, 37n.

CHAPTER 8

1. Capt. William L. Trask's boat was already loaded with commissary stores.

2. Company commander Capt. C. W. Frazer reported men in Freeman's 21st Tennessee were each issued forty cartridges. *OR*, 3:306, 355, 360, 362; Wright, "Belmont," p. 70; Polk, *Polk*, 1:306; Frazer Letter, Nov. 9, 1861, in personal collection of Thomas P. Sweeney, Springfield, Mo.; Johnson, "Reminiscences," TSLA.

3. *Daily Picayune* (New Orleans), Nov. 14, 1861; Wright, "Belmont," p. 70; Polk, *Polk*, 2:39; Evans, *Confederate Military History*, 10:162; Dillon Diary, in personal collection of Mrs. N. E. Ward, Prescott, Ark.; *New Orleans Daily Crescent*, Nov. 13, 1861; *OR*, 3:350, 353.

4. *Daily Picayune* (New Orleans), Nov. 14, 1861.

5. Trouble would plague Stewart's battery at Columbus. A week later a caisson would explode, burning severely two more members of the battery. *New Orleans Daily Crescent*, Nov. 13, 1861; Nov. 7, 1861, entry, Dillon Diary, in personal collection of Mrs. N. E. Ward, Prescott, Ark.; J. B. Battle to Flora B. Turley, Nov. 19, 1861, in Rosser, "Battle," pp. 23–24; *Memphis Avalanche*, Nov. 12, 1861; C. J. Johnson to Lou Johnson, Nov. 15, 1861, Johnson Letters, LSU.

6. *Daily Confederate News* (Columbus, Ky.), Nov. 12, 1861.

7. Dillon Diary, in personal collection of Mrs. N. E. Ward, Prescott, Ark.; *OR*, 3:276, 352–53; Walke, *Naval Scenes*, p. 42; *Daily Picayune* (New Orleans), Nov. 14, 1861; Claiborne Memoirs, USAMHI; *Daily Nashville Patriot*, Nov. 15, 1861.

8. G. J. Pillow to L. Polk, Nov. 6, 1861, W. W. Mackall to L. Polk, Nov. 4,

1861, Polk Papers, NARS; *CV* 16:345–46; Nov. 7, 1861, entry, Fielder Diary, TSLA; Singletary, "Belmont," p. 507; Ray Reminiscences, UAL; Carnes, "Belmont," p. 369.

9. Law, "Diary," p. 175; *CV* 2:105. Many were to call Sallie Gordon Law of Memphis "Mother of the Confederacy." "Over forty" members of her family were in the Confederate army, including her brother George W. Gordon of the 11th Tennessee, later a Confederate brigadier general and still later a member of Congress.

10. Nov. 1, 1861, entry, Fielder Diary, TSLA. Eight of the ten companies were from Gibson, another was from Dyer County, and still another, Company E, under Capt. Drew A. Outlaw, was a Kentucky company.

11. Robert Milton Russell (1825–93) has eluded Confederate chroniclers. Having graduated from West Point, class of 1848, he was somehow overlooked by the thorough Ellsworth Eliot. Until 1850 he served in the 5th Infantry at East Pascagoula, Miss.; Fort Towson, Indian Territory; and Benicia, Calif. This young lieutenant made a contribution to American place names while riding with a superior officer in California by suggesting that a mountain in the distance be named in honor of an officer named Whitney. Russell resigned from the army in 1850 to become a merchant and miner near Mariposa, Calif. From 1853 to 1855 he farmed in Austin, Tex., and is believed to have returned to Gibson County, Tenn., before the war began. He never achieved higher rank than colonel in the Confederate army although he rendered conspicuous service at Shiloh and seems to have served effectively as the commander of the 20th Tennessee Cavalry under Forrest. In the postwar era he lived in Trenton, Tenn., but he seems to have identified with California (Tyree Bell would also) and lived at least the last few years of his life in Tulare, Calif., with his two brothers. *Weekly Delta* (Visalia, Calif.), Jan. 17, 1886, Dec. 21, 1893; Menefee and Dodge, *Tulare and Kings Counties*; *Daily Confederate News* (Columbus, Ky.), Nov. 12, 1861; Tulare County, Calif., Death Certificates; Cadets Admitted, USMA; *CV* 6:529; Lindsley, *Annals*, p. 307; Cullom, *Biographical Register*, 358; Family Group Record, Robert M. Russell, in possession of Brent A. Cox, Milan, Tenn.; *Visalia* (Calif.) *Daily Times*, May 5, 1893; Stephenson, "My War Autobiography," LSU.

12. *OR*, 3:306, 361–62; Bell Report, SIU; *Memphis Daily Appeal*, Nov. 19, 1861; Nov. 7, 1861, entry, Fielder Diary, TSLA; U.S. Government, *Union and Confederate Navies*, 22:425.

13. At the same time that he offered his services to Davis, Beltzhoover approached the Louisiana State Seminary of Learning and Military Academy at Alexandria, Louisiana, seeking the position that William T. Sherman had resigned. Beltzhoover confessed he had also applied for a commission in the Confederate army. "I must obtain employment as soon as possible for the sake of my little children." D. Beltzhoover to George M. Graham, Apr. 12, 1861, Fleming Collection, LSU. *New Orleans Commercial Bulletin*, Nov. 19, 1870; *Daily Picayune* (New Orleans), Nov. 9, 1861; *New Orleans Bee*, n.d., quoted in

Daily Nashville Patriot, Nov. 14, 1861; Eliot, *West Point*, p. 300; General Order 6, Department of Louisiana, May 5, 1861, General Order 3, Department of Louisiana, May 31, 1861, D. Beltzhoover to Jefferson Davis, Mar. 1, 1861, Adj. Gen. M. Grivot to Jefferson Davis, Apr. 16, 1861, D. Beltzhoover to C. G. Memminger, Apr. 18, 1861, Compiled Service Records of Confederate Soldiers, NARS; C. C. Jones Notes, Jones Papers, DU; Heitman, *Historical Register*, 1:209.

14. Ivers represented the Tredegar Foundry of Richmond and subcontracted the manufacture of the guns to the company of John Clark in New Orleans.

15. Arthur W. Bergeron, Jr., *Louisiana Confederate Military Units*, pp. 36–37; *New Orleans Daily Crescent*, Oct. 29, 1861; *Daily Picayune* (New Orleans), Nov. 9, 1861; *New Orleans Bee*, n.d., quoted in *Daily Nashville Patriot*, Nov. 14, 1861; James W. Maddox, Confederate Questionnaire, MDAH; Daniel, *Cannoneers*, pp. 10, 16, 21–22; Goodspeed Publishing Company, *Memoirs of Mississippi*, pp. 992–96; Montgomery, *Reminiscences*, pp. 68–70; Sgt. Maj. Amelius M. Haydel to sister, Oct. 1, 1861, Andry Papers, LSU; Winters, *Civil War in Louisiana*, p. 38; Deupree, "Reminiscences," p. 23.

16. *New Orleans Daily Crescent*, Oct. 29, 1861.

17. *Daily Picayune* (New Orleans), Nov. 14, 1861; *New Orleans Daily Crescent*, Oct. 29, 1861. During these critical weeks, a bored Gus Watson decided to seek action with his friend Frank Montgomery, captain of the Bolivar Troop. On October 14, they managed to find a nice little fight just above Beckwith Farm. *OR*, 3:245.

18. This letter, well-known to the soldiers of the Army of Tennessee, was captured by Union soldiers at Belmont and published, not only embarrassing Colonel Beltzhoover at the moment but hanging over his head in the years to come. *St. Louis Sunday Republican*, Nov. 10, 1861; C. J. Johnson to Lou Johnson, Nov. 7, 1861, Johnson Letters, LSU.

19. Tappan's men knew Hunter's Farm well. "We took two or three trips 'foraging and scouting' in the interior, going several miles up the river to Col. Andrew or Daniel Hunter's farm. . . . That old farmer, Dan'l Hunter, was staunchly southern. When the battle came on, he gave all the information he could, scouting himself, and taking part, in his shirt sleeves and with a double barrelled shot gun. A big fat red faced determined looking, Israel Putnam like old fellow. I do not know what became of him. No doubt he was ruined, probably killed during the war. A typical Missouri Southerner!" Stephenson, "My War Autobiography," LSU.

20. Another dramatic report has the *Grampus*, the tiny Confederate gunboat that steamed between Columbus and Cairo, coming downriver "under full head of steam, whistle blowing all the while." Unfortunately no reliable substantiating reference to the *Grampus* being present at the time of the battle has been found. If the little black stern-wheeler had been available, surely the daring Capt. Marsh Miller would have had his two brass six-pounders "pop-

ping away." *CV* 16:191; Kinnison ms., SHC; Stephenson, "My War Autobiography," LSU.

21. *St. Louis Sunday Republican*, Nov. 10, 1861.

22. Hubbard, "Belmont," p. 459; Stephenson, "My War Autobiography," LSU; *OR*, 3:350, 355, 358, 360; Conger, *Rise of U.S. Grant*, p. 89; Evans, *Confederate Military History*, 10:61–62; Barnwell, "Belmont," p. 370; *Daily Picayune* (New Orleans), Nov. 17, 1861.

23. In his report Beltzhoover said three sections were made of the Watson Battery, each covering a road. Apparently contradicting Tappan's account of the dispositions, Beltzhoover probably meant that two of his sections, close together, commanded the Hunter's Farm Road that forked as it approached Belmont. *OR*, 3:360.

24. Tappan says his line was about 100 yards from the river. He must have meant the flank of the company on his extreme right, because he took position facing west beyond Camp Johnston, which would have placed him at least 400 yards from the riverbank. Ibid., 3:355.

25. Nine of the companies were made up "of Arkansas men: some companies out of the 'backwoods' and 'swamps,' hunters, trappers etc—unlettered, hardly knowing the use of shoes! Others from more settled portions . . . well mannered and often religious! Hymns and Prayer Meetings often would be heard from these latter. All of them made as fine fighting material as the world could produce." The tenth company, Company K, the Erin Guards, were Irish laborers who had been building levees on the Mississippi. In their midst were sprinkled thirty to forty men "run out" of St. Louis by the Yankees. Stephenson, "My War Autobiography," LSU.

26. Tappan, "Tappan"; Janie M. Nichols, "Tappan," pp. 330–32; Evans, *Confederate Military History*, 10:416–17; Eliot, *Yale*, pp. 66–68, 101; Wakelyn, *Biographical Directory*, p. 405; Hallum, *Arkansas*, pp. 450–51; Warner, *Generals in Gray*, pp. 298–99, Stephenson, "My War Autobiography," LSU.

27. In his report Pillow states he first put out skirmishers then formed his line of battle. Since he did not use skirmishers from the 12th Tennessee, the first to arrive, it would seem that the regiments (12th, 21st, and 22d at least) remained massed on the river for a while, perhaps until their officers found the positions they were to occupy and received their orders from Pillow. *OR*, 3:325.

28. Ibid., 3:325.

29. Nov. 7, 1861, entry, Fielder Diary, TSLA.

30. Kinnison ms., SHC.

31. *OR*, 3:358; Bell, Report, SIU; *Memphis Daily Appeal*, Nov. 10, 1861.

32. At this time Pillow returned to Tappan his three companies guarding Beltzhoover's guns.

33. Without comment Beltzhoover reported the critical shift ordered by Pillow, "uniting my battery at the edge of the woods and the bend of the right hand road from the usual landing of the enemy's gunboats." *OR*, 3:360.

34. *Memphis Daily Appeal*, Nov. 14, 1861.

35. *Daily Confederate News* (Columbus, Ky.), Nov. 12, 1861; Frazer Letter, Nov. 9, 1861, in personal collection of Thomas P. Sweeney, Springfield, Mo.; *Memphis Daily Appeal*, Nov. 10, 1861.

36. Kinnison ms., SHC.

37. *OR*, 3:325–26, 340–41; *Memphis Daily Appeal*, Nov. 19, 1861; Evans, *Confederate Military History*, 10:61–62; R. H. Wood to Mary Wood, Nov. 10, 1861, Wood Letters, TSLA; Kinnison ms., SHC.

38. Vaughan, *Thirteenth Regiment*, pp. 12–14, 73; *OR*, 3:333–35.

39. *OR*, 3:356; Deupree, "Noxubee Squadron," pp. 18–19.

40. Stephenson, "My War Autobiography," LSU.

41. "Peerless as a prince," Pickett "threw off brilliant editorials and many thunderbolts into the ranks of the old Whig party. Then he turned his attention to Blackstone and worked off many high pressure, polished forensics to the delight of his admirers." Hallum, *Arkansas*, p. 242; Tennessee Civil War Commission, *Tennesseans in the Civil War*, 1:219–20; *Nashville Union and American*, Nov. 12, 1861; Mathes, *Old Guard in Gray*, pp. 241, 274–75; Pickett MSR, NARS; Wingfield, *Memphis*, p. 17; *Mississippi Free Trader* (Natchez), Aug. 29, 1854.

42. *OR*, 3:350.

43. Ibid., 360.

44. Ibid., 325.

45. Ibid., 333, 358.

46. R. H. Wood to Mary Wood, Nov. 7, 1861, Wood Letters, TSLA; Polk, *Polk*, 1:354.

47. Conger, *Rise of U. S. Grant*, p. 90.

48. *OR*, 3:341.

49. Ibid., 342; Wright, "Belmont," 73; Polk, *Polk*, 1:354; Kinnison ms., SHC; Peter Franklin Walker, "Holding the Tennessee Line," p. 230.

CHAPTER 9

1. Private Trueman to Elizabeth Simpson, Nov. 11, 1861, Simpson Letters, ISHL.

2. Jansen Reminiscences, ISHL.

3. Brinton, *Memoirs*, pp. 70, 73–74.

4. *OR*, 3:149.

5. It would be more accurate, perhaps, to refer to this road as the Charleston Road, but since Grant called it the Bird's Point Road, it will be referred to by that name throughout. The Bird's Point Road ran roughly south to north; the Charleston Road, west to east.

6. Grant maintained he put Detrich in position himself. Captain Detrich, however, reported that he received his orders not from Grant but "from one of General Grant's aides."

7. Seaton, "Belmont," p. 310; *Chicago Daily Tribune*, Nov. 15, 1861; Grant, *Memoirs*, 1:272; Iowa AGO, *Roster and Record*, 1:911; *St. Louis Sunday Republican*, Nov. 10, 1861; *Daily Missouri Republican* (St. Louis), Nov. 14, 15, 1861; Austin Diary, ISHL; *OR*, 3:291, 294–96.

8. *Daily Missouri Republican* (St. Louis), Jan. 16, 1886; *Louisville Daily Journal*, Nov. 15, 1861.

9. *OR*, 3:278.

10. *Chicago Daily Tribune*, Nov. 15, 1861; *OR*, 4:174; *Daily Missouri Republican* (St. Louis), Nov. 15, 1861; *OR*, 3:278, 283.

11. Singletary, "Belmont," p. 506; Edward Prince to R. J. Oglesby, Dec. 7, 1861, in Simon, *Papers of Ulysses S. Grant*, 3:261n; Marshall-Cornwall, *Grant*, p. 40.

12. It would be difficult to overemphasize the density of the forest surrounding Belmont. Unlike the hilly Kentucky land across the river, the Belmont vicinity is "low-lying made-land. The river in ages gone by had moved to the eastward, and left behind the low, rich bottom land . . . generally heavily wooded. There are dense forests, few large farms, few and difficult roads." Kinnison ms., SHC.

13. A buttonwood is a large plane tree similar to a sycamore.

14. Singletary, "Belmont," p. 506; Nov. 6–7, 1861, entries, Fielder Diary, TSLA; *Daily Missouri Republican* (St. Louis), Nov. 7, 1861; Brinton, *Memoirs*, pp. 84–86; Grant, *Memoirs*, 1:272; Force, *Fort Henry to Corinth*, pp. 20–21.

15. Force, *Fort Henry to Corinth*, p. 21.

16. The very name of the place delighted John Fiske who could not resist the quip that Belmont received its grand name "on the same principle that will some times lead well-meaning parents to christen a little brunette daughter 'Blanche.'" Fiske did not realize, perhaps, the accuracy and irony of his aside. This humble steamboat landing with its two log cabins had been incorporated in 1854, named for the august American agent of the Rothchilds, and at the time of the battle belonged to the Belmont Company.

By 1895 Belmont's population would explode to 150. It became the southern terminus of the Iron Mountain Railroad, and a transfer steamer enabled trains to connect with the Mobile and Ohio. Repair shops, a roundhouse, a large grain elevator, and the Hotel Belmont showed the ambitions of speculators and promoters who believed "Belmont was intended to be the metropolis of the state." The Mississippi had other ideas. All that remains of Belmont at the close of the twentieth century is a forlorn relic of a grain elevator manacled with vines and a muddy bank that a ferry boat uses now and then. See Powell, *Mississippi County*, p. 156.

17. Survey of Belmont Peninsula, 1843; Mississippi County, Mo., Deed Book 4, p. 622.

18. In the 1850s ferry traffic increased with the establishment of the Belmont and Kentucky City Ferry Company. Roth, "Civil War at the Confluence," p. 11.

19. Before the end of the nineteenth century two railroads, the St.

Louis–Iron Mountain Railroad and the Cairo and Fulton Road, would extend to Belmont in order to connect with the Mobile and Ohio.

20. Catton, *Grant*, p. 71; Parks, *Polk*, p. 192; Kinnison ms., SHC; Marshall-Cornwall, *Grant*, p. 40; Powell, *Mississippi County*, p. 156; Brinton, *Memoirs*, p. 85; James P. Jones, *"Black Jack,"* p. 110; Hubbard, "Belmont," p. 459.

21. On the other hand the plank road could have been seen as a device of Polk's engineers giving Pillow's defenders a handy, concealed route by which to strike an encroaching amphibious force in the flank. Catton, *Grant*, p. 71; Hubbard, "Belmont," p. 459; *OR*, 3:358; Missouri, Maps 4, 5; Cowles, *Atlas*, plate 4, map 2; McClernand Campaign Maps, 1861; Private Trueman to Elizabeth Simpson, Nov. 11, 1861, Simpson Letters, ISHL; Survey of Belmont Peninsula, 1843.

22. Brinton, *Memoirs*, pp. 77, 79; Hubbard, "Belmont," p. 459; Simon, *Papers of Ulysses S. Grant*, 3:261n; Conger, *Rise of U. S. Grant*, p. 88; James P. Jones, *"Black Jack,"* p. 110; Polk, "Belmont," p. 348; *OR*, 3:270; David L. Wilson and Simon, *Ulysses S. Grant*, p. 50.

23. It was only six and a half feet above the low-water mark of December 1860.

24. Hubbard, "Belmont," p. 459; Marshall-Cornwall, *Grant*, p. 40; Grant, *Memoirs*, 1:279; *Daily Missouri Republican* (St. Louis), Nov. 10, 1861; U. S. Grant to A. H. Foote, Nov. 22, 1861, in Simon, *Papers of Ulysses S. Grant*, 3:213; Seaton, "Belmont," p. 310; Carnes, "Belmont," p. 369.

25. Byers, *Iowa*, p. 83; *OR*, 3:278, 282–83; McClernand Autobiography, CHS; Schwartz, Report, CHS; Kinnison ms., SHC; Hubbard, "Belmont," p. 459; *Daily Missouri Republican* (St. Louis), Nov. 15, 1861; Morris, Kuykendall, and Harwell, *31st Regiment*, p. 23; Force, *Fort Henry to Corinth*, p. 21.

26. Actually Detrich's reserve battalion held the extreme left of Grant's force deployed along the Bird's Point Road. They remained a quarter of a mile above Belmont Point almost at the end of the great slough at the junction of the Bird's Point Road and a narrow wood road running along the bank.

27. One may question Brinton's placing the hospital so far forward, but the landing site he considered unsecured. "As I considered our rear unprotected, I ordered our hospital up nearer the main body." Brinton, *Memoirs*, p. 76.

28. Schwartz, Report, CHS; *OR*, 3:271, 278, 283, 291–292; Henry I. Smith, *Seventh Iowa*, p. 252; Crippin, "Diary," p. 231; *Chicago Daily Tribune*, Nov. 15, 1861; Kinnison ms., SHC; *St. Louis Sunday Republican*, Nov. 10, 1861; Morris, Kuykendall, and Harwell, *31st Regiment*, p. 23; Brinton, *Memoirs*, p. 76; Byers, *Iowa*, p. 83.

29. *Daily Missouri Republican* (St. Louis), Nov. 15, 1861; *OR*, 3:278, 283; McClernand Autobiography, CHS.

30. Morris, Kuykendall, and Harwell, *31st Regiment*, p. 23.

31. Schwartz, Report, CHS.

32. Buford rode up to Logan, according to Capt. Lewis Hansback of the 27th, and "said, rather pompously, 'Colonel Logan, remember, if you please,

that I have the position of honor.' Without turning to the right or left, Logan instantly replied, 'I don't care a d——n where I am, so long as I get into this fight.' " Dawson, *Logan*, p. 19.

33. *OR*, 3:283, 287; Morris, Kuykendall, and Harwell, *31st Regiment*, p. 23.

34. A Madison County widower with a ten-year-old daughter, this Philadelphia-born machinist was known to some as "Harrison E." Hart but to most as "the courteous gentleman and gallant soldier."

35. *OR*, 3:291–92; Byers, *Iowa*, p. 83; Seaton, "Belmont," p. 311.

36. Seaton, "Belmont," p. 311.

37. Eddy, *Patriotism*, 1:162, 170, 307–9, 316; Dell, *Lincoln*, p. 92; *Chicago Daily Tribune*, Nov. 9, 1861; James Grant Wilson, *Sketches*, pp. 103–4; Aug. 19, 1861, entry, Austin Diary, ISHL; Henry Dougherty Pension Application, NARS; Illinois AGO, *Report*, 2:218–43.

38. Coatesworth, *Loyal People*, pp. 318–21; Travis MSR, NARS; Travis Biographical Sketch, ISHL; James Wilson and Fiske, *Appleton's Cyclopedia of American Biography*, 17:6; McBride and Robison, *Biographical Directory*, 1:734.

39. Amid this thrashing and crashing about in the woods, an unidentified Federal soldier found an infant, a female, abandoned and "sleeping sweetly on the bare ground" beside an "old road." The baby was taken to the rear and seen there by Confederate prisoners. The soldier who had found her took her with him aboard one of the transports back to Bird's Point. He advertised about her in newspapers in Columbus and Cairo, but no one responded. Eventually the baby was placed at Bird's Point in the home of a childless German couple, "delighted to take charge of the little waif." They adopted her and she reached adulthood. Her German parents named her Emma Sylvester ("found in the woods"). Ray Reminiscences, UAL; *Cairo* (Ill.) *Argus*, May 26, 1896.

40. Morris, Kuykendall, and Harwell, *31st Regiment*, p. 23.

41. Jansen Reminiscences, ISHL; L. Ozburn to Diza Ozburn, Nov. 10, 1861, Ozburn Letters, ISHL; McFeely, *Grant*, p. 83.

42. Morris, Kuykendall, and Harwell, *31st Regiment*, p. 19; Seaton, "Belmont," p. 312; J. B. Battle to Flora B. Turley, Nov. 9, 1861, in Rosser, "Battle," p. 22; Austin Diary, ISHL; *Chicago Daily Tribune*, Nov. 15, 1861.

43. *OR*, 3:283; Rosser, "Battle," pp. 33, 34n; Jansen Reminiscences, ISHL.

44. Eddy, *Patriotism*, 2:54; Jansen Reminiscences, ISHL; *OR*, 3:283.

45. All this reordering of alignments in the wilderness took its toll. Two companies of the 7th Iowa passed through to the front of Logan's 31st, remained there through the skirmishing phase, and apparently attached themselves to Logan for most of the battle. *OR*, 3:183–84.

46. Schwartz directed that the caissons be left in the rear at an open spot near the "lake." *Daily Missouri Republican* (St. Louis), Nov. 15, 1861; Schwartz, Report, CHS.

47. *OR*, 3:287–88.

48. One observer noted that by so doing, Grant's line "failed to reach the

river above Belmont." This allowed the enemy the great advantage of being able to land reinforcements there. "Biography of McClernand," Wallace Papers, ISHL.

49. Seaton, "Belmont," p. 311; *OR*, 3:292.

50. Brinton, *Memoirs*, pp. 76, 87.

51. Adams, "Memoirs," ISHL.

52. Hicken, *Illinois*, p. 21; William E. Woodward, *Meet General Grant*, p. 210; U. S. Grant to Jesse Root Grant, Nov. 8, 1861, in Simon, *Papers of Ulysses S. Grant*, 3:137.

53. U. S. Grant to Jesse Root Grant, Nov. 8, 1861, in Simon, *Papers of Ulysses S. Grant*, 3:137; *OR*, 3:270; Greeley, *American Conflict*, 1:596n.

54. Henry I. Smith, *Seventh Iowa*, p. 19; Morris, Kuykendall, and Harwell, *31st Regiment*, p. 23.

55. Morris, Kuykendall, and Harwell, *31st Regiment*, p. 23.

56. *Chicago Daily Tribune*, Nov. 15, 1861; Schwartz, Report, CHS; *St. Louis Sunday Republican*, Nov. 10, 1861; Henry I. Smith, *Seventh Iowa*, p. 19.

57. *OR*, 3:283.

58. *Chicago Daily Tribune*, Nov. 15, 1861.

59. *OR*, 3:292; Kinnison ms., SHC.

60. One of the often quoted Belmont stories concerns a captured Tennessean. One version includes Grant, another does not. According to the Grant story, two Union soldiers had worked their way behind the Tennessean, "a long, lank, loose-jointed rebel, who had become so interested in shooting as to remain behind a tree until cut off from his command." The soldiers brought him in and delivered him to Grant, who asked, "How large is the force fighting against us?"

" 'To God, stranger,' exclaimed the terrified Tennessean, lifting both his hands above his head, 'I can't tell. This yer ground was just kivered with men this morning. Swar me in, stranger; I'll fight for you; swar me in, but *don't* kill me.' " Albert D. Richardson, *Grant*, p. 199; Frank Moore, *Anecdotes*, p. 139.

CHAPTER 10

1. Nov. 8, 1861, entry, Fielder Diary, TSLA.

2. R. H. Wood to Mary Wood, Nov. 10, 1861, Wood Letters, TSLA.

3. "The first man in our Company, shot, was 'Wm Bulger,' shot in the leg. He was right by me. I can see the expression of his face now. He looked indignant! He walked off with a limp, his lips stuck out, as he made his way to the rear, but he did not say a word." Stephenson, "My War Autobiography," LSU; Nov. 8, 1861, entry, Fielder Diary, TSLA.

4. Nov. 8, 1861, entry, Austin Diary, ISHL.

5. J. B. Battle to Flora B. Turley, Nov. 9, 1861, in Rosser, "Battle," p. 22; J. F. Henry to G. A. Henry, Nov. 8, 1861, Henry Papers, SHC; Rennolds, *Henry County Commands*, p. 27; *CV* 16:190.

6. Collins, "Morgan," p. 277.

7. *OR*, 3:288; James Grant Wilson, *Sketches*, pp. 96–98.

8. Brinton, *Memoirs*, pp. 78–80.

9. Lt. Patrick White, advancing his section of guns to Logan's left, wrote in his diary: "I noticed our own dead who had dyed in the full flush of health, had turned black and we had to move them so as not to crush them with our cannon wheels. I will frankly say to you the thoughts that came to my mind then were: this may be my last day and I may see my mother before night." White, "Diary," p. 646; *OR*, 3:279; *Daily Missouri Republican* (St. Louis), Nov. 15, 1861; J. A. McClernand to U. S. Grant, Nov. 12, 1861, McClernand Papers, ISHL.

10. Tyree Bell maintains that he charged before "having fired a gun." Pillow, on the other hand, states that he ordered the charge only after Beltzhoover ran out of ammunition and after Bell and Wright had reported to him that they had exhausted theirs. Alfred Fielder's version backs Pillow. Bell's report is most curious. Why would he state that he did not fire, with White's men close upon him, firing volleys into his position? *OR*, 3:278, 287–88, 326; Bell, Report, SIU; Nov. 7, 1861, entry, Fielder Diary, TSLA.

11. Nov. 8, 1861, entry, Fielder Diary, TSLA; *OR*, 3:326, 332–33; Bell, Report, SIU; Ray Reminiscences, UAL; *CV* 13:468; Mathes, *Old Guard in Gray*, p. 22.

12. *OR*, 3:358; Stephenson, "My War Autobiography," LSU.

13. Ibid. Despite Pillow's contention of a number of bayonet charges by his line of battle, Tappan states that "this was the only charge made by my regiment while under command of Brigadier General Pillow." This seems to have been the case for the entire Confederate line although periodically there were faltering advances and retreats by individual units. Tappan's men as well as others, however, would participate in bayonet charges that afternoon under Cheatham or Samuel Marks.

14. Bell, Report, SIU; *OR*, 3:326, 333; *CV* 16:346; Mathes, *Old Guard in Gray*, p. 22.

15. Jansen Reminiscences, ISHL; *OR*, 3:288, 333, 356; Stephenson, "My War Autobiography," LSU; Evans, *Confederate Military History*, 10:62; L. Ozburn to Diza Ozburn, Nov. 10, 1861, Ozburn Letters, Odum, "Reminiscences," ISHL.

16. Conger, *Rise of U. S. Grant*, p. 90; *OR*, 3:298–99; Richard J. Person to G. J. Pillow, Nov. 12, 1861, Snyder Collection, UMKC.

17. John Brinton while searching for Grant came upon a Union soldier wounded by the Watson Battery. "I have never seen a worse wound, before or since. The whole of the skin and muscles of the back from the nape of the neck to the thighs and on both sides of the spine had been torn away, as if the tissues had been scooped out by a clean-cutting curved instrument." The surface of the man's body was "raw and bleeding." Brinton could do nothing, say nothing, but just watch the soldier die. Brinton, *Memoirs*, p. 75.

18. U.S. Government, *Medical and Surgical History*, 1 (appendix): 18–19;

OR, 3:286, 342; Greeley, *American Conflict*, 1:596n; Adams, "Memoirs," ISHL; McClernand Autobiography, CHS; Estvan, *War Pictures*, pp. 179–80; Hubbard, "Belmont," p. 459; Squier, *Leslie's Pictorial History*, 1:195.

19. *OR*, 3:292.

20. Seaton, "Belmont," p. 312; Henry I. Smith, *Seventh Iowa*, p. 252; Kurtz, "Belmont," p. 20.

21. *Chicago Daily Tribune*, Nov. 15, 1861.

22. Adams, "Memoirs," ISHL; *OR*, 3:292.

23. *St. Louis Sunday Republican*, Nov. 10, 1861; Frank Moore, *Anecdotes*, p. 426; "Biography of McClernand," Wallace Papers, ISHL.

24. Conger, *Rise of U. S. Grant*, p. 88.

25. R. H. Wood to Mary Wood, Nov. 10, 1861, Wood Letters, TSLA; *Memphis Daily Appeal*, Nov. 9, 10, 1861.

26. Observers wandering the battlefield found Confederate casualties had many more wounds below the waist than the Federals. *Memphis Daily Appeal*, Nov. 14, 1861.

27. *Nashville Union and American*, Nov. 14, 1861.

28. *OR*, 3:337, 339.

29. *Nashville Banner*, Nov. 12, 1861; Lindsley, *Annals*, p. 315; *OR*, 3:337; *Memphis Daily Appeal*, Nov. 10, 1861; Frazer Letter, Nov. 9, 1861, in personal collection of Thomas P. Sweeney, Springfield, Mo.

30. Staff officer Gustavus A. Henry, Jr., watched a Yankee take aim at Pillow. Henry "spoke to the Genl & he spurred his horse & the fellow fired & down went my horse." Linderman, *Embattled Courage*, p. 35; *Daily Picayune* (New Orleans), Nov. 15, 1861; G. A. Henry, Jr., to G. A. Henry, Sr., Nov. 11, 1861, Henry Papers, SHC; Estvan, *War Pictures*, p. 184.

31. *OR*, 3:339–40; R. H. Wood to Mary Wood, Nov. 10, 1861, Wood Letters, TSLA.

32. *OR*, 3:340.

33. R. H. Wood to Mary Wood, Nov. 10, 1861, Wood Letters, TSLA.

34. Ibid.

35. The rammer-missile "pulled out" Ory's eye, he lost the hearing in both ears, and his left arm, hand, and fingers were crippled. Clement Ory's Application for Land Grant, LSA.

36. Adams, "Memoirs," ISHL; *OR*, 3:342.

37. *Chicago Daily Tribune*, Nov. 15, 1861; *Reunions of Taylor's Battery*, p. 20; White, "Diary"; Schwartz, Report, CHS.

38. White, "Diary," p. 646.

39. *St. Louis Sunday Republican*, Nov. 10, 1861; *Chicago Evening Journal*, quoted in Eddy, *Patriotism*, 1:183; Greeley, *American conflict*, 1:596n. After the battle, at the approaches to the position of the Watson Battery were found "numerous bodies of men who had been slain by round shot, grape or canister." U.S. Government, *Medical and Surgical History*, 1 (Appendix): 18.

40. Drivers as well as cannoneers made up a Civil War battery. The Watson

Battery, larger than most, in the fall of 1861 possessed 150 cannoneers and 40 drivers. James W. Maddox, Confederate Questionnaire, MDAH.

41. Another member of the Chicago Battery maintains that the gun went off prematurely because it was so hot from rapid firing. The discharge badly burned George White's eyes. Lt. Patrick White relates that in the excitement of the battle, the section moved on and "the poor fellow walked back to the landing." In the apocryphal meandering of veterans' stories, the indomitable George Q. White made his way across the country. Eventually he gained an audience with President Lincoln who commissioned his one-armed cannoneer a quartermaster. White, "Diary," pp. 648–49.

42. *CV* 16:191.

43. *OR*, 3:360; *Chicago Daily Tribune*, Nov. 15, 1861.

44. *Chicago Daily Tribune*, Nov. 15, 1861; *OR*, 3:309, 326, 360; *Daily Picayune* (New Orleans), Nov. 14, 1861; G. J. Pillow to Judah Benjamin, Jan. 16, 1862, Pillow MSR, NARS; Jansen Reminiscences, ISHL.

45. White, "Diary."

46. Frazer Letter, Nov. 9, 1861, in personal collection of Thomas P. Sweeney, Springfield, Mo.; Wright, "Belmont," p. 73; *OR*, 3:326, 337; R. H. Wood to Mary Wood, Nov. 7, 10, 1861, Wood Letters, TSLA; *Memphis Daily Appeal*, Nov. 9, 10, 1861.

47. Stanley, *Autobiography*, p. 175.

48. *OR*, 3:278, 284; "Biography of McClernand," Wallace Papers, ISHL; J. A. McClernand to U. S. Grant, Nov. 12, 1861, McClernand Papers, ISHL; Force, *Fort Henry to Corinth*, p. 21.

49. *OR*, 3:284; Conger, *Rise of U. S. Grant*, p. 88; Edward H. Bowman to William S. Rosecrans, June 28, 1882, Rosecrans Papers, UCLA.

50. *OR*, 3:283–84; Eddy, *Patriotism*, 2:54; Private Trueman to Elizabeth Simpson, Nov. 11, 1861, Simpson Letters, ISHL; Conger, *Rise of U. S. Grant*, p. 88.

51. *OR*, 3:333; Vaughan, *Thirteenth Regiment*, p. 14.

52. *OR*, 3:326, 333–34.

53. Ibid., 333–34.

54. There may have been perhaps forty servants in the fight at Belmont. Most were slaves. Some like William Stains, McClernand's body servant, played a conspicuous role. Grant had his servant Bob along throughout the day as did Patrick White of the Chicago Battery. A black father and son, "armed with muskets and knives," fought in the ranks with the 13th Arkansas. "I asked them if they were volunteers, they said they were for that day & looked as cool as the bravest." Jack, the servant of Lieutenant Shelton, fired twenty-seven times before he was incapacitated with three wounds. He was taken to the Overton Hospital in Memphis with the other wounded Confederates and died there of his wounds on November 18. His son, George W. Shelton, was captured "with a musket in his hand, a cartridge box on," and taken to Cairo where he and another servant "Rob" were delivered to Company A, 31st Illinois, to be used for "camp purposes."

Capt. R. H. Wood in a letter to his wife Mary reported that Colonel Tappan told him angrily of the fate of a wounded slave: "When the Lincolnites found him they wrapped him up in leaves & wood & burned him to death." Pvt. John B. Battle reported seeing on the battlefield "several dead and wounded negros who had fought beside their master as bravely as any man."

The servant of Capt. James A. Ventress, Jr., of the Lebauve Guards, 11th Louisiana, "fought like a tiger, killing several yankees." He brought the body of one man he had killed, a "red-whiskered one," to Columbus and "exhibited him."

55. *CV* 16:131; Vaughan, *Thirteenth Regiment*, pp. 13–14, 51; Lindsley, *Annals*, p. 315.

56. Vaughan, *Thirteenth Regiment*, p. 63; S. R. Latta to Mary Latta, Nov. 8, 1861, Latta Papers, TSLA.

57. S. R. Latta to Mary Latta, Nov. 8, 1861, Latta Papers, TSLA.

58. *OR*, 3:334.

59. Ibid.

60. Ibid., 326, 335; G. J. Pillow to J. P. Benjamin, Jan. 16, 1862, Pillow MSR, NARS.

61. Following the battle of Belmont controversy would rage between Pillow and Polk about the responsibility for the failure to adequately replenish ammunition. Generally it was accepted that many units exhausted their supply early. Freeman of the 22d, however, contended that his men had an average of twenty-five rounds per man, and he said, "I don't think any company was out of ammunition entirely during the day." Tappan maintained he did not run out. Captain Frazer said his men had forty rounds. Yet, it does appear that the shortage was serious. Most Confederates seem to have entered the fight with six to nine cartridges, which, even if carefully conserved, would not have sufficed. There was also the problem, in the 12th at least, of ammunition being too small to be serviceable. Later, Confederates would go into battle with 60 rounds, sometimes even 100.

Beltzhoover's short supply is mysterious. He knew better, and having been on the Missouri shore a month, he had had time to store up a supply. Perhaps he underestimated the amount required and wasted too many rounds early in the fight.

Without question there was a supply of ammunition at the riverbank. A number of soldiers write of dropping back to the river to pick up what they needed. Pillow requested ammunition early, but Captain Butler of the *Prince*, who brought his request to Polk, asserted that "ammunition had been sent for and brought over to the battlefield by 'Prince' previous to my being sent by General Pillow." Indeed, Butler pointed out that boxes of ammunition lay by the river when he started back with the request to Polk.

Polk seems to have acted on Pillow's request promptly. He detailed Col. Preston Smith to see to the resupply. Smith asserted that plenty was sent over and that when he arrived at the riverbank he saw "large quantities of ammunition at different places on the river bank, some fifty boxes being untouched."

The fault lies, it seems, with careless and inexperienced officers who did not make sure that their units, be they companies or regiments, had an adequate supply on hand.

62. Vaughan, *Thirteenth Regiment*, p. 12; S. R. Latta to Mary Latta, Nov. 8, 1861, Latta Papers, TSLA.

CHAPTER 11

1. J. B. Battle to Flora B. Turley, Nov. 9, 1861, in Rosser, "Battle," pp. 22–23.

2. Fielder Diary, TSLA; *OR*, 3:288, 337.

3. *Memphis Daily Appeal*, Nov. 12, 1861; *OR*, 3:334.

4. *Pike County Democrat* (Pittsfield, Ill.), Nov. 28, 1861; *OR*, 3:280, 284, 288; Crippin, "Diary," p. 231; Private Trueman to Elizabeth Simpson, Nov. 11, 1861, Simpson Letters, ISHL.

5. Private Trueman to Elizabeth Simpson, Nov. 11, 1861, Simpson Letters, ISHL.

6. The sword was inscribed, "Presented by Gen. Greene to Matthew Rhea— the last man to retreat from the battle of Guilford Court House." Fifty-four members of Company A became prisoners, but some of these would escape later in the afternoon. *Memphis Daily Appeal*, Nov. 12, 1861; Vaughan, *Thirteenth Regiment*, p. 14.

7. Private Trueman to Elizabeth Simpson, Nov. 11, 1861, Simpson Letters, ISHL; *OR*, 3:284, 288; Odum, "Reminiscences," ISHL; Eddy, *Patriotism*, 2:54.

8. *OR*, 3:350–51; Deupree, "Noxubee Squadron," p. 25.

9. Deupree, "Reminiscences," pp. 95–96; Deupree, "Noxubee Squadron," pp. 12, 25, 95–97; Miller Biographical Sketch, MDAH; Rowland, *Mississippi*, 1:377; *CV* 18:27; Winston, *Story of Pontotoc*, p. 159; M. Jeff Thompson to G. J. Pillow, Aug. 19, 1861, CSA Papers, DU.

10. *OR*, 3:350–51; Deupree, "Noxubee Squadron," p. 25; *Daily Missouri Republican* (St. Louis), Nov. 15, 1861; Evans, *Confederate Military History*, 12:34.

11. *OR*, 3:286, 288; *Daily Missouri Republican* (St. Louis), Nov. 15, 1861; Odum, "Reminiscences," ISHL; *Chicago Daily Tribune*, Nov. 15, 1861; Henry I. Smith, *Seventh Iowa*, p. 12.

12. Henry I. Smith, *Seventh Iowa*, p. 12; Brinton, *Memoirs*, pp. 77, 84–85; *Chicago Daily Tribune*, Nov. 15, 1861; Seaton, "Belmont," p. 314; Hubbard, "Belmont," p. 459.

13. Brinton, *Memoirs*, pp. 76–77.

14. *OR*, 3:279, 292; White, "Diary," p. 647; *Chicago Daily Tribune*, Nov. 15, 1861; Schwartz, Report, CHS.

15. Controversy arose regarding who captured the rebel flag. Logan gave the honor to Pvt. E. D. Winters of Company A, a skirmisher company of the

31st that spent most of the day operating with Dougherty's regiments. Logan says that in the act of pulling down the flag, Winters was wounded and one of Buford's men took it. Logan carefully, petulantly, points out that Buford and his men "were at all times protected in every movement by the advance of my cavalry company, who were detached from my command, and had led Colonel Buford through the woods to the battle-field." Another source maintains that Logan himself "tore down the flag of treason." Sergeant Sample of the 7th Iowa is also credited with its capture. In any case, after the battle, the Confederate flag turned up in Lauman's sickroom at Bird's Point, where privileged visitors were allowed to view it. *OR*, 3:288–89; Squier, *Leslie's Pictorial History*, 1:196; Stephenson, "My War Autobiography," LSU.

16. *Louisville Daily Journal*, Nov. 15, 1861; *Chicago Daily Tribune*, Nov. 15, 1861; *Daily Missouri Republican* (St.Louis), Nov. 14, 1861; Squier, *Leslie's Pictorial History*, 1:195–96; Byers, *Iowa*, pp. 84–85; *OR*, 3:289, 292, 297; *Weekly Missouri Democrat* (St. Louis), Nov. 19, 1861; *Chicago Post*, n.d., quoted in *Memphis Daily Appeal*, Nov. 13, 1861; Fielder Diary, TSLA.

17. *OR*, 3:286, 288, 292–93; *Chicago Daily Tribune*, Nov. 15, 1861; Henry I. Smith, *Seventh Iowa*, p. 19.

18. Yale College seems to have been well represented at Belmont: Hillyer, Knox Walker, John Brinton, John C. Burch of Pillow's staff and James Tappan and Capt. James G. Hamilton of the Southern Guards, 154th Senior Tennessee, were alumni.

19. *New York Herald*, Nov. 12, 1861; Albert D. Richardson, *Grant*, pp. 198–99; James Grant Wilson, *Rawlins*, p. 66; *Weekly Missouri Democrat* (St. Louis), Nov. 19, 1861; G. A. Henry, Jr., to G. A. Henry, Sr., Nov. 11, 1861, Henry Papers, SHC.

20. Beltzhoover's Watson Battery seems to have played no role in the defense of Camp Johnston. It appears, as stated in Beltzhoover's report and confirmed in Polk's, that once the Confederate initial line of battle was abandoned, the battery displaced to the rear and re-formed there, but without ammunition; in effect, it was parked in camp. Union reports, however, emphasize attacking and seizing the battery in the center of the camp and describe the mounds of dead and wounded found around the guns.

One speculates about where Taylor and Schwartz found the ammunition to turn the Watson guns on the retreating Confederates later in the battle. Seaton mentions loads left in the New Orleans guns; if he is correct, Beltzhoover and Polk notwithstanding, one must assume that the gunners, drivers, and Beltzhoover himself pulled the Watson guns into battery in the camp, abandoned them there, and fled over the riverbank with some of the panicked infantry.

21. *Daily Missouri Republican* (St. Louis), Nov. 14, 1861.

22. W. H. Onstot to Lizzie Onstot, Nov. 16, 1861, Onstot Papers, ISHL.

23. Frazer Letter, Nov. 9, 1861, in personal collection of Thomas P. Sweeney, Springfield, Mo.; R. H. Wood to Mary Wood, Nov. 10, 1861, Wood Letters, TSLA; J. B. Battle to Flora B. Turley, Nov. 9, 1861, in Rosser, "Battle," p. 23; *Memphis Daily Appeal*, Nov. 12, 1861.

24. Twain, *Life on the Mississippi*, p. 205; Estvan, *War Pictures*, pp. 181–82; *OR*, 3:326.

25. Feb. 11, 1839, entry, W. F. Cooper Diary, Cooper Family Papers, TSLA.

26. Jan. 20, 1847, entry, in Quaife, *Diary of James K. Polk*, 2:345–46.

27. Inevitably he became involved in politics, not only in Tennessee but nationally. As a James Buchanan ally and spokesman he sought Gideon Pillow's support in 1856, offering in return Buchanan's support for the vice presidential nomination. Walker entered the Tennessee Senate in 1858 and was noted for his attacks on "the apostate & traitor" John Bell. He edited the *Memphis Daily Appeal* in 1859 and became an important supporter of Douglas in 1860. McBride and Robison, *Biographical Directory*, 2:754; Yale University, *Obituary Record*, pp. 133–34; *Nashville Dispatch*, Aug. 29, 1863; Watson, "Walker," pp. 34, 34n, 35; Boone, "Belmont," TSLA; Graf, *Papers of Andrew Johnson*, 3:294, 295n, 402, 412; Nevins, *Ordeal of the Union*, 2:9–10; Gower, *Pen and Sword*, pp. 414, 540; Paul H. Bergeron, "All in the Family," p. 11.

28. Sally Walker Boone, Knox Walker's daughter, reported in her memoir "After the Battle of Belmont," written in the 1880s, that in the battle "Lieutenant Bob Hitt, now representative from Illinois, was shot in the hip." She mentioned just five casualties in her father's regiment: her cousin Jimmie, Capt. F. A. Strocky, Capt. J. Welby Armstrong, Capt. John Saffarans, and Hitt. Robert Roberts Hitt (1834–1906) was a veteran and respected Illinois congressman (1882–1906), perhaps best known as a young man who reported the Lincoln-Douglas debates.

After checking the usual sources in Illinois to confirm Boone's report, inquiries were made of Hitt family members. They, quite naturally, were astonished at the suggestion that their forebear could have been a Confederate officer. And it was beyond belief that if Boone was correct he could have been elected to Congress from Illinois in 1882, successfully concealing his past, particularly from John Logan who was on a rampage about conspiring rebels.

Ultimately David Wigdor, assistant chief of the Manuscript Division at the Library of Congress, ended the need for further investigation. Hitt's diary in the Library of Congress, records that he was in Milwaukee, Wis., at the time of Belmont, actively pursuing his career as a court reporter. Boone, "Belmont," TSLA.

29. Dennigan served in Mexico as a member of the 2d Kentucky Volunteers. He remarked that "Belmont was his seventh battle but he said in no battle in the Mexican War was there such fighting done." Dillon Diary, in personal collection of Mrs. N. E. Ward, Prescott, Ark.

30. Boone, "Belmont," TSLA; *New Orleans Daily Crescent*, Oct. 29, 1861; Stevenson, *Thirteen Months*, pp. 41, 43–48; *Nashville Daily Gazette*, Nov. 10, 1861; Dillon Diary, in personal collection of Mrs. N. E. Ward, Prescott, Ark.; Fakes, "Memphis and the Mexican War," p. 120; Tennessee Civil War Commission, *Tennesseans in the Civil War*, 1:174–76; Lindsley, *Annals*, pp. 173–75; *Nashville Union and American*, Nov. 13, 1861.

31. "Some stopped the tubes on their guns, and filled the barrel with liquor. The colonel, while passing a tent one day, saw one of the men elevate his gun and take a long pull at the muzzle. He called out 'Pat, what have you got in your gun? Whiskey?'

"He answered—'Colonel, I was looking into the barrel of my gun to see whether she was clean.'

"The colonel walked on, muttering something about the curiosity of man's eyes being located in his mouth." Stevenson, *Thirteen Months*, p. 40.

32. Boone, "Belmont," TSLA.

33. Stevenson, *Thirteen Months*, p. 70.

34. *OR*, 3:334; *Daily Confederate News* (Columbus, Ky.), Nov. 12, 1861; Rosser, "Battle," p. 38; Stevenson, *Thirteen Months*, pp. 72–73; Vaughan, *Thirteenth Regiment*, p. 51; Conger, *Rise of U. S. Grant*, p. 93; Force, *Fort Henry to Corinth*, pp. 21–22.

35. Boone, "Belmont," TSLA.

36. *Southern Bivouac*, 3:89–90.

37. Boone, "Belmont," TSLA.

38. Twain, *Life on the Mississippi*, p. 206.

39. *Daily Confederate News* (Columbus, Ky.), Nov. 12, 1861.

40. S. R. Latta to Mary Latta, Nov. 8, 1861, Latta Papers, TSLA; *Memphis Daily Appeal*, Nov. 13, 1861; *OR*, 3:356; Twain, *Life on the Mississippi*, p. 96.

41. These men seem to have been individual squads led by men such as Sgt. Jeff Crookham, Company I, of the ever eager 7th Iowa. Some came from Buford's 27th Illinois and others from the 22d. They not only dragged the Watson guns into position, they manned them: loading, aiming and firing. Schwartz, Report, CHS; Byers, *Iowa*, p. 85; Schmitt, *Twenty-Seventh Illinois*, p. 30; Seaton, "Belmont," p. 313.

42. Schwartz, Report, CHS; *Nashville Union and American*, Nov. 14, 1861; *New Orleans Daily Crescent*, Nov. 11, 1861; D. B. Frierson to unidentified correspondent, Cooper Family Papers, TSLA; Seaton, "Belmont," p. 313; Byers, *Iowa*, p. 85.

43. *Daily Missouri Republican* (St. Louis), Jan. 16, 1886; *Memphis Daily Appeal*, Nov. 12, 1861.

44. Frazer Letter, Nov. 9, 1861, in personal collection of Thomas P. Sweeney, Springfield, Mo.

45. R. H. Wood to Mary Wood, Nov. 10, 1861, Wood Letters, TSLA.

46. Ibid.; D. B. Frierson to unidentified correspondent, Nov. 11, 1861, Cooper Family Papers, TSLA; Evans, *Confederate Military History*, 10:62; J. F. Henry to G. A. Henry, Sr., Nov. 8, 1861, Henry Papers, Fielder Diary, TSLA.

47. *Memphis Daily Appeal*, Nov. 9, 1861; Frank Moore, *Anecdotes*, pp. 455–56.

48. Private Trueman to Elizabeth Simpson, Nov. 11, 1861, Simpson Letters, ISHL.

49. E. Woodward to A. Woodward, Nov. 8, 1861, in *Memphis Daily Appeal*, Nov. 10, 1861.

50. *CV* 5:391.

51. Stevenson, *Thirteen Months*, p. 70.

52. White, "Diary," p. 647.

53. *Chicago Daily Tribune*, Nov. 15, 1861.

54. Seaton, "Belmont," p. 314; *Memphis Avalanche*, n.d., quoted in *Daily Nashville Patriot*, Nov. 12, 1861; *New Orleans Daily Crescent*, Nov. 13, 1861; *Chicago Daily Tribune*, Nov. 15, 1861; *OR*, 3:363; R. H. Wood to Mary Wood, Nov. 10, 1861, Wood Letters, TSLA; *Memphis Daily Appeal*, Nov. 10, 12, 1861.

55. Twain, *Life on the Mississippi*, p. 206.

56. It is interesting and puzzling that despite the vigorous and successful efforts of the Chicago Battery, Grant maintained his "efforts were in vain" to get his artillery to fire on the Confederate transports. After Belmont Leonidas Polk asked Henry Dougherty about the battery and complimented them. "He said we took all the conceit out of theirs." Grant, *Memoirs*, 1:276; White, "Diary," p. 647.

57. *Chicago Daily Tribune*, Nov. 15, 1861; *Daily Missouri Republican* (St. Louis), Nov. 15, 16, 1861; *OR*, 3:280; C. J. Johnson to Lou Johnson, Nov. 8, 1861, Johnson Letters, LSU.

58. Singletary, "Day."

59. Private Trueman to Elizabeth Simpson, Nov. 11, 1861, Simpson Letters, ISHL; Henry I. Smith, *Seventh Iowa*, p. 260.

60. Law, "Diary," p. 178; Rennolds, *Henry County Commands*, p. 27; *CV* 16:190.

61. Brinton, *Memoirs*, p. 80.

62. Austin Diary, ISHL; Squier, *Leslie's Pictorial History*, 1:195.

63. Eddy, *Patriotism*, 1:183.

64. Force, *Fort Henry to Corinth*, p. 22; *OR*, 3:279–80, 337; Seaton, "Belmont," p. 313.

65. Grant, *Memoirs*, 1:274; *OR*, 3:293; John Alexander Logan, *Volunteer Soldier*, p. 623; Henry I. Smith, *Seventh Iowa*, p. 19; Albert D. Richardson, *Grant*, p. 200.

66. Crippin, "Diary"; *Daily Missouri Republican* (St. Louis), Nov. 14, 1861; *OR*, 3:288, 297; Odum, "Reminiscences," ISHL; *Louisville Daily Journal*, Nov. 16, 1861; *New York Tribune*, Nov. 12, 1861.

67. Grant, *Memoirs*, 1:274; *Reunions of Taylor's Battery*, p. 20.

68. Schwartz, Report, CHS.

69. Albert D. Richardson, *Grant*, p. 200; Morris, Kuykendall, and Harwell, *31st Regiment*, p. 24; *St. Louis Sunday Republican*, Nov. 10, 1861; John Alexander Logan, *Volunteer Soldier*, p. 623; Schwartz, Report, CHS; *New York Herald*, Nov. 12, 1861; *OR*, 3:284.

70. Adams, "Memoirs," ISHL; *Daily Missouri Republican* (St. Louis), Nov. 14, 1861.

71. Schwartz, Report, CHS; *OR*, 3:280.

72. Brinton commented on the two or three quartermaster wagons placed

at his disposal: "These being destitute of springs, and the country over which they passed being wooded and rough, our wounded suffered much unnecessary anguish." Brinton, *Memoirs*, pp. 77–78; Henry I. Smith, *Seventh Iowa*, p. 252; U.S. Government, *Medical and Surgical History*, 1 (appendix): 19; *OR*, 3:275, 297.

73. Seaton, "Belmont," p. 319; *Weekly Missouri Democrat* (St. Louis), Nov. 19, 1861.

74. Grant, *Memoirs*, 1:274.

75. *OR*, 3:270, 280, 284; Schwartz, Report, CHS; John Alexander Logan, *Volunteer Soldier*, p. 623; Wright, "Belmont," p. 72; Morris, Kuykendall, and Harwell, *31st Regiment*, p. 24; Frank Moore, *Anecdotes*, p. 456; Albert D. Richardson, *Grant*, p. 200; *St. Louis Sunday Republican*, Nov. 10, 1861; Kurtz, "Belmont," p. 21.

76. Private Stephenson reported,

> Our Adjutant then, was William Mercer Otey, the son of Bishop Otey (P.E.) of Tenn. and adopted son of Wm Mercer a wealthy merchant of New Orleans. Stepping into his tent, on returning from the battle, he uttered an exclamation! Some of our men, near by, ran to him, and there, stretched full length on the floor, with a stick of some combustible in hand, lay a grey headed but vigorous determined looking old yankee, on his back, face up and eyes staring! He had evidently been shot by one of our men in the very act of firing the tent! Mercer Otey knelt down by his side and putting the candle to the man's face (it was then dark) indulged in a long soliloquy half taunting, which rather disgusted me, and I turned away.

Stephenson, "My War Autobiography," LSU; E. M. Graham to W. B. Mattox, Nov. 1861, in Thompson, "Graham," pp. 29, 30n; R. H. Wood to Mary Wood, Nov. 10, 1861, Wood Letters, TSLA; *Memphis Daily Appeal*, Nov. 9, 10, 1861; *OR*, 3:325; Stevenson, *Thirteen Months*, pp. 67–68; J. B. Battle to Flora B. Turley, Nov. 9, 1861, in Rosser, "Battle," p. 23.

77. R. H. Wood to Mary Wood, Nov. 10, 1861, Wood Letters, TSLA; *Daily Picayune* (New Orleans), Nov. 14, 1861; *OR*, 3:334, 356, 361; Barnwell, "Belmont," p. 370; Horn, *Army of Tennessee*, p. 65; Singletary, "Belmont," p. 507; E. Woodward to A. Woodward, in *Memphis Daily Appeal*, Nov. 10, 1861.

78. R. H. Wood to Mary Wood, Nov. 10, 1861, Wood Letters, TSLA.

79. The chain of cowardice, hung around Gideon Pillow's neck by circumstances or by enemies, choked him throughout the Civil War, indeed the remainder of his life. Abandoning his fellow Tennesseans at Fort Donelson was unforgivable. What actually occurred with him on the last day of the battle of Murfreesboro has never been resolved conclusively. Nevertheless, there is sufficient evidence from a number of reliable sources to conclude that Pillow, at least at Belmont, was a brave soldier, willing to expose himself to death.

80. *Memphis Avalanche*, n.d., quoted in *Daily Nashville Patriot*, Nov. 12,

1861; *OR*, 3:326, 361; Davis, *Rise and Fall*, 1:404; Carnes, "Belmont," p. 369; Twain, *Life on the Mississippi*, p. 206; Durham, "Civil War Letters," p. 41.

81. L. Polk to Secretary of War George Randolph, July 22, 1862, in *OR*, 3:324.

82. Singletary, "Belmont," p. 507.

CHAPTER 12

1. "This was Pillow talk for an army of equal size." Simon, "Grant at Belmont," p. 164; *OR*, 3:315, 326, 328.

2. The field batteries of Capt. William H. "Red" Jackson and Capt. Marshall T. Polk had not arrived, however. "The steamer transporting these batteries, in her attempt to land them on the Missouri shore, by some means lost her stage planks, and the landing at that moment became impossible. She was forced to return to the Kentucky shore." *OR*, 3:307; Parks, *Polk*, p. 191.

3. Polk's indecision, understandable considering the intelligence he received, was observed by many and freely admitted by Polk himself. Surgeon Lunsford Yandell, Jr., summed up the situation as seen by a junior officer: "But General Polk would not allow it [crossing over to Missouri to engage the enemy], as he expected an attack from this side of the river, which was certainly the plan of the enemy." L. P. Yandell, Jr., to L. P. Yandell, Sr., Nov. 10, 1861, Yandell Family Papers, FC.

4. Polk may have remembered ordering Marks to land upriver, but it seems the transports headed straight for the camp. Marks, however, agreed that Polk ordered him to flank the enemy. *OR*, 3:307; *Daily Picayune* (New Orleans), Nov. 14, 1861.

5. James P. Jones, *"Black Jack,"* p. 84; Evans, *Confederate Military History*, 10:486, 683–84; Carroll MSR, NARS; *Memphis, Tennessee, City Directory*, 1885; Tennessee Civil War Commission, *Tennesseans in the Civil War*, 1:205–8; *CV* 9:154; Lindsley, *Annals*, p. 332; Ridley, *Battles and Sketches*, p. 173; Mathes, *Old Guard in Gray*, p. 292; Young, *Memphis*, p. 337; *OR*, ser. 2, 5:264, 23:25; Graf, *Papers of Andrew Johnson*, 4:294n; *Tennessee Historical Quarterly* 34:163.

6. Tyler puzzled historian Ezra Warner "perhaps more than any other Confederate general. . . . Who was he?" Warner became so intrigued that he wrote an article about his Tyler research adventures. Exasperated, he concluded that Tyler was clouded by "a mystery of circumstances or a gigantic conspiracy of silence reaching from the highest echelon of governmental, social and political life to the lowest." Warner, "Who Was General Tyler?," pp. 15–18, and *Generals in Gray*, pp. 312–13; Evans, *Confederate Military History*, 10:304, 335–37; Wright, *Tennessee in the War*.

7. *Daily Picayune* (New Orleans), Nov. 14, 1861.

8. *Daily Missouri Republican* (St. Louis), Jan. 16, 1886.

9. The pilot of the *Hill* explained the sensation of being under fire to cub pilot Samuel Clemens:

I was sitting with my legs hanging out of the pilot-house window. All at once I noticed a whizzing sound passing my ear. Judged it was bullet. I didn't stop to think about anything, I just tilted over backward and landed on the floor, and stayed there. The balls came booming around. Three cannon balls went through the chimney; one ball took off the corner of the pilot-house; shells were screaming and bursting all around. Mighty warm times—I wished I hadn't come. I lay there on the pilot-house floor, while the shots came faster and faster. I crept in behind the big stove, in the middle of the pilot-house. Presently a minie-ball came through the stove and just grazed my head and cut my hat. I judged it was time to go away from there. The captain was on the roof with a red-headed major from Memphis—a fine looking man. I heard him say he wanted to leave here, but "that pilot is killed." I crept over to the starboard side to pull the bell to set her back; raised up and took a look, and I saw about fifteen shot-holes through the window-panes; had come so lively I hadn't noticed them. I glanced out on the water, and the splattering shot were like a hail-storm. I thought best to get out of that place. I went down the pilot-house guy head first—not feet first but head first—slid down—before I struck the deck, the captain said we must leave there. So I climbed up the guy and got on the floor again. About that time they collared my partner and were bringing him up to the pilot-house between two soldiers. Somebody had said I was killed. He put his head in and saw me on the floor reaching for the backing-bells. He said, "Oh, h—l! he ain't shot," and jerked away from the men who had him by the collar, and ran below. . . . Pretty soon after that I was sick, and used up, and had to go off to the Hot Springs. (Twain, *Life on the Mississippi*, pp. 206–7)

10. R. H. Wood to Mary Wood, Nov. 10, 1861, Wood Letters, TSLA.

11. Tom Arliskas of Chicago, Ill., who investigated Confederate uniforms worn at Belmont, believes Tyler's men must have fired on Walker's Legion (2d Tennessee), some of whom were wearing blue. Tom Arliskas to author, Dec. 28, 1989.

12. *Daily Picayune* (New Orleans), Nov. 14, 1861; *Daily Missouri Republican* (St. Louis), Jan. 16, 1886.

13. Young, *Seventh Cavalry*, pp. 21–23; Tennessee Civil War Commission, *Tennesseans in the Civil War*, 1:28; *OR*, 3:363; *Nashville Union and American*, Nov. 14, 1861.

14. *Battlefields of the South*, p. 119.

15. Henry Walke claimed a share of the credit for creating mayhem among the Confederate reinforcements as they attempted to cross. He maintained that his gunboats fired *over* the wooded point at Belmont and scored hits on the transports, which "dispersed a whole company of artillerists. . . . This it was

thought caused the enemy's transports to cross the river at a point almost beyond the reach of our shot and land their troops lower down; which was the very thing we desired to accomplish." Walke, *Naval Scenes*, p. 36.

16. *New Orleans Daily Crescent*, Nov. 11, 1861; Seaton, "Belmont," p. 314; *OR*, 3:270, 363; *Battlefields of the South*, p. 119; *Memphis Daily Appeal*, Nov. 12, 1861.

17. *OR*, 3:363.

18. *Daily Picayune* (New Orleans), Nov. 13, 14, 1861; Floyd, *Barrow Family*, p. 36; *OR*, 3:354, 359, 361, 363.

19. The *Hill* seems to have later become disabled and lain to against the shore where, according to one account, stragglers by the hundreds took refuge. Jansen Reminiscences, ISHL; *New Orleans Daily Crescent*, Nov. 13, 1861.

20. C. J. Johnson to Lou Johnson, Nov. 8, 1861, Johnson Letters, LSU; *OR*, 3:363.

21. *Battlefields of the South*, p. 119; *OR*, 3:270, 327, 307; Evans, *Confederate Military History*, 10:12; *New Orleans Daily Crescent*, Nov. 13, 1861.

22. Mathes, *Old Guard in Gray*, p. 70; Young, *Seventh Cavalry*, p. 22; *New Orleans Daily Crescent*, Nov. 13, 1861.

23. These troops were probably the fragments of the 12th Tennessee commanded by Tyree Bell. He mentions Marks coming up on his right in the counterattack. Bell, Report, SIU.

24. *OR*, 3:354; Roscoe G. Jennings to Orville Jennings, Nov. 19, 1861, Jennings Letters, UAMS; Frazer Letter, Nov. 9, 1861, in personal collection of Thomas P. Sweeney, Springfield, Mo.; C. J. Johnson to Lou Johnson, Nov. 8, 1861, Johnson Letters, LSU; *Battlefields of the South*, p. 119; *New Orleans Daily Crescent*, Nov. 11, 13, 1861.

25. *OR*, 3:309, 353, 354; *Memphis Daily Appeal*, Nov. 13, 1861.

26. The 1st Mississippi Infantry Battalion became the 44th Mississippi Infantry Regiment. The 154th Senior Tennessee was a fashionable and honored Memphis militia unit before the war that had been allowed to retain its regimental number.

27. *OR*, 3:343; White, "Diary," p. 647.

28. The Kentucky-born captain of the Yazoo packet *Charm*, William L. Trask, had been on the river most of his thirty-two years. He delighted in entertaining the ladies and newspaper reporters on board. Trask would continue to command the *Charm* until the fall of Island 10. Then he undertook the assignment of towing the *Arkansas* to a sheltered haven up the Yazoo River. His success in doing so was considered a "great feat" by rivermen.

The *Charm* itself met an inglorious death following the battle of the Big Black, May 17, 1863. Perhaps her most notable hour, other than her service at Belmont, came in the summer of 1861 when, downriver near Helena, she became for a moment a "suddenly manufactured man-of-war." H. A. Gosnell tells this exciting and amusing story in his *Guns on Western Waters*, p. 29.

29. *OR*, 3:363.

30. Ibid., 308.

31. Ibid., 343–44; *New Orleans Delta*, n.d., quoted in *Daily Nashville Patriot*, Nov. 12, 1861.

32. The "tremendous roar" of the Lady Polk had an electrifying effect on the Confederates crouched beneath the riverbank. Private Stephenson wrote:

> At its voice our men give a yell! They are not whipped—only worried, and as their new friends jump on shore, bringing loads of ammunition, they readily form in line to attack the enemy a second time. I see all this going around me as I rush along the river bank. It is like a photograph still upon my mind. And as I run along the bank hunting for the rest of my command, I come across Hammett [Stephenson's older brother] breaking open ammunition boxes and giving out cartridges. "Be a man Phil," says he as he loads me down, and away I start.

Estvan, *War Pictures*, pp. 182–83; *Memphis Daily Appeal*, Nov. 10, 1861; *CV* 3:260; *OR*, 3:324; Lindsley, *Annals*, p. 66; Wright, "Belmont," p. 72; R. H. Wood to Mary Wood, Nov. 10, 1861, Wood Letters, TSLA; Conger, *Rise of U. S. Grant*, p. 93; Stephenson, "My War Autobiography," LSU.

33. *Memphis Avalanche*, n.d., quoted in *Daily Nashville Patriot*, Nov. 12, 1861; Cartmell, "Witness," p. 190; Hubbard, "Belmont," p. 459; Twain, *Life on the Mississippi*, p. 206; *Daily Confederate News* (Columbus, Ky.), Nov. 12, 1861; Quintard, "Cheatham," p. 351.

34. Author's interview with Cheatham's daughter, Mrs. Telfair Hodgson, July 22, 1957, Sewanee, Tenn.; Graber, *Life Record*, pp. 182–83; Newspaper clipping, n.p., n.d., in personal collection of T. R. Hay, Locust Valley, N.Y.; *New York Herald*, n.d., quoted in *Charleston Daily Courier*, Aug. 15, 1864; *CV* 8:373; Evans, *Confederate Military History*, 10:302–4; B. F. Cheatham to father, Feb. 14, 1848, Cheatham Family Papers, UNSO; Timothy D. Johnson, "Cheatham: The Early Years," pp. 269–88; Losson, *Forgotten Warriors*, pp. 15–31; B. F. Cheatham, Summary of Military Career, Cheatham Biography, Cheatham Collection, UNSO; *Tennessee Magazine*, Nov. 18, 1934; Claiborne Memoirs, USAMHI; Jefferson Davis to L. Polk, Sept. 2, 1861, Polk Papers, UNSO.

35. R. H. Wood to Mary Wood, Nov. 10, 1861, Wood Letters, TSLA.

36. Pollard, *First Year*, p. 201; J. F. Henry to G. A. Henry, Nov. 8, 1861, Henry Papers, SHC; Bell, Report, SIU; Carnes, "Belmont," p. 369; *OR*, 3:334, 344, 356, 361; R. H. Wood to Mary Wood, Nov. 10, 1861, Wood Letters, TSLA; Vaughan, *Thirteenth Regiment*, pp. 12–14; S. R. Latta to Mary Latta, Nov. 8, 1861, Latta Papers, TSLA; *New Orleans Delta*, n.d., quoted in *Daily Nashville Patriot*, Nov. 12, 1861; Quintard, "Cheatham," p. 351; Hubbard, "Belmont," p. 459; Evans, *Confederate Military History*, 10:12; Stephenson, "My War Autobiography," LSU.

37. LaBree, *Camp Fires*, p. 120.

38. *Memphis Daily Appeal*, Nov. 12, 1861.

39. R. H. Wood to Mary Wood, Nov. 7, 1861, Wood Letters, TSLA; *New Orleans Delta*, n.d., quoted in *Daily Nashville Patriot*, Nov. 12, 1861; Timothy D. Johnson, "Cheatham at Belmont," p. 167.

40. Professor Armstrong had operated the boys school in Memphis for the Walkers and other prominent, wealthy families. After the battle of Belmont, Mrs. W. S. Pickett (Knox Walker's sister) wanted to have Armstrong's body brought back to Memphis. "He taught our boys. . . . He shall be buried from Calvary and sleep in my lot." Then she learned that Armstrong had been "shot to pieces" by cannon fire and that what remained of him had been placed in a common grave. Boone, "Belmont," TSLA; Frank Moore, *Anecdotes*, p. 456; *OR*, 3:344; Walke, *Naval Scenes*, p. 42; *Nashville Banner*, Nov. 13, 1861; Evans, *Confederate Military History*, 10:703; *Nashville Daily Gazette*, Nov. 10, 1861; J. Welby Armstrong to E. Blake, Nov. 1, 1861, Armstrong MSR, NARS.

41. Bell, Report, SIU.

42. *Memphis Daily Appeal*, Nov. 12, 1861.

43. White, "Diary," p. 647; *OR*, 3:334, 344, 356; *Battlefields of the South*, p. 119; Cartmell, "Witness," p. 190; R. H. Wood to Mary Wood, Nov. 10, 1861, Wood Letters, TSLA; Quintard, "Cheatham," p. 351; Roland, *Johnstton*, p. 280; Evans, *Confederate Military History*, 10:12; J. B. Battle to Flora B. Turley, Nov. 9, 1861, in Rosser, "Battle," p. 23; L. P. Yandell, Jr., to L. P. Yandell, Sr., Nov. 10, 1861, in *Memphis Avalanche*, Nov. 12, 1861.

44. Nov. 7, 1861 entry, Fielder Diary, TSLA.

45. *OR*, 3:331; *New Orleans Daily Crescent*, Nov. 13, 1861; Evans, *Confederate Military History*, 10:62–63.

46. C. J. Johnson to Lou Johnson, Nov. 8, 1861, Johnson Letters, LSU; *Daily Picayune* (New Orleans), Nov. 14, 1861; *OR*, 3:354.

47. *Daily Picayune* (New Orleans), Nov. 14, 1861.

48. Robert J. Alexander was the first member of a New Orleans hose company to die. Associates and friends learned of his death from "the sound of the funeral tappings on the bell of the Louisiana Hose Company." When the fireman's body was returned to the city, all the fire companies turned out for the funeral. *New Orleans Daily Crescent*, Nov. 11, 1861; *OR*, 3:354–55.

49. Among Tyler's casualties was his newest recruit, Pvt. Robert Tyler (no relation) of the 5th Tennessee. Rennolds, *Henry County Commands*, p. 27; Stephenson, "My War Autobiography," LSU.

50. A disgusted member of the 11th Louisiana reported: "Had our Regiment acted as they should we should have killed and captured nearly the entire force." Then he remembered that they had been thrown into confusion by firing into their own troops, almost surrounded by the enemy, "all mixed up in the woods," and "ignorant of the country." Taking all things into account, he rethought his statement and decided that after all, "they did pretty well." C. J. Johnson to Lou Johnson, Nov. 8, 1861, Johnson Letters, LSU; *New Orleans Daily Crescent*, Nov. 13, 1861.

51. C. J. Johnson to Lou Johnson, Nov. 8, 1861, Johnson Letters, LSU.

52. *Memphis Daily Appeal*, Nov. 21, 1861; Mathes, *Old Guard in Gray*, p. 147; Carnes, "Belmont," p. 369; Singletary, "Belmont," p. 507; C. J. Johnson to Lou Johnson, Nov. 8, 1861, Johnson Papers, LSU; Singletary, "Day"; J. F. Henry to G. A. Henry, Nov. 8, 1861, Henry Papers, SHC; *Daily Picayune* (New Orleans), Nov. 14, 1861; *New Orleans Daily Crescent*, Nov. 11, 1861; Nov. 7, 1861, entry, Fielder Diary, TSLA.

CHAPTER 13

1. Henry I. Smith, *Seventh Iowa*, p. 17.

2. *OR*, 3:286.

3. Austin Diary, ISHL; Lindsley, *Annals*, p. 66; Henry I. Smith, *Seventh Iowa*, p. 19; L. Ozburn to Diza Ozburn, Nov. 10, 1861, Ozburn Letters, ISHL; Crippin, "Diary"; White, "Diary," p. 647; *OR*, 3:284; U.S. Government, *Medical and Surgical History*, 1 (appendix): 18; Brinton, *Memoirs*, pp. 84–85; Schwartz, Report, CHS; *Daily Picayune* (New Orleans), Nov. 14, 1861; *CV* 16:190; *Memphis Daily Appeal*, Nov. 10, 1861.

4. *Chicago Daily Tribune*, Nov. 8, 1861; *Nashville Union and American*, Nov. 14, 1861; Lindsley, *Annals*, p. 66; *CV* 3:260, 16:190; Eddy, *Patriotism*, 1:183; Ridley, *Battles and Sketches*, pp. 25–26; Greeley, *American Conflict*, 1:396n.

5. Brinton, *Memoirs*, p. 77.

6. Grant, *Memoirs*, 1:274.

7. It appears likely from Grant's and McClernand's reports that Buford was ordered to take his place in the column, probably between Fouke's regiment and Dougherty's Brigade. *Daily Missouri Republican* (St. Louis), Jan. 16, 1886; *OR*, 3:280, 284; Odum, "Reminiscences," ISHL; D. C. Smith to Carrie Pieper, Nov. 14, 1861, Smith Letters, ISHL.

8. Schwartz, Report, CHS; *OR*, 3:280, 284, 290.

9. White, "Diary," p. 647.

10. Brinton, *Memoirs*, pp. 77–78; *Weekly Missouri Democrat* (St. Louis), Nov. 19, 1861; U. S. Grant to Jesse Root Grant, Nov. 8, 1861, in Simon, *Papers of Ulysses S. Grant*, 3:137–38; *OR*, 3:284; Seaton, "Belmont," p. 315; Crippin, "Diary," p. 232.

11. Brinton, *Memoirs*, p. 78.

12. Wentz had distinguished himself earlier at Springfield but admitted during the course of the fighting that, compared to Belmont, "Springfield was nothing to it." Henry I. Smith, *Seventh Iowa*, p. 16; D. C. Smith to Carrie Pieper, Nov. 14, 1861, Smith Letters, ISHL; *OR*, 3:298; Ingersoll, *Iowa*, p. 134; *Chicago Daily Tribune*, Nov. 15, 1861; Stuart, *Iowa Colonels*, p. 172.

13. Stuart, *Iowa Colonels*, p. 172; *OR*, 3:297; *Weekly Missouri Democrat* (St. Louis), Nov. 19, 1861.

14. The 150 men of the Reverend John Miller's command moved in single file below the enemy seeking Dollins's horsemen. Although they themselves

felt cut off, some of Grant's infantry thought they "had the appearance of being innumerable." Frazer Letter, Nov. 9, 1861, in personal collection of Thomas P. Sweeney, Springfield, Mo.

15. Brinton, *Memoirs*, pp. 77–79; White, "Diary," pp. 647–48; Henry I. Smith, *Seventh Iowa*; Grant, *Memoirs*, 1:276; Odum, "Reminiscences," ISHL; Society of the Army of the Tennessee, *Proceedings*, p. 28.

16. Schwartz, Report, CHS; *Chicago Post*, n.d.,quoted in *Memphis Daily Appeal*, Nov. 11, 1861; White, "Diary," p. 647; *OR*, 3:280; Brinton, *Memoirs*, p. 79.

17. A Logan biographer presents another account, most unflattering to McClernand: "When Logan saw the position we were in and McClernand saw it, and the latter didn't know what to do, and made the remark, 'I don't know what we are going to do,' Logan said, 'You give me permission and I will show you what I will do.' McClernand said, 'All right you go ahead.' " Logan's report of the battle, however, negates this account. Byron Andrews, *Logan*, p. 397, quoted in James P. Jones, *"Black Jack,"* p. 114; *Louisville Daily Journal*, Nov. 16, 1861; *OR*, 3:289.

18. *OR*, 3:280.

19. G. R. Vanhorn to C. W. Pierce, Oct. 26, 1886, in *Reunions of Taylor's Battery*, p. 95.

20. John Alexander Logan, *Volunteer Soldier*, p. 624; Brinton, *Memoirs*, p. 78; *OR*, 3:270, 289, 308; *Weekly Missouri Democrat* (St. Louis), Nov. 19, 1861; *Chicago Daily Tribune*, Nov. 15, 1861.

21. It was McClernand's bravery the *New York Herald* chose to emphasize. It thrilled its readers with a description of the breakout in terms of McClernand "making himself a road of blood." Nolte, "Downeasters," p. 19; *New York Herald*, Nov. 12, 1861.

22. Henry I. Smith, *Seventh Iowa*, p. 16; Singletary, "Belmont," p. 507; John Alexander Logan, *Volunteer Soldier*, p. 623; *OR*, 3:280–81; Grant, *Memoirs*, 1:276; Brinton, *Memoirs*, pp. 79–80.

23. James Grant Wilson, *Sketches*, p. 97; Frank Moore, *Anecdotes*, p. 426; *OR*, 3:281; *Louisville Daily Journal*, Nov. 16, 1861.

24. Private Trueman to Elizabeth Simpson, Nov. 11, 1861, Simpson Letters, ISHL; *OR*, 3:286; *Daily Missouri Republican* (St. Louis), Nov. 15, 1861.

25. *Reunions of Taylor's Battery*, pp. 20–21; Schwartz, Report, CHS; *Chicago Daily Tribune*, Nov. 11, 1861; *OR*, 3:270.

26. Adams, "Memoirs," ISHL; *OR*, 3:286–87, 293; Odum, "Reminiscences," ISHL.

27. *St. Louis Sunday Republican*, Nov. 10, 1861.

28. *OR*, 3:354; C. J. Johnson to Lou Johnson, Nov. 11, 1861, Johnson Letters, LSU.

29. *OR*, 3:295; Byers, *Iowa*, p. 86.

30. *Reunions of Taylor's Battery*, pp. 20–21; Schwartz, Report, CHS; *Chicago Daily Tribune*, Nov. 11, 1861; *OR*, 3:270.

31. *Chicago Daily Tribune*, Nov. 15, 1861; *St. Louis Sunday Republican*,

Nov. 10, 1861; Cartmell, "Witness," p. 190; J. F. Henry to G. A. Henry, Nov. 8, 1861, Henry Papers, SHC; *OR*, 3:293, 297; Henry I. Smith, *Seventh Iowa*, p. 80; Stuart, *Iowa Colonels*, p. 164.

32. Henry I. Smith, *Seventh Iowa*, p. 252.

33. *Louisville Daily Journal*, Nov. 15, 1861; Frank Moore, *Rebellion Record*, 3:289.

34. U. S. Grant to Jesse Root Grant, Nov. 8, 1861, in Simon, *Papers of Ulysses S. Grant*, 3:138.

35. "The retreat was a route, for our men were scattered every where. I don't care what the papers say, the men that were in it say that every man took care of himself, and hardly two men of a regiment were together. The men ran because they were scattered, but the universal testimony is that there was no panic, nine out of ten of the men came on the boats laughing and joking. They had been fighting six or seven hours, and cannon and musketry couldn't scare them any more." Nov. 13, 1861, entry, in Wills, *Army Life*, p. 43.

36. Kurtz, "Belmont," p. 21; Simon, "Grant at Belmont," p. 161; *St. Louis Sunday Republican*, Nov. 10, 1861.

37. L. Ozburn to Diza Ozburn, Nov. 10, 1861, Ozburn Letters, ISHL.

38. *Chicago Daily Tribune*, Nov. 11, 1861.

39. Squier, *Leslie's Pictorial History*, 1:196.

40. Private Trueman to Elizabeth Simpson, Nov. 11, 1861, Simpson Letters, ISHL.

41. U.S. Government, *Medical and Surgical History*, 1 (Appendix): 19.

42. D. C. Smith to Carrie Pieper, Nov. 14, 1861, Smith Letters, ISHL.

43. Young Pvt. Boggan Cash of the Secession Guards, 13th Tennessee, the great-grandson of Capt. Patrick Boggan of North Carolina revolutionary war fame, shot a Yankee officer and tried to take him prisoner. The man would not surrender "and made the mistake of tantalizing his would-be-captor on his boyish appearance." Cash killed him then, "appalled at what he had done, tried to stanch the blood of his expiring foeman and wept as he failed." Colonel Wright of the 13th sent the dead officer's sword to Cash's mother. In his note Wright wrote, "You are the mother of a hero." Cash would be killed a year later at Murfreesboro. Mathes, *Old Guard in Gray*, p. 239; Vaughan, *Thirteenth Regiment*, p. 49.

44. U.S. Government, *Medical and Surgical History*, 1 (appendix): 19.

45. John Knight to brother and sister, Nov. 13, 1861, Brown Letters, ISHL. William Knight and Dave Wallace would later be exchanged for Confederate prisoners, but William would die of his wound in December.

46. Austin Diary, ISHL.

47. E. M. Graham to W. B. Maddox, Nov. 1861, in Thompson, "Graham," p. 29.

48. Nolte, "Downeasters," pp. 19–20.

49. S. R. Latta to Mary Latta, Nov. 8, 1861, Latta Papers, TSLA.

50. *Memphis Daily Appeal*, Nov. 19, 1861; Frazer Letter, Nov. 9, 1861, in personal collection of Thomas P. Sweeney, Springfield, Mo.

51. L. Ozburn to Diza Ozburn, Nov. 10, 1861, Ozburn Letters, ISHL.

52. *Memphis Argus*, Nov. 10, 1861; C. J. Johnson to Lou Johnson, Nov. 8, 1861, Johnson Letters, LSU.

53. *Memphis Daily Appeal*, Nov. 13, 1861; *CV* 16:190.

54. Brinton, *Memoirs*, pp. 80–81.

55. Ibid., p. 82.

56. As Brinton rode on, he collected stray soldiers and stray mules. He mounted several wounded on this string of "secesh mules," including a boy who died while mounted. The manner of the young soldier's death prompted a study by Brinton published in the *American Journal of the Medical Sciences.* Brinton, *Memoirs*, p. 88.

57. Ibid., pp. 82–86.

58. *OR*, 3:280.

59. Ibid., 284–85, 271, 280; Private Trueman to Elizabeth Simpson, Nov. 11, 1861, Simpson Letters, ISHL.

60. *Memphis Daily Appeal*, Nov. 14, 1861.

61. Ibid.

62. Lt. William Shipley of Quincy, Ill., a "young man of rare talents," had been ill in camp for some time. He insisted on coming along on the Belmont expedition and performed his duties "radiant with smiles." Shipley was mortally wounded as Buford's straggling column passed Hunter's Farm. *OR*, 3:285.

63. Capt. A. K. Bozarth to J. A. McClernand, Nov. 30, 1861, McClernand Papers, ISHL; *OR*, 3:272, 285; Private Trueman to Elizabeth Simpson, Nov. 11, 1861, Simpson Letters, ISHL; Eddy, *Patriotism*, 2:54; Squier, *Leslie*'s *Pictorial History*, 1:196.

64. Crippin, "Diary," p. 232.

65. J. A. Rawlins to E. B. Washburne, n.d., in Simon, *Papers of Ulysses S. Grant*, 7:302n.

66. Jansen Reminiscences, ISHL.

CHAPTER 14

1. Maj. Henry Winslow, Polk's trouble-shooting aide-de-camp, returned from the Missouri side about 2 P.M. and supported Pillow's plea for reinforcements. He also told Polk that "my opinion was that the battle was lost unless re-enforcements were sent across; that the troops were in full retreat and appeared to have lost all confidence in their officers, and I thought your presence alone would restore order and save the day." *OR*, 3:361.

2. Other Confederate regiments watched Smith's Brigade prepare to cross. They "bewailed their fate when they found they were not to be included." Rennolds, *Henry County Commands*, p. 27; *OR*, 3:308; T. J. Walker, "Reminiscences," p. 44; Law, "Diary," p. 176.

3. Law, "Diary," p. 176; *OR*, 3:344, 348, 362, 364; *Daily Confederate News*

(Columbus, Ky.), Jan. 1862; *New Orleans Delta*, n.d., quoted in *Daily Nashville Patriot*, Nov. 21, 1861; Davis, *Rise and Fall*, 1:404.

4. The only official mention of the halt ordered by Cheatham is in Pillow's and Marks's reports. One would assume from Cheatham's and Polk's reports that the pursuit was continuous. Considering Cheatham's presence at the riverbank, however, and the time needed for the reembarkation, it seems likely that the chase was interrupted for some reason. It is plausible Cheatham thought it "prudent" to wait for Smith's Brigade to land and come up. Several sources state that Polk stopped the pursuit himself, perhaps in the name of human decency but more probably to allow the pursuers time to re-form and then continue on, prepared to meet anticipated organized resistance at the landing. *OR*, 3:327, 354; Frazer Letter, Nov. 9, 1861, in personal collection of Thomas P. Sweeney, Springfield, Mo.; Timothy D. Johnson, "Cheatham at Belmont," pp. 169–72.

5. *Memphis Daily Appeal*, Nov. 10, 13, 1861; Timothy D. Johnson, "Cheatham at Belmont," pp. 169–72; *OR*, 3:308.

6. *OR*, 3:327, 308.

7. Ibid., 344, 346, 348; Wright, "Belmont," pp. 78, 82.

8. Tending the Union wounded to the last were Surgeons Edward H. Bowman, 27th Illinois, and Amos Witter, 7th Iowa. *OR*, 3:327; U.S. Government, *Medical and Surgical History*, 1 (appendix): 19.

9. Waiting near the captured Federal hospital, Capt. R. H. Wood of the 22d Tennessee found himself with J. B. Teague of his company. They had been estranged, Teague voting against Wood in the regimental elections.

> He [Teague] had a good reason for it. He had lied on me & I told him of it before the company. He was mad about it & voted for my opponent. He, however, fought bravely at Belmont & I freely forgave him. He would now vote for me if I were a candidate. After the battle was over & we had pursued the enemy away up the river & we were pausing for breath I felt grateful to him for the bravery he had exhibited and extended my hand telling him that after such a days work all differences should be buried. He burst into tears & expressed great regret that there should have been any differences.

R. H. Wood to Mary Wood, Nov. 7, 25, 1861, Wood Letters, TSLA; Quintard, "Cheatham," p. 351; S. R. Latta to Mary Latta, Nov. 8, 1861, Latta Papers, TSLA; *OR*, 3:354, 356; *Memphis Daily Appeal*, Nov. 21, 1861.

10. *OR*, 3:346.

11. Hardly has there been a more carefully monitored lieutenant colonel than Marcus J. Wright, commanding the 154th. With him on the road at the field hospital were his regimental commander, Preston Smith, now in charge of the brigade; his division commander, Frank Cheatham; and the department commander, Leonidas Polk, not to mention Gideon Pillow who continued to give orders throughout the day to company- and regimental-size units.

12. *OR*, 3:346, 348, 270; *Memphis Daily Appeal*, Nov. 13, 21, 1861; Seaton, "Belmont," p. 315.

13. Phil Fouke would often tell the story that he was that officer and that John V. Wright, his friend and fellow congressional Democrat, "had recognized him and then spared his life." Fouke met Wright in New Orleans after the war and thanked him. "I knew he was mistaken," said Wright, "but the illusion was too good a one to be dissipated, and he died with the belief." The *Memphis Daily Appeal* learned of the incident less than a week after the battle and credited the Fouke version. The editors criticized Wright for his "excess of courtesy." *OR*, 3:348–49; *CV* 17:400; *Louisville Daily Journal*, Nov. 16, 1861; John Vines Wright, Apr. 13, 1907, Wright Scrapbooks, SHC; *Memphis Daily Appeal*, Nov. 12, 1861.

14. *Memphis Daily Appeal*, Nov. 9, 1861; *OR*, 3:344–45.

15. It proved difficult to reconcile observation with experience, but one observer tried, believing that the Yankee steamers backed into the river and headed "upstream without guidance." *Memphis Daily Appeal*, Nov. 9, 10, 13, 21, 1861; *Daily Confederate News* (Columbus, Ky.), Nov. 1861; Quintard, "Cheatham," p. 351.

16. Observers on the bluffs at Columbus at dusk could see nothing except flashes from the cannon of the gunboats. But they could hear the "battle still raging" and noted the time was five o'clock, as did a few of the participants. *New Orleans Daily Crescent*, Nov. 13, 1861.

17. *OR*, 3:308.

18. Pillow's role in the pursuit and fight at the landing is difficult to reconstruct and appraise. He is mentioned as being present but does not appear to have been in command, deploying the "victorious commands as they arrived, . . . directing the different corps entering [the cornfield] opposite the ground they would occupy on the river bank, and lining the bank for more than a mile," as he maintained in his report. It seems that Cheatham and Smith, not Pillow, led the Confederate forces in the fight against the boats. Ibid., 327.

19. *Memphis Avalanche*, n.d., quoted in *Daily Nashville Patriot*, Nov. 12, 1861; R. H. Wood to Mary Wood, Nov. 7, 1861, Wood Letters, TSLA; Mathes, *Old Guard in Gray*, p. 147; *OR*, 3:345, 351; *Nashville Union and American*, Nov. 14, 1861; Young, *Seventh Cavalry*, pp. 21–22.

20. *OR*, 3:345.

21. The 4th and 9th Tennessee regiments also crossed and marched out from Belmont that night but never saw action.

22. *Memphis Daily Appeal*, Nov. 10, 1861.

23. Buford's 27th Illinois and Dollins's cavalry, more than a mile west of the Mississippi, worried almost as much about being hit by gunboat salvos. A number of shells passed well over the Confederates, continuing on deep into the Missouri countryside. R. H. Wood to Mary Wood, Nov. 7, 1861, Wood Letters, TSLA; *OR*, 3:354; *Memphis Daily Appeal*, Nov. 9, 13, 1861; Walke, *Naval Scenes*, p. 41.

24. *Daily Missouri Republican* (St. Louis), Jan. 26, 1861; *OR*, 3:281.

25. Grant, *Memoirs*, 1:277.

26. Austin Diary, ISHL.

27. It should be noted that Captain Detrich maintained in his report to Dougherty that he established a defensive line at the landing: "There I formed the detachment on open ground, above the lane and below the point of timber where the steamer Memphis lay, and in which the enemy soon appeared, but kept out of range." Walke, *Naval Scenes*, p. 37; *OR*, 3:295, 281.

28. White, "Diary," p. 648; Schwartz, Report, CHS.

29. Morris, Kuykendall, and Harwell, *31st Regiment*, p. 25; *Reunions of Taylor's Battery*, p. 21; *Chicago Tribune*, Nov. 11, 1861.

30. *Daily Missouri Republican* (St. Louis), Jan. 26, 1886.

31. *St. Louis Sunday Republican*, Nov. 10, 1861; *Chicago Daily Tribune*, Nov. 11, 1861; L. Ozburn to Diza Ozburn, Nov. 10, 1861, Ozburn Letters, ISHL.

32. Grant, *Memoirs*, 1:278.

33. Richardson credits John Rawlins with having the captain run out a plank for Grant. Rawlins and Grant's servant Bob had just come aboard themselves. Albert D. Richardson, *Grant*, p. 202.

34. Schwartz, Report, CHS; *OR*, 3:281; "Biography of McClernand," Wallace Papers, ISHL; Seaton, "Belmont," p. 315; Grant, *Memoirs*, 1:278–79. Mrs. Grant, back at home and alone in her room at this hour, "saw" her husband. Grant remarked when she told him: "That is singular. Just about that time I was on horseback and in great peril, and I thought of you and the children, and what would become of you if I were lost." Simon, *Memoirs of Julia Dent Grant*, p. 93.

35. Centered on the hurricane deck was "a long narrow house called a 'texas.' The officers and clerks had their quarters here as well as those river gods, the pilots." Lane, *American Paddle Steamboats*, p. 33.

36. Henry I. Smith, *Seventh Iowa*, p. 260.

37. River people use "wrack" to refer to a tangle of driftwood, not to submerged boat wreckage.

38. *Daily Missouri Republican* (St. Louis), Jan. 16, 1886; White, "Diary," p. 648; Austin Diary, ISHL.

39. White, "Diary," p. 648; *Daily Missouri Republican* (St. Louis), Jan. 16, 1886; *Chicago Tribune*, Nov. 11, 1861.

40. Union Battle Reports, NARS.

41. Boynton, *Navy*, 1:513.

42. White, "Diary," p. 648.

43. Walke, *Naval Scenes*, p. 37; Stuart, *Iowa Colonels*, p. 164; *Weekly Missouri Democrat* (St. Louis), Nov. 19, 1861; D. C. Smith to Carrie Pieper, Nov. 14, 1861, Smith Letters, ISHL; Boynton, *Navy*, 1:513.

44. Austin Diary, ISHL.

45. *Chicago Daily Tribune*, Nov. 15, 1861.

NOTES TO PAGES 173-77 * 267

46. *Reunions of Taylor's Battery*, p. 21; *Weekly Missouri Democrat* (St. Louis), Nov. 19, 1861; *OR*, 3:281; *Chicago Daily Tribune*, Nov. 11, 1861.

47. *OR*, 3:271, 281, 289; *St. Louis Sunday Republican*, Nov. 10, 1861; Seaton, "Belmont," p. 315; *Chicago Daily Tribune*, Nov. 11, 1861; L. Ozburn to Diza Ozburn, Nov. 10, 1861, Ozburn Letters, ISHL; *Weekly Missouri Democrat* (St. Louis), Nov. 19, 1861.

48. Grant reported "three men wounded, one of whom belonged to one of the boats." *OR*, 3:271.

49. Seaton, "Belmont," p. 315; Austin Diary, ISHL.

50. Henry I. Smith, *Seventh Iowa*, p. 12.

51. Grant, *Memoirs*, 1:279; *St. Louis Sunday Republican*, Nov. 10, 1861.

52. Brinton, *Memoirs*, p. 89; Seaton, "Belmont," p. 315; Private Trueman to Elizabeth Simpson, Nov. 11, 1861, Simpson Letters, and Austin Diary, ISHL.

53. A week after the battle, Grant informed a correspondent that his troops "are continuing to return every day to Bird's Point. Yesterday twenty returned and they reported that eighteen others who had taken a different route would shortly arrive in camp." *OR*, 3:281; Schwartz, Report, CHS; Austin Diary, ISHL; *Chicago Daily Tribune*, Nov. 11, 1861; Seaton, "Belmont," p. 315; *Louisville Daily Journal*, Nov. 15, 1861.

54. *Chicago Daily Tribune*, Nov. 11, 1861; Seaton, "Belmont," p. 316.

55. Union Battle Reports, NARS.

56. *Ohio State Journal* (Columbus), n.d., quoted in Walke, *Naval Scenes*, p. 41.

57. Walke remained at Island 1 as he was directed. Cook returned to Fort Holt about 10 P.M. An hour after Cook's safe return Walke "weighed anchor and proceeded to Cairo." *OR*, 3:276; Walke, *Naval Scenes*, pp. 40–47.

58.

Cairo Nov 7, 1861

Capt C. McKeever A. A. G.

We met the rebels about nine oclock this morning two & half 2 1/2 miles from Belmont, drove them step by step into their camp & across the river. We burned their tents & started on our return with all their artillery but for lack of transportation had to leave four pieces in the woods. The rebels recrossed the river & followed in our rear to place of embarkation. Loss heavy on both sides.

U. S. Grant
Brig. Gen.

Simon, *Papers of Ulysses S. Grant*, 3:128.

59. Jansen Reminiscences, ISHL; Mrs. John Alexander Logan, *Reminiscences*, p. 115; Austin Diary, ISHL; *Chicago Daily Tribune*, Nov. 11, 1861; Brinton, *Memoirs*, p. 89.

CHAPTER 15

1. L. P. Yandell, Jr., to L. Yandell, Sr., Nov. 10, 1861, in Frank Moore, *Rebellion Record*, 3:289–90.

2. E. Woodward to A. Woodward, Nov. 8, 1861, in *Memphis Daily Appeal*, Nov. 10, 1861.

3. U.S. Government, *Medical and Surgical History*, 1 (appendix): 22.

4. Crippin, "Diary."

5. Edward H. Bowman to William S. Rosecrans, June 28, 1882, Rosecrans Papers, UCLA.

6. L. P. Yandell, Jr., to L. P. Yandell, Sr., Nov. 10, 1861, in Frank Moore, *Rebellion Record*, 3:289–90; *CV* 16:190.

7. Frank Moore, *Anecdotes*, p. 518.

8. Crippin, "Diary."

9. Stevenson, *Thirteen Months*, p. 75; Deupree, "Noxubee Squadron," p. 26; *Daily Missouri Republican* (St. Louis), Nov. 14, 1861.

10. Rosser, "Battle," p. 23. Horrified Charles Johnson of the 11th Louisiana went back to his tent and tore up all of his wife's letters that he had been saving carefully. "Several letters were taken from the foe . . . and exhibited throughout the camp and I had no idea of letting your letters fall into Yankee hands." C. J. Johnson to Lou Johnson, Nov. 17, 1861, Johnson Letters, LSU.

11. *St. Louis Sunday Republican*, Nov. 10, 1861.

12. Frank Moore, *Anecdotes*, pp. 138–39; D. C. Smith to Carrie Pieper, Nov. 14, 1861, Smith Letters, ISHL.

13. *Memphis Daily Appeal*, Nov. 12, 1861; Squier, *Leslie's Pictorial History*, 1:196.

14. The brother was the doctor who fought beside the skirmishers earlier in the day and the mysterious officer who had ridden up behind Capt. R. H. Wood's company in the cornfield and issued outrageous commands. Capt. McHenry Brooks had not seen his brother "since the breaking out of the Mexican War, when our doctor, leaving his northern home in Ill. or Ohio, went to Mexico, after the war remained in the south, never returning home and when our war broke out joined our southern forces. And so, the two brothers met." According to Pvt. Phil Stephenson, the doctor "had been wounded in the leg . . . and had crawled down to the river's edge, for a drink, I suppose. Some yankee had followed him and killed him. the man had evidently put his gun to the doctor's head and fired, for the powder blackened all the side of the head where the bullet entered." Squier, *Leslie's Pictorial History*, 1:196; Stephenson, "My War Autobiography," LSU.

15. Frank Moore, *Anecdotes*, p. 518.

16. Neither Congress, the War Department, nor Belmont could escape Anna Ella Carroll. She claimed she had been present and "saw the dead and dying as they lay upon the field." Her Irish confidant, river pilot Charles M. Scott, however, ruined her story. When Scott returned to St. Louis from Belmont "so infernally scared that I could neither write, nor stand, nor sleep,"

Mrs. Carroll, who was in St. Louis, not at Belmont, sent for him and received a report of doings downriver. Greenbie, *My Dear Lady*, p. 145; U.S. Government, *House Miscellaneous Document 179*, pp. 9, 17.

17. *CV* 16:190.

18. U.S. Government, *Medical and Surgical History*, 1 (appendix): 22.

19. Henry I. Smith, *Seventh Iowa*, p. 253. Thirteen wounded Federals picked up on the field the morning of November 8 were allowed to be placed on the *Belle Memphis* and returned to Cairo the night of November 8. Frank Cheatham seems to have been responsible for their release. Major Webster, who brought the flag of truce downriver, reported Lieutenant Colonel Hart's detail had buried sixty-eight men. The *St. Louis Sunday Republican* of November 10, 1861, reported eighty-five buried on the field.

20. The next day other steamers took up the task, and the *Charm* was "ordered down river after corn." *Memphis Daily Appeal*, Nov. 9, 1861; *OR*, 3:363; *CV* 2:105.

21. Butler was buried in Live Oak Cemetery, Pas Christian, Miss. L. Polk to E. G. W. Butler, Sr., Nov. 9, 1861, Polk Papers, UNSO; Charles L. Sullivan to author, Sept. 5, 1989; Polk, *Polk*, 2:57–58; *New Orleans Daily Crescent*, Nov. 13, 1861; *Memphis Daily Appeal*, Nov. 13, 1861; Wilbur E. Meneray to author, May 12, 1988.

22. Nov. 9, 1861, entry, Harper Diary, USAMHI; J. Knight to brother and sister, Nov. 30, 1861, Brown Letters, ISHL; Henry I. Smith, *Seventh Iowa*, p. 253; *Memphis Daily Appeal*, Nov. 17, 1861.

23. Dougherty would be well enough to be moved and exchanged in December. Mrs. Dougherty was sworn in as a nurse at Bird's Point "so that she could remain with her husband in camp." Dec. 6, 1861, entry, Austin Diary, ISHL; *CV* 2:106; *Memphis Daily Appeal*, Nov. 17, 1861; U. S. Grant to L. Polk, Nov. 10, 1861, L. Polk to U. S. Grant, Nov. 10, 1861, in Simon, *Papers of Ulysses S. Grant*, 3:139–40, 140n.

24. William G. Stevenson reported Irish soldiers had whiskey in their canteens and behaved as "ruffians" to their wounded and dying foes. Stevenson, *Thirteen Months*, p. 71; U.S. Government, *Medical and Surgical History*, 1 (appendix): 19.

25. Nolte, "Downeasters," p. 20; *Memphis Daily Appeal*, Nov. 17, 1861.

26. Adams, "Memoirs," ISHL.

27. *Memphis Daily Appeal*, Nov. 14, 16, 1861.

28. James M. Keller to L. Polk, Nov. 8, 1861, Polk Papers, NARS.

29. *Memphis Daily Appeal*, Nov. 14, 1861; LaPointe, "Military Hospitals," p. 327.

30. *CV* 7:445–46; Dec. 6, 21, 1861, entries, in Law, "Diary," pp. 179–80; Keating, *Memphis*, 1:501–3; *Memphis Daily Appeal*, Nov. 10, 1861; Young, *Memphis*, p. 341.

31. Young, *Memphis*, p. 341; Henry I. Smith, *Seventh Iowa*, pp. 260–61; Brinton, *Memoirs*, pp. 83–84; Ingersoll, *Iowa*, p. 135.

32. U.S. Government, *Medical and Surgical History*, 1:22–23; *St. Louis*

Weekly Missourian, Nov. 10, 1861; *OR*, 3:275; Barton, *Angels*, p. 298; James Grant Wilson, *Sketches*; Hicken, *Illinois*, p. 23; W. H. Osborn to M. Brayman, Nov. 12, 1861, McClernand Papers, ISHL.

33. Adams, "Memoirs," ISHL.

34. Ibid.

35. James Grant Wilson, *Sketches*.

36. Surgeon John Brinton tells the story of a poorly trained Illinois surgeon at Cairo who not only had never performed an amputation but "had never seen one." After Belmont, one had to be performed in his regiment, and he tried every means to avoid it. He begged Brinton to spare him and do the amputation himself, but Brinton refused, having faith in him and knowing the man's usefulness was at stake. Somehow, with Brinton at his side, the surgeon got through the ordeal. And, as Brinton wryly points out, by the time of Fort Donelson the following winter this doctor had established a reputation among the enlisted men as perhaps the most skillful surgeon in the western army. Brinton, *Memoirs*, pp. 90–91; Barton, *Angels*, p. 298; U. S. Grant to J. A. McClernand, Nov. 15, 1861, McClernand Papers, ISHL; Simon, *Papers of Ulysses S. Grant*, 3:171; James Grant Wilson, *Sketches*; Henry I. Smith, *Seventh Iowa*, p. 254; J. Knight to sister, Nov. 13, 1861, Brown Letters, ISHL.

37. Mrs. John Alexander Logan, *Reminiscences*, p. 116.

38. White, "Diary," p. 649.

39. The total number of casualties range from Grant's estimate of 485 to 607, the latter figure reported by *Harper's Magazine* in January 1862, in W. M. Polk's article in Robert Underwood Johnson and Buel, *Battles and Leaders*, and in Simon, "Grant at Belmont," p. 161. For lists of individual casualties by regiment, see *Daily Missouri Republican* (St. Louis), Nov. 12, 1861, and *St. Louis Missouri Weekly Democrat*, Nov. 19, 1861.

40. Many of the missing from the 7th were killed or wounded, perhaps as many as 74 killed and 127 wounded. Veteran Henry I. Smith of the 7th believed the loss suffered by his regiment at Belmont was unusually high, "frightful to contemplate." It also should be kept in mind that two of the ten companies of the 7th Iowa remained with the boat guard and suffered only minor loss.

41. *OR*, 3:310; *Daily Confederate News* (Columbus, Ky.), Nov. 12, 1861; *Daily Missouri Republican* (St. Louis), Nov. 15, 1861; *Daily Nashville Patriot*, Nov. 15, 1861; Polk, "Belmont," pp. 355n, 356; Simon, "Grant at Belmont," p. 161; Joseph Jones, "Medical History," p. 128; *Memphis Daily Appeal*, Nov. 17, 1861; Fox, *Regimental Losses*, p. 543; Dyer, *Compendium*, 2:587; Force, *Fort Henry to Corinth*, p. 22; Drake, *Annals*, appendix, p. 4.

42. This approximation of Confederate regimental strength (3,000) can be calculated on the basis of about 600 per regiment minus 100 to 400 men (bands, etc.) left on the Columbus side during the furious ferrying operation from 8:30 to 9:30 A.M. Pillow contended his regiments numbered less than 500 "as shown by the daily morning report." *OR*, 3:325.

43. The total of Confederates reported killed in individual regiments does not match the total killed for Polk's force. There are many reasons for such inaccuracy. Two that should be kept in mind are the staggered dates of the reports and the fact that names of men who died of wounds tend to be found in the columns of the dead and the wounded, and perhaps the missing as well.

44. Five company commanders were wounded in the 13th, and Rhea's Company A, facing Buford's flank attack unsupported, lost five killed, eight wounded, and thirty captured. For good measure John Vines Wright's law partner, "a very sensible man" according to his captors, fell into Phil Fouke's hands.

45. This estimate from some fifteen fragments of information seems low, particularly the number of wounded.

46. *Memphis Daily Appeal*, Nov. 10, 1861.

47. Many animals were killed or injured on November 7. Dollins's company lost thirteen horses. When Dollins returned and examined the remaining mounts, he declared several unfit for additional service. J. J. Dollins to J. A. McClernand, Nov. 22, 1861, McClernand Papers, ISHL.

48. *OR*, 3:282; J. A. McClernand, receipt, Nov. 12, 1861, McClernand Papers, ISHL; Brinton, *Memoirs*, pp. 92-93.

49. Sandburg, *Lincoln*, 1:465; Mathes, *Old Guard in Gray*, p. 285; U. S. Grant to Jesse Root Grant, Nov. 27, 1861, in Simon, *Papers of Ulysses S. Grant*, 3:227.

50. *Daily Nashville Patriot*, Nov. 12, 1861; *Memphis Daily Appeal*, Nov. 10, 1861.

51. Brinton, *Memoirs*, p. 92. Brinton tried hard to retrieve the instruments through negotiation but failed. A Confederate soldier ultimately swapped them to a Mississippi doctor for a horse. The fate of the orderly who went "scudding off" with Brinton's precious cargo when the shells began to fly is unknown.

52. Force, *Fort Henry to Corinth*, p. 22; *OR*, 3:290; T. J. Freeman to W. R. Hunt, Nov. 19, 1861, in *Nashville Daily Gazette*, Nov. 14, 1861; *New Orleans Daily Crescent*, Nov. 13, 1861; Barnwell, "Belmont," pp. 370-71.

53. *Daily Picayune* (New Orleans), Nov. 14, 1861.

54. *Nashville Daily Gazette*, Nov. 12, 27, 1861; *OR*, 3:310.

55. Law, "Diary," p. 177.

56. J. Cooper to P. Fouke, Nov. 10, 1861, McClernand Papers, ISHL.

57. Simon, *Papers of Ulysses S. Grant*, 3:131, 132n; Henry I. Smith, *Seventh Iowa*, p. 260.

58. *OR*, ser. 2, 1:530.

59. Judge Breese was along to pick up and bring home his son-in-law, Maj. Thomas McClurken, 30th Illinois, who had been severely wounded. McClurken would die of his wounds within the month. N. B. Buford to L. Polk, Nov. 13, 1861, Polk Papers, UNSO.

60. *Daily Missouri Republican* (St. Louis), Nov. 16, 1861; *Daily Nashville Patriot*, Nov. 15, 1861.

61. L. Polk to Frances D. Polk, Nov. 15, 1861, Polk Papers, UNSO.

62. L. P. Yandell, Jr., to L. P. Yandell, Sr., Nov. 18, 1861, in Baird, "No Sunday," p. 320; *OR*, ser. 2, 1:530.

63. *Daily Nashville Patriot*, Nov. 15, 1861.

64. Losson, *Forgotten Warriors*, p. 38.

65. Polk, "Belmont," p. 357; *CV* 8:374.

66. Polk, "Belmont," pp. 355n, 356; L. Polk to Frances D. Polk, Nov. 15, 1861, Polk Papers, UNSO.

67. L. Polk to Frances D. Polk, Nov. 15, 1861, Polk Papers, UNSO.

68. A weary Polk would reflect that evening that he and his friend Buford parted "ready to return to the same work of wholesale and sweeping destruction" tomorrow. Ibid.

69. Polk, "Belmont," p. 356; L. Polk to Frances D. Polk, Nov. 15, 1861, Polk Papers, UNSO; *CV* 8:374; N. B. Buford to L. Polk, Nov. 13, 1861, Polk Papers, UNSO; Polk, *Polk*, 2:49; *Nashville Banner*, Nov. 16, 1861.

CHAPTER 16

1. *Memphis Daily Appeal*, Nov. 9, 1861.

2. Bruce Catton observed that Confederates "who read their Bibles" and who realized that these Federals had come from "Egypt" might underline the prophecy "Egypt shall gather them, and Memphis shall bury them." Catton, *Terrible Swift Sword*, p. 68.

3. G. J. Pillow to Mary Pillow, Nov. 7, 1861, in *New York Times*, Nov. 19, 1861.

4. *OR*, 3:308–9; General Orders 20, Nov. 12, 1861, First Division, Western Department, NARS.

5. *Nashville Banner*, Nov. 10, 1861.

6. Boone, "Belmont," TSLA.

7. Ibid.

8. Young, *Memphis*, p. 341.

9. Boone, "Belmont," TSLA.

10. *Nashville Banner*, Nov. 9, 10, 1861; Estvan, *War Pictures*, p. 186; *New Orleans Daily Crescent*, Nov. 11, 1861; Horn, *Army of Tennessee*, pp. 63, 66; John Buford to Nannie Wilson, Nov. 26, 1861, Confederate Collection, TSLA; Silver, *A Life for the Confederacy*, p. 78; Folmar, *From That Terrible Field*, p. 8.

11. *OR*, 3:311.

12. Ibid., 312; James D. Richardson, *Papers of the Confederacy*, 1:168.

13. Benson, "Belmont Quick Step"; Signaigo, "Battle of Belmont," pp. 217–20.

14. The *Nashville Daily Gazette* joined the *Memphis Argus* and the *Memphis Daily Appeal* in protesting the "restrictions placed upon the Telegraph" at Co-

lumbus. Polk's clumsy and futile attempt at censorship cost him dearly with the Tennessee press. New Orleans papers, however, tended to take Polk's part and stormed at the *Daily Appeal* for deemphasizing the contributions of the Louisiana troops at Belmont.

15. *Memphis Argus*, Nov. 14, 1861.

16. L. P. Yandell, Jr., to L. P. Yandell, Sr., Dec. 15, 1861, in Baird, "No Sunday," p. 326.

17. Gosnell, *Guns on Western Waters*, p. 32; Nov. 8, 1861, entry, in C. Vann Woodward, *Mary Chestnut's Civil War*, p. 233.

18. G. J. Pillow to J. J. Pettus, Nov. 12, 1861, G. J. Pillow to L. S. Dixon, Nov. 17, 1861, G. J. Pillow to I. G. Harris, Nov. 17, 1861, Pillow MSR, NARS.

19. *OR*, 4:560–61.

20. R. H. Wood to Mary Wood, Nov. 28, 1861, Wood Letters, TSLA; C. J. Johnson to Lou Johnson, Nov. 15, 17, 1861, Johnson Letters, LSU.

21. *OR*, 52, pt. 2:222.

22. Pillow was reinstated just in time for Fort Donelson. Meanwhile, during the winter and spring, Polk set about gathering testimony about Belmont, delaying his response to Pillow's charges until July 1862. His letter to Secretary of War George Randolph at that time contains a devastating attack on Pillow. *OR*, 3:317–60.

23. Jefferson Davis would display genius in the eventual appointment of Pillow to the Conscript Bureau, a post where his initiative, his organizational talent, and his enthusiasm could be channeled effectively. Thus Davis allowed the Confederacy to make use of this Confederate patriot of high energy and special abilities who allowed himself to be consumed by ambition and jealousy.

24. J. A. McClernand to G. B. McClellan, Nov. 8, 1861, McClernand Papers, ISHL.

25. *St. Louis Sunday Republican*, Nov. 10, 1861; General Order 15, Nov. 8, 1861, McClernand Papers, ISHL.

26. *St. Louis Sunday Republican*, Nov. 10, 1861; *OR*, 3:274; U.S. Government, *Union and Confederate Navies*, 22:398.

27. John Simon points out that "everything after the first paragraph is in another hand. The entire letter, except for the first paragraph and the last sentence, was printed in the *Cincinnati Gazette*, Nov. 11, 1861, identified as a letter from USG to his father." Simon, *Papers of Ulysses S. Grant*, 3:138n.

28. Simon, *Papers of Ulysses S. Grant*, 3:137–38.

29. Simon, "Grant at Belmont," p. 165.

30. *OR*, 3:507; Simon, *Papers of Ulysses S. Grant*, 3:134.

31. "Though his stated reasons for the attack changed sufficiently to require Rawlins to rewrite the official report three years after it occurred, Grant insisted to the end of his days the battle was a success." Anderson and Anderson, *The Generals*, p. 212.

32. For a thorough and well-reasoned discussion of these reports, see

Simon, *Papers of Ulysses S. Grant*, 3:143n–156n, and "Grant at Belmont," pp. 163–65.

33. Wills, *Army Life*, p. 43.

34. Simon, *Papers of Ulysses S. Grant*, 3:135.

35. Ibid., 122; *OR*, 3:272; J. Plummer to L. F. Ross, Nov. 8, 1861, McClernand Papers, ISHL.

36. W. H. L. Wallace to Ann Wallace, Nov. 14, 1861, Wallace-Dickey Papers, ISHL.

37. Merrill, *Battle Flags South*, p. 46. Henry Walke was even angrier about how the gunboats had been neglected in the accounts of Belmont. "It is very evident that he [the secretary of navy] had no particular friends on board those two gunboats, otherwise we would have had a glowing description of their performance." Walke, *Naval Scenes*, pp. 43, 47; *OR*, 22:399.

38. Merrill, *Battle Flags South*, p. 46.

39. Nov. 13, 1861, entry, in Wills, *Army Life*, p. 41.

40. Ibid., p. 42.

41. Fiske, *Mississippi Valley*, pp. 49–50.

42. Cole, *Era of the Civil War*, p. 266.

43. David L. Wilson and Simon, *Ulysses S. Grant*, p. 53.

44. Smith called for a court of inquiry to investigate Col. Eleazer Paine's conduct, charging he ventured too close to Columbus and brought his column back in a demoralized condition.

45. J. Cutler Andrews, *North Reports*, p. 119; *St. Louis Sunday Republican*, Nov. 10, 1861; *Weekly Missouri Democrat* (St. Louis), Nov. 8, 1861; *Chicago Tribune*, Nov. 9, 1861; *Columbus* (Ohio) *Crisis*, Nov. 14, 1861, quoted in Anna Maclay Green, "Civil War Opinion," p. 6; Byers, *Iowa*, pp. 87–88; *Illinois State Journal* (Springfield), Nov. 12, 1861.

46. *Keokuk* (Iowa) *Gate City*, Nov. 8, 1861, quoted in *Chicago Daily Tribune*, Nov. 9, 1861; Simon, *Papers of Ulysses S. Grant*, 3:239n.

47. *Congressional Globe*, 37th Cong., 2d sess., pt. 3:2036, quoted in Anna Maclay Green, "Civil War Opinion," p. 23; Byers, *Iowa*, p. 87.

48. Hicken, "From Vandalia to Vicksburg," pp. 164–65; A. Lincoln to J. A. McClernand, Nov. 10, 1861, quoted in Williams, *Lincoln Finds a General*, 3:90, 92; *Columbus* (Ohio) *Crisis*, Nov. 14, 1861, quoted in Anna Maclay Green, "Civil War Opinion," p. 6; McFeely, *Grant*, p. 95.

49. *Columbus* (Ohio) *Crisis*, Nov. 14, 1861, quoted in Anna Maclay Green, "Civil War Opinion," p. 6; J. Cutler Andrews, *North Reports*, p. 119.

50. Grant, *Memoirs*, 1:281.

51. *St. Louis Sunday Republican*, Nov. 10, 1861.

52. Frank Moore, *Rebellion Record*, 2:287–88, quoted in Williams, *Lincoln Finds a General*, 3:90.

53. W. H. Onstot to Lizzie Onstot, Nov. 16, 1861, Onstot Letters, ISHL.

54. Frank Moore, *Rebellion Record*, 3:288.

55. Ibid.

56. *New York Herald*, Nov. 19, 1861.

57. U. S. Grant to Brig. Gen. Seth Williams, Nov. 20, 1861, in *OR*, 3:272–73.

CHAPTER 17

1. Johnston, *Johnston*, p. 377.

2. *Daily Picayune* (New Orleans), Nov. 14, 1861.

3. Belmont began the combat partnership of Leonidas Polk and Frank Cheatham. This special relationship, arguably the axis of the Army of Tennessee, lasted three years. Polk admired Cheatham enormously, seeing in the man's honesty, simplicity, bravery, and patriotism the prototype Tennessee soldier.

4. W. H. L. Wallace to Gov. Richard Yates, Nov. 15, 1861, Yates Papers, ISHL.

5. Reed, *Combined Operations*, p. 72.

6. Kinnison ms., SHC.

7. Byers, *Iowa*, p. 87.

8. *Ohio State Journal* (Columbus), Nov. 12, 1861.

9. *Chicago Daily Tribune*, Nov. 11, 1861.

10. Wills, *Army Life*, p. 43. During the winter that followed and into the spring, the men of Logan's "Dirty-first" would be drilling and an officer would give the command, "Belmont Charge!" This never failed to lift the men's spirits, and they would execute the double-quick with a "wild cheer." Morris, Kuykendall, and Harwell, *31st Regiment*, p. 26.

11. *Daily Confederate News* (Columbus, Ky.), Nov. 12, 1861.

12. John Alexander Logan, *Volunteer Soldier*, p. 625.

13. *Ohio State Journal* (Columbus), Nov. 12, 1861.

14. Horace Maynard (unionist congressman) to Andrew Johnson, Nov. 13, 1861, in Graf, *Papers of Andrew Johnson*, 5:33, 34n.

BIBLIOGRAPHY

MANUSCRIPT COLLECTIONS

Atlanta, Ga.
  Emory University, Robert W. Woodruff Library
    John T. Champneys Letters
    Frank Richardson Letters, Bell I. Wiley Papers
Austin, Tex.
  University of Texas, Eugene C. Barker Texas History Center
    Confederate States of America Records Collection
Baton Rouge, La.
  Louisiana State Archives
    Applications for Land Grants, State Land Office Records
  Louisiana State University Libraries, Louisiana and Lower Mississippi
    Valley Collections
    Michel Thomassin Andry and Family Papers
    Edward George Washington Butler Letters
    Walter L. Fleming Collection
    Charles James Johnson Letters
    Liddell Family Papers
    Phillip D. Stephenson, "My War Autobiography"
Boston, Mass.
  Harvard University, Houghton Library
    Frederick M. Dearborn Collection
  Massachusetts Historical Society
    Gideon Johnson Pillow Papers
Carbondale, Ill.
  Southern Illinois University, Morris Library
    Tyree H. Bell, Report of the Battle of Belmont
Carlisle, Pa.
  U.S. Army Military History Institute
    L. B. Claiborne Memoirs, *Civil War Times Illustrated* Collection
    Stuart Goldman Collection
    Aaron C. Harper Diary, Harrisburg Civil War Roundtable Collection
Chapel Hill, N.C.
  University of North Carolina, Southern Historical Collection
    Gustavus A. Henry Papers
    H. L. Kinnison ms.
    William Whann Mackall Papers

Leonidas Polk Papers (microfilm)
M. Jeff Thompson Reminiscences (typed copies)
John Vines Wright Scrapbooks
Marcus Joseph Wright Papers
Chicago, Ill.
  Chicago Historical Society
    Mason Brayman Papers
    Philip Bond Fouke Collection
    John Alexander McClernand, Autobiography
    John Alexander McClernand, Report of the Battle of Belmont
    Gideon Johnson Pillow Collection
    Adolphus Schwartz, Report of the Battle of Belmont
Cleveland, Ohio
  Western Reserve Historical Society
    Civil War Miscellany
    Gideon Johnson Pillow Papers
Columbia, Mo.
  University of Missouri–Columbia Library
    M. Jeff Thompson Papers
Durham, N.C.
  Duke University, William R. Perkins Library
    Edward George Washington Butler Papers
    Confederate States of America Papers
    Flowers Collection
    Charles C. Jones Papers
    John Euclid Magee Diary
    Solomon Scrapbook
Fayetteville, Ark.
  University of Arkansas Libraries
    William Stephen Ray Reminiscences
Iowa City, Iowa
  State Historical Society of Iowa
    Jacob G. Lauman Papers
    James C. Parrott Papers
    7th Iowa Volunteer Infantry Regiment Papers
Jackson, Miss.
  Mississippi Department of Archives and History
    Confederate Questionnaires
    John H. Miller Biographical Sketch
Kansas City, Mo.
  University of Missouri–Kansas City, Western Historical Collection
    Robert M. Snyder, Jr., Collection
Little Rock, Ark.
  University of Arkansas for Medical Sciences Library
    Roscoe G. Jennings Letters

Los Angeles, Calif.
  Personal collection of Harry G. Shepherd, Jr.
    Hazen Churchill Ladd Diary
  University of California at Los Angeles
    William S. Rosecrans Papers
Louisville, Ky.
  Filson Club
    Yandell Family Papers
Memphis, Tenn.
  Memphis–Shelby County Public Library
    Goodman Collection
    Gideon Johnson Pillow Papers
Milan, Tenn.
  Personal collection of Brent A. Cox
    Family Group Record, Robert M. Russell
Nashville, Tenn.
  Tennessee State Library and Archives
    Sally Walker Boone, "After the Battle of Belmont," Civil War Collection
    Cheatham Family Papers
    Confederate Collection, Civil War Collection
    Cooper Family Papers
    James Caswell Edenton Diary, Civil War Collection
    Alfred Tyler Fielder Diary
    Thomas Firth Diary
    George Washington Gordon and William Tecumsah Avery Papers
    Governor Isham Green Harris Papers
    William Hicks Jackson Papers
    John Johnson, "Civil War Reminiscences," Civil War Collection
    Samuel R. Latta Papers
    Register, Southern Mothers Hospital
    Robert Hancock Wood Letters, Bills Family Papers
  Vanderbilt University, Jean and Alexander Heard Library
    James G. Stahlman Collection
New Haven, Conn.
  Yale University, Sterling Library
    Civil War Manuscript Collection
    Leonidas Polk Family Papers
New Orleans, La.
  Historic New Orleans Collection
    Butler Family Papers
New York, N.Y.
  New-York Historical Society
    Gideon Johnson Pillow Correspondence
Philadelphia, Pa.
  Historical Society of Pennsylvania

    Dreer Collection
    Gideon Johnson Pillow Letters
Prescott, Ark.
  Personal collection of Mrs. N. E. Ward
    William Sylvester Dillon Diary
Princeton, N.J.
  Princeton University Library
    de Coppet Collection
St. Louis, Mo.
  Missouri Historical Society
    Civil War Collection
    Gideon Johnson Pillow Papers
    Thompson-Pillow-Polk Papers
San Marino, Calif.
  Huntington Library
    William J. Hardee Papers
Sewanee, Tenn.
  University of the South, DuPont Library
    Cheatham Family Papers
    Benjamin Franklin Cheatham Collection
    Leonidas Polk Papers
Springfield, Ill.
  Illinois State Historical Library
    Lemuel Adams, "Memoirs of Lemuel Adams"
    William Montgomery Austin Diary (typed copies)
    Bailache-Brayman Family Papers
    Brown Letters
    Thomas J. Frazee Letters
    Samuel Bateman Hood Papers
    Theodore H. Jansen Reminiscences (photocopies)
    Lewis F. Lake, "My War Service as a Member of 'Taylor's Battery,'
      Company B, 1st Illinois Light Artillery"
    John Alexander McClernand Papers
    Addison Odum, "Reminiscences bout the Battle of Belmont"
    Richard J. Oglesby Papers
    William H. Onstot Papers (typed copies and photocopies)
    Lindorf Ozburn Letters
    David W. Poak Papers (photocopies)
    Leonidas Polk Letters
    Adolphus Schwartz Collection
    Elizabeth Simpson Letters
    Dietrich C. Smith Letters
    William D. T. Travis Papers and Sketches
    27th Illinois Infantry Association Proceedings

   Wallace-Dickey Papers
   Joseph Wallace Papers
   Richard Yates Papers
Springfield, Mo.
  Personal collection of Thomas P. Sweeney
    Capt. C. W. Frazer Letter and Map
Washington, D.C.
  Library of Congress
    Andrew Hull Foote Papers
    Ulysses S. Grant Papers
    John Alexander Logan Papers
    Leonidas Polk Papers
  National Archives and Record Service
    J. Welby Armstrong MSR (RG 109)
    Mrs. Alexander Bielaski Pension Application (RG 94)
    Charles Montgomery Carroll MSR (RG 109)
    Compiled Service Records of Confederate Soldiers (RG 109)
    Confidential and Unofficial Letters Sent (RG 107)
    District of Southeast Missouri, Letters Received (RG 393)
    Henry Dougherty Pension Application (RG 94)
    Ulysses S. Grant, Letters Sent (RG 109)
    Albert S. Johnston's Command, Letters Sent, Telegrams Sent and Received (RG 109)
    Letters to Generals in the Field (RG 107)
    Samuel F. Marks MSR (RG 109)
    Ed Pickett, Jr., MSR (RG 109)
    Gideon Johnson Pillow MSR (RG 109)
    Gideon Johnson Pillow Papers (RG 109)
    Brig. Gen. Gideon Johnson Pillow's Command, Letterbook (RG 109)
    Brig. Gen. Gideon Johnson Pillow's Command, Special Order Book (RG 109)
    Leonidas Polk MSR (RG 109)
    Leonidas Polk Papers (RG 109)
    Marshall T. Polk MSR (RG 109)
    Register of Sick and Wounded, Overton General Hospital at Memphis (RG 109)
    7th Iowa Letterbook (RG 94)
    Rebecka McMurty Roberts Pension Application (RG 94)
    William D. T. Travis MSR (RG 94)
    Union Battle Reports (RG 94)
    J. Knox Walker MSR (RG 109)
    Augustus Wentz MSR (RG 94)
    Western Department, First Division, General Orders (RG 109)
    Western Department, Letters Received (RG 393)

Western Department, Records (Dept. 2) (RG 393)
Western Department, Telegrams (RG 393)
John Vines Wright MSR (RG 109)
West Point, N.Y.
    U.S. Military Academy Archives
        Cadets Admitted to the U.S. Military Academy, 1800–1848

NEWSPAPERS

Burlington (Iowa) *Hawk-Eye*
Cairo (Ill.) *Argus*
Chicago Chronicle
Chicago Daily Tribune
Cincinnati Daily Inquirer
Daily Arkansas Gazette (Little Rock)
Daily Confederate News (Columbus, Ky.)
Daily Missouri Republican (St. Louis)
Daily Nashville Patriot
Daily Picayune (New Orleans)
Frank Leslie's Illustrated Newspaper (New York, N.Y.)
Illinois State Journal (Springfield)
Louisville Daily Journal
Memphis Argus
Memphis Daily Appeal
Memphis Daily Avalanche
Mississippi Free Trader (Natchez)
Nashville Banner
Nashville Daily Gazette
Nashville Dispatch
Nashville Union and American
New Orleans Commercial Bulletin
New Orleans Daily Crescent
New York Times
Ohio State Journal (Columbus)
Pike County Democrat (Pittsfield, Ill.)
St. Louis Sunday Republican
Visalia (Calif.) *Daily Times*
Weekly Missouri Democrat (St. Louis)

POEMS AND SONGS

Benson, Joseph C., arranger. "Belmont Quick Step." Nashville, 1861.
Moore, B. J. Samuel. *Battle of Belmont*. N.p., 1861.

Rutherford, George S. *The Poetic History of the Seventh Iowa Regiment.* Muscatine, Iowa, 1863.
Signaigo, J. Augustine. "Battle of Belmont." In *War Songs and Poems of the Southern Confederacy, 1861–1865,* edited by H. M. Wharton. Washington, 1904.

MAPS

Belmont, Missouri, Maps 4 and 5 (RG 109), National Archives and Record Service, Washington, D.C.
Cowles, Calvin D., ed. *Atlas to Accompany the Official Records of the Union and Confederate Armies.* Washington, D.C., 1891–95. Reprint. New York, 1958.
Emory, W. H. Hydrographic Basin of Upper Mississippi River, 1843, Map 1829, Tennessee State Library and Archives, Nashville, Tenn.
McClernand Campaign Maps, 1861, McClernand Papers, Illinois State Historical Library, Springfield, Ill.
Mississippi River Strip, Map 417, 1861–65, Tennessee State Library and Archives, Nashville, Tenn.
Survey of Belmont Peninsula, 1843, Surveyor General's Office (RG 49), National Archives and Record Service, Washington, D.C.
Suter, Charles R. Map of a Reconnaissance of the Mississippi River from Cairo, Ill. to New Orleans, La., June 23, 1874 (RG 77), National Archives and Record Service, Washington, D.C.

OFFICIAL DOCUMENTS

Illinois Adjutant General's Office. *Report of the Adjutant General of the State of Illinois, 1861–1866.* 10 vols. Springfield, Ill., 1900.
Iowa Adjutant General's Office. *Report of Brig. Gen. Nathaniel B. Baker, Adjutant General.* Des Moines, 1867.
———. *Roster and Record of Iowa Soldiers in the War of the Rebellion, Together with Historical Sketches of Volunteer Organizations, 1861–1866.* 6 vols. Des Moines, 1908–11.
Mississippi County, Mo., Deed Book 4, Charleston, Mo.
Tulare County, Calif. Death Certificates, Visalia, Calif.
U.S. Government. *Biographical Directory of the American Congress, 1774–1949.* Washington, 1950.
———. *Civil War Chronology.* 5 vols. Washington, 1963.
———. 1860 Census, Maury County, Tenn.
———. *House Miscellaneous Document 179.* 44th Cong., 1st sess.
———. *The Medical and Surgical History of the War of the Rebellion, 1861–1865.* 3 vols. Washington, 1870–88.

———. *Official Records of the Union and Confederate Navies in the War of the Rebellion.* 30 vols. Washington, 1896.

———. *The War of the Rebellion: A Compilation of the Official Records of the Union and Confederate Armies.* 128 vols. Washington, 1880–1901.

ACCOUNTS BY PARTICIPANTS

Baird, Nancy D. "There Is No Sunday in the Army: Civil War Letters of Lundsford P. Yandell, 1861–62." *Filson Club Historical Quarterly* 53 (July 1979): 317–27.

Barnwell, Robert W. "The Battle of Belmont." *Confederate Veteran* 39:370–71.

Basler, Roy P., Marion D. Pratt, and Lloyd A. Dunlaps, eds. *Collected Works of Abraham Lincoln.* 9 vols. New Brunswick, N.J., 1953–55.

Battlefields of the South, from Bull Run to Fredericksburgh; with Sketches of Confederate Commanders, and Gossip of the Camps. By an English Combatant, Lieutenant of Artillery in the Field Staff. New York, 1864.

Brinton, John H. *Personal Memoirs.* New York, 1914.

Brown, Lucy E., comp. *Civil War Letters of John Knight, First Lieutenant, 7th Iowa Infantry, July 30, 1861–May 31, 1865.* Oak Park, Ill., 1951.

Browning, Orville Hickman. *The Diary of Orville Hickman Browning.* Edited by Theodore Calvin Pease and James G. Randall. 2 vols. Springfield, Ill., 1925–33.

Burr, Barbara. "Letters from Two Wars." *Journal of the Illinois State Historical Society* 30 (April 1937): 135–58.

Carnes, W. W. "In the Battle of Belmont." *Confederate Veteran* 39:369–70.

Cartmell, J. M. "Witness to the Battle of Belmont." *Confederate Veteran* 16:190.

Chetlain, Augustus Lewis. *Recollections of Seventy Years.* Galena, Ill., 1899.

Cramer, Jesse Grant, ed. *Letters of Ulysses S. Grant to His Father and His Youngest Sister, 1857–78.* New York, 1912.

Crippin, Edward W. "The Diary of Edward W. Crippin, Private, 27th Illinois Volunteers, War of the Rebellion, August 7, 1861, to September 19, 1863." *Transactions of the Illinois State Historical Society* 14 (1909): 220–84.

Crist, Lynda L., ed. *Papers of Jefferson Davis.* 6 vols. Baton Rouge, 1971– .

Davidson, N. P. "Maj. John H. Miller, a 'Fighting Parson.' " *Confederate Veteran* 18:27.

Davis, Jefferson. *The Rise and Fall of the Confederate Government.* 2 vols. New York, 1881.

Deupree, J. G. "Reminiscences of Service with the First Mississippi Cavalry." *Publications of the Mississippi Historical Society* 7:85–100.

Durham, Walter T., ed. "Civil War Letters to Wynnewood." *Tennessee Historical Quarterly* 34 (Spring 1975): 32–47.

Eads, James B. "Recollections of Foote and the Gun-boats." In *Battles and Leaders of the Civil War*, edited by Robert Underwood Johnson and Clarence Clough Buel, 1:338–46. New York, 1887.

Eby, Henry H. *Observations of an Illinois Boy in Battle, Camp and Prison—1861 to 1865*. Mendota, Ill., 1910.

Erickson, Edgar L., ed. "Hunting for Cotton in Dixie: From the Civil War Diary of Captain Charles E. Wilcox." *Journal of Southern History* 4 (November 1938): 493–514.

Folmar, John Kent, ed. *From That Terrible Field: Civil War Letters of James M. Williams, Twenty-First Alabama Infantry Volunteers*. University, Ala., 1981.

Force, Manning F. *From Fort Henry to Corinth*. New York, 1881.

Gorgas, Josiah. *Civil War Diary*. Edited by Frank Vandiver. Tuscaloosa, Ala., 1947.

Gower, Herschel. *Pen and Sword: The Life and Journals of Randall McGavock*. Nashville, 1959.

Graber, Henry W. *The Life Record of H. W. Graber, a Terry Texas Ranger, 1861–1865: Sixty-Two Years in Texas*. 1912. Reprint. Austin, Tex., 1987.

Graf, LeRoy A., ed. *The Papers of Andrew Johnson*. 7 vols. Knoxville, 1967– .

Grant, Ulysses Simpson. *Personal Memoirs of U. S. Grant*. 2 vols. New York, 1885–86.

Hubbard, George H. "In the Battle of Belmont, Mo." *Confederate Veteran* 30:459.

Johnson, Robert Underwood, and Clarence Clough Buel, eds. *Battles and Leaders of the Civil War* 4 vols. New York, 1887.

Law, the Reverend J. G. "Diary of the Rev. J. G. Law." *Southern Historical Society Papers* 11:175–81, 297–304, 460–65, 12:538–43.

Logan, John Alexander *The Volunteer Soldier of America. By John A. Logan. With Memoir of the Author and Military Reminiscences from General Logan's Private Journal*. Chicago, 1887.

Logan, Mrs. John A. "Illinois in the Councils of the Nation." *Transactions of the Illinois State Historical Society* 9 (1916): 230–39.

———. *Reminiscences of a Soldier's Wife: An Autobiography*. New York, 1913.

Montgomery, Frank A. *Reminiscences of a Mississippian in Peace and War*. Cincinnati, 1901.

Moore, Frank, ed. *Anecdotes, Poetry and Incidents of the War: North and South, 1860–1865*. New York, 1867.

———. *Rebellion Record: A Diary of American Events, with Documents, Narratives, Illustrative Incidents, Poetry, etc.* 10 vols. New York, 1861–63.

Nolte, Eugene A., ed. "Downeasters in Arkansas: Letters of Roscoe G. Jennings to His Brother." *Arkansas Historical Quarterly* 18 (Spring 1959): 3–25.

Pillow, Gideon J. *Speech of Gen. Gideon J. Pillow, Delivered at the Mass Meeting of the Democracy, Near Columbia, Tenn. On the 13th of July, 1844, on the Annexation of Texas*. Columbia, Tenn., 1844.

Quaife, Milo M. *The Diary of James K. Polk during His Presidency, 1845 to 1849.* 4 vols. Chicago, 1910.

Reunions of Taylor's Battery, 18th Anniversary of the Battle of Fort Donelson, Feb. 14, 1880, 25th Anniversary of the Battle of Belmont, Nov. 6, 1886. Chicago, 1890.

Richardson, James D. *The Messages and Papers of the Confederacy, Including Diplomatic Correspondence, 1861–1865.* 2 vols. Nashville, 1905.

Ridley, Bromfield Lewis *Battles and Sketches of the Army of Tennessee.* Mexico, Mo., 1906.

Rosser, R. W., ed. "The Battle of Belmont: Pvt. John Bell Battle's Eyewitness Account." *Confederate Chronicles of Tennessee* 2 (1987): 21–54.

Seaton, John "The Battle of Belmont." In Military Order of the Loyal Legion of the United States, Kansas Commandery, *War Talks in Kansas.* Kansas City, 1906.

Shanks, William F. G. *Personal Recollections of Distinguished Generals.* New York, 1866.

Silver, James W., ed. *A Life for the Confederacy as Recorded in the Pocket Diaries of Pvt. Robert A. Moore.* Jackson, Tenn., 1959.

Simon, John Y., ed. *The Papers of Ulysses S. Grant.* 14 vols. Carbondale, Ill., 1967– .

———. *Personal Memoirs of Julia Dent Grant.* New York, 1975.

Singletary, Don. "The Battle of Belmont." *Confederate Veteran* 23:506–7.

———. "The Day of the Battle of Belmont." *Hickman County Gazette*, September 30, 1971.

Smith, Henry I. *History of the Seventh Iowa Veteran Volunteer Infantry.* Mason City, Iowa, 1903.

Smith, Susan "The Soldier's Friend." *Confederate Veteran* 7:444–46.

Society of the Army of the Tennessee. *Report of the Proceedings of the Society of the Army of the Tennessee at the First Annual Meeting, Held at Cincinnati, O., November 14th and 15th, 1866.* Cincinnati, 1877.

Squier, Ephriam George, ed. *Frank Leslie's Pictorial History of the American Civil War.* 2 vols. New York, 1861–62.

Stanley, Henry Morton. *The Autobiography of Sir Henry Morton Stanley.* Edited by Dorothy Stanley. New York, 1909.

Stevenson, William G. *Thirteen Months in the Rebel Army.* New York, 1862.

Taylor, William. "About the Battle of Belmont." *Confederate Veteran* 16:345–46.

Twain, Mark. *Life on the Mississippi.* New York, 1883.

Thompson, William Y., ed. "E. M. Graham, North Louisianian." Center for Louisiana Studies, University of Southwestern Louisiana, Lafayette, La.

Vaughan, Alfred J. *Personal Record of the Thirteenth Regiment Tennessee Infantry.* Memphis, 1897.

Walke, Henry. "The Gun-boats at Belmont and Fort Henry." In *Battles and Leaders of the Civil War*, edited by Robert Underwood Johnson and Clarence Clough Buel, 1:358–67. New York, 1887.

———. *Naval Scenes and Reminiscences of the Civil War in the United States.* New York, 1877.

Walker, T. J. "Reminiscences of the Civil War." *Confederate Chronicles of Tennessee* 1 (June 1986): 37–94.

Wallace, Isabel. *Life and Letters of W. H. L. Wallace.* Chicago, 1909.

Wallace, Lew. "The Capture of Ft. Donelson." In *Battles and Leaders of the Civil War*, edited by Robert Underwood Johnson and Clarence Clough Buel, 1:398–428. New York, 1887.

West, J. D. "The 13th Tennessee Regiment." *Tennessee Historical Magazine* 7 (1921–23): 180–93.

White, Patrick H. "Civil War Diary of Patrick H. White." Edited by J. E. Boos. *Journal of the Illinois State Historical Society* 15 (October 1922–January 1923): 640–63.

Wilds, George B. "Battle of Belmont, Mo." *Confederate Veteran*, 32:485–86.

Wills, Charles Wright. *Army Life of an Illinois Soldier.* Edited by Mary E. Kellogg. Washington, 1906.

Woodward, C. Vann. *Mary Chestnut's Civil War.* London, 1981.

Wright, Marcus Joseph. "The Battle of Belmont." *Southern Historical Society Papers* 16:69–82.

———. *Diary of General Marcus J. Wright, C.S.A.* N.p., n.d.

———. "Personal Recollections of General Grant." *Confederate Veteran* 17:400–402.

BOOKS

Allen, Hall. *Center of Conflict: A Factual Story of the War between the States in Western Kentucky and Tennessee.* Paducah, Ky., 1961.

Allen, John W. *Legends and Lore of Southern Illinois.* Carbondale, Ill., 1963.

Anderson, Nancy Scott, and Dwight Anderson. *The Generals: Ulysses S. Grant and Robert E. Lee.* New York, 1988.

Andrews, Byron. *A Biography of General John A. Logan: With an Account of His Public Service in Peace and War.* New York, 1884.

Andrews, J. Cutler. *The North Reports the Civil War.* Pittsburgh, 1955.

———. *The South Reports the Civil War.* Princeton, 1979.

Badeau, Adam. *Military History of Ulysses S. Grant, from April, 1861 to April, 1865.* 3 vols. New York, 1881.

Barton, George. *Angels of the Battlefield.* Philadelphia, 1898.

Bateman, Newton. *Historical Encyclopedia of Illinois with Commemorative Biographies.* Chicago, 1926.

Bergeron, Arthur W., Jr. *Guide to Louisiana Confederate Military Units, 1861–1865.* Baton Rouge, 1989.

Boynton, Charles Brandon. *The History of the Navy During the Rebellion.* 2 vols. New York, 1866.

Brown, Dee Alexander. *Grierson's Raid.* Urbana, Ill., 1954.

Brown, Leonard. *American Patriotism*. Des Moines, 1869.

Byers, Samuel H. M. *Iowa in War Times*. Des Moines, 1888.

Caldwell, Joshua William. *Sketches of the Bench and Bar of Tennessee*. Knoxville, 1898.

Carter, Samuel, III. *The Final Fortress: The Campaign for Vicksburg, 1862–1863*. New York, 1980.

Catton, Bruce. *Grant Moves South*. Boston, 1960.

———. *Never Call Retreat*. Garden City, N.Y., 1965.

———. *Terrible Swift Sword*. Garden City, N.Y., 1963.

———. *This Hallowed Ground: The Story of the Union Side of the Civil War*. Garden City, N.Y., 1956.

———. *U. S. Grant and the American Military Tradition*. Boston, 1954.

Coatesworth, Stella S. *The Loyal People of the North-west*. Chicago, 1869.

Cole, Arthur Charles *The Era of the Civil War, 1848–1870*. Vol. 3, *Centennial History of Illinois*. Springfield, Ill., 1919.

Conger, A. L. *The Rise of U. S. Grant*. New York, 1931.

Connelly, Thomas Lawrence. *Army of the Heartland: The Army of Tennessee, 1861–1862*. Baton Rouge, 1967.

Conrad, Glenn R. *A Dictionary of Louisiana Biography*. 2 vols. New Orleans, 1988.

Cooling, Benjamin Franklin. *Forts Henry and Donelson: the Key to the Confederate Heartland*. Knoxville, 1987.

Coulter, E. Merton. *Civil War and Reconstruction in Kentucky*. Chapel Hill, 1926.

Cullom, George W. *Biographical Register of the Officers and Graduates of the U. S. Military Academy*. 6 vols. New York, 1879–1920.

Daniel, Larry J. *Cannoneers in Gray: The Field Artillery of the Army of Tennessee, 1861–1865*. University, Ala., 1984.

Dawson, George Francis. *Life and Services of Gen. John A. Logan as Soldier and Statesman*. Chicago, 1887.

Dell, Christopher. *Lincoln and the War Democrats: The Gradual Erosion of Conservative Tradition*. London, 1975.

Drake, Edwin L., ed. *Annals of the Army of Tennessee*. Nashville, 1878.

Dyer, Frederick H. *A Compendium of the War of the Rebellion*. 3 vols. New York, 1959.

Eaton, Clement. *A History of the Southern Confederacy*. New York, 1954.

Eckenrode, Hamilton J. *George B. McClellan*. Chapel Hill, 1936.

Eddy, Thomas Mears. *The Patriotism of Illinois*. 2 vols. Chicago, 1865–66.

Eisenschimml, Otto. *The Celebrated Case of Fitz John Porter*. Indianapolis, 1950.

Eliot, Ellsworth, Jr. *West Point in the Confederacy*. New York, 1941.

———. *Yale in the Civil War*. New Haven, 1932.

Erwin, Milo. *The History of Williamson County, Illinois*. Macon, Ill., 1876.

Estvan, Bela. *War Pictures from the South*. New York, 1863.

Evans, Clement Anselm. *Confederate Military History*. 12 vols. Atlanta, 1899.

Fiske, John. *The Mississippi Valley in the Civil War*. New York, 1902.

Floyd, William Barrow. *The Barrow Family of Old Louisiana*. Lexington, Ky., 1963.

Fox, William F. *Regimental Losses in the American Civil War, 1861–1865*. Albany, N.Y., 1889.

Frost, John. *The Mexican War and Its Warriors*. New York, 1848.

Goodspeed Publishing Company. *Biographical and Historical Memoirs of Mississippi*. Chicago, 1891.

Gosnell, Harpur Allen. *Guns on Western Waters: The Story of River Gunboats in the Civil War*. Baton Rouge, 1949.

Greeley, Horace. *The American Conflict: A History of the Great Rebellion in the United States of America, 1860–1864*. 2 vols. Hartford, Conn., 1865.

Green, William Mercer. *Memoir of Rt. Rev. James Hervey Otey*. New York, 1885.

Greenbie, Marjorie Barstow. *My Dear Lady: The Story of Anna Ella Carroll, the "Great Unrecognized Member of Lincoln's Cabinet."* New York, 1974.

Hallum, John. *Biographical and Pictorial History of Arkansas*. Albany, N.Y., 1887.

Hamilton, James. *The Battle of Fort Donelson*. New York, 1968.

Harrison, Lowell H. *The Civil War in Kentucky*. Lexington, 1975.

Heitman, Francis B. *Historical Register and Dictionary of the United States Army*. 2 vols. Washington, 1903.

Hicken, Victor. *Illinois in the Civil War*. Urbana, Ill., 1966.

Horn, Stanley Fitzgerald. *The Army of Tennessee*. Norman, Okla., 1941.

Illinois Civil War Centennial Commission. *Civil War Medal of Honor Winners from Illinois*. Springfield, Ill., 1962.

Ingersoll, Lurton Dunham. *Iowa and the Rebellion*. Philadelphia, 1866.

Iowa Civil War Centennial Commission. *The Undying Procession: Iowa's Civil War Regiments*. Edited by Edith W. McElroy. Springfield, Ill., n.d.

Johanssen, Robert W. *Stephen A. Douglas*. New York, 1973.

Johnston, William Preston *Life of General Albert Sidney Johnston*. New York, 1878.

Jones, James P. *"Black Jack": John A. Logan and Southern Illinois in the Civil War Era*. Tallahassee, 1967.

Keating, J. M. *History of the City of Memphis and Shelby County, Tennessee*. 2 vols. Syracuse, N.Y., 1888.

LaBree, Ben, ed. *Camp Fires of the Confederacy*. Louisville, 1899.

Lane, Carl D. *American Paddle Steamboats*. New York, 1943.

Lewis, Lloyd. *Captain Sam Grant*. Boston, 1950.

———. *Sherman, Fighting Prophet*. New York, 1932.

Liddell Hart, Basil Henry. *Sherman: Soldier, Realist, American*. New York, 1929.

Linderman, Gerald P. *Embattled Courage: The Experience of Combat in the American Civil War*. New York, 1987.

Lindsley, John Berrien, ed. *The Military Annals of Tennessee*. Nashville, 1896.

Livermore, Thomas Leonard. *Numbers and Losses in the Civil War in America, 1861–1865*. New York, 1901.

Livingston, John. *Sketches of Eminent Americans*. 2 vols. New York, 1853.

Losson, Christopher. *Tennessee's Forgotten Warriors: Frank Cheatham and His Confederate Division*. Knoxville, 1990.

McBride, Robert M., and Daniel M. Robison, eds. *Biographical Directory of the Tennessee General Assembly*. 2 vols. Nashville, 1975.

McCartney, Clarence Edward. *Grant and His Generals*. New York, 1953.

McFeely, William S. *Grant: A Biography*. New York, 1981.

McMurry, Richard M. *Two Great Rebel Armies: An Essay in Confederate Military History*. Chapel Hill, 1989.

McPherson, James M. *Battle Cry of Freedom: The Civil War Era*. New York, 1988.

Marshall-Cornwall, James. *Grant as a Military Commander*. London, 1970.

Mathes, James Harvey. *The Old Guard in Gray*. Memphis, 1897.

Menefee, Eugene L., and Fred A. Dodge. *History of Tulare and Kings Counties California*. Los Angeles, 1913.

Merrill, James M. *Battle Flags South: The Story of the Civil War Navies on Western Waters*. Rutherford, N.J., 1970.

Michael, William Henry. *Iowa Soldiers and Sailors in the War of the Rebellion*. Des Moines, 1904.

Milton, George Fort. *The Eve of Conflict: Stephen A. Douglas and the Needless War*. Boston, 1934.

Monaghan, Jay. *Swamp Fox of the Confederacy: The Life and Military Services of M. Jeff Thompson*. Tuscaloosa, Ala., 1957.

Morris, William S., J. B. Kuykendall, and L. D. Harwell. *History of the 31st Regiment Volunteers, Organized by John A. Logan*. Evansville, Ind., 1902.

Nebelsick, Alvin L. *History of Belleville*. Belleville, Ill., 1951.

Nevins, Allan. *Ordeal of the Union*. 2 vols. New York, 1947.

Nichols, James L. *Confederate Engineers*. Tuscaloosa, Ala., 1957.

Parks, Joseph H. *General Leonidas Polk, C.S.A.* Baton Rouge, 1962.

Perry, W. S. *The History of the American Episcopal Church*. 2 vols. Boston, 1885.

Polk, William Mecklenburg. *Leonidas Polk, Bishop and General*. 2d ed. 2 vols. New York, 1915.

Pollard, Edward A. *The First Year of the War*. Richmond, Va., 1862.

Porter, David Dixon. *Naval History of the Civil War*. New York, 1886.

Potter, David M. *The Impending Crisis, 1848–1861*. New York, 1963.

Powell, Betty F. *History of Mississippi County, Missouri, Beginning through 1972*. Independence, Mo., 1975.

Reed, Rowena. *Combined Operations in the Civil War*. Annapolis, Md., 1978.

Rennolds, Edwin Hansford. *A History of the Henry County Commands Which Served in the Confederate States Army*. Jacksonville, Fla., 1904.

Richardson, Albert D. *A Personal History of Ulysses S. Grant*. Chicago, 1868.

Roland, Charles P. *Albert Sidney Johnston*. Austin, Tex., 1964.

Rowland, Dunbar, ed. *Mississippi: Comprising Sketches of Counties, Towns, Events, Institutions, and Persons, Arranged in Cyclopedic Form*. 4 vols. Spartanburg, S.C., 1976.

Sandburg, Carl. *Abraham Lincoln: The War Years*. 4 vols. New York, 1939.

Scharf, J. Thomas. *History of the Confederate States Navy*. New York, 1887.

Schmitt, William A. *History of the Twenty-Seventh Illinois Volunteers*. Winchester, Ill., 1892.

Smith, George W. *A History of Southern Illinois*. 3 vols. Chicago, 1912.

Smith, Justin H. *The War with Mexico*. 2 vols. New York, 1929.

Speer, William S. *Sketches of Prominent Tennesseans*. Nashville, 1888.

Stickles, Arndt M. *Simon Bolivar Buckner*. Chapel Hill, 1940.

Stuart, Addison A. *Iowa Colonels and Regiments: Being a History of Iowa Regiments in the War of the Rebellion*. Des Moines, 1865.

Sword, Wiley. *Shiloh: Bloody April*. New York, 1974.

Tennessee Civil War Commission. *Tennesseans in the Civil War*. 2 vols. Nashville, 1964–65.

Thomas, Benjamin Platt, and Harold M. Hyman. *Stanton: The Life and Times of Lincoln's Secretary of War*. New York, 1962.

U.S. Infantry School. *Battle of Belmont*. Camp Benning, Ga., 1921.

Wakelyn, Jon L. *Biographical Directory of the Confederacy*. Edited by Frank Vandiver. Westover, Conn., 1977.

Warner, Ezra J. *Generals in Blue: Lives of the Union Commanders*. Baton Rouge, 1964.

———. *Generals in Gray: Lives of the Confederate Commanders*. Baton Rouge, 1959.

Way, Frederick J. *Way's Packet Directory, 1848–1983*. Athens, Ohio, 1983.

Way, Virgil, and Isaac H. Elliott. *History of the Thirty-first Regiment Illinois Volunteer Infantry in the Civil War*. Gibson City, Ill., 1902.

Williams, Kenneth P. *Lincoln Finds a General*. 5 vols. New York, 1949–59.

Wilson, David L., and John Y. Simon, eds. *Ulysses S. Grant: Essays and Documents*. Carbondale, Ill., 1981.

Wilson, James Grant. *Biographical Sketches of Illinois Officers Engaged in the War Against the Rebellion of 1861*. Chicago, 1862.

———. *Life of John A. Rawlins*. New York, 1916.

———. *Life of Ulysses S. Grant*. Springfield, Mass., 1868.

Wilson, James Grant, and John Fiske, eds. *Appleton's Cyclopedia of American Biography*. 17 vols. New York, 1900.

Wingfield, Marshall. *Literary Memphis: A Survey of Its Writers and Writings*. Memphis, 1942.

Winston, E. T. *Story of Pontotoc*. Pontotoc, Miss., 1931.

Winters, John D. *The Civil War in Louisiana*. Baton Rouge, 1963.

Woodward, William E. *Meet General Grant*. New York, 1928.

Wright, Marcus Joseph. *Tennessee in the War, 1861–1865*. New York, 1908.

Yale University. *Obituary Record of Graduates of Yale College Deceased from June, 1860 to June, 1880*. New Haven, 1880.

Young, J. P. *The Seventh Cavalry*. Nashville, 1890.

——. *Standard History of Memphis, Tennessee*. Knoxville, 1912.

ARTICLES

Bell, Patricia. "Gideon Pillow: A Personality Profile." *Civil War Times Illustrated* 6 (June 1967): 12–19.

Bergeron, Paul H. "All in the Family: President Polk in the White House." *Tennessee Historical Quarterly* 46 (Spring 1987): 10–20.

Briggs, John E. "The Enlistment of Iowa Troops during the Civil War." *Iowa Journal of History and Politics* 15 (July 1917): 323–92.

Brinkman, E. C. "They Wronged John A. Logan." *Filson Club Historical Quarterly* 41 (1967): 154–68.

Calbert, Jack. "The Jackson Purchase and the End of the Neutrality Policy in Kentucky." *Filson Club Historical Quarterly* 38 (July 1964): 206–23.

Carpenter, C. C., and G. W. Crossley. "Seventh Iowa Volunteers in the Civil War Gave Valiant Service." *Annals of Iowa* 34 (1957): 100–111.

Castel, Albert. "Black Jack Logan." *Civil War Times Illustrated* 15 (November 1976): 4–10, 41–45.

Collins, William H. "Biographical Sketch of Maj. Gen. James D. Morgan." *Transactions of the Illinois State Historical Society* 11:274–85.

Cooling, Benjamin F. "Gideon Johnson Pillow." In *Dictionary of American Military Biography*, edited by Roger J. Spiller, 3:861–65. Westport, Conn., 1985.

Cross, Jasper W. "The Civil War Comes to Egypt." *Journal of the Illinois State Historical Society* 44 (Summer 1951): 160–69.

Cunningham, S. A. "Mother of the Confederacy." *Confederate Veteran* 2: 176–77.

——. "Tyree H. Bell." *Confederate Veteran* 6:529.

Deupree, J. G. "The Noxubee Squadron of the First Mississippi Cavalry, C.S.A., 1861–1865." *Publications of the Mississippi Historical Society* 2:12–143.

Fakes, Turner J., Jr. "Memphis and the Mexican War." *West Tennessee Historical Society Papers* 11 (1948): 119–44.

"Forgotten Likeness of Captain Alexander Bielaski Uncovered." *American Polonia Reporter* 7 (November–December 1962): 15.

Gillespie, Michael L. "The Novel Experiment: Cottonclads and Steamboatmen." *Civil War Times Illustrated* 22 (December 1983): 34–39.

Green, Anna Maclay. "Civil War Opinion of General Grant." *Journal of the Illinois State Historical Society* 22 (April 1929): 1–64.

Hicken, Victor. "John A. McClernand and the House Speakership Struggle of 1859." *Illinois State Historical Society Journal* 53 (1960): 163–78.

Hogan, Don L. "General Pillow's Body Rests in Lonely Grave." *Memphis Press Scimitar*, March 11, 1927.

Jacobs, Mrs. Eloise Tyler. "Commodore Montgomery, a Confederate Naval Hero, and His Adventures." *Confederate Veteran* 25:26–27.

Johnson, Timothy D. "Benjamin Franklin Cheatham: The Early Years." *Tennessee Historical Quarterly* 42 (Fall 1983): 269–75.

————. "Benjamin Franklin Cheatham at Belmont." *Missouri Historical Review* 81 (1986–87): 159–72.

Jones, James P. "Brig. General James Camp Tappan, C.S.A." *Phillips County Historical Quarterly* 3 (June 1965).

Jones, Joseph. "Medical History of the Southern Confederacy." *Southern Historical Society Papers* 20:121–32.

Keiser, Thomas J. "The St. Louis Years of Ulysses S. Grant." *Gateway Heritage* 6 (Winter, 1985–86): 10–21.

Kilmer, George L. "War to the Death: The Seventh Iowa in the Battles of the West." War Department Library, pamphlet 270. Washington, n.d.

Kurtz, Henry I. "The Battle of Belmont." *Civil War Times Illustrated* 3 (June 1963): 18–24.

LaPointe, Patricia M. "Military Hospitals in Memphis, 1861–1865." *Tennessee Historical Quarterly* 42 (Winter 1983): 329–42.

Levene, Helene H. "Illinois Catholics in the Civil War." *Illinois Civil War Sketches* 2 (June 1963): 15–19.

Long, E. B. "The Paducah Affair: Bloodless Action That Altered the Civil War in the Mississippi Valley." *Register of the Kentucky Historical Society* 70 (1972): 250–60.

Longacre, Edward G. "Congressman Becomes General: The Rise of John A. McClernand." *Civil War Times Illustrated* 21 (November 1982): 30–39.

Lufkin, Charles L. "Divided Loyalties: Sectionalism in Civil War McNairy County, Tennessee." *Tennessee Historical Quarterly* 47 (Fall 1988): 169–77.

McGhee, James E. "The Neophyte General: U. S. Grant and the Belmont Campaign." *Missouri Historical Review* 47 (July 1973): 465–83.

McIlvaine, Charles Pettit. "Leonidas Polk." *Southern Historical Society Papers* 18:371–81.

Mullen, Jay Carlton. "The Turning of Columbus." *Register of the Kentucky Historical Society* 44 (July 1966): 209–55.

Nichols, Janie M. "Gen. James C. Tappan, C.S.A." *Confederate Veteran* 39:330–32.

Polk, William Mecklenburg. "General Polk and the Battle of Belmont." In *Battles and Leaders of the Civil War*, edited by Robert Underwood Johnson and Clarence Clough Buel, 1:348–57. New York, 1887.

Porter, James Davis. "A Sketch of the Life and Services of Gen. B. F. Cheatham." *Southern Bivouac* 2 (1883–84): 145–50.

Quintard, Rev. Charles. "B. F. Cheatham, C.S.A." *Southern Historical Society Papers* 16:349–54.

Randall, William H. F. "General Lauman, a Rift in the Cloud." *Annals of Iowa* 5 (1867): 897–902.

Rawlings, Mrs. Isaac D. "Polish Exiles in Illinois." *Transactions of the Illinois State Historical Society* 34:83–104.

Roth, David E. "The Civil War at the Confluence, Where the Ohio Meets the Mississippi." *Blue and Gray Magazine* 2 (July 1985): 6–20.

Sears, David. "David B. Sears, Pioneer in the Development of the Water Power of the Mississippi River." *Journal of the Illinois State Historical Society* 8 (July 1915): 300–315.

Sewell, Alan. "The Loyalty of Illinois." *Civil War Times Illustrated* 20 (December 1981): 14–21.

Simon, John Y. "Grant at Belmont." *Military Affairs* 45 (December 1981): 161–66.

———. "John Alexander McClernand." In *Historical Times Illustrated Encyclopedia of the Civil War*, edited by Patricia L. Faust, pp. 56–457. New York, 1986.

Snyder, J. F. "Charles Dickens in Illinois." *Journal of the Illinois State Historical Society* 3 (October 1910): 7–22.

Spence, Philip B. "Leonidas Polk." *Confederate Veteran* 8:373.

Stonesifer, Roy P., Jr. "Gideon J. Pillow: A Study in Egotism." *Tennessee Historical Quarterly* 25 (December 1966): 340–50.

Strawn, Halbert J. "The Attitude of General John A. Logan on the Question of Secession in 1861." *Journal of the Illinois State Historical Society* 6 (July 1913): 256–57.

Tappan, Thomas Edmund, Jr. "General James Camp Tappan." Unpublished ms. in possession of Thomas C. Tappan, Memphis, Tenn.

Throne, Mildred. "Iowans and the Civil War." *Palimpsest* 50 (February 1969): 65–143.

———. "Letter from Jacob Lauman at Shiloh." *Iowa Journal of History* 52 (July 1954): 273.

Upham, Cyril B. "Arms and Equipment for the Iowa Troops in the Civil War." *Iowa Journal of History and Politics* 16 (January 1918): 3–52.

Wade, Stephen. "Prospects for Cairo, Ill., Heading Down." *News Free Press* (Chattanooga, Tenn.), August 6, 1989.

Walker, Peter Franklin. "Building a Tennessee Army: Autumn, 1861." *Tennessee Historical Quarterly* 16 (June 1957), 99–116.

———. "Holding the Tennessee Line: Winter, 1861–1862." *Tennessee Historical Quarterly* 16 (September 1957): 228–49.

Warner, Ezra J. "Who Was General Tyler?" *Civil War Times Illustrated* 9 (October 1970): 15–19.

Watson, Elbert L. "James Walker of Columbia, Polk's Critic and Compatriot." *Tennessee Historical Quarterly* 23 (March 1964): 24–37.

Weinert, Richard P. "The Little Known Story of the Illinois Confederates." *Civil War Times Illustrated* 1 (October 1962): 44–45.

Whitesell, Robert D. "Military and Naval Activity between Cairo and Colum-
bus." *Register of the Kentucky Historical Society* 61 (April 1963): 107–21.
Wilson, Bluford. "Southern Illinois and the Civil War." *Transactions of the
Illinois State Historical Society* 16:93–103.

DISSERTATIONS

Eidson, William Gene. "John Alexander Logan: Hero of the Volunteers."
Ph.D. dissertation, Vanderbilt University, 1967.
Hicken, Victor. "From Vandalia to Vicksburg: The Political and Military Ca-
reer of John A. McClernand." Ph.D. dissertation, University of Illinois at
Urbana, 1955.
Holliday, Charles Lloyd. "The Military Career of General John Alexander
Logan, 1861–1865." Ph.D. dissertation, Washington University, 1948.
Messamore, Ford. "John A. Logan: Democrat and Republican." Ph.D. dis-
sertation, University of Kentucky, 1939.
Watters, George Wayne. "Isham Green Harris, Civil War Governor and
Senator from Tennessee, 1818–1897." Ph.D. dissertation, Florida State
University, 1965.

INDEX

Adams, Lt. Lemuel, 102, 182–83, 215

Aleck Scott, 48, 50, 57, 173, 186–87, 235 (n. 3)

Alexander, Lt. Robert J., 145, 259 (n. 48)

Alexandria, La., 237 (n. 13)

Alle, Pvt. William, 232 (n. 12)

Alton, Ill., 216

Annapolis, Md., 182

Apache Indians, 87

Arkansas. See CSS *Arkansas*

Arliskas, Thomas, 256 (n. 11)

Armstrong, Capt. J. Welby, 124, 144, 251 (n. 27), 259 (n. 40)

Army of Louisiana, 69

Army of Northern Virginia, 34

Army of Tennessee, 34, 220, 238 (n. 18), 275 (n. 3)

Army of the Cumberland, 206

Army of the Potomac, 21

Austin, Capt. John, 137

Austin, Pvt. William M., 49, 94, 157, 172, 215

Austin, Tex., 237 (n. 11)

"Babe of Belmont," 243 (n. 39)

Ball, Lt. C. P., 107

Barrett, Lieutenant, 170

Barrow, Alexander, 42

Barrow, Batt, 42

Barrow, Clifford, 42

Barrow, George W., 42

Barrow, Hilliard, 42

Barrow, Capt. John J., 42, 138, 215

Barrow, Mrs. Mary, 42

Barrow, Lt. Col. Robert H., 42, 138–39, 145, 202, 215

Barrow family, 42

Battle, Pvt. John Bell, 114, 248 (n. 54)

Bayou Lafourche, La., 27

Beckwith Farm (Landing), 2, 175, 238 (n. 17)

Bee, Gen. Bernard, 69

Bell, Sen. John, 251 (n. 27)

Bell, Lt. Col. Tyree H., 68–69, 74–75, 77, 95–99, 113, 143–44, 202, 215, 237 (n. 11), 245 (n. 10)

Belle Memphis, 49, 51, 56, 79–81, 155–56, 171–75, 186, 232 (nn. 12, 18), 267 (n. 27), 269 (n. 19)

Belleville, Ill., 15, 216

Belleville Advocate, 15

Belmont, Mo., 46, 48, 51, 53, 55–56, 58–59, 69, 74–75, 80–84, 117, 136, 199, 240 (n. 12), 242 (n. 19)

Belmont and Kentucky City Ferry Co., 240 (n. 18)

"Belmont Charge!," 275 (n. 10)

Belmont Company, 240 (n. 16)

Belmont Point, 60, 62–63, 155, 165, 236 (n. 10), 242 (n. 26), 256 (n. 15)

"Belmont Quick Step," 191

Beltzhoover, Lt. Col. Daniel, 69–71, 73–74, 77, 99, 101, 105, 107, 111, 113, 130, 138, 145, 200, 202, 215, 237 (n. 13), 238 (n. 18), 239 (nn. 23, 32, 33)

Benicia, Calif., 237 (n. 11)

Benton, Ill., 217

Bickerdyke, Mother Mary A., 183

Bielaski, Agnes, 224 (n. 14)

Bielaski, Capt. Alexander, 13, 22, 109–10, 115, 203, 224 (n. 14)

Bielaski, Rosie, 224 (n. 14)

Big Black, battle of, 257 (n. 28)
Bird's Point, Mo., 2, 4–5, 22–23,
  45–46, 48–49, 53, 117, 175, 177,
  181, 193, 232 (n. 12), 243 (n. 39),
  250 (n. 15), 267 (n. 53), 269 (n. 23)
Bird's Point Road, 79, 88, 162, 183
Black Hawk War, 9
Blake, Capt. Edward, 186
Blandville, Ky., 38, 44, 66
Bloomfield, Mo., 45, 47, 48, 51,
  53–55, 193, 232 (n. 12)
Blythe, Lt. Col. Andrew K., 139, 165,
  201, 215
Blythe's Mississippi Battalion. See
  1st Mississippi Volunteer Infantry
  Battalion
Bob (Grant's servant), 247 (n. 54),
  266 (n. 33)
Boggan, Capt. Patrick, 262 (n. 43)
Bolivar Troop, 76, 117, 238 (n. 17)
Boone, Mrs. Sally Walker, 123, 190,
  251 (n. 28)
Bowen, Col. John S., 38, 71
Bowles, Capt. A. J., 76, 81, 92
Bowling Green, Ky., 47
Bowman, Surg. Edward H., 264
  (n. 8)
Boyne, battle of, 29
Bracelet, 182
Bragg, Gen. Braxton, 44, 217
Bratcher cabin, 84
Brayman, Maj. Mason, 13, 161
Brazos-Santiago, Mex., 87
Breese, Judge Sidney, 187, 271
  (n. 59)
Brinton, Surg. John H., 21, 49, 57,
  59, 63, 78, 84, 90, 95, 118, 127,
  130, 148, 155, 158, 161, 174, 181,
  235 (n. 3), 242 (n. 17), 250 (n. 18),
  253 (n. 72), 263 (n. 56), 270 (n. 36),
  271 (n. 51)
Brooks, Surgeon (13th Arkansas),
  94, 104–5, 179, 268 (n. 14)
Brooks, Capt. McHenry, 179, 268
  (n. 14)

Brooks, Capt. Thorndike, 135
Brown, Gov. Aaron V., 73
Browning, Sen. Orville, 21
Buchanan, Pres. James, 31, 251
  (n. 27)
Buckner, Gen. Simon B., 228 (n. 12),
  229 (n. 17)
Buena Vista, battle of, 192
Buffington, Mo., 54–55
Buford, Col. Napoleon B., 19–21,
  78, 89–90, 92, 109–11, 116, 149,
  161–63, 168, 201, 203, 206, 215,
  242 (n. 32), 250 (n. 15), 260 (n. 7),
  263 (n. 62), 272 (n. 68)
Bulger, Pvt. William, 244 (n. 3)
Bull Run, battle of, 19
Burch, Col. John C., 73, 250 (n. 18)
Burlington, Iowa, 23
Burlington Hawkeye, 195
Burton, Capt. William C., 114–15
Butler, Capt. B. J., 68, 140, 164, 215,
  248 (n. 61)
Butler, Edward G. W., Sr., 180
Butler, Maj. Edward G. W., Jr., 35,
  41, 139, 158–59, 180, 269 (n. 21)

Cadwalader, Gen. George, 31
Cairo, Ill., 1, 3, 5, 12, 14, 19, 21,
  23–25, 36, 48, 50, 55, 56, 115,
  148, 175, 183, 225 (n. 2), 231
  (n. 8), 235 (n. 3), 238 (n. 20), 247
  (n. 54), 269 (n. 19), 270 (n. 36)
Cairo and Fulton Railroad, 242 (n. 19)
Camargo, Mex., 33
Campbell, Col. William B., 142
Camp Johnston, Mo., 63, 65, 71, 73,
  75, 77, 83, 99, 100, 107, 108, 111,
  113–14, 116–27, 130–33,
  136–39, 147, 162, 172, 199,
  200–206, 234 (n. 47), 239 (n. 24),
  250 (n. 20)
Camp Moore, La., 41
Camp Yates, Ill., 19
Canby, Gen. Edward, 119
Cannon Guards, 137, 145

Cape Girardeau, Mo., 3–4, 45, 47, 55–56, 194, 232 (n.12)
Carlin, Col. William P., 45
Carlyle, Ill., 87
Carroll, Anna Ella, 268 (n.16)
Carroll, Col. Charles M., 135, 215
Carroll, Gov. William, 31
Carroll County, Tenn., 42
Carroll Guards, 41
Cash, Pvt. Patrick Boggan, 215, 262 (n.43)
Casualties (CSA), 184–85, 270 (n.42), 271 (nn.43, 44, 45)
Casualties (USA), 184, 270 (nn.39, 40)
Catahoula Guards, 41
Catlin, Lt. James K., 49
Catton, Bruce, 272 (n.2)
Centralia, Ill., 16
Cerro Goro, battle of, 31
Chalk Bluffs, 2, 36, 39
Chancellor, 49, 171, 173–75
Charleston, Mo., 45–46, 48, 51, 56
Charleston, Mo., battle of, 88
Charleston Road, 71, 83, 240 (n.5)
Charm, 65, 68–69, 120, 126, 134, 136–37, 139, 150, 164–65, 180, 185, 204, 257 (n.28), 269 (n.20)
Chase, Sgt. David, 126
Chase, Salmon P., 21
Cheatham, Brig. Gen. Benjamin F., 5, 38, 65, 131, 135, 139–44, 146, 161, 164–65, 167–68, 174, 186–88, 191, 202–4, 215, 245 (n.13), 264 (nn.4, 11), 265 (n.18), 269 (n.19), 275 (n.3)
Chester, Ill., 16
Chestnut, Mrs. Mary, 191
Chicago, Ill., 15
Chicago Light Battery (Taylor's battery), 48–49, 59, 90–91, 95, 105–8, 118, 124–26, 152, 155–56, 170, 173, 177, 185, 201, 203, 204, 247 (nn.41, 54), 253 (n.56)

Chicago Tribune, 195–96
Chickamauga, battle of, 218
Cincinnati, Ohio, 22
Cincinnati Daily Commercial, 236 (n.10)
Cincinnati Gazette, 273 (n.27)
Clark, John, 237 (n.14)
Clark County, Va., 158
Clarksville, Tenn., 47–48, 65, 192
Clayton, Mr. (pilot of Charm), 139
Clemens, Samuel (Mark Twain), 124, 225 (n.1), 256 (n.9)
Clinton, Gen. Henry, 75
Columbus, Ky., 1, 3–5, 7, 25, 29, 33–39, 41–42, 46–48, 50–51, 53, 57–58, 62, 66–68, 71, 76, 81–83, 118, 121, 125, 132, 134, 139, 163, 180, 186, 189, 191–94, 196–97, 200, 222 (n.2), 229 (n.1), 231 (nn.5, 6), 234 (n.47), 238 (n.20), 265 (n.16), 270 (n.42), 272 (n.14), 274 (n.44)
Commerce, Mo., 2, 44, 55, 232 (n.12)
Conscript Bureau (CSA), 273 (n.23)
Continental Guards (Orleans Guards), 40
Contreras, battle of, 31
Cook, Col. John, 46, 56, 174, 194, 267 (n.57)
Cooper, Pvt. John, 186
Cooper, Gen. Samuel, 227 (n.1)
Cooper, William F., 122
Crabb, Capt. Ben, 99
Crippin, Cpl. Edward W., 21, 216
Crookham, Sgt. Jeff, 252 (n.41)
Crowley, Pvt. John, 215
CSS Arkansas, 257 (n.28)
Cumberland River, 196
Cunningham, Capt. Hilbert B., 135
Curry, Captain, 232 (n.12)

Dagnan, Lt. John, 123
Daly, Father (chaplain of 2d Tennessee), 123

Dana, Charles A., 12
Davenport, Iowa, 23
Davis, Pres. Jefferson, 3, 5, 10, 27,
    29, 31, 34, 38, 47, 69, 142, 191,
    237 (n. 13), 273 (n. 23)
DeHeuss, Lt. William, 119
Delano, Capt. Sterling P., 153, 170,
    216
Delano's Adams County cavalry, 49,
    80
Democratic party, 10, 16, 18, 30,–31,
    41–42, 142, 207
Dennigan, Private, 122, 251 (n. 29)
Detrich, Capt. John E., 79–81, 86,
    155, 170, 206, 240 (n. 6), 242
    (n. 26), 266 (n. 27)
Dickens, Charles, 14, 15
Dillon, Polk, 68
Dillon Guards, 39–41, 137, 145
District of Southeast Missouri, 3
Dixie Greys, 108
Dollins, Capt. James J., 17, 49, 80,
    109–11, 114, 117, 150, 153, 161,
    176, 216, 271 (n. 47)
Dougherty, Col. Henry, 5, 50, 56, 80,
    86–88, 90, 101, 107, 117, 119,
    154–55, 181, 202–5, 216, 219,
    234 (n. 52), 253 (n. 56), 266 (n. 27),
    269 (n. 23)
Dougherty, Mrs. Henry, 181, 269
    (n. 23)
Dougherty's Bird's Point Brigade
    (Second Brigade), 56, 79–80, 86,
    90, 92, 94, 101, 119, 148, 152,
    155, 171, 184, 202–3, 234 (n. 52),
    260 (n. 7)
Douglas, Sen. Stephen A., 9–10, 12,
    15, 18, 251 (n. 27)
Dresser, Capt. James, 16
DuPont, Admiral, 191
Dyer County, Tenn., 42, 237 (n. 10)
Dyer Grays, 112, 157

Eagle Iron Works, 22
East Pascagoula, Miss., 237 (n. 11)

"Egypt," 12, 14, 18, 223 (n. 3), 225
    (nn. 3, 49), 272 (n. 2)
81st Illinois Volunteer Infantry Regi-
    ment, 216
11th Illinois Volunteer Infantry Regi-
    ment, 46
11th Louisiana Volunteer Infantry
    Regiment, 35, 40–41, 135–39,
    144–46, 155, 157, 165, 167, 259
    (n. 50)
Eliot, Ellsworth, 237 (n. 11)
Elliott, the Right Reverend Stephen,
    29
Elliott's Mill, Ky., 2, 47, 54, 56, 66,
    67, 199
Episcopal church, 27
Erin Guards, 239 (n. 25)

Falls, H. H., 112
Farrow, Pvt. John P., 112
Favrot, Lieutenant, 39
Feliciana, Ky., 54, 71
Fielder, Pvt. Albert, 68, 93, 97, 114,
    144, 245 (n. 10)
15th Tennessee Volunteer Infantry
    Regiment, 134–36, 138, 145–46,
    167, 256 (n. 11)
5th Infantry, 237 (n. 11)
5th Louisiana Volunteer Infantry
    Battalion, 66
5th Tennessee Volunteer Infantry
    Regiment, 259 (n. 49)
1st Dragoons, 87
1st Iowa Volunteer Infantry Regi-
    ment, 149
1st Mississippi Volunteer Cavalry
    Battalion, 66, 71, 117
1st Mississippi Volunteer Infantry
    Battalion (Blythe's Mississippi Bat-
    talion), 139, 161, 164, 174, 184,
    257 (n. 26)
1st Regiment of Artillery, 69
1st Tennessee Volunteer Infantry
    Regiment, 142
Fish Lake, 82

Fiske, John, 29, 195, 228 (n. 8), 240 (n. 16)

Fitzgerald, Capt. Ed, 166

Fleming, Capt. John G., 40

Foote, Capt. Andrew H., 52, 194, 223 (n. 13), 234 (n. 51), 235 (n. 10)

Forbes, Surg. John, 138

Forrest, Gen. Nathan B., 215–19

Fort Blakely, Ala., 119

Fort Donelson, Tenn., 197

Fort Donelson, battle of, 208, 217–20, 228 (n. 12), 229 (n. 17), 254 (n. 79), 270 (n. 36), 273 (n. 22)

Fort Henry, battle of, 197, 208

Fort Holt, Ky., 2, 38, 46, 50, 55–56, 267 (n. 57)

Fort Jefferson, Ky., 50, 67

Fort Pemberton, Miss., 216

Fort Pillow, Tenn., 48, 229 (n. 5)

Fort Prentiss, Ill., 175

Fort Towson, Indian Territory, 237 (n. 11)

44th Mississippi Volunteer Infantry Regiment, 257 (n. 26)

Fouke, Col. Philip B., 15–16, 23, 90, 92, 99, 101, 104, 106, 117, 148, 154, 162, 186, 202–3, 205, 207, 216, 260 (n. 7), 264 (n. 13), 271 (n. 44)

4th Tennessee Volunteer Infantry Regiment, 37, 66, 178, 265 (n. 21)

Frazer, Capt. Charles W., 103, 105, 216, 236 (n. 2), 248 (n. 61)

Fredericktown, Mo., 4

Freeman, Col. Thomas J., 42, 77, 102–3, 127, 132, 185, 201–2, 216, 248 (n. 61)

Frémont, Maj. Gen. John C., 3–5, 7, 22, 45–46, 55, 87, 195

Friendship Volunteers, 68, 93, 95

Fugitive Slave Act, 18

Gailor, Pvt. William H., 138, 145

Gaines Invincibles, 112

Galena, Ill., 8, 9

Gantt, Col. E. W., 66

General Hospital (Brick Hospital, Cairo, Ill.), 183

Gibson County, Tenn., 69, 93, 237 (nn. 10, 11)

Gillespie, Mother Angela, 183

Glass, Lt. Matt, 99

Gordon, Gen. George W., 237 (n. 9)

Gorgas, Gen. Josiah, 33

Grace, Father, 123

Graham, Pvt. Albert K., 138

Graham, Pvt. Tom, 71

Grampus, 238 (n. 20)

Granger, Gen. Gordon, 33

Grant, Jesse R., 193

Grant, Brig. Gen. Ulysses S., 3–9, 13–14, 18–19, 21–25, 33, 45–53, 55, 57, 60, 63, 69, 78, 80, 84, 86–88, 92, 95, 109, 121, 126, 131, 133, 148–49, 152, 155, 156, 158, 161, 163, 166, 170–75, 183–84, 186–88, 192–96, 198–201, 203–8, 216–17, 223 (nn. 3, 13), 229 (n. 17), 231 (nn. 5, 8), 232 (nn. 12, 16), 233 (n. 26), 234 (n. 51), 240 (nn. 5, 6), 243 (n. 60), 247 (n. 54), 253 (n. 56), 257 (n. 58), 260 (n. 7), 266 (n. 33, 34), 267 (n. 53), 273 (n. 31)

Grant, Mrs. Ulysses S., 266 (n. 34)

Gray, Capt. A. B., 187

Green, Pvt. Caleb, 22, 180–81

Greene, Gen. Nathanael, 249 (n. 6)

Greenville, Mo., 45

Guilford Courthouse, battle of, 249 (n. 6)

Halleck, Gen. Henry W., 208

Hamilton, Capt. James G., 250 (n. 18)

Hamilton, Capt. S. D. H., 66–67

Hansback, Capt. Lewis, 21, 216, 242 (n. 32)

Hardee, Brig. Gen. William J., xiv, 3, 7

Hardeman County, Tenn., 42, 93
Harlan, Sen. James, 195
Harper, Pvt. Aaron C., 180
Harper's Weekly, 88, 270 (n. 39)
Harris, Gov. Isham G., 1, 27, 34, 88,
    191, 222 (n. 2)
Harris, Col. Tom, 8, 88
Harris Guards, 124
Harry W. R. Hill, 68–69, 122, 124,
    126, 136, 182, 204, 256 (n. 9), 257
    (n. 19)
Hart, Lt. Col. Harrison E., 86, 101,
    106, 156, 202, 216, 243 (n. 34),
    269 (n. 19)
Harvard Law School, 19
Hatch, Capt. Reuben B., 171, 174,
    187
Hatchie Hunters, 93
"Hawkeyes," 22
Hay, John, 12
Hebert, Col. Paul O., 69
Helena, Ark., 73, 257 (n. 28)
Henry, Maj. Gustavus A., Jr., 121,
    246 (n. 30)
Hickman, Ky., 2, 4, 51
Hillyer, Capt. William S., 121, 250
    (n. 18)
Hitt, Robert Roberts, 251 (n. 28)
Horn, Stanley F., 52
Hotel Belmont, 240 (n. 16)
Houston, Pvt. Arch, 112–13
Hume, Lt. W. Y. C., 178
Hunt, George, 70
Hunt, Private, 144–45
Hunt, Col. W. R., 186
Hunter, Andrew, 238 (n. 19)
Hunter, Daniel, 238 (n. 19)
Hunter's Farm, Mo., 2, 53, 57, 60,
    62, 66, 71, 73–74, 78–80, 82,
    111, 148, 155, 162–63, 165, 166,
    168–70, 199, 202, 204, 238
    (n. 19), 263 (n. 62)
Hunter's Farm Road, 82–84,
    153–54, 239 (n. 23)

Hurst, Col. Fielding, 217
Hutsonville, Ill., 16

Illinois State Journal (Springfield),
    195
Indianapolis, Ind., 183
Indian Ford, Mo., 45
Indian Territory, 27
Ingomar, 68
Iron Banks, Ky., 2, 5, 25, 36, 60,
    79–80, 84, 136, 140, 201, 208
Iron Banks Ferry, 82
Iron Mountain Railroad, 240 (n. 16)
Ironton, Mo., 23
Island No. 1, 194, 267 (n. 57)
Island No. 10, 215, 218–19
Ivers, Edmund J., 70, 238 (n. 14)

Jack (servant of Lieutenant Shelton),
    247 (n. 54)
Jackson, Pres. Andrew, 27, 30
Jackson, Capt. William H., 138–39,
    145, 216, 255 (n. 2)
Jackson, Miss., 41
Jackson Purchase, Ky., 4
Jackson's Battery, 182
James Montgomery, 49, 57
"Jeff Davis," 185
Jefferson, Ill., 16
Johnson, Pres. Andrew, 228 (n. 12)
Johnson, Lt. Charles, 39, 268 (n. 10)
Johnson, Lt. John, 33
Johnson, Capt. Sam, 87–88
Johnston, Gen. Albert Sidney, 3, 5,
    27, 47, 67, 190, 197–98, 208, 215,
    228 (n. 12)
Johnston, William Preston, 198
Jolliet, Louis, 36
Jones, Lt. Lafayette, 76, 81

Kaskaskia District, Ill., 15
Kearny, Col. Phil, 87
Kennedy, Lt. Col. J. B., 66
Kentucky, 68, 137, 182

Kentucky Military Institute, 76
Keystone State, 49
Kirkwood, Governor, 195
Knight, Pvt. John, 157
Knight, Pvt. William, Jr., 157, 216, 262 (n. 45)
Knights of the Golden Circle, 14
Kurtz, Henry I., 52
Kuykendall, Maj. Andrew J., 16

"Lady Polk," 36, 67, 81, 140, 147, 160, 191, 258 (n. 32)
Lake Bruin, La., 70
Lake County, Tenn., 135
Laomi, Ill., 16
Latta, Capt. Sam, 112, 124
Lauman, Col. Jacob G., 23–24, 49, 91–92, 101, 107, 118–19, 121, 123, 126, 130, 152, 156, 202, 205, 217
Law, Cpl. John G. (the Reverend), 68, 186
Law, Mrs. Sallie G., 68, 181, 126–27, 182, 186, 237 (n. 9)
Layton, Capt. J. D., 103, 105, 108, 180
Lebauve Guards, 248 (n. 54)
"Leighton," 27
Lexington. See USS *Lexington*
Liberty Guards, 103, 105, 108, 180
Library of Congress, 251 (n. 28)
Liddell, Gen. St. John R., 227 (n. 1)
Limburger, Pvt. W. C., 112
Limerick, siege of, 228 (n. 8)
Lincoln, Pres. Abraham, 7, 9, 11, 13, 15, 18–19, 195, 205, 223 (n. 13), 224 (n. 14), 225 (n. 14), 247 (n. 41)
Lincoln-Douglas debates, 251 (n. 28)
Logan, Col. John A., 12, 14–19, 23, 51, 86, 92, 95, 98, 102, 106, 117, 135, 153–54, 162, 171, 179, 183, 187, 202–3, 205, 207–8, 217–18, 223 (n. 3), 242 (n. 32), 245 (n. 9), 249 (n. 15), 251 (n. 28), 260 (n. 17)

Logan Negro Law, 18
Logwood, Lt. Col. Thomas H., 217
Logwood's Tennessee Cavalry Battalion, 136
Looney, Capt. William A., 183
Louisiana Hose Company, 259 (n. 48)
Louisiana State Seminary of Learning and Military Academy, 237 (n. 13)
Louisville and Nashville Railroad, 218
Louisville Daily Journal, 195, 231 (n. 5)
Lucas Bend, Mo., 2, 5, 54, 57, 67, 234 (n. 47)
Lynch, Sgt. Dennis, 144
Lyon, Gen. Nathaniel, 3, 23
Lytle, Gen. W. H., 219

McAdams, Capt. Sam, 119
McClellan, Gen. George B., 33, 49, 192
McClellan, Mrs. George B., 158
McClernand, Brig. Gen. John A., 9–15, 17–19, 22–23, 31, 48–50, 56, 79–80, 84, 86, 89–91, 95, 102, 109, 125, 127, 152–54, 161, 163, 170–71, 174–75, 183, 185, 192, 195–96, 203, 205, 207, 217, 223 (nn. 3, 13), 232 (n. 16), 247 (n. 54), 260 (n. 7), 261 (nn. 17, 21)
McClernand's Cairo Brigade (First Brigade), 12, 15–16, 18, 48–49, 56, 80, 86, 94, 102, 148, 161
McClurken, Maj. Thomas, 271 (n. 59)
McCook, Gen. Alexander, 219
McCook, Capt. Edwin S., 90, 153, 217
McCown, Brig. Gen. John P., 37–38, 42, 65–68, 71, 77, 164, 187, 198, 201, 217
McCoy, Sgt. William J., 126, 173

McDonald, Lt. John, 38
McDowell, Lt. William W., 98
McFeely, William S., 52
McGhee, James E., 52
Mackall, Gen. William W., 39
McKeever, Capt. Chauncey, 231
    (n. 5), 267 (n. 58)
McMurry, Richard, 34
McNairy, Maj. F. H., 165
McNairy County, Tenn., 44
McPherson, Maj. Gen. James,
    219
Macon, Ga., 182
Madeline, Pvt. E., 67
Madison County, Ill., 243 (n. 34)
Madrid Bend Guards, 135
Margetson, the Right Reverend
    John, 228 (n. 8)
Mariposa, Cal., 237 (n. 11)
Marks, Col. Samuel F., 40–42,
    134–40, 145–46, 161, 165,
    200–201, 217, 245 (n. 13), 255
    (n. 4), 257 (n. 23), 264 (n. 4)
Marquette, Fr. Jacques, 36
Marsh, Col. C. Carroll, 48, 193
Marshall, Captain, 125
Maury County, Tenn., 122
Mayfield, Ky., 2, 5, 47–48, 54, 66
Mayfield Creek, Ky., 233 (n. 26)
Mayfield Road, 46, 67
Memphis, Tenn., 3, 68, 70, 122–23,
    125, 135, 182, 187, 189–92, 208,
    216, 219, 230 (n. 9), 247 (n. 54),
    256 (n. 9), 257 (n. 26), 259 (n. 40),
    272 (n. 2)
Memphis Argus, 191, 272 (n. 14)
Memphis Avalanche, 219, 234 (n. 47)
Memphis City Hospital, 182
Memphis Daily Appeal, 76, 189, 251
    (n. 27), 265 (n. 12), 272 (n. 14)
Memphis Light Dragoons, 136–37
Memphis Public Ledger, 219
Mercer, William, 254 (n. 76)
Mexican War, 16, 18, 23, 30–31, 33,
    35, 37, 41–43, 60, 66, 69, 86–87,

122, 142, 192, 229 (n. 17), 251
    (n. 29), 268 (n. 14)
Mexico City, Mex., 87
Milburn, Ky., 2, 46, 48, 54, 56,
    66–67, 199
Miller, Lt. Col. John H., 66, 76,
    116–17, 168, 185, 202, 217, 260
    (n. 14)
Miller, Capt. Marsh, 238 (n. 20)
Milwaukee, Wis., 251 (n. 28)
Missionary Ridge, battle of, 216
Mississippi and Ohio Railroad De-
    pot, 190
Mississippi Free Trader, 76
Mississippi River, 1, 36–37, 58, 83,
    131, 161, 175, 208, 225 (n. 1), 239
    (n. 25), 240 (n. 16)
Mississippi Valley, 27, 29–31
Mitchell, Pvt. James A., 112
Mitchell, Surg. R. W., 180
Mobile, Ala., 215
Mobile and Ohio Railroad, 36, 82,
    229 (n. 1), 240 (n. 16), 242 (n. 19)
Montgomery, Capt. Frank, 199, 238
    (n. 17)
Montgomery, Gen. Richard, 135
Montreal, Can., 17
Morgan, Colonel (10th Illinois), 94
Mosby's Cotton Shed, 182
Mound City, Ill., 2, 94, 183
Mount St. Mary's College, 69
Mount Whitney, Cal., 237 (n. 11)
Murfreesboro, battle of, 217–18, 254
    (n. 79), 262 (n. 43)
Muscatine, Iowa, 23

Nashville, Tenn., 27
Nashville Banner, 188, 228 (n. 12)
Nashville Daily Gazette, 272 (n. 14)
Natchez, Miss., 71
Navajo Indians, 87
Naval Scenes, 204, 219
Neely, Mark E., Jr., 224 (n. 14)
Negro Wool Swamp (Nigger-Wool
    Swamp), 47, 54, 55

New Albany, Ind., 117
Newell, Capt. Tom H., 136
New Madrid, Mo., 46, 51, 53, 55, 83
New Madrid earthquake, 82
New Madrid Road, 75
New Orleans, La., 254 (n. 76), 259
   (n. 48), 265 (n. 13), 273 (n. 14)
New Orleans *Daily Picayune*, 198
New York, N.Y., 23
New York Herald, 26, 196, 261
   (n. 21)
New York Times, 88
9th Tennessee Volunteer Infantry
   Regiment, 265 (n. 21)
Norfolk, Mo., 2, 45

Odum, Addison, 217
Odum, Martin, 217
Oglesby, Col. Richard J., 46, 51–53,
   55, 193–94, 217, 231 (n. 8), 232
   (n. 12)
Ohio River, 5, 63
Ohio State Journal, 208
154th Senior Tennessee Volunteer
   Infantry Regiment, 45, 68, 139,
   160, 164–67, 174, 182, 257 (n. 26)
Onstot, Cpl. William H., 57, 121,
   217
Ory, Pvt. Clement, 105, 246 (n. 35)
Oskaloosa, Iowa, 23
Otey, the Right Reverend James, 30,
   190
Otey, Capt. William Mercer, 254
   (n. 76)
Outlaw, Capt. Drew A., 237 (n. 10)
Overton Hospital (Overton Hotel),
   182, 247 (n. 54)
Ozburn, Pvt. Lindorf, 171, 218

Paducah, Ky., 1, 4–5, 9, 47, 50, 53,
   135, 193, 199, 204, 216, 232
   (n. 12)
Paine, Brig. Gen. Eleazer A., 46, 56,
   195, 218, 233 (n. 26), 274 (n. 44)
Parrott, Capt. James C., 22, 156, 218

Pearson, Pvt. Robert N., 16
Perczel, Col. Nicholas, 55
Pettus, Gov. John J., 191
Peyton, Lt. Thomas W., 40
Phillips Academy (Exeter, N.H.), 73
Pickens, Gen. Andrew, 116
Pickett, Col. Ed, 76, 102–4, 108,
   201–2, 240 (n. 41)
Pickett, Capt. W. D., 162
Pickett, Mrs. W. S., 259 (n. 40)
Pierce, Pres. Franklin, 31
Pierson, Pvt. John W., 171–72, 182
Pillow, Brig. Gen. Gideon J., xiv, 1,
   3, 5, 7, 12, 30–35, 37, 42–44, 47,
   53, 65, 67–69, 71, 73–77, 83, 85,
   97, 102–4, 107, 111, 113–14,
   116, 121–22, 124, 132, 134–35,
   138, 142–43, 164–65, 168, 189,
   191–92, 196, 198–201, 204–5,
   207–8, 218, 222 (n. 2), 228 (n. 12),
   229 (nn. 5, 17), 239 (nn. 27, 32,
   33), 242 (n. 21), 245 (nn. 10, 13,
   30), 248 (n. 61), 251 (n. 27), 254
   (n. 79), 263 (n. 1), 264 (nn. 4, 11),
   265 (n. 18), 270 (n. 42), 273
   (nn. 22, 23)
"Pillow talk," 255 (n. 1)
Pilot Knob, Mo., 45
Pinckneyville, Ill., 16
Pine Mountain, Ga., 218
Pittman, Lieutenant, 148
Plummer, Col. Joseph, 4, 45–47, 55,
   194, 218
Poak, Pvt. David, 16
Pointe Coupee Battery, 66–67, 70,
   236 (n. 5)
Polk, Pres. James K., 30–31, 122
Polk, Maj. Gen. Leonidas, 3–5,
   25–30, 34–39, 41–42, 44, 48, 50,
   53, 55, 65–66, 69–71, 107, 126,
   132, 134–35, 138–40, 142, 157,
   164–66, 168–70, 180–82,
   186–93, 196, 198–200, 207–8,
   218, 223 (n. 13), 227 (n. 1), 229
   (n. 8), 232 (n. 17), 242 (n. 21), 248

Polk, Maj. Gen. Leonidas (*continued*)
(n.61), 250 (n.20), 253 (n.56), 255
(nn.3, 4), 264 (n.4, 11), 272
(n.68), 273 (n.22), 275 (n.3)
Polk, Capt. Marshall T., 168, 255
(n.2)
Polk, Dr. William M., 77, 270 (n.39)
Pond, Pvt. Frank, 126
Pontotoc, Miss., 116–17
Pontotoc Dragoons, 117
Porter, Comdr. W. D., 223 (n.13)
Port Royal, battle of, 190–91
Prentiss, Brig. Gen. Benjamin, 23
Price, Maj. Gen. Sterling, 4, 7, 21,
46–47, 51, 53, 193–94, 196, 232
(n.12)
Prince, 68–69, 120, 122, 126, 140,
142, 150, 164, 180, 187, 215, 248
(n.61)
Provisional Army of Tennessee, 34,
37, 142
Purdy, Tenn., 42
Purdy Whig, 42

Quincy, Ill., 8

Randolph, Secretary of War George,
273 (n.22)
Rawlins, Capt. John A., 9, 52, 56,
121, 163, 193, 203, 234 (n.52),
266 (n.33), 273 (n.31)
Reeder, Mr. (clerk of the *Scott*), 235
(n.3)
Republican party, 15
Reynolds, Lt. Gov. Thomas C., 33
Rhea, Capt. Matthew (grandfather of
Capt. Matthew), 249 (n.6)
Rhea, Capt. Matthew, 75, 111,
113–16, 271 (n.44)
Rice, Maj. Elliott W., 23, 152, 202,
218
Richardson, Albert D., 121, 266
(n.33)
Roberts, Charles, 112–13

Rob Roy, 49, 175
Rock Island, Ill., 19–20
Rock Island and Peoria Railroad, 20
Rodgers, Comdr. John, 63
Rogers, Pvt. John W., 112
Rosale Guards, 42, 138
Ross, Col. L. F., 194
Ross, Lt. Col. William B., 122, 218
Rumsey, Lt. Israel P., 50
Russell, Col. Robert M., 68, 124,
138, 201, 218, 219, 237 (n.11)
Rust, Lt. H. A., 174

Sacramento, battle of, 87
Saffarans, Capt. John, 125, 251
(n.28)
St. Agnes Academy, 182
St. Francis River, 45
St. Francis Swamp, 47
St. Joseph, La., 70
St. Louis, Mo., 15, 45, 55, 177, 223
(n.13), 239 (n.25), 268 (n.16)
St. Louis *Daily Missouri Republican*,
49
St. Louis–Iron Mountain Railroad,
242 (n.19)
St. Louis Missouri Weekly Democrat,
53, 195
St. Louis Republican, 37
St. Louis Sunday Republican, 53,
195, 269 (n.19)
St. Patrick's Church, 123
Sample, Sergeant, 250 (n.15)
Sampson, Pvt. Frank, 157
Sanderson, Col. W. L., 46, 56
Sanitary Commission, 183
Schmitt, Capt. William A., 86, 89
Schwartz, Capt. Adolphus, 79,
106–7, 118, 124, 130, 148, 150,
170, 174, 202, 218, 243 (n.46),
250 (n.20)
Scott, Charles M., 49, 57, 79–80,
170, 232 (nn.12, 17), 268 (n.16)
Scott, Gen. Winfield, 31, 87, 142, 192

Scott, Mrs. Winfield, 69
Seaton, Capt. John, xii, 86–87, 90,
    101, 104, 119, 127, 175, 234
    (n. 47), 250 (n. 20)
Sebastian brothers (pilots of the *Ty-
    ler*), 60
Secession Guards, 262 (n. 43)
2d Illinois Light Artillery, 79
2d Kentucky Volunteer Regiment,
    251 (n. 29)
2d Tennessee Volunteer Infantry
    Regiment, 121–23, 143–44, 190,
    199, 204, 219, 252 (n. 31), 256
    (n. 11)
2d U.S. Artillery Regiment, 23
Sedgwick, Gen. John, 33
Seminole War, 37, 41
7th Illinois Volunteer Infantry Regi-
    ment, 175, 194
7th Iowa Volunteer Infantry Regi-
    ment, 22–23, 48–49, 79–81, 84,
    86, 91, 92, 99, 101, 107, 111,
    117–19, 144, 149, 152, 155–57,
    173, 204, 243 (n. 45), 250 (n. 15),
    252 (n. 41), 270 (n. 40)
Shawneetown, Ill., 9
Shawneetown Democrat, 9
Shelby Light Dragoons, 138
Shelton, Lieutenant, 247 (n. 54)
Shelton, George W., 247 (n. 54)
Sherman, Gen. William T., 19, 33,
    191, 217, 219, 237 (n. 13)
Shiloh, battle of, 216–19
Shipley, Lt. William, 21, 263 (n. 62)
Sikeston, Mo., 45–46, 48, 55
Simon, John Y., 53, 231 (n. 5), 233
    (n. 32), 273 (n. 27)
Simpson, Elizabeth, 226 (n. 20)
Sisters of Mercy, 183
Sisters of the Holy Cross, 183
6th Arkansas Volunteer Infantry
    Regiment, 108
6th Tennessee Volunteer Infantry
    Regiment, 38

Smith, Brig. Gen. C. F., 9, 46, 50,
    56, 193, 195, 217, 232 (n. 12), 274
    (n. 44)
Smith, Pvt. Henry I., 147, 218, 270
    (n. 40)
Smith, Capt. Melancthon, 139–40,
    164, 199
Smith, Col. Preston, 42, 139–40,
    165–68, 201, 218, 248 (n. 61), 264
    (nn. 4, 11), 265 (n. 18)
Smith, Mrs. Susan Kirby, 182
Smith's battery, 201
Society of the Army of the Tennes-
    see, 52
Sons of Erin, 144
Southern Mothers Home, 182
Springfield, Ill., 12–13, 23
Springfield, battle of, 149, 260 (n. 12)
Stains, William, 154, 247 (n. 54)
Stanley, Pvt. Henry M., 62, 108, 126,
    219
Stanton, Secretary of War Edwin, 21
Stembel, Comdr. Roger N., 60, 63,
    175, 194, 204
Stephenson, Pvt. Hammett, 258
    (n. 32)
Stephenson, Pvt. Phillip, 73, 97–98,
    145–46, 219, 254 (n. 76), 258
    (n. 32), 268 (n. 14)
Stevenson, Pvt. William G., 269
    (n. 24)
Stewart, Maj. Alexander P., 66–67,
    140
Stewart, Capt. Francis M., 124, 143
Stewart, Capt. Richard A., 66–67, 70
Stith, Capt. F., 74, 76
Stonefort, Ill., 16
Strocky, Capt. F. A., 251 (n. 28)
"Suckers," 22
Sumner, Col. Edwin V., 87
Sumner County, Tenn., 68

Tangipahoa Parish, La., 41
Taos, battle of, 87

Tappan, Col. James C., 66–67, 71–74, 76–77, 95, 97–99, 124–25, 143–44, 200–201, 219, 238 (n. 19), 239 (nn. 23, 24, 32), 245 (n. 13), 248 (nn. 54, 61), 250 (n. 18)

Tarleton, Col. Bonastre, 27

Tate, Sam, 30, 192

Taylor, Capt. Ezra, 48–50, 119, 124, 131, 148, 152, 154, 173, 202, 219, 250 (n. 20)

Taylor, Gen. Richard, 73

Taylor, Capt. William F., 136, 219

Taylor, Gen. Zachary, 87, 192

Taylor's battery. See Chicago Light Battery

Taylor's cavalry, 168

Teague, Pvt. J. B., 264 (n. 9)

Temple, Pvt. John C., 99

Tennessee Mounted Rifles, 162, 168

Tennessee River, 196

Tensas Parish, La., 69

10th Iowa Volunteer Infantry Regiment, 55–56

"Texas," 171, 266 (n. 35)

Thayer, Bandmaster, 101, 155

13th Arkansas Volunteer Infantry Regiment, 71, 73–74, 93–95, 99, 105, 117, 125, 131, 143, 145, 179, 239 (n. 25)

13th Tennessee Volunteer Infantry Regiment, 42, 44, 74–75, 77, 111–16, 122, 138, 143, 201, 271 (n. 44)

30th Illinois Volunteer Infantry Regiment, 15, 48, 80–81, 84, 89, 99, 101, 104, 117, 119, 148, 154, 155

31st Illinois Volunteer Infantry Regiment, 16–17, 80–81, 84, 90, 94, 99, 101, 113–14, 119, 121, 138, 153, 156–57, 183, 218, 243 (n. 45), 247 (n. 54), 250 (n. 15), 275 (n. 10)

Thomas, Gen. George H., 19

Thompson Cavalry, 76

Thompson, Gen. M. Jeff, 3–4, 7, 45–48, 51, 53, 55–56, 65, 117, 222 (n. 4)

Thurmond, Lieutenant, 124

Tilman, Lt. Col. Hiram, 187

Tracey, Mrs., 41

Trask, Capt. William L., 68, 137, 165, 180, 185, 219, 236 (n. 1), 257 (n. 28)

Travis, Pvt. William D. T., 88, 128–29, 156, 181, 219

Tredegar Foundry, 238 (n. 14)

Trent Affair, 191

Trenton, Tenn., 237 (n. 11)

Trueman, Private, 49–50, 78, 226 (n. 20)

Tulare, Cal., 237 (n. 11)

12th Arkansas Volunteer Infantry Regiment, 66

12th Tennessee Volunteer Infantry Regiment, 68–69, 74–75, 93–95, 97–98, 105, 114, 117, 143, 144, 239 (n. 27), 257 (n. 23)

20th Tennessee Volunteer Cavalry Regiment, 237 (n. 11)

28th Illinois Volunteer Infantry Regiment, 194

21st Illinois Volunteer Infantry Regiment, 8, 223 (n. 3)

21st Tennessee Volunteer Infantry Regiment, 74–75, 99, 102–3, 105, 108, 111, 113, 116, 122, 124, 127, 143, 236 (n. 2), 239 (n. 27)

22d Illinois Volunteer Infantry Regiment, 48–49, 50, 79, 80–81, 84, 86, 88, 90, 92, 102, 106, 111, 117, 119, 127, 149, 152, 155, 156, 173, 232 (n. 12), 234 (n. 47), 252 (n. 41)

22d Tennessee Volunteer Infantry Regiment, 42, 74, 75, 93–94, 102–5, 111, 116, 124, 143, 239 (n. 27)

27th Illinois Volunteer Infantry Regiment, 19, 21, 48, 57, 78, 80–81, 84, 89–91, 109, 114–17, 119,

121, 149, 153, 161, 163, 168, 174
Twiggs, Brig. Gen. David E., 69
Tyler, Pvt. Robert, 136, 259 (n. 49)
Tyler, Lt. Col. Robert C., 135–36,
  145, 167, 201, 219, 255 (n. 6), 259
  (n. 49)
Tyler (Taylor). See USS Tyler

Union City, Tenn., 135
U.S. General Land Office, Depart-
  ment of the Interior, 13
United States Military Academy. See
  West Point, N.Y.
USS Carondolet, 63
USS Lexington, 5, 49, 56, 60,
  62–63, 169, 172, 175
USS Tyler (Taylor), 49, 50, 56, 60,
  62–64, 169, 172, 175, 233 (n. 22)
University of Louisville, 18
University of Tennessee, 44
University of the South, 29
University of Virginia, 44

Vaughan, Lt. Col. Alfred J., 44,
  111–13, 125, 201, 219
Ventress, Capt. James A., Jr., 248
  (n. 54)
Vicksburg, Miss., 208, 215, 222 (n. 2)
Vicksburg, battle of, 217, 220
Vienna, Ill., 16
Vining Station, battle of, 219
Viola, Ky., 46, 54, 56
Virginia Military Institute, 44
Vollmer, Pvt. David, 143–44
Vroom, Samuel, 60

Waagner, Col. Gustav, 4, 79
Walke, Comdr. Henry, 5, 49, 50,
  56–57, 60–64, 162, 172–75, 192,
  194, 203–6, 219, 223 (n. 13), 234
  (n. 51), 235 (n. 10), 256 (n. 15), 267
  (n. 57), 274 (n. 37)
Walker, Mrs. Elizabeth, 82
Walker, Col. J. Knox, 31, 44,
  121–24, 126, 134, 143, 199,

201–2, 219–20, 250 (n. 18), 251
  (n. 27), 259 (n. 40)
Walker, James, 122
Walker, Mrs. Jane Marie Polk, 122
Walker, Lt. Jimmie, 123, 190, 219,
  251 (n. 28)
Walker, Sam, 122–23, 190
Walker, William, 135
Walker's Legion, 122
Wallace, Pvt. Dave, 233 (n. 32), 262
  (n. 45)
Wallace, Gen. Lew, 33
Wallace, Col. W. H. L., 46, 51–52,
  55–56, 193–94, 202, 218–19
Waller, Lt. Leroy R., 194
Warner, Ezra, 255 (n. 6)
Washburne, Elihu B., 8, 163
Washington, D.C., 122
Washington Battery, 70
Washington Rifles, 135
Watson, Pvt. Augustus C., 69–70,
  237 (n. 17)
Watson Battery, 67, 70, 73–77, 83,
  99, 101, 105–8, 111–13, 119,
  121, 124, 130–31, 144–45, 148,
  154, 164, 166, 185, 202, 204, 239
  (n. 23), 245 (n. 17), 246 (n. 39), 250
  (n. 20), 252 (n. 41)
Waveland Collegiate Institute, 88
Waxhaw, S.C., 27
Webster, Maj. Joseph D., 9, 121,
  186, 269 (n. 19)
Welles, Secretary of the Navy
  Gideon, 52, 234 (n. 51), 274 (n. 37)
Wentz, Lt. Col. Augustus, 23, 149
Wentz, Mrs. Rebecka McMurty, 23,
  179, 220
West Feliciana Parish, La., 39, 42
West Point, battle of, 219
West Point, N.Y., 8, 12, 19, 27, 37,
  69, 219, 237 (n. 11)
Whig party, 240 (n. 41)
White, Pvt. George Q., 106–7, 247
  (n. 41)
White, Lt. Col. John H., 16, 86,

White, Lt. Col. John H. (*continued*)
94–95, 202, 218, 220, 245 (n. 10)
White, Capt. Josiah S., 162, 165
White, Lt. Patrick H., 106–7, 118,
125–26, 148, 170, 184, 220, 245
(n. 9), 247 (nn. 41, 54)
Wigdor, David, 251 (n. 28)
Wilcox, Sgt. John, 89
Williams, Kenneth P., 51, 231 (n. 8)
Williamson County, Ill., 135
Wills, Charles, 194
Wilson's Creek, battle of, 3, 23
Winslow, Maj. Henry, 65–66,
76–77, 137, 263 (n. 1)
Winters, Pvt. E. D., 249 (n. 15)
Wisdom, Capt. Dew Moore, 42, 220
Witter, Surg. Amos, 264 (n. 8)
Wood, Mrs. Mary, 248 (n. 54)
Wood, Capt. Robert H., 93, 102,
104, 124–25, 132, 143, 248
(n. 54), 264 (n. 9), 268 (n. 14)
Wrack heap, 172, 266 (n. 37)
Wright, Col. John V., 42–44, 75,
111–13, 115, 201, 207, 220, 245
(n. 10), 262 (n. 43), 265 (n. 13), 271
(n. 44)
Wright, Lt. Col. Marcus J., 77, 139,
165–66, 174, 202, 220, 264 (n. 11)
Wright's Boys, 44

Yale College, 73, 122, 250 (n. 18)
Yandell, Surg. Lunsford P., Jr., 178,
191, 222 (n. 4), 255 (n. 3)
Yandell, Sally, 222 (n. 4)
Yates, Gov. Richard, 8, 12, 23
Yazoo, 182
Yazoo River, 68, 257 (n. 28)